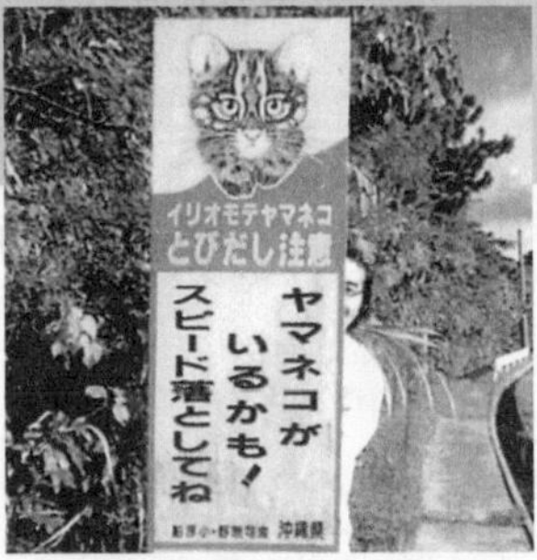
イリオモテヤマネコ
とびだし注意
ヤマネコがいるかも！
スピード落としてね
沖縄県

冨樫義博

Note: The sign says "Iriomote Wildcats Crossing. Watch out! Please slow down." –Ed.

We didn't see any.

Yoshihiro Togashi

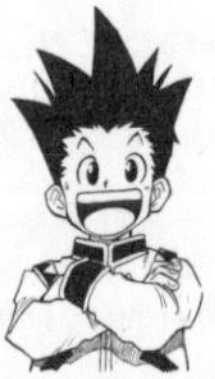

Yoshihiro Togashi's manga career began in 1986 at the age of 20, when he won the coveted Osamu Tezuka Award for new manga artists. He debuted in the Japanese **Weekly Shonen Jump** magazine in 1989 with the romantic comedy **Tende Shôwaru Cupid**. From 1990 to 1994 he wrote and drew the hit manga **YuYu Hakusho**, which was followed by the dark comedy science-fiction series **Level E,** and finally this adventure series, **Hunter x Hunter**, available from VIZ Media's SHONEN JUMP Advanced imprint. In 1999 he married the manga artist Naoko Takeuchi.

HUNTER X HUNTER Volume 10
SHONEN JUMP Manga Edition

STORY AND ART BY
YOSHIHIRO TOGASHI

English Adaptation & Translation/Lillian Olsen
Touch-up Art & Lettering/Mark Griffin
Design/Amy Martin
Editor/Yuki Takagaki

Printed in Italy

Published by VIZ Media, LLC
P.O. Box 77010
San Francisco, CA 94107

11
First printing, September 2006
Eleventh printing, June 2022

VIZ MEDIA
viz.com

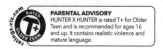

PARENTAL ADVISORY
HUNTER X HUNTER is rated T+ for Older Teen and is recommended for ages 16 and up. It contains realistic violence and mature language.

ratings.viz.com RATED T+ OLDER TEEN

SHONEN JUMP

SHONEN JUMP ADVANCED MANGA

HUNTER×HUNTER

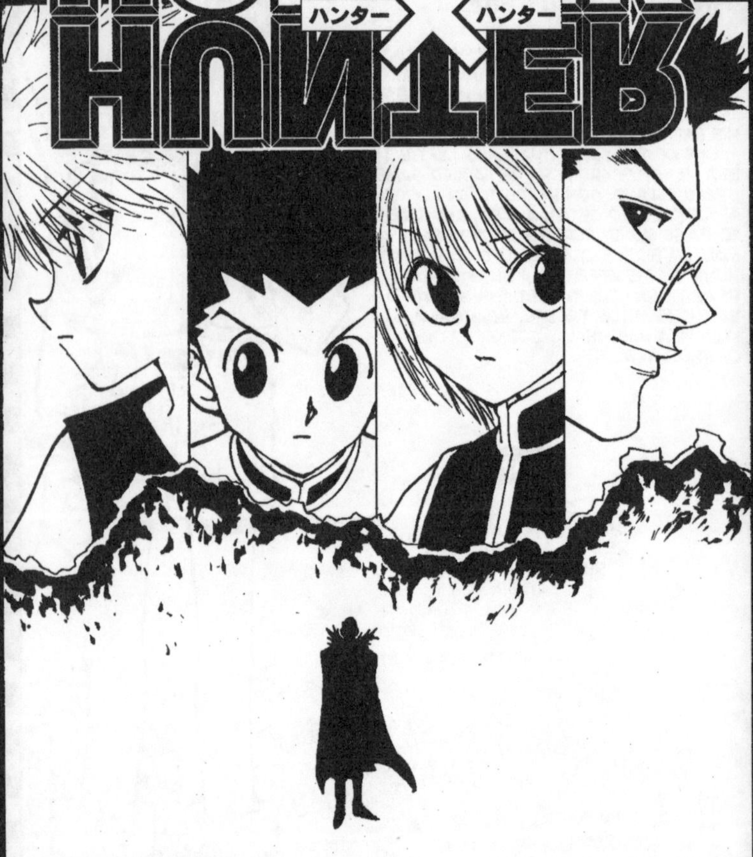
ハンター × ハンター

Story & Art by
Yoshihiro Togashi

Volume 10

CHARACTERS

The Story Thus Far

GON ONCE DREAMED OF BECOMING A HUNTER LIKE HIS LONG-LOST FATHER, THE GREAT GING FREECCS. NOW THAT GON HAS PASSED THE HIGHLY SELECTIVE LICENSING EXAM, FINDING HIS FATHER WILL PROVE TO BE EVEN HARDER.

ONE OF THE CLUES THAT GING LEFT BEHIND IS A MEMORY CARD FOR THE FABLED GAME GREED ISLAND. GON HEADS TO AN AUCTION IN YORKNEW TO OBTAIN A COPY, AND TRIES TO RAISE MONEY FOR THE EXORBITANT MINIMUM BID. HE CHANCES UPON A BOUNTY HUNT THAT IS OFFERING A SUBSTANTIAL REWARD, BUT THE TARGET TURNS OUT TO BE THE PHANTOM TROUPE. MEANWHILE, KURAPIKA HAS FINALLY CORNERED ONE OF THEIR MEMBERS...

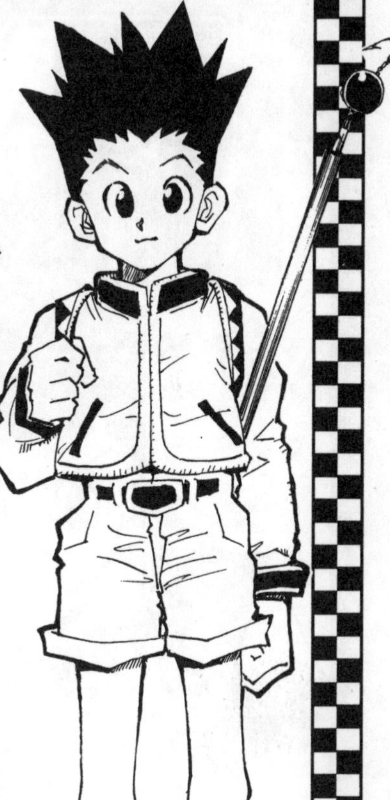

Gon

OUR EAGER HERO. NOW A HUNTER, HE'S ON A QUEST TO BE REUNITED WITH HIS FATHER!

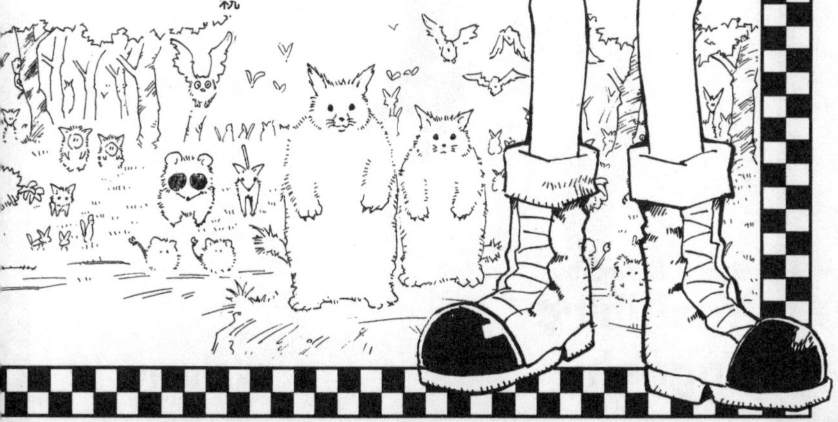

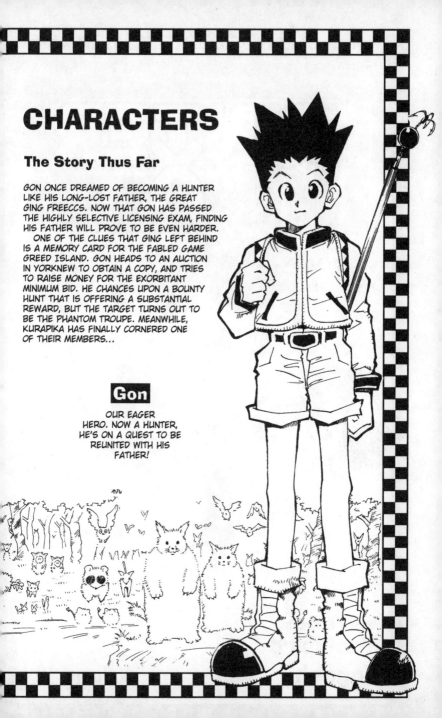

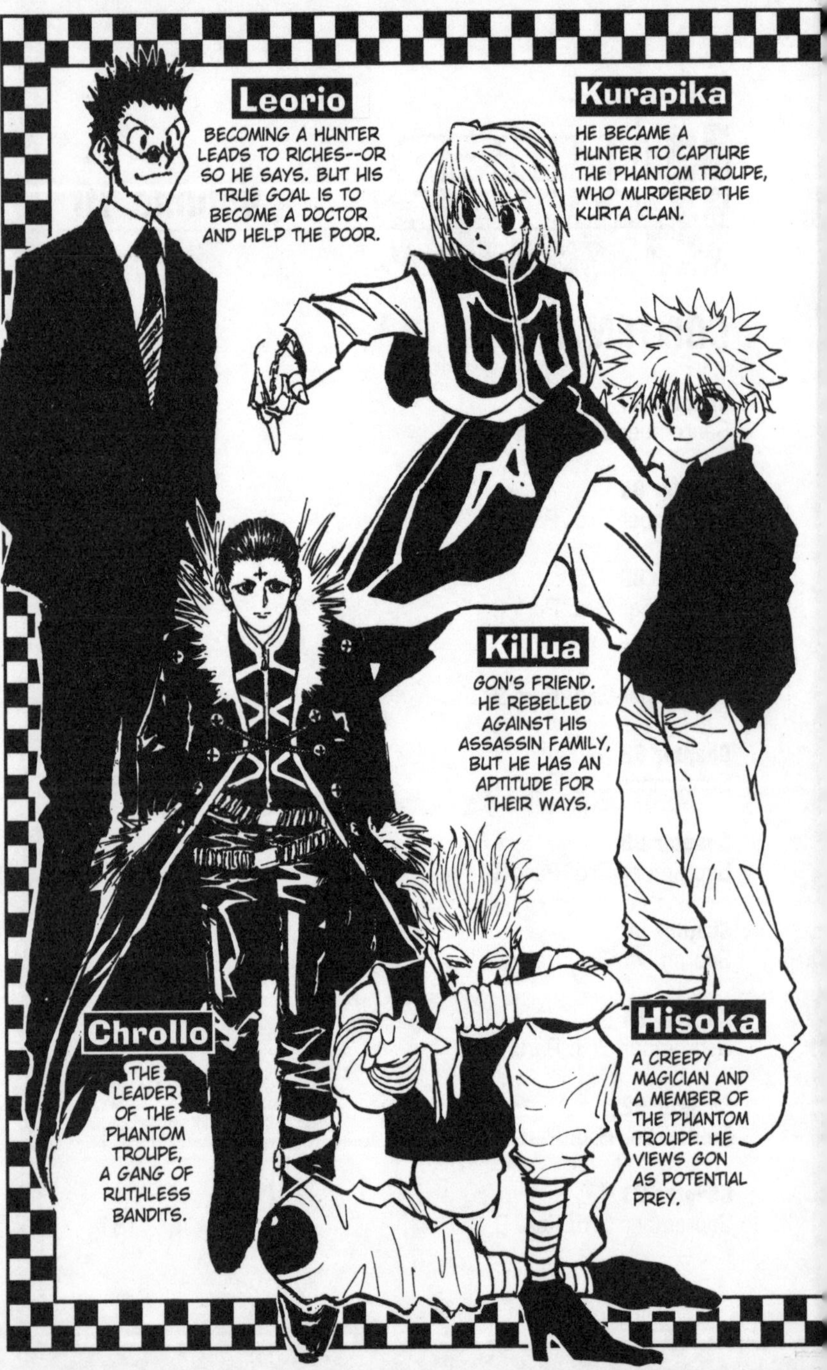
Kurapika
HE BECAME A HUNTER TO CAPTURE THE PHANTOM TROUPE, WHO MURDERED THE KURTA CLAN.
Leorio
BECOMING A HUNTER LEADS TO RICHES--OR SO HE SAYS. BUT HIS TRUE GOAL IS TO BECOME A DOCTOR AND HELP THE POOR.
Killua
GON'S FRIEND. HE REBELLED AGAINST HIS ASSASSIN FAMILY, BUT HE HAS AN APTITUDE FOR THEIR WAYS.
Hisoka
A CREEPY MAGICIAN AND A MEMBER OF THE PHANTOM TROUPE. HE VIEWS GON AS POTENTIAL PREY.
Chrollo
THE LEADER OF THE PHANTOM TROUPE, A GANG OF RUTHLESS BANDITS.

Volume 10

CONTENTS

Chapter 84
September 2nd: Part 6

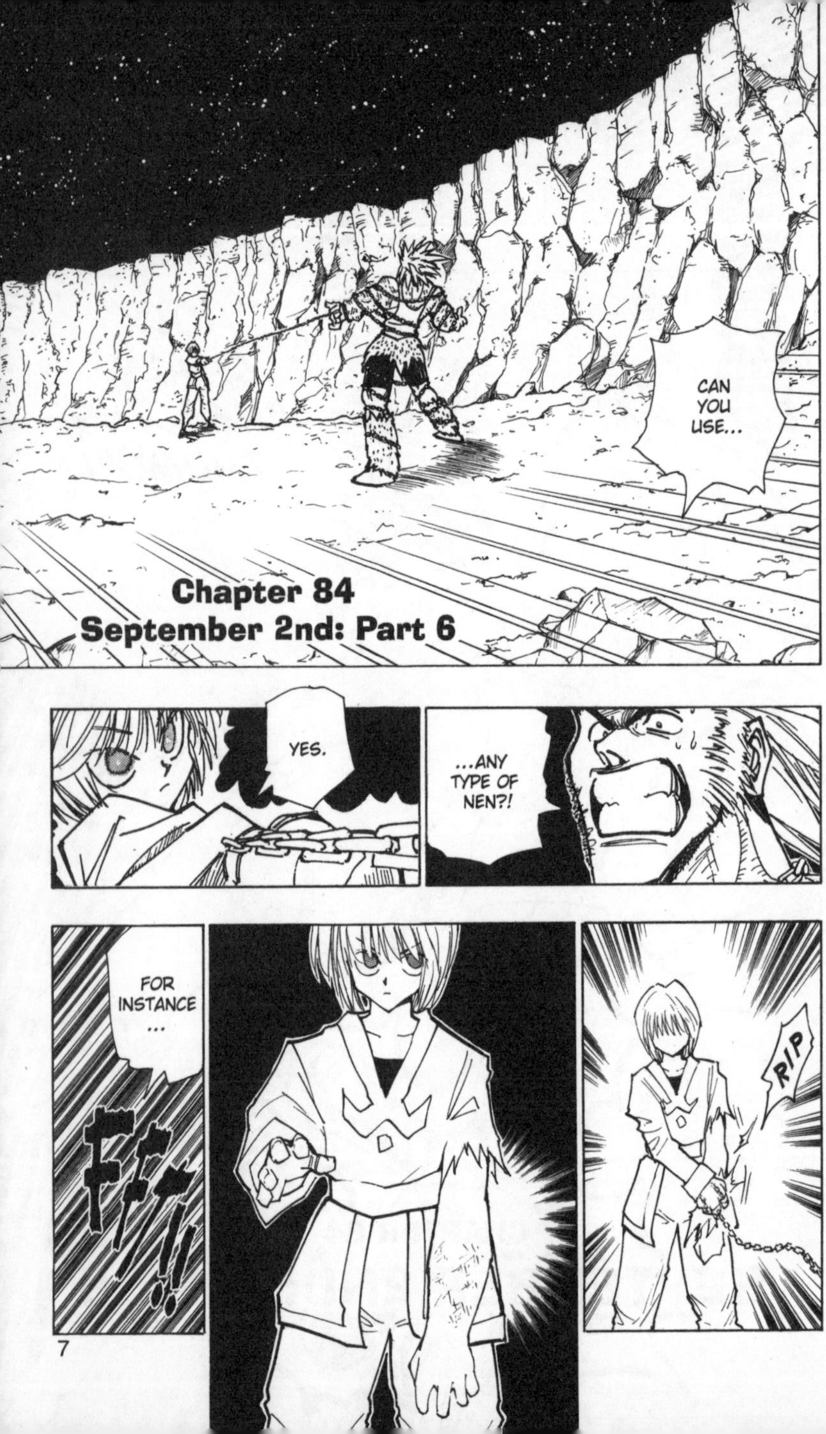
CAN YOU USE...
...ANY TYPE OF NEN?!
YES.
RIP
FOR INSTANCE ...

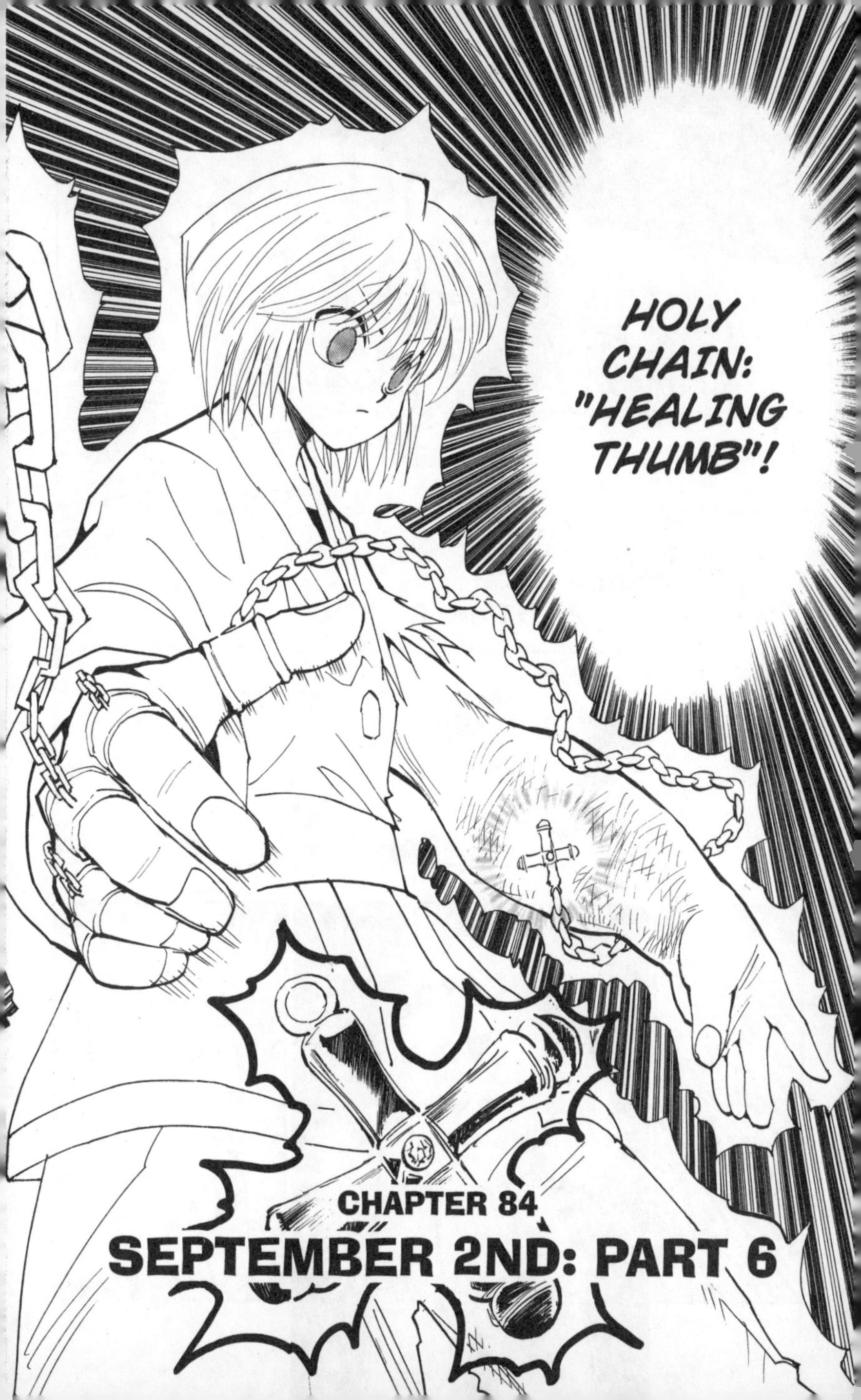
HOLY CHAIN: "HEALING THUMB"!

CHAPTER 84
SEPTEMBER 2ND: PART 6

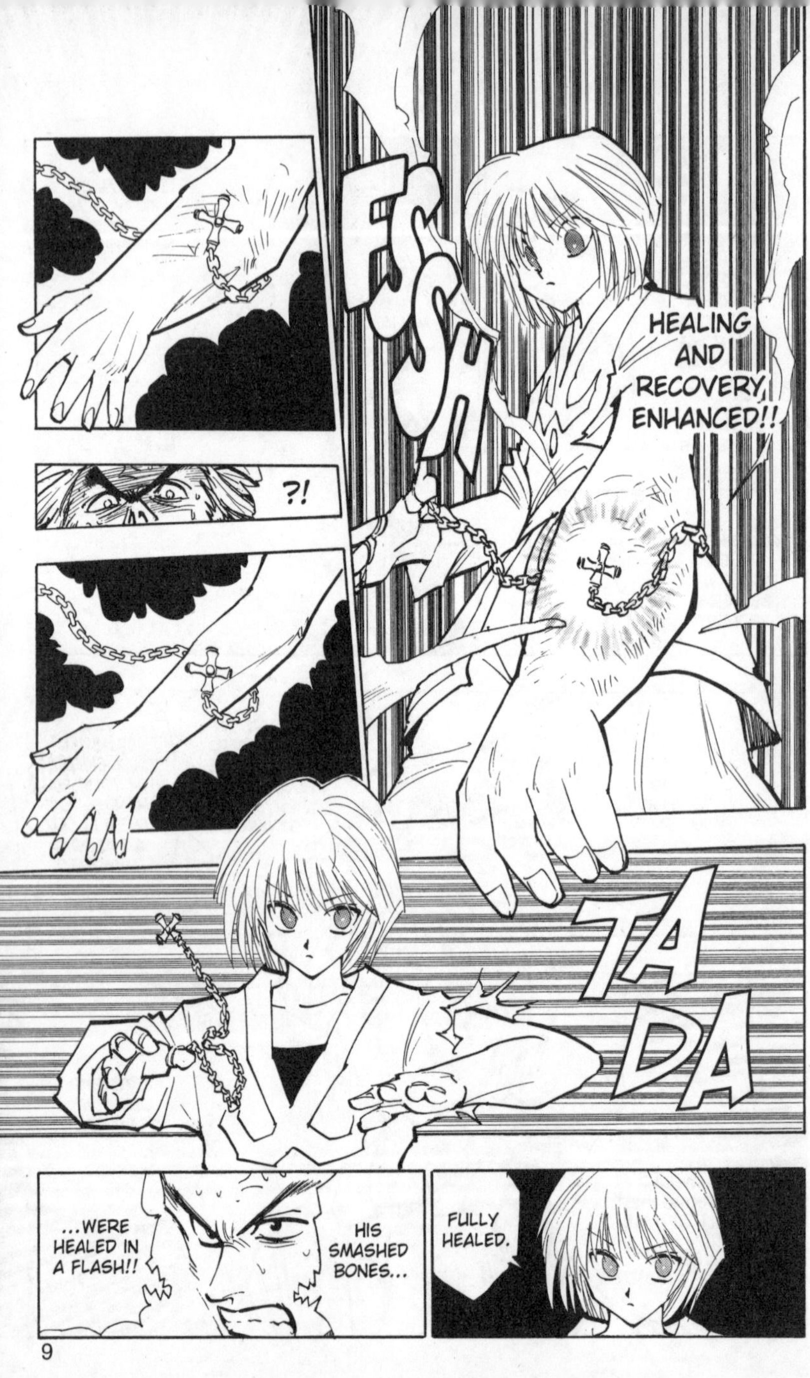
FSH
HEALING AND RECOVERY ENHANCED!!
?!
TA DA
FULLY HEALED.
HIS SMASHED BONES...
...WERE HEALED IN A FLASH!!

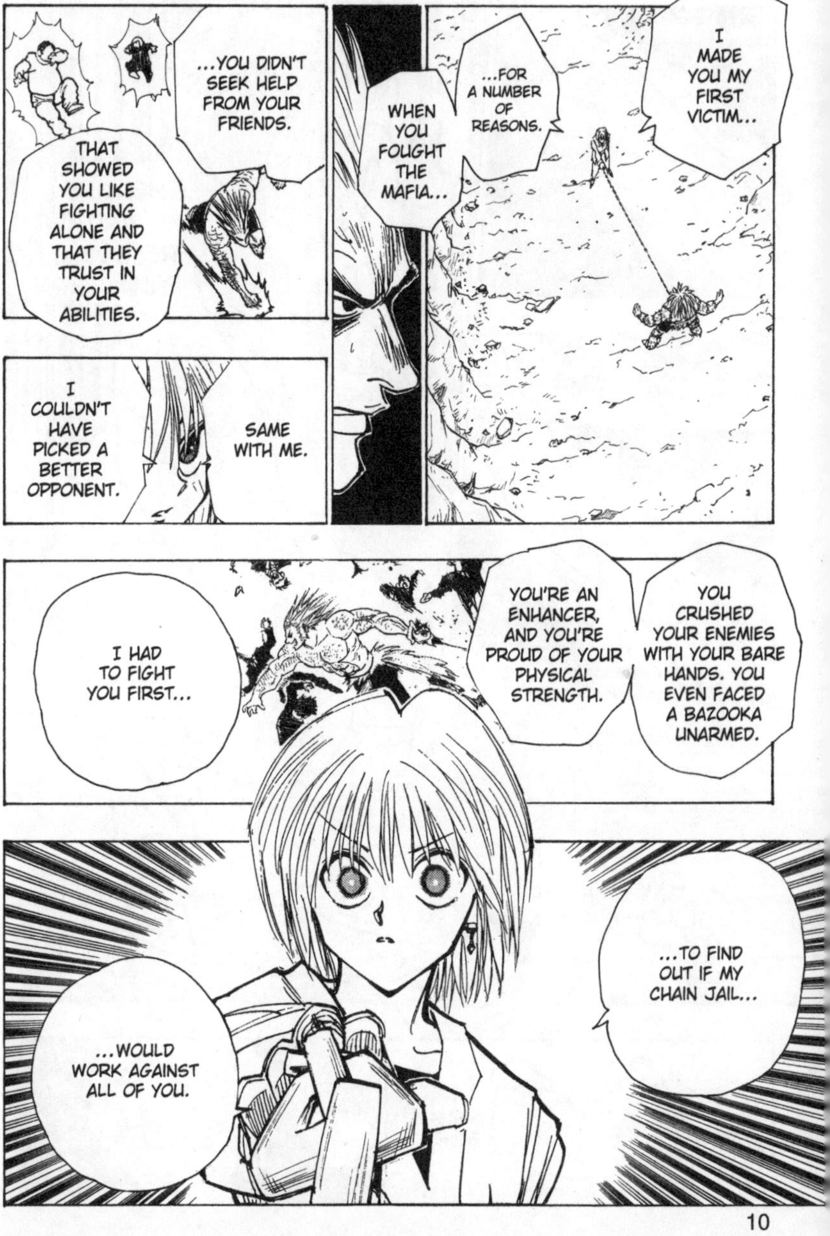
I MADE YOU MY FIRST VICTIM...
...FOR A NUMBER OF REASONS.
WHEN YOU FOUGHT THE MAFIA...
...YOU DIDN'T SEEK HELP FROM YOUR FRIENDS.
THAT SHOWED YOU LIKE FIGHTING ALONE AND THAT THEY TRUST IN YOUR ABILITIES.
I COULDN'T HAVE PICKED A BETTER OPPONENT.
SAME WITH ME.
YOU CRUSHED YOUR ENEMIES WITH YOUR BARE HANDS. YOU EVEN FACED A BAZOOKA UNARMED.
YOU'RE AN ENHANCER, AND YOU'RE PROUD OF YOUR PHYSICAL STRENGTH.
I HAD TO FIGHT YOU FIRST...
...TO FIND OUT IF MY CHAIN JAIL...
...WOULD WORK AGAINST ALL OF YOU.

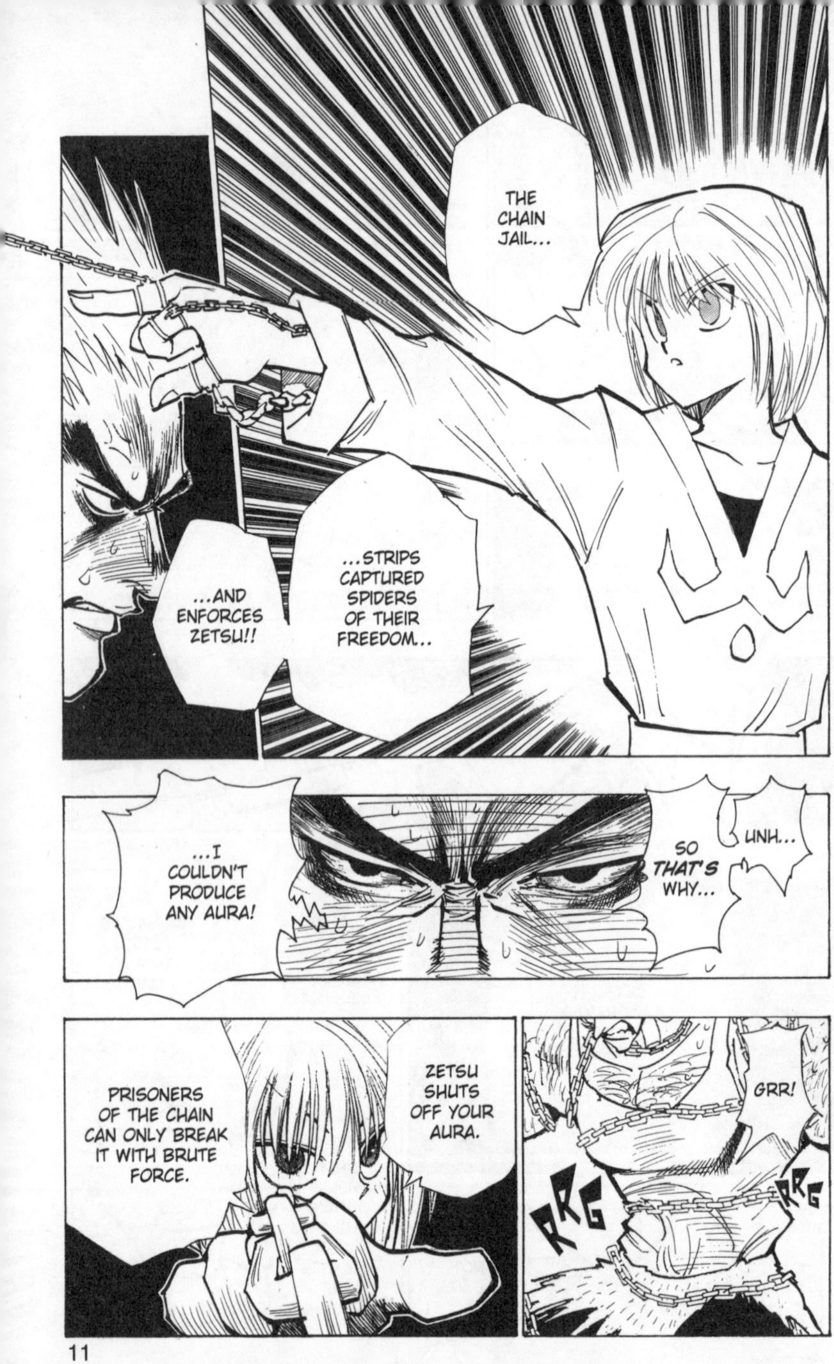
THE CHAIN JAIL...
...STRIPS CAPTURED SPIDERS OF THEIR FREEDOM...
...AND ENFORCES ZETSU!!
UNH...
SO *THAT'S* WHY...
...I COULDN'T PRODUCE ANY AURA!
GRR!
RRG
RRG
ZETSU SHUTS OFF YOUR AURA.
PRISONERS OF THE CHAIN CAN ONLY BREAK IT WITH BRUTE FORCE.

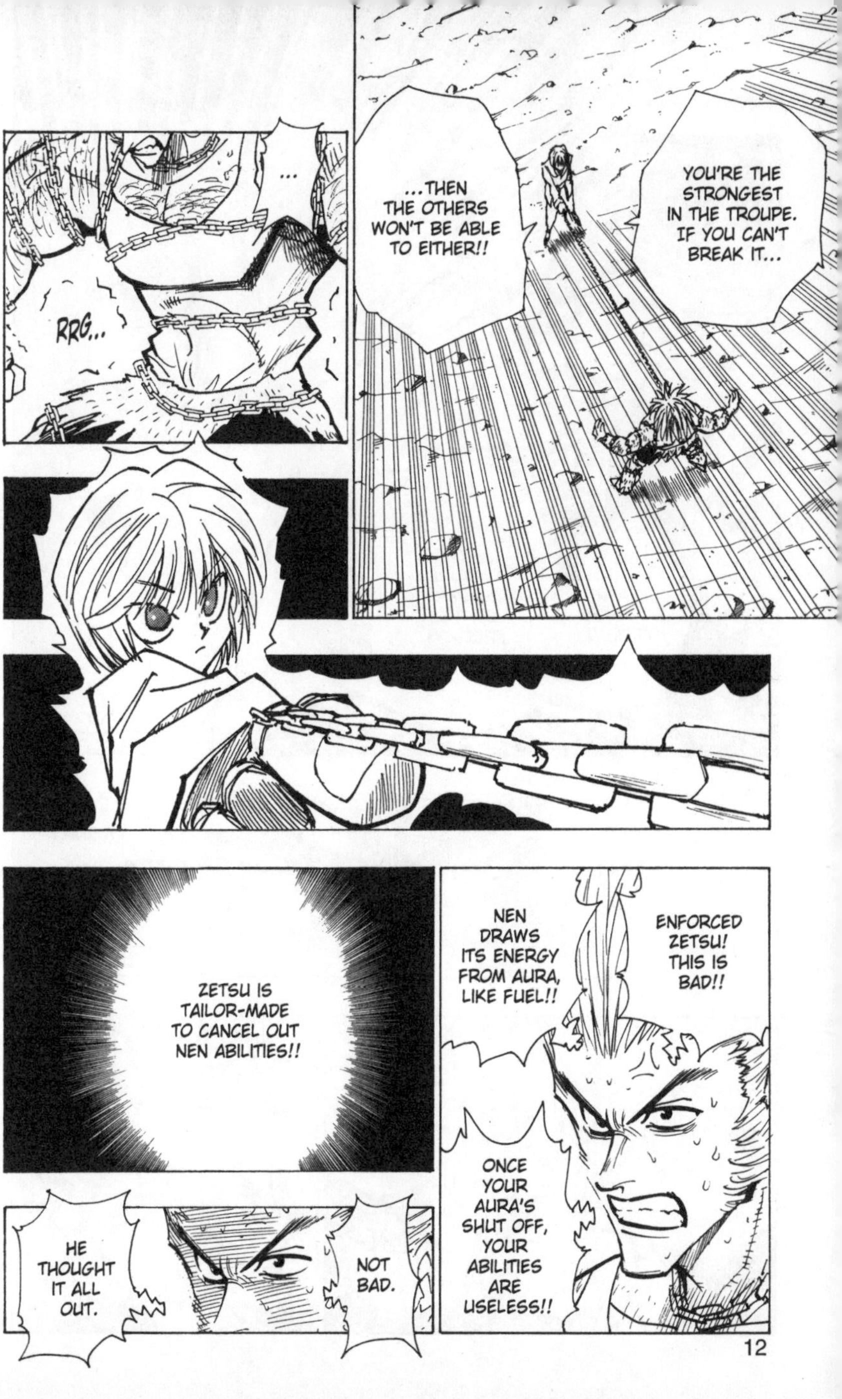
YOU'RE THE STRONGEST IN THE TROUPE. IF YOU CAN'T BREAK IT...
...THEN THE OTHERS WON'T BE ABLE TO EITHER!!
...
RRG...
ENFORCED ZETSU! THIS IS BAD!!
NEN DRAWS ITS ENERGY FROM AURA, LIKE FUEL!!
ONCE YOUR AURA'S SHUT OFF, YOUR ABILITIES ARE USELESS!!
ZETSU IS TAILOR-MADE TO CANCEL OUT NEN ABILITIES!!
NOT BAD.
HE THOUGHT IT ALL OUT.

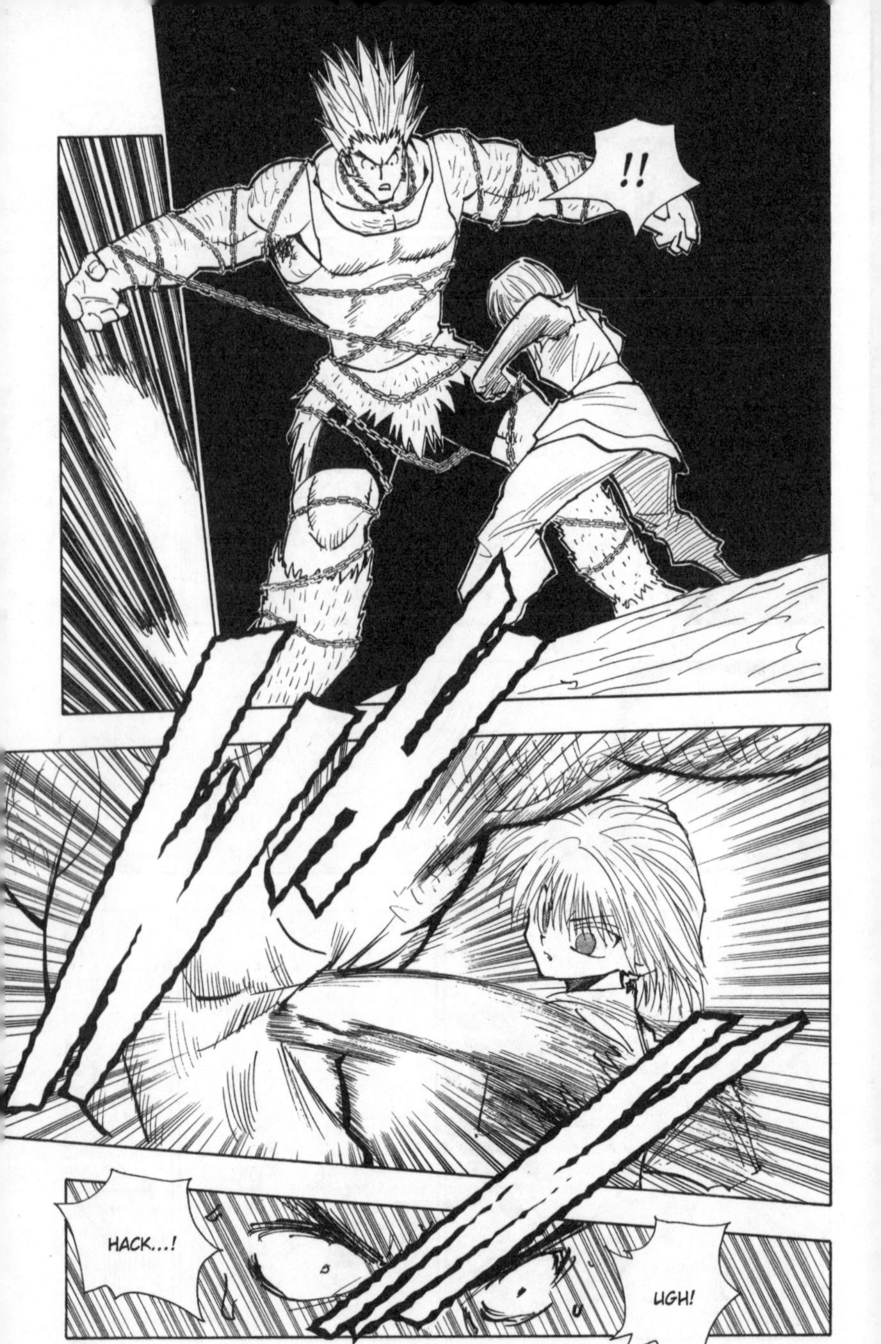
!!
UGH!
HACK...!

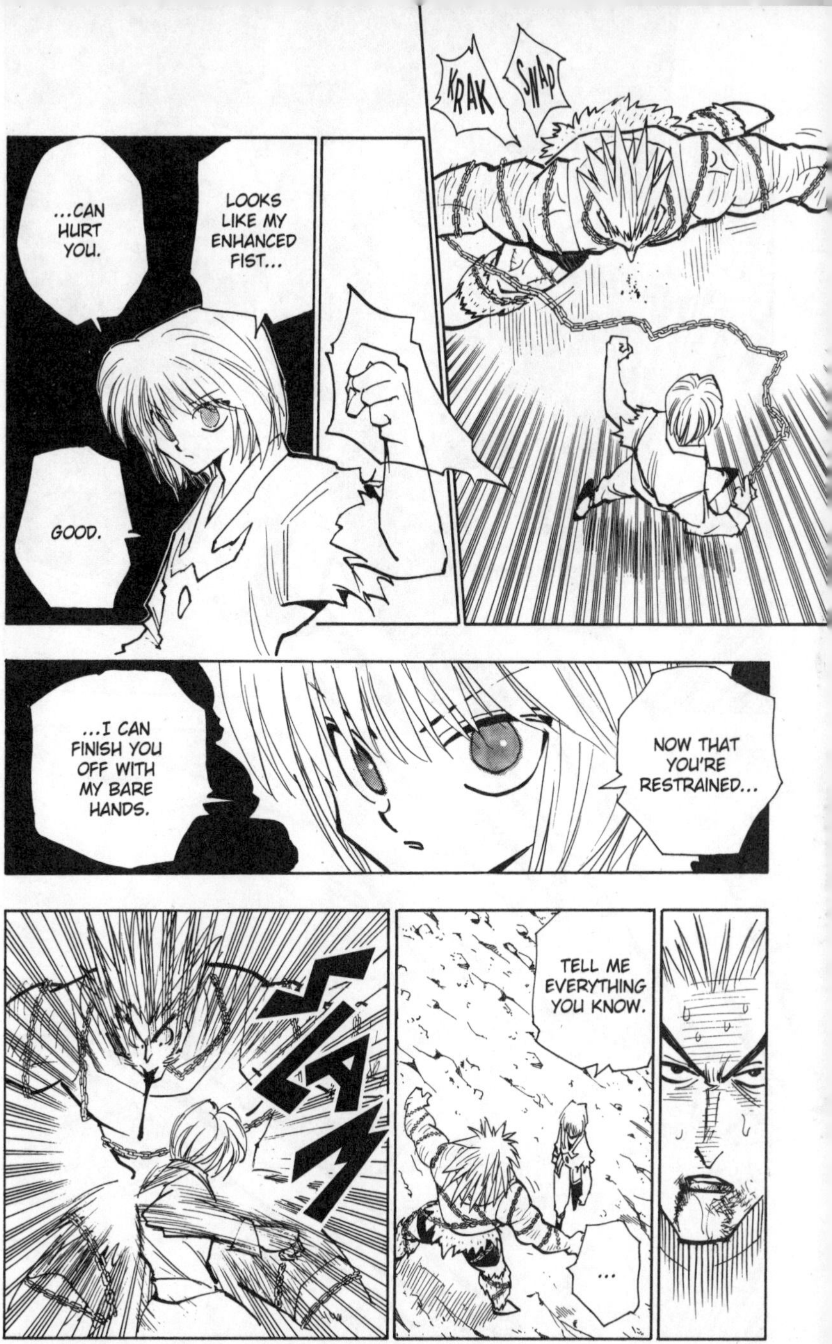
KRAK
SNAP
LOOKS LIKE MY ENHANCED FIST...
...CAN HURT YOU.
GOOD.
NOW THAT YOU'RE RESTRAINED...
...I CAN FINISH YOU OFF WITH MY BARE HANDS.
TELL ME EVERYTHING YOU KNOW.
...
SLAM

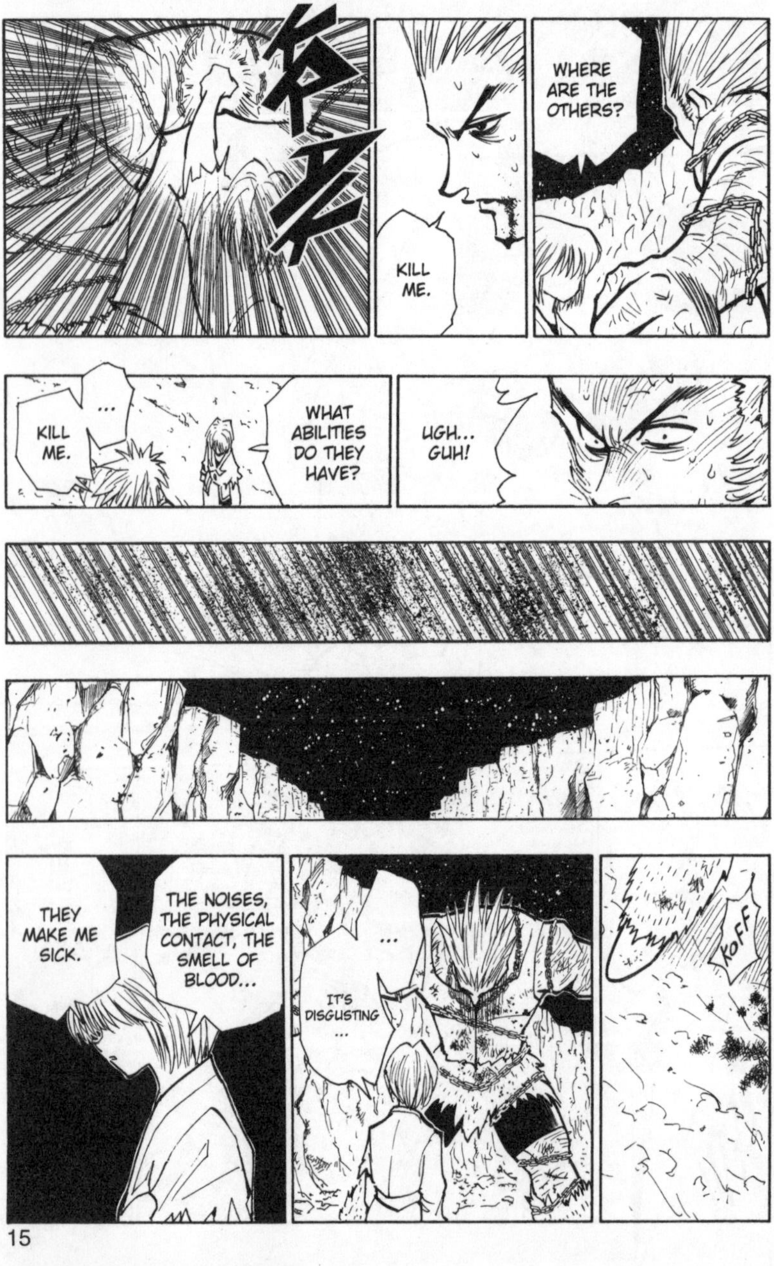
WHERE ARE THE OTHERS?
KILL ME.
UGH... GUH!
WHAT ABILITIES DO THEY HAVE?
...
KILL ME.
KOFF
...
IT'S DISGUSTING ...
THE NOISES, THE PHYSICAL CONTACT, THE SMELL OF BLOOD...
THEY MAKE ME SICK.

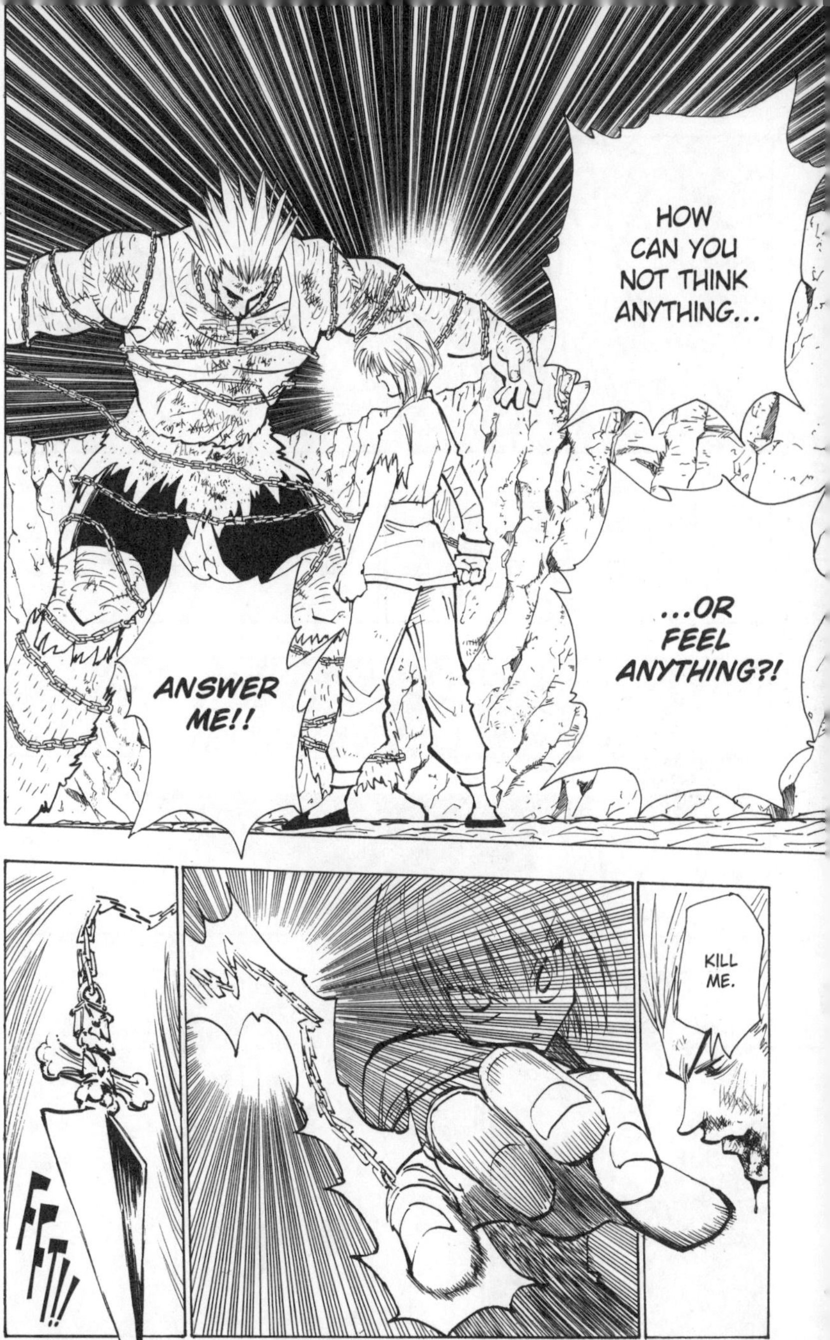
HOW CAN YOU NOT THINK ANYTHING...
...OR FEEL ANYTHING?!
ANSWER ME!!
KILL ME.
FFT!!

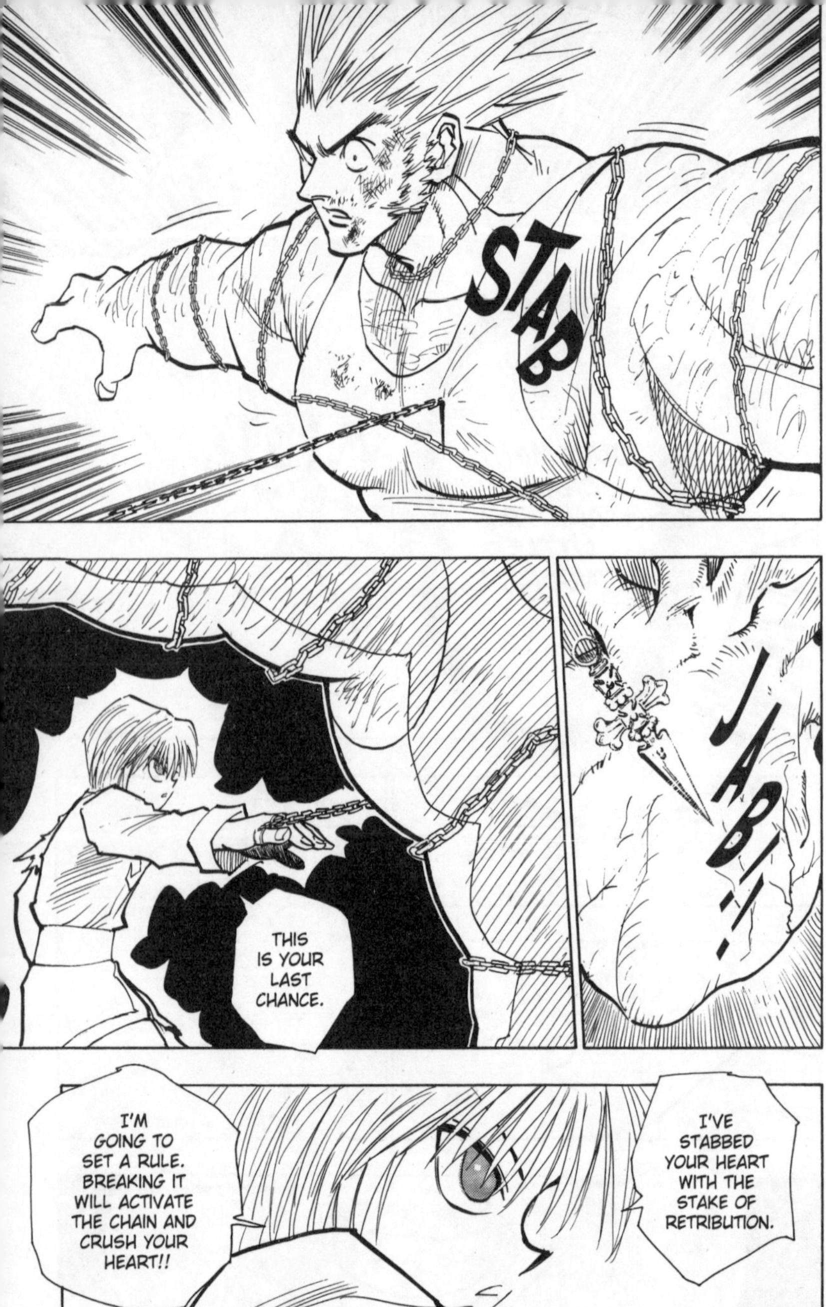
STAB
JAB!!!
THIS IS YOUR LAST CHANCE.
I'VE STABBED YOUR HEART WITH THE STAKE OF RETRIBUTION.
I'M GOING TO SET A RULE. BREAKING IT WILL ACTIVATE THE CHAIN AND CRUSH YOUR HEART!!

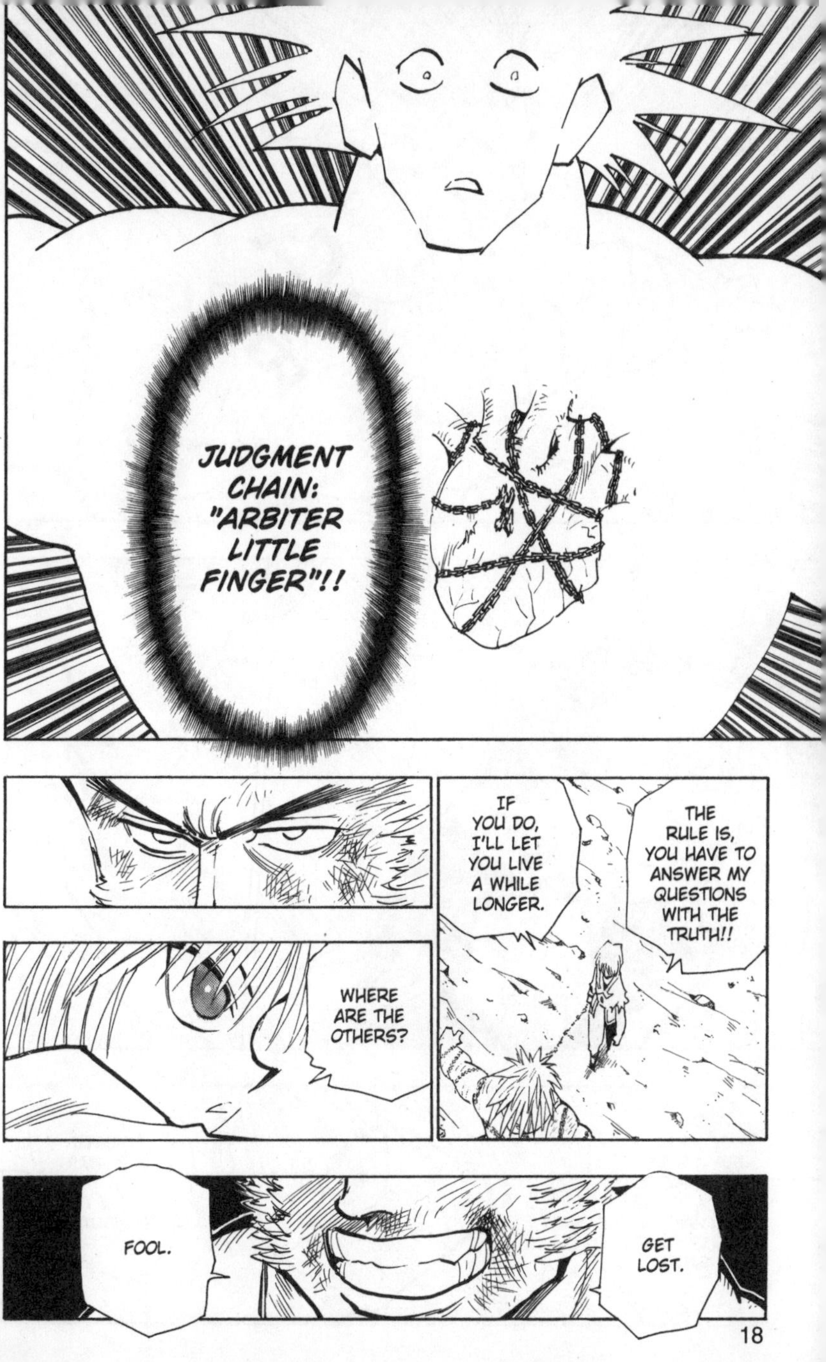
JUDGMENT CHAIN: "ARBITER LITTLE FINGER"!!
THE RULE IS, YOU HAVE TO ANSWER MY QUESTIONS WITH THE TRUTH!!
IF YOU DO, I'LL LET YOU LIVE A WHILE LONGER.
WHERE ARE THE OTHERS?
GET LOST.
FOOL.

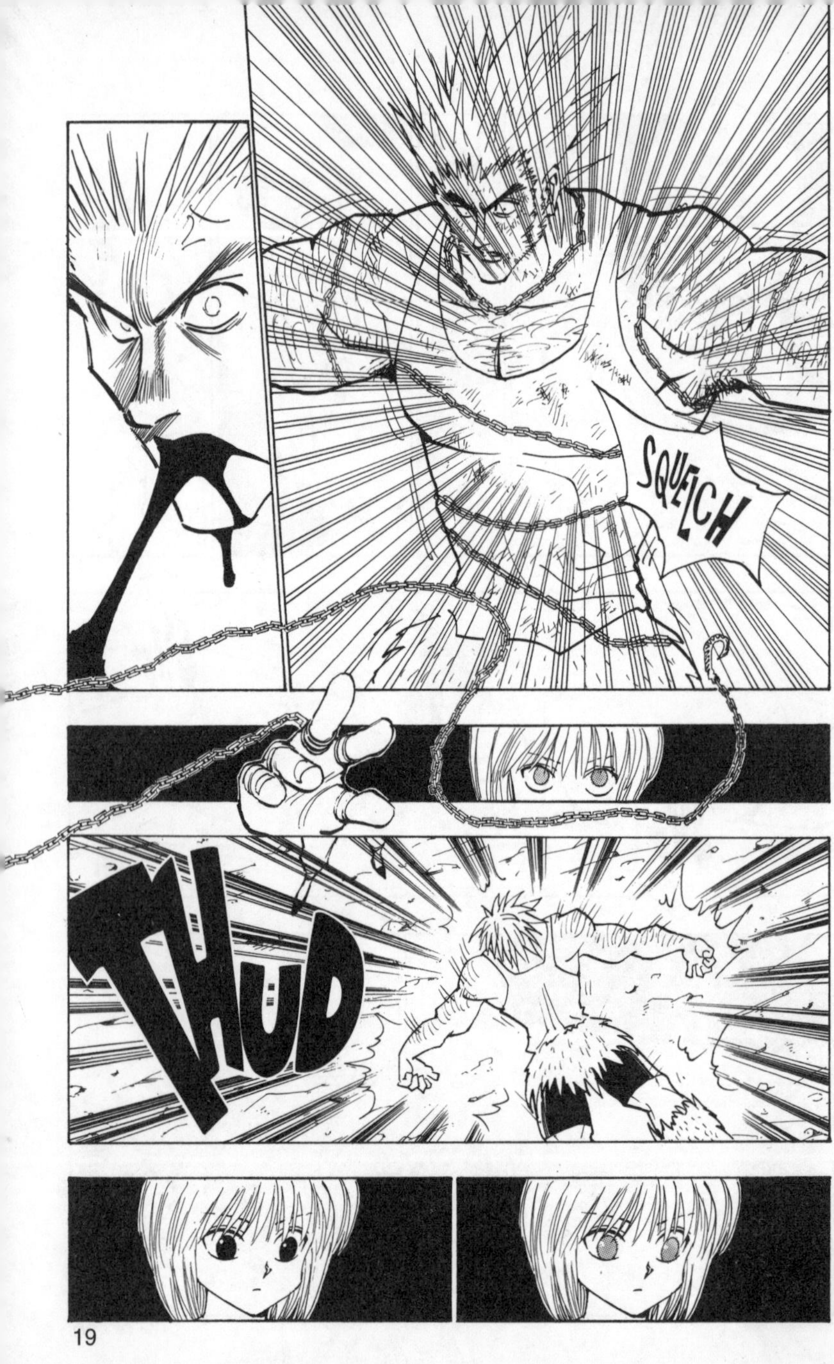
SQUELCH
THUD

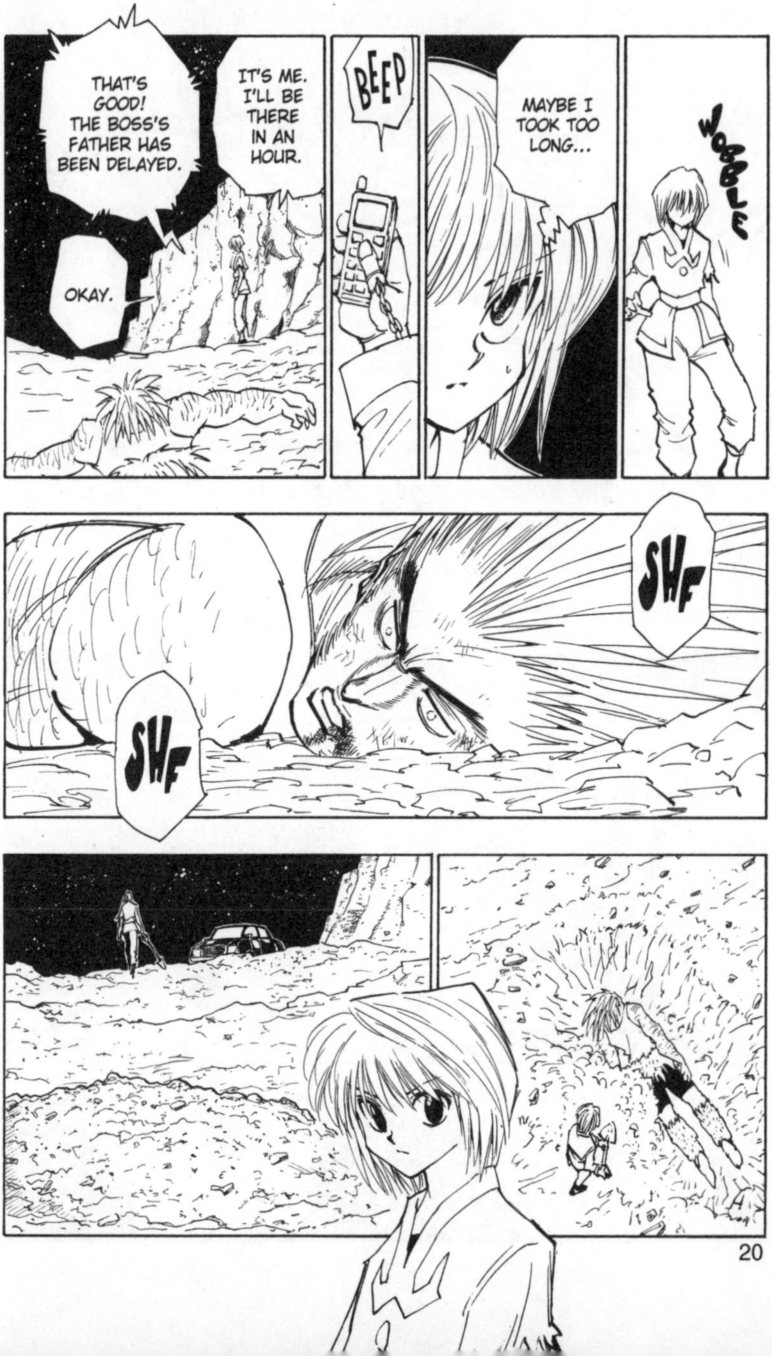
WOBBLE
MAYBE I TOOK TOO LONG...
BEEP
IT'S ME. I'LL BE THERE IN AN HOUR.
THAT'S GOOD! THE BOSS'S FATHER HAS BEEN DELAYED.
OKAY.
SHF
SHF

READ THIS WAY

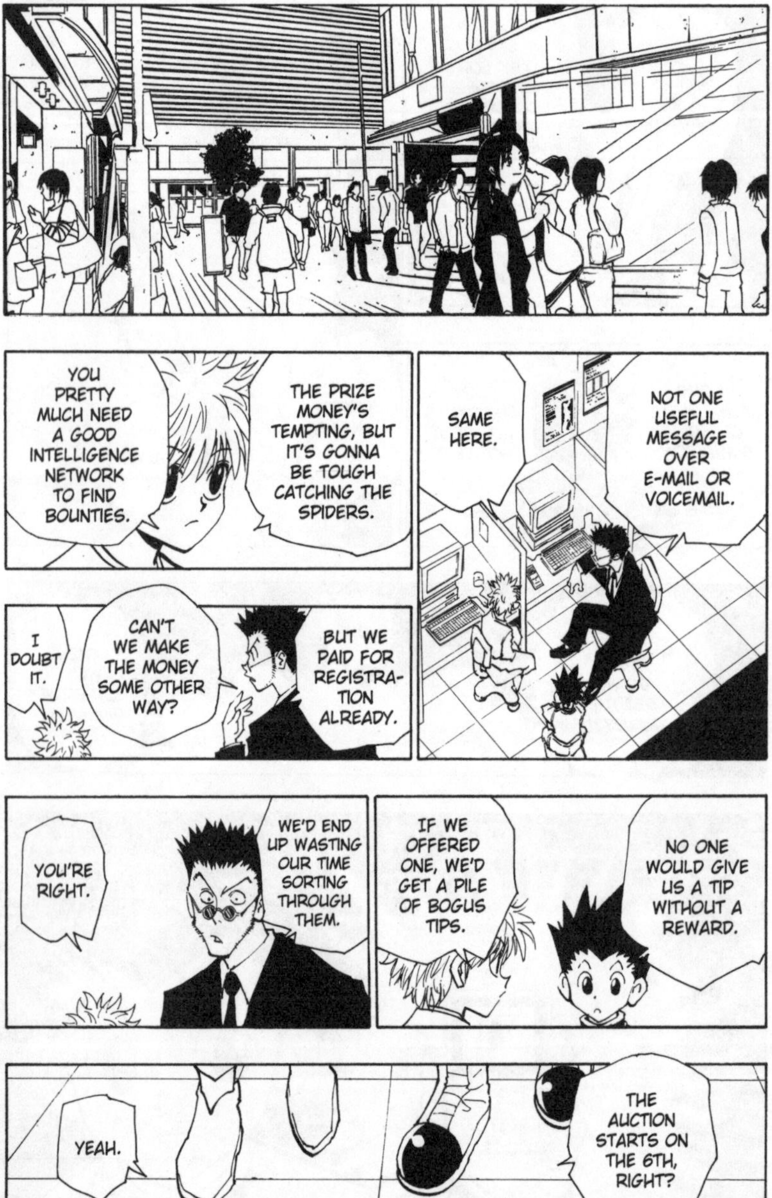
NOT ONE USEFUL MESSAGE OVER E-MAIL OR VOICEMAIL.
SAME HERE.
THE PRIZE MONEY'S TEMPTING, BUT IT'S GONNA BE TOUGH CATCHING THE SPIDERS.
YOU PRETTY MUCH NEED A GOOD INTELLIGENCE NETWORK TO FIND BOUNTIES.
BUT WE PAID FOR REGISTRATION ALREADY.
CAN'T WE MAKE THE MONEY SOME OTHER WAY?
I DOUBT IT.
NO ONE WOULD GIVE US A TIP WITHOUT A REWARD.
IF WE OFFERED ONE, WE'D GET A PILE OF BOGUS TIPS.
WE'D END UP WASTING OUR TIME SORTING THROUGH THEM.
YOU'RE RIGHT.
THE AUCTION STARTS ON THE 6TH, RIGHT?
YEAH.

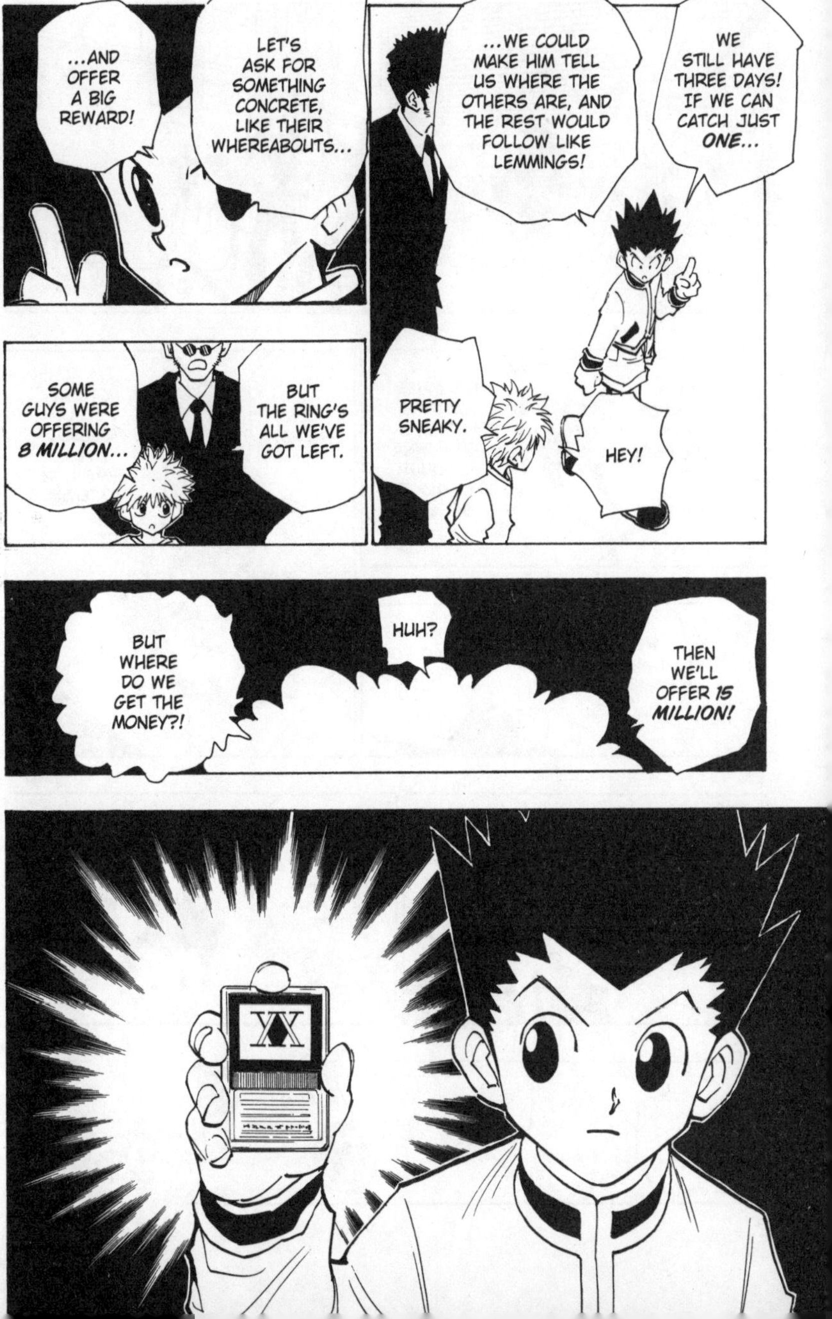
WE STILL HAVE THREE DAYS! IF WE CAN CATCH JUST *ONE*...
...WE COULD MAKE HIM TELL US WHERE THE OTHERS ARE, AND THE REST WOULD FOLLOW LIKE LEMMINGS!
HEY!
PRETTY SNEAKY.
LET'S ASK FOR SOMETHING CONCRETE, LIKE THEIR WHEREABOUTS...
...AND OFFER A BIG REWARD!
BUT THE RING'S ALL WE'VE GOT LEFT.
SOME GUYS WERE OFFERING ***8 MILLION***...
THEN WE'LL OFFER ***15 MILLION!***
HUH?
BUT WHERE DO WE GET THE MONEY?!

READ THIS WAY

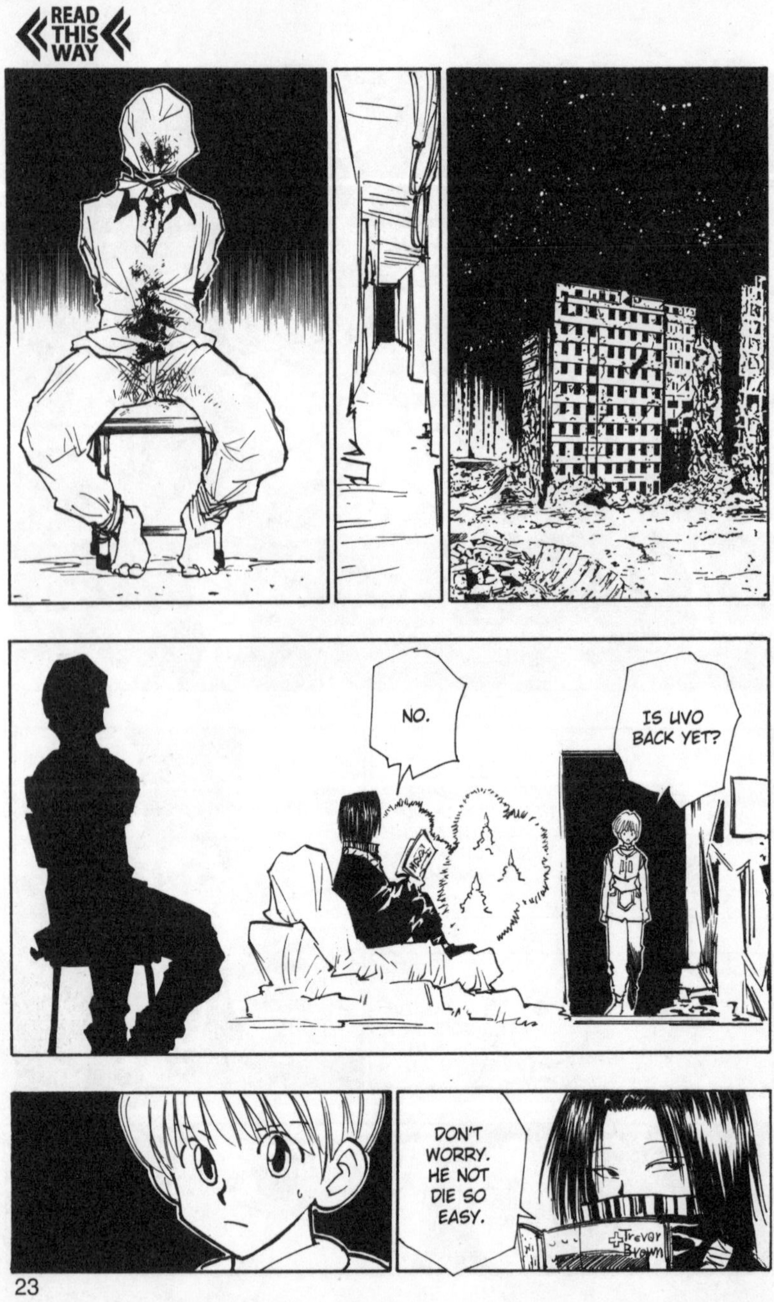
IS UVO BACK YET?
NO.
DON'T WORRY. HE NOT DIE SO EASY.
Trevor Brown

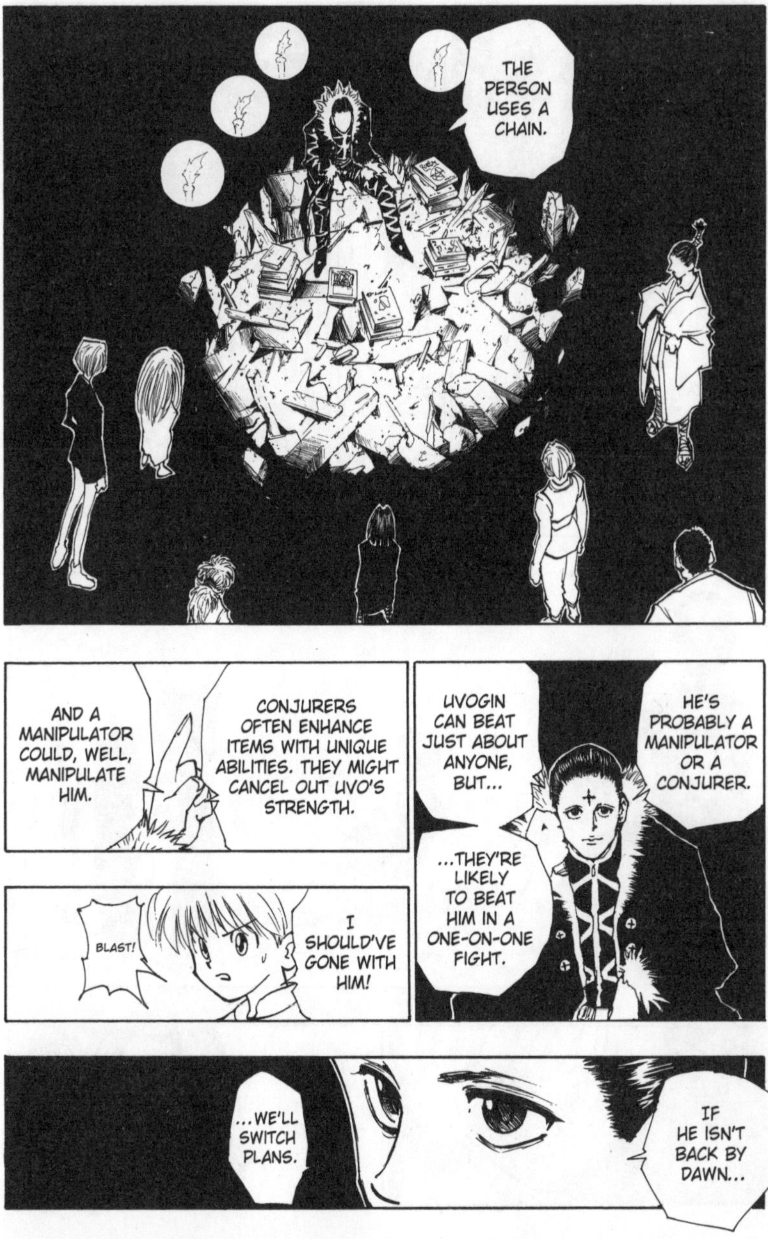
THE PERSON USES A CHAIN.
HE'S PROBABLY A MANIPULATOR OR A CONJURER.
UVOGIN CAN BEAT JUST ABOUT ANYONE, BUT...
...THEY'RE LIKELY TO BEAT HIM IN A ONE-ON-ONE FIGHT.
CONJURERS OFTEN ENHANCE ITEMS WITH UNIQUE ABILITIES. THEY MIGHT CANCEL OUT UVO'S STRENGTH.
AND A MANIPULATOR COULD, WELL, MANIPULATE HIM.
I SHOULD'VE GONE WITH HIM!
BLAST!
IF HE ISN'T BACK BY DAWN...
...WE'LL SWITCH PLANS.

READ THIS WAY

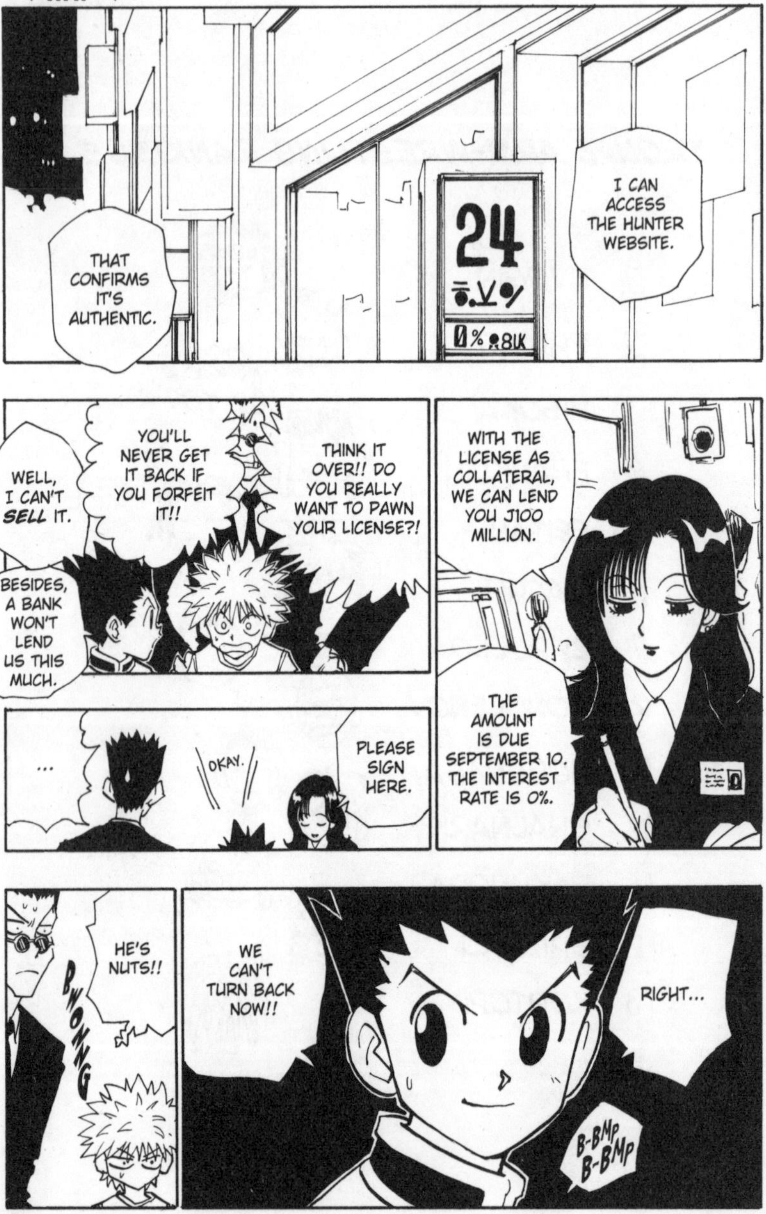

I CAN ACCESS THE HUNTER WEBSITE.
24
THAT CONFIRMS IT'S AUTHENTIC.
WITH THE LICENSE AS COLLATERAL, WE CAN LEND YOU J100 MILLION.
THE AMOUNT IS DUE SEPTEMBER 10. THE INTEREST RATE IS 0%.
THINK IT OVER!! DO YOU REALLY WANT TO PAWN YOUR LICENSE?!
YOU'LL NEVER GET IT BACK IF YOU FORFEIT IT!!
WELL, I CAN'T **SELL** IT.
BESIDES, A BANK WON'T LEND US THIS MUCH.
PLEASE SIGN HERE.
OKAY.
...
RIGHT...
WE CAN'T TURN BACK NOW!!
B-BMP B-BMP
HE'S NUTS!!
BWONNG

TROUPE ARM-WRESTLING RANKINGS

1 UVOGIN
2 PHINKS
3 HISOKA
4 FRANKLIN
5 FEITAN
6 MACHI
7 CHROLLO
8 BONOLENOV
9 NOBUNAGA
10 SHALNARK
11 PAKUNODA
12 SHIZUKU
13 KORTOPI

Chapter 85 September 3rd: Part 1

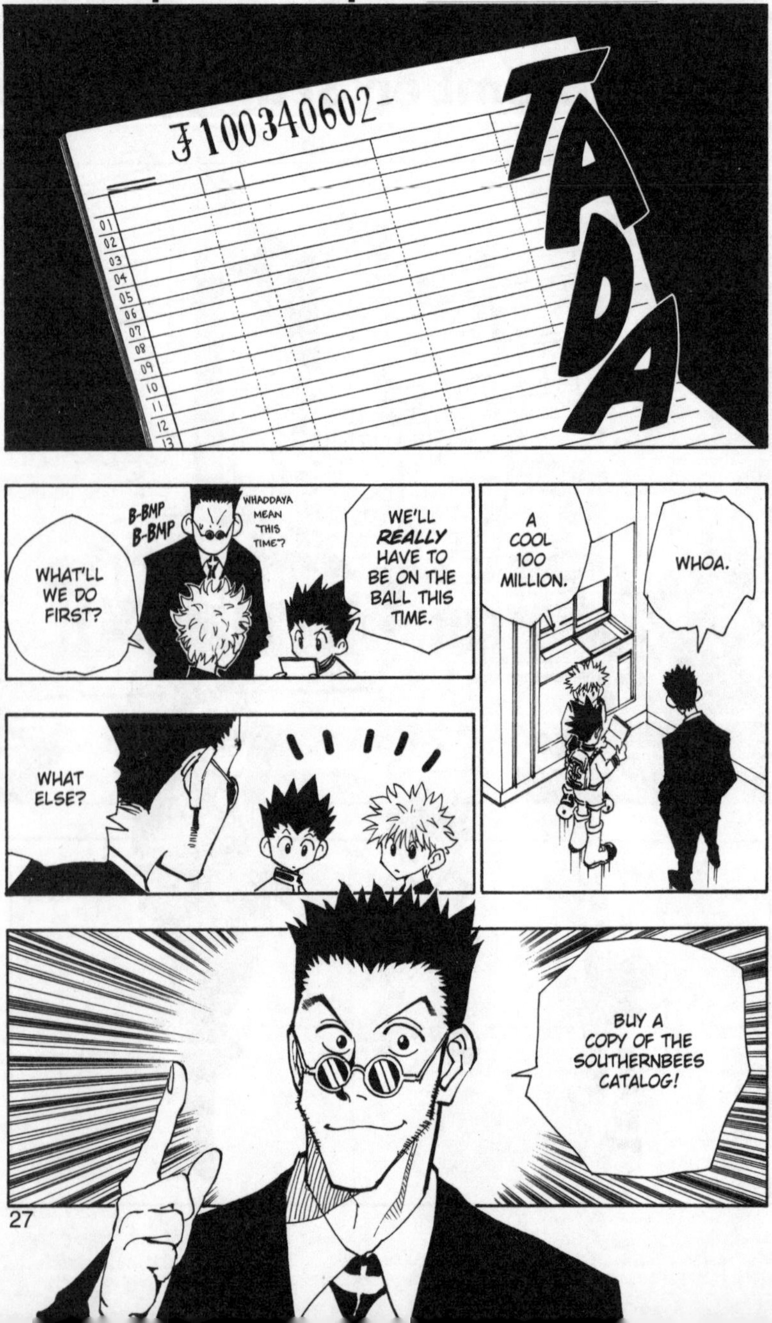
Ɉ100340602-
TADA
A COOL 100 MILLION.
WHOA.
WE'LL *REALLY* HAVE TO BE ON THE BALL THIS TIME.
WHADDAYA MEAN "THIS TIME"?
B-BMP B-BMP
WHAT'LL WE DO FIRST?
WHAT ELSE?
BUY A COPY OF THE SOUTHERNBEES CATALOG!

Chapter 85
September 3rd: Part 1

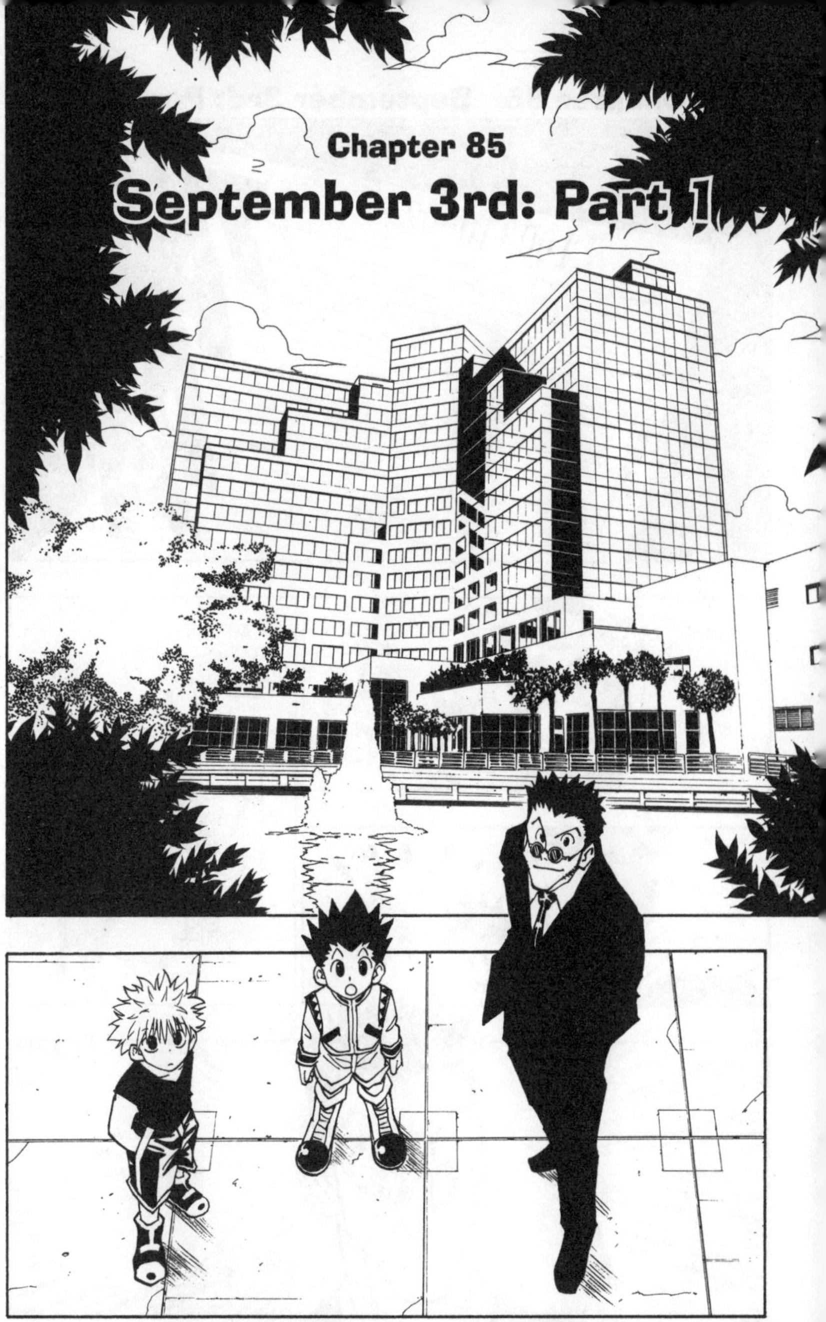

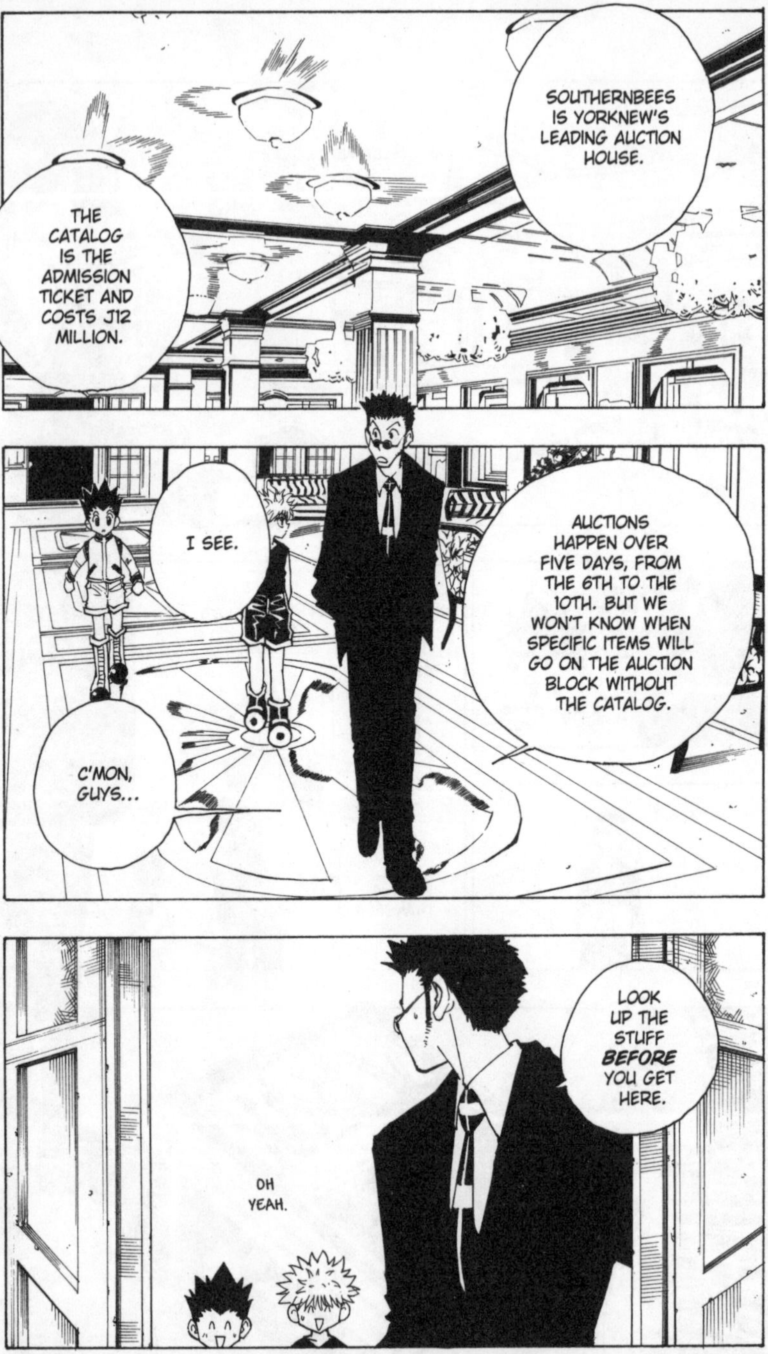
SOUTHERNBEES IS YORKNEW'S LEADING AUCTION HOUSE.
THE CATALOG IS THE ADMISSION TICKET AND COSTS J12 MILLION.
AUCTIONS HAPPEN OVER FIVE DAYS, FROM THE 6TH TO THE 10TH. BUT WE WON'T KNOW WHEN SPECIFIC ITEMS WILL GO ON THE AUCTION BLOCK WITHOUT THE CATALOG.
I SEE.
C'MON, GUYS...
LOOK UP THE STUFF *BEFORE* YOU GET HERE.
OH YEAH.

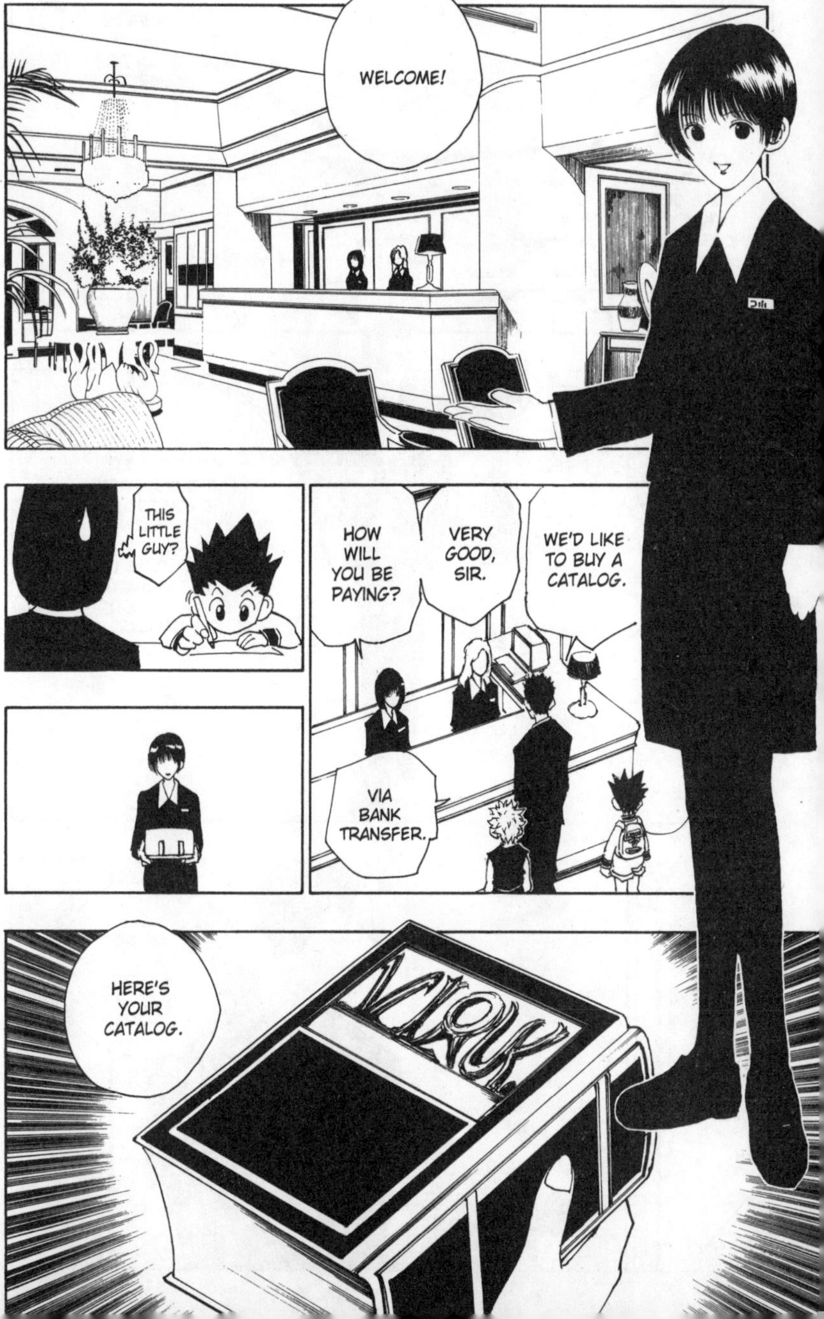
WELCOME!
WE'D LIKE TO BUY A CATALOG.
VERY GOOD, SIR.
HOW WILL YOU BE PAYING?
VIA BANK TRANSFER.
THIS LITTLE GUY?
HERE'S YOUR CATALOG.

READ THIS WAY

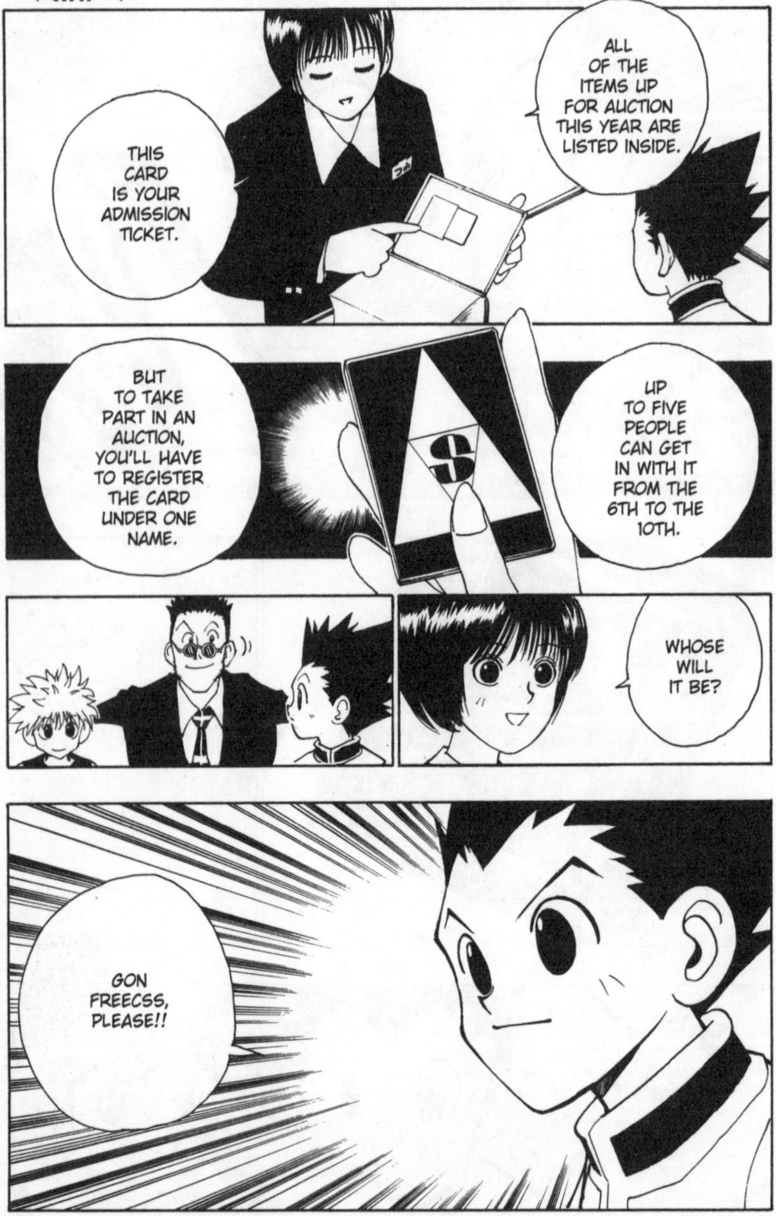
ALL OF THE ITEMS UP FOR AUCTION THIS YEAR ARE LISTED INSIDE.
THIS CARD IS YOUR ADMISSION TICKET.
UP TO FIVE PEOPLE CAN GET IN WITH IT FROM THE 6TH TO THE 10TH.
BUT TO TAKE PART IN AN AUCTION, YOU'LL HAVE TO REGISTER THE CARD UNDER ONE NAME.
WHOSE WILL IT BE?
GON FREECSS, PLEASE!!

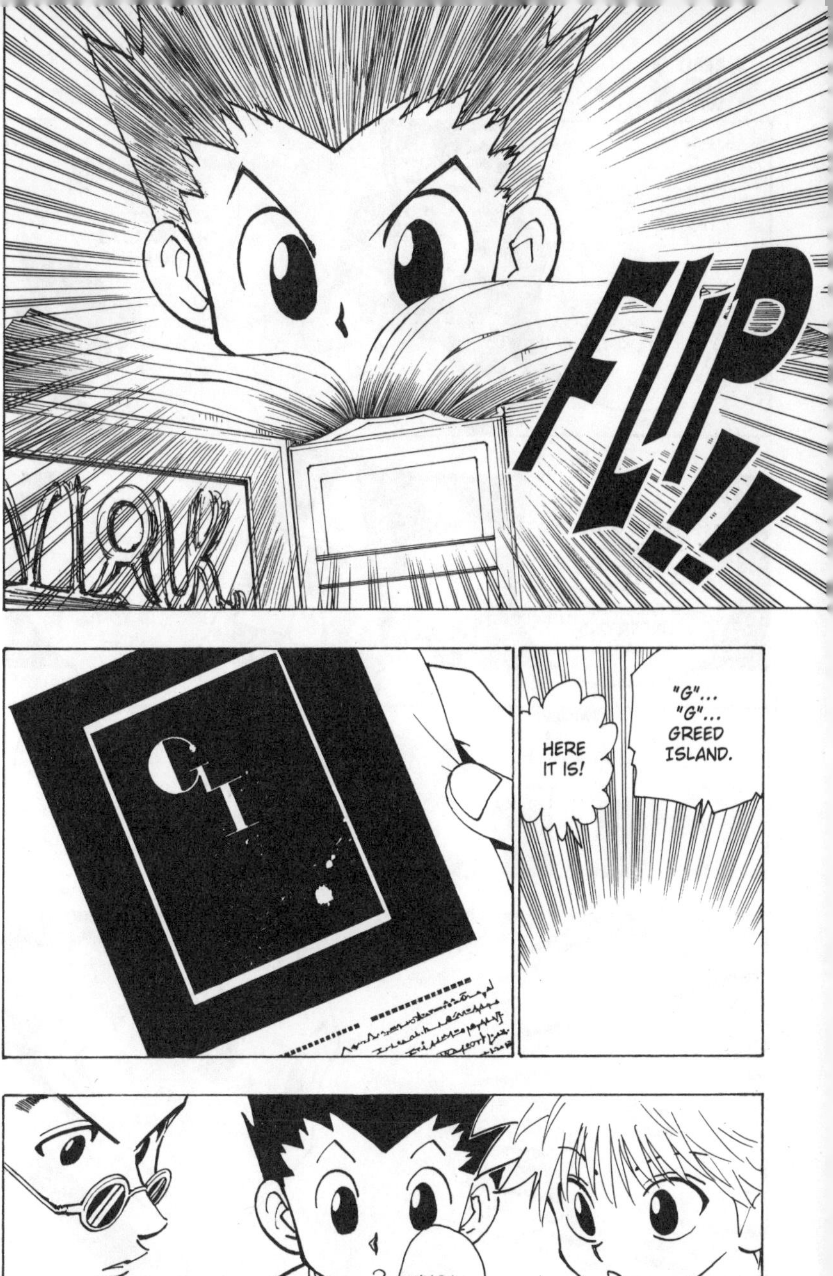
FLIP!!
"G"... "G"... GREED ISLAND.
HERE IT IS!
GI
WHOA...

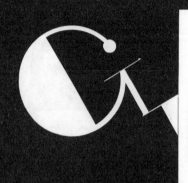

Greed Island
A Game for Hunters

In 1987, a mere 100 cartridges were sold for J5.8 billion each. Very little is known about the game's contents, as you'll discover by reading the instruction manual, the entirety of which is scanned below. Please bear this in mind when bidding on this item.

"Greed Island" has not appeared on the market for the past few years, but Southernbees has successfully acquired seven copies. Authenticity was verified in the following ways:
1) Confirmation with the manufacturer (verification of the serial number)
2) Confirmation of ownership history (records of sale)
3) Actual condition of the item
The condition of the games speaks for itself. As to their authenticity, there can be no doubt after seeing them in person. We urge that you see for yourself; they are a must-see.

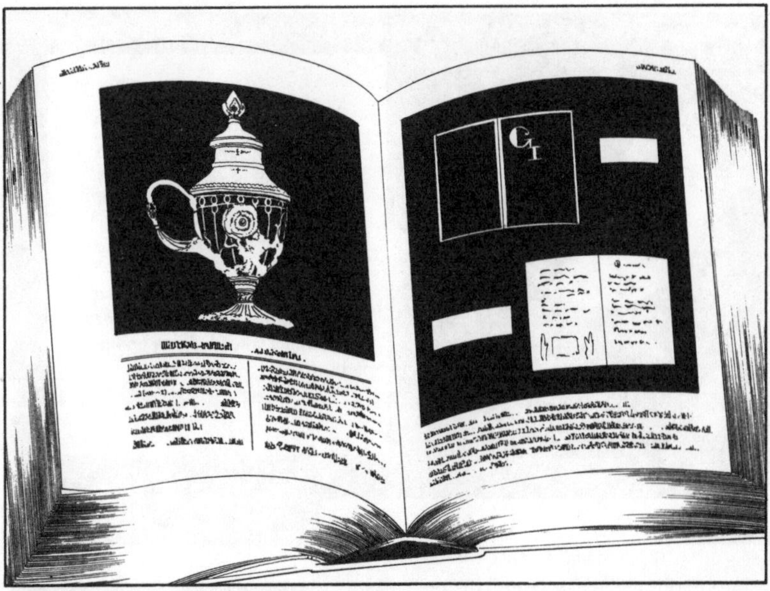

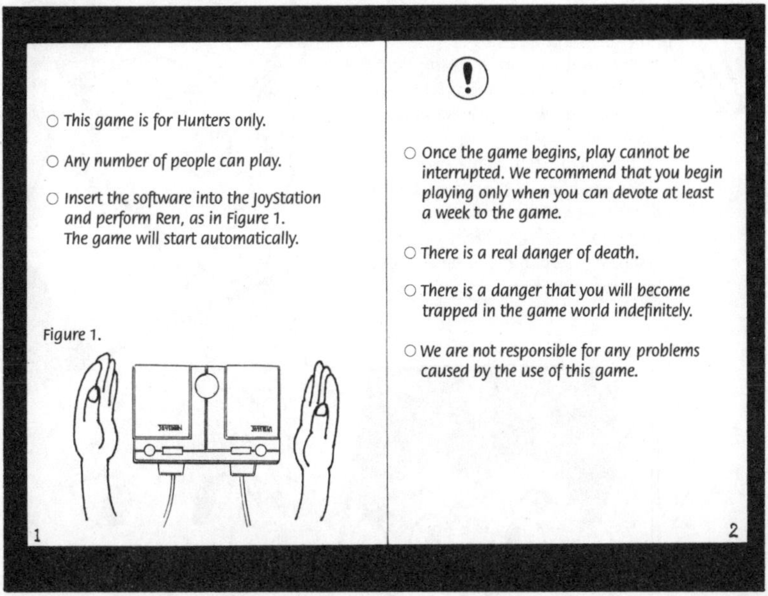
○ This game is for Hunters only.

○ Any number of people can play.

○ Insert the software into the JoyStation and perform Ren, as in Figure 1. The game will start automatically.

Figure 1.

1

○ Once the game begins, play cannot be interrupted. We recommend that you begin playing only when you can devote at least a week to the game.

○ There is a real danger of death.

○ There is a danger that you will become trapped in the game world indefinitely.

○ We are not responsible for any problems caused by the use of this game.

2

READ THIS WAY

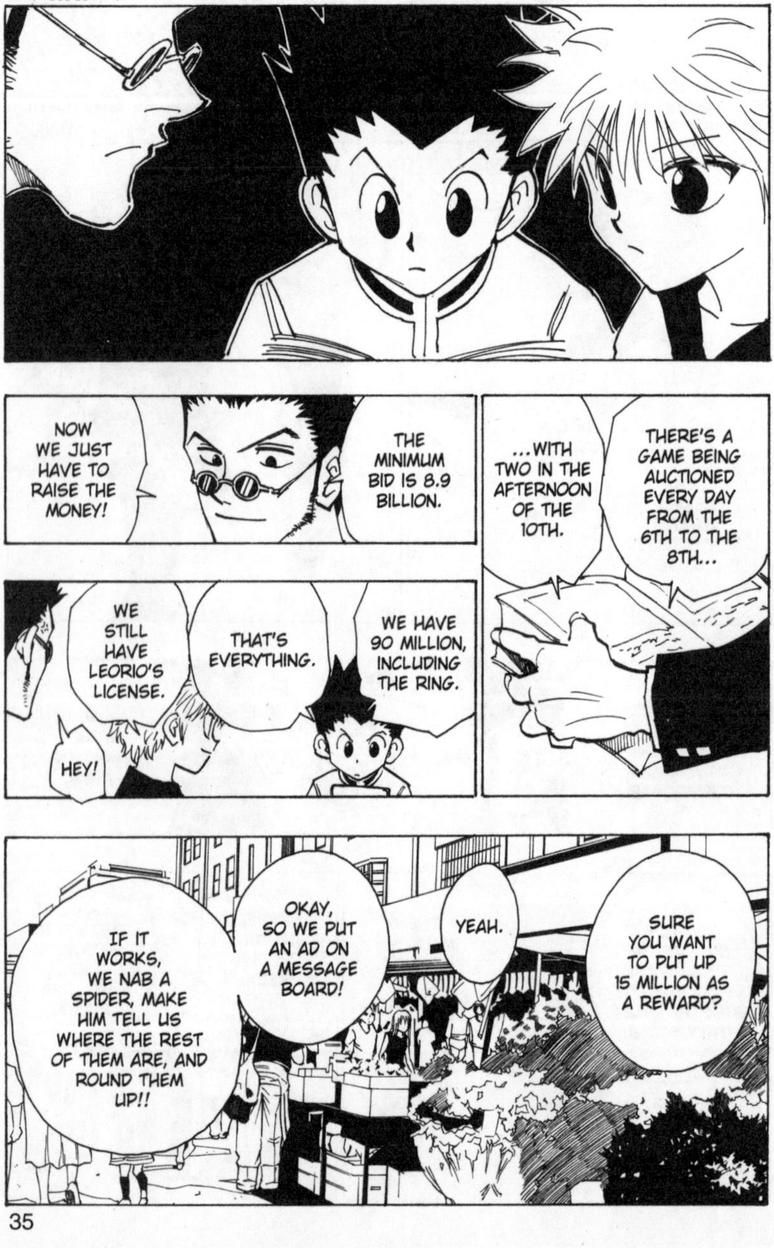
THERE'S A GAME BEING AUCTIONED EVERY DAY FROM THE 6TH TO THE 8TH...
...WITH TWO IN THE AFTERNOON OF THE 10TH.
THE MINIMUM BID IS 8.9 BILLION.
NOW WE JUST HAVE TO RAISE THE MONEY!
WE HAVE 90 MILLION, INCLUDING THE RING.
THAT'S EVERYTHING.
WE STILL HAVE LEORIO'S LICENSE.
HEY!
SURE YOU WANT TO PUT UP 15 MILLION AS A REWARD?
YEAH.
OKAY, SO WE PUT AN AD ON A MESSAGE BOARD!
IF IT WORKS, WE NAB A SPIDER, MAKE HIM TELL US WHERE THE REST OF THEM ARE, AND ROUND THEM UP!!

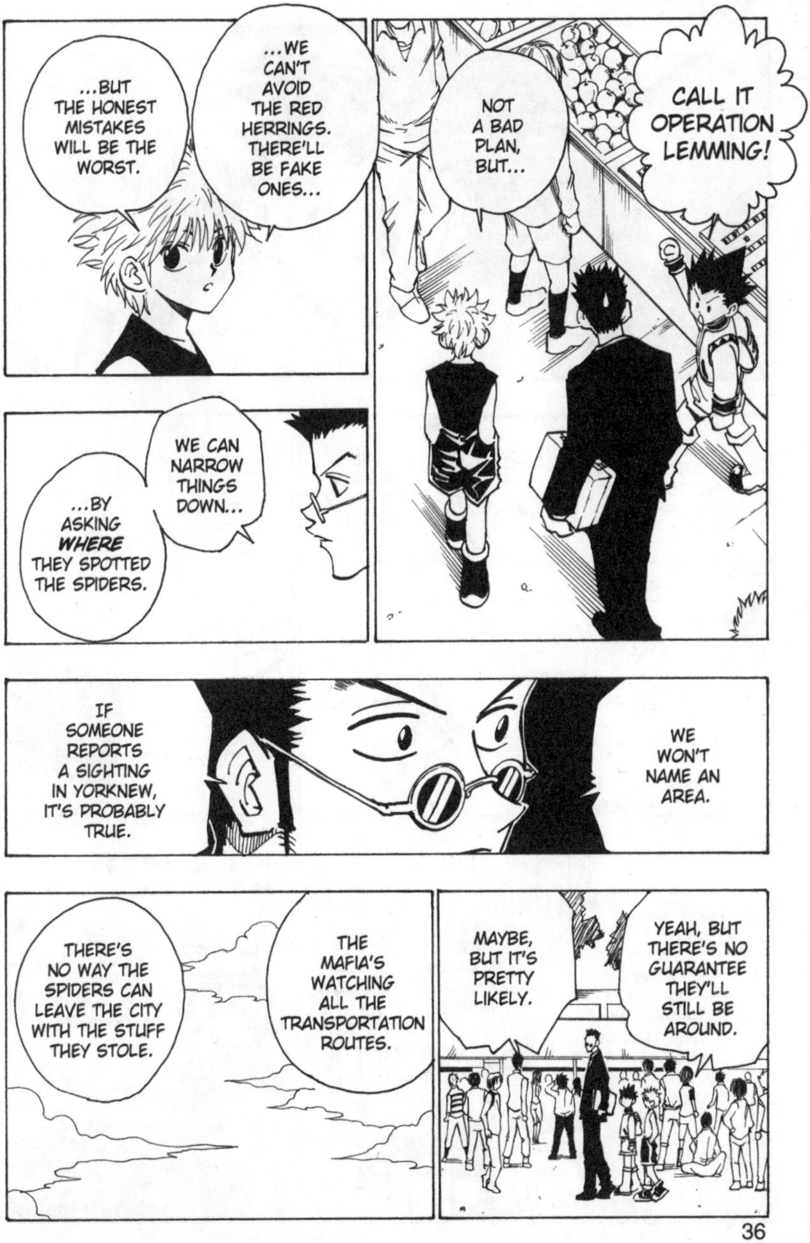
CALL IT OPERATION LEMMING!
NOT A BAD PLAN, BUT...
...WE CAN'T AVOID THE RED HERRINGS. THERE'LL BE FAKE ONES...
...BUT THE HONEST MISTAKES WILL BE THE WORST.
WE CAN NARROW THINGS DOWN...
...BY ASKING *WHERE* THEY SPOTTED THE SPIDERS.
WE WON'T NAME AN AREA.
IF SOMEONE REPORTS A SIGHTING IN YORKNEW, IT'S PROBABLY TRUE.
YEAH, BUT THERE'S NO GUARANTEE THEY'LL STILL BE AROUND.
MAYBE, BUT IT'S PRETTY LIKELY.
THE MAFIA'S WATCHING ALL THE TRANSPORTATION ROUTES.
THERE'S NO WAY THE SPIDERS CAN LEAVE THE CITY WITH THE STUFF THEY STOLE.

READ THIS WAY

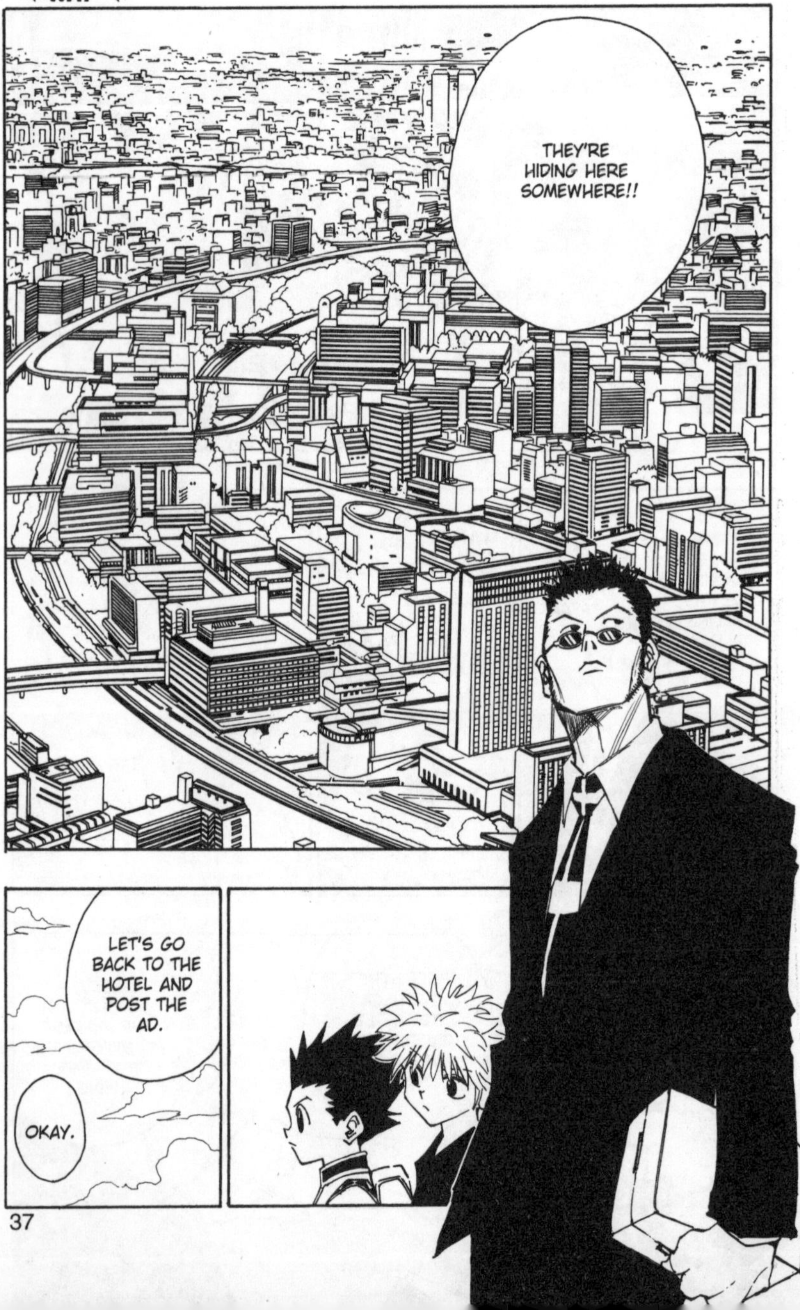
THEY'RE HIDING HERE SOMEWHERE!!
LET'S GO BACK TO THE HOTEL AND POST THE AD.
OKAY.

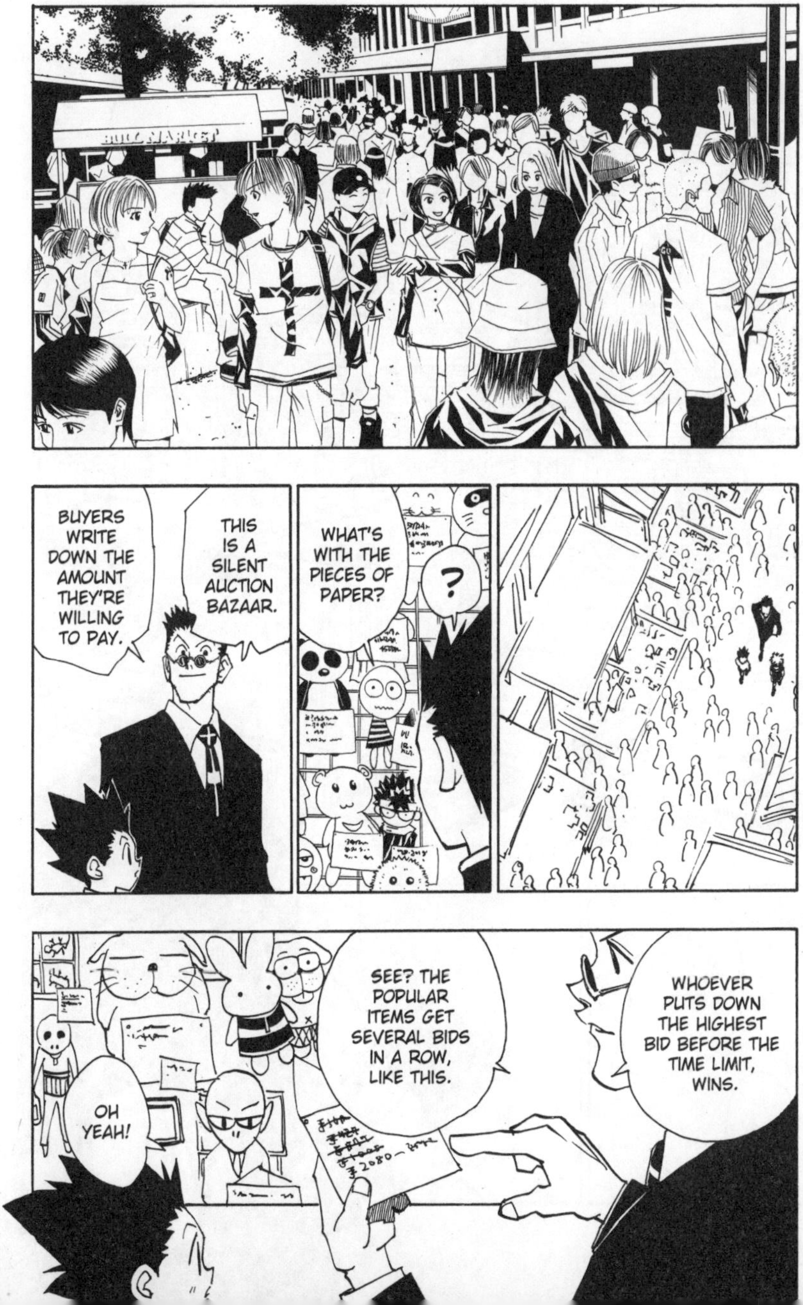
BULL MARKET
WHAT'S WITH THE PIECES OF PAPER?
?
THIS IS A SILENT AUCTION BAZAAR.
BUYERS WRITE DOWN THE AMOUNT THEY'RE WILLING TO PAY.
WHOEVER PUTS DOWN THE HIGHEST BID BEFORE THE TIME LIMIT, WINS.
SEE? THE POPULAR ITEMS GET SEVERAL BIDS IN A ROW, LIKE THIS.
OH YEAH!

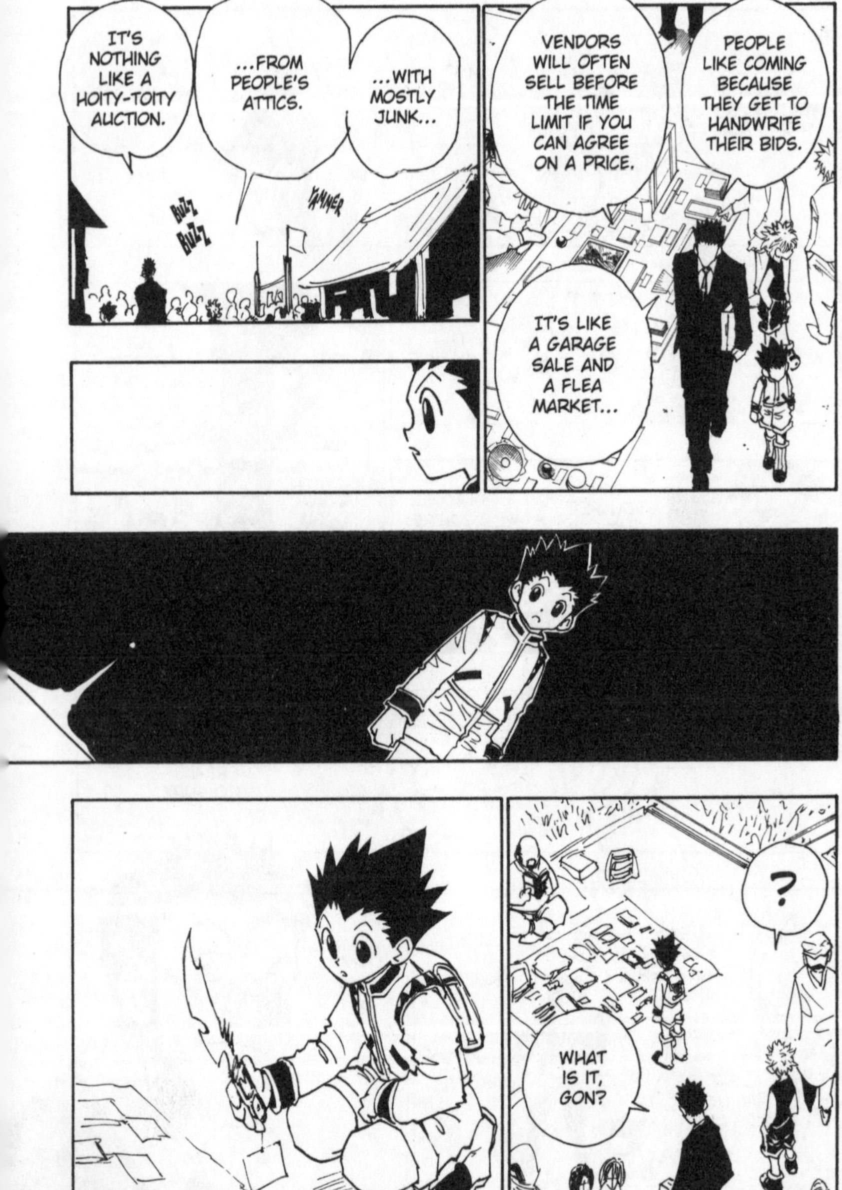
PEOPLE LIKE COMING BECAUSE THEY GET TO HANDWRITE THEIR BIDS.
VENDORS WILL OFTEN SELL BEFORE THE TIME LIMIT IF YOU CAN AGREE ON A PRICE.
IT'S LIKE A GARAGE SALE AND A FLEA MARKET...
...WITH MOSTLY JUNK...
...FROM PEOPLE'S ATTICS.
IT'S NOTHING LIKE A HOITY-TOITY AUCTION.
YAMMER
BUZZ BUZZ
?
WHAT IS IT, GON?

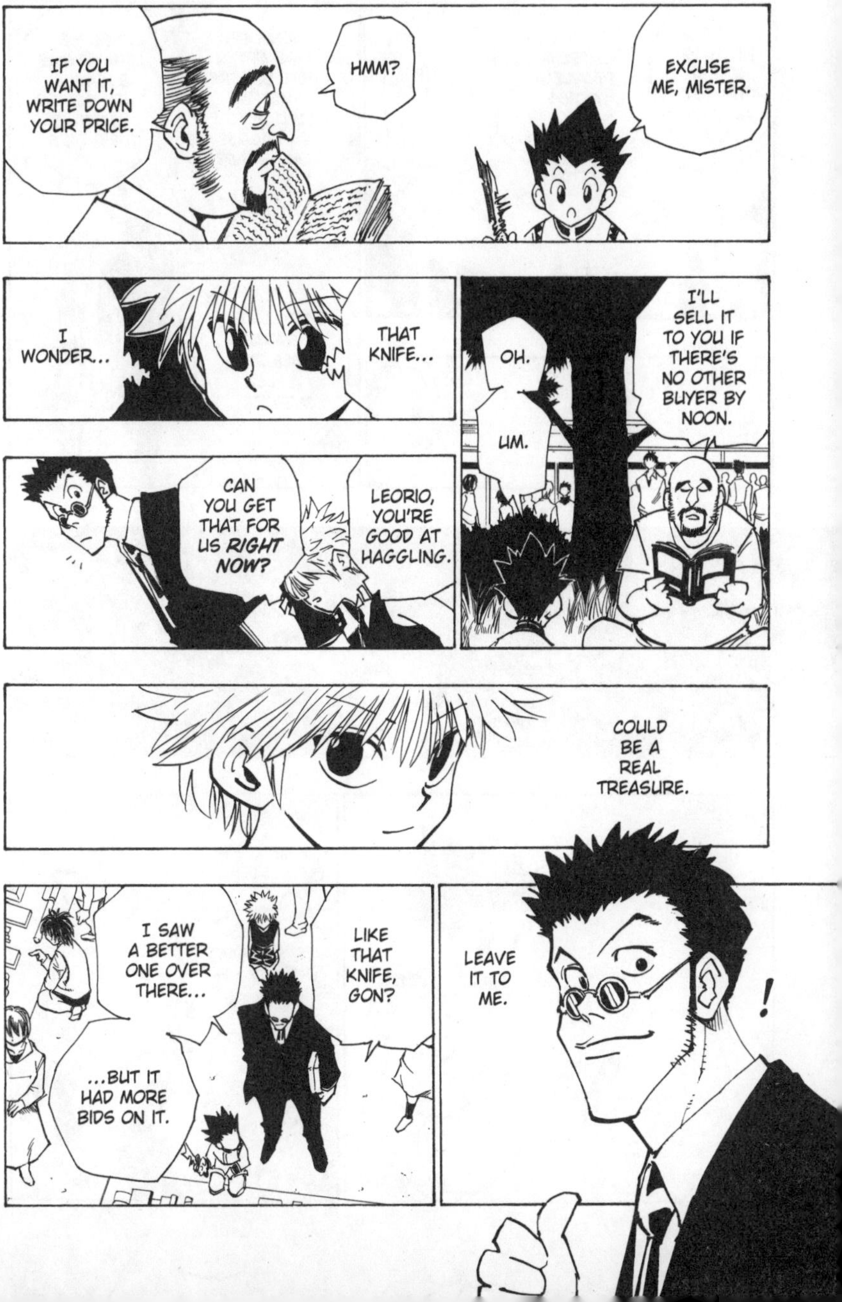
EXCUSE ME, MISTER.
HMM?
IF YOU WANT IT, WRITE DOWN YOUR PRICE.
I'LL SELL IT TO YOU IF THERE'S NO OTHER BUYER BY NOON.
OH.
UM.
THAT KNIFE...
I WONDER...
LEORIO, YOU'RE GOOD AT HAGGLING.
CAN YOU GET THAT FOR US *RIGHT NOW?*
COULD BE A REAL TREASURE.
LEAVE IT TO ME.
!
LIKE THAT KNIFE, GON?
I SAW A BETTER ONE OVER THERE...
...BUT IT HAD MORE BIDS ON IT.

READ THIS WAY

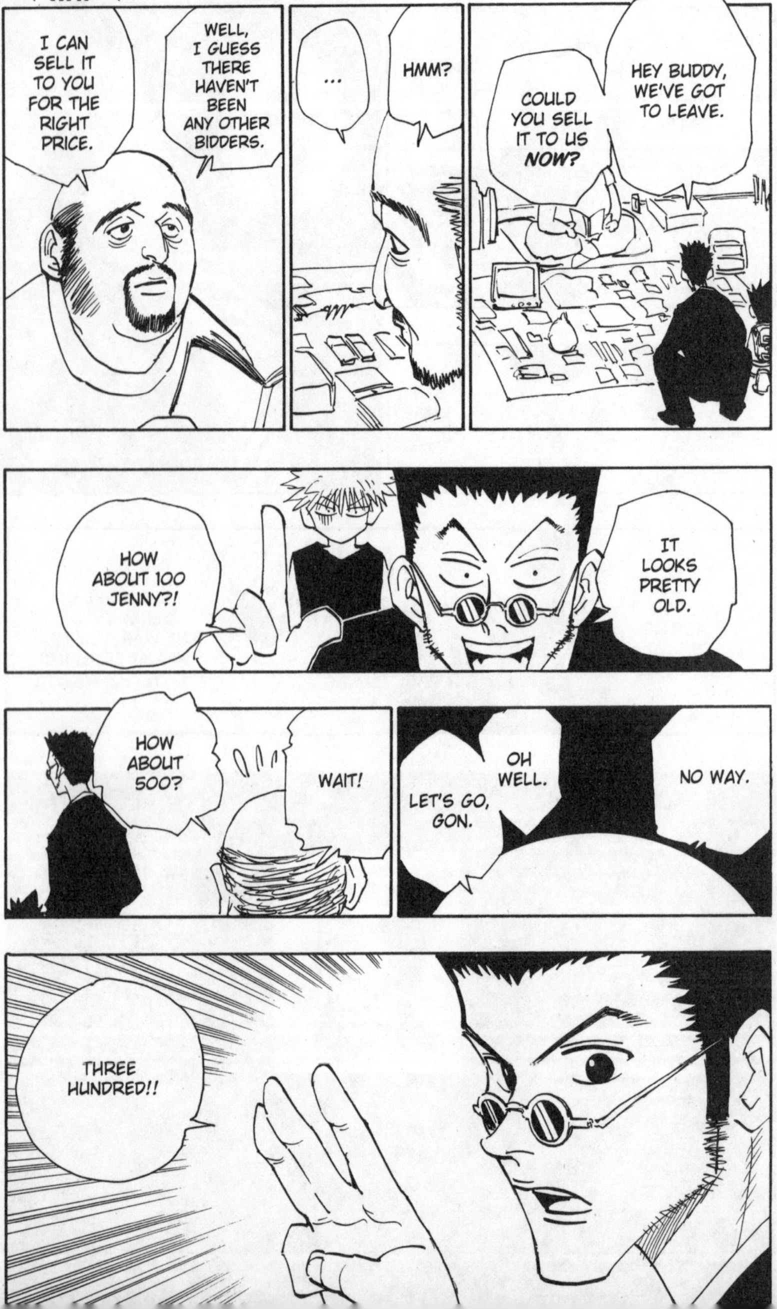
HEY BUDDY, WE'VE GOT TO LEAVE.
COULD YOU SELL IT TO US *NOW?*
HMM?
...
WELL, I GUESS THERE HAVEN'T BEEN ANY OTHER BIDDERS.
I CAN SELL IT TO YOU FOR THE RIGHT PRICE.
IT LOOKS PRETTY OLD.
HOW ABOUT 100 JENNY?!
NO WAY.
OH WELL.
LET'S GO, GON.
WAIT!
HOW ABOUT 500?
THREE HUNDRED!!

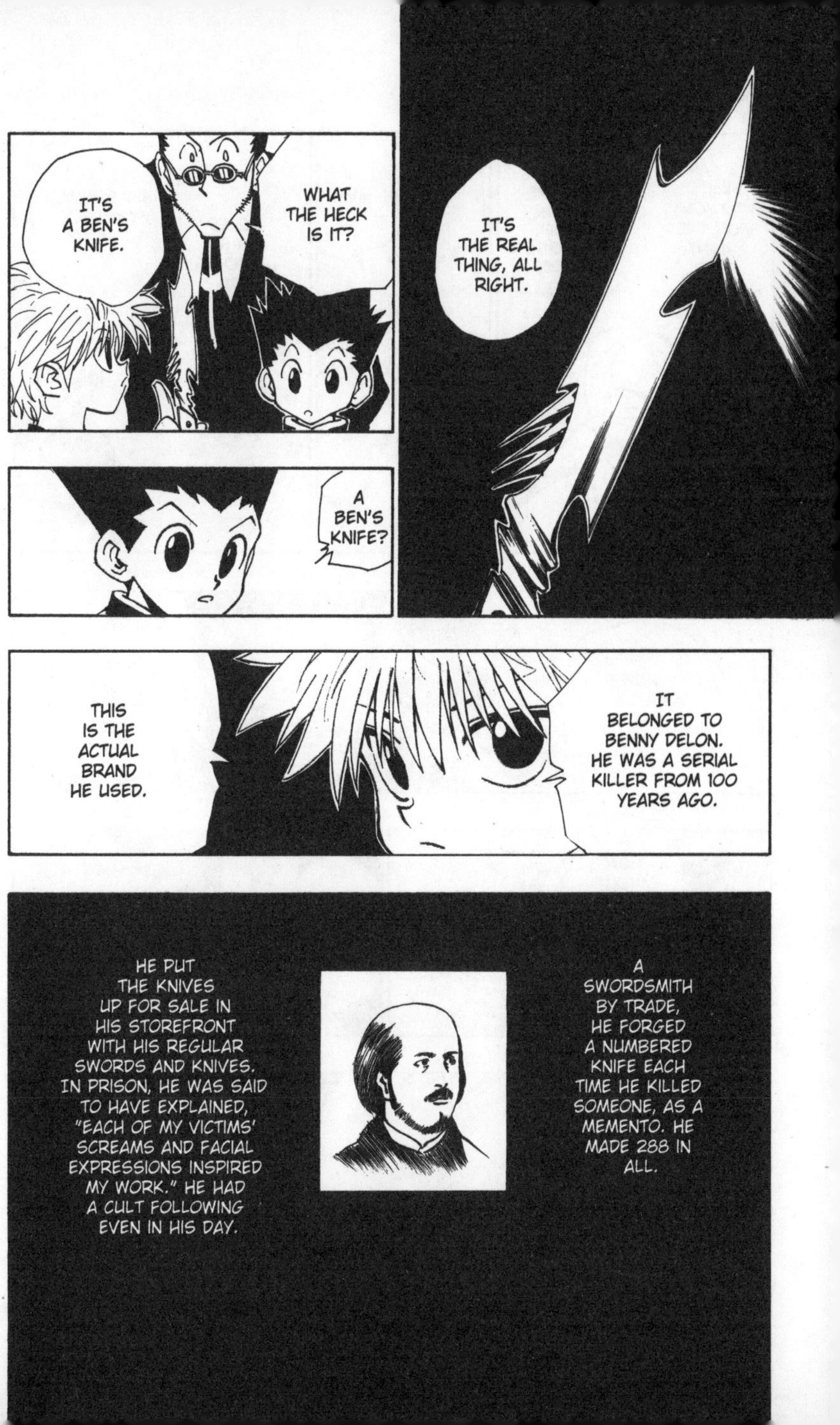
IT'S THE REAL THING, ALL RIGHT.
WHAT THE HECK IS IT?
IT'S A BEN'S KNIFE.
A BEN'S KNIFE?
IT BELONGED TO BENNY DELON. HE WAS A SERIAL KILLER FROM 100 YEARS AGO.
THIS IS THE ACTUAL BRAND HE USED.
A SWORDSMITH BY TRADE, HE FORGED A NUMBERED KNIFE EACH TIME HE KILLED SOMEONE, AS A MEMENTO. HE MADE 288 IN ALL.
HE PUT THE KNIVES UP FOR SALE IN HIS STOREFRONT WITH HIS REGULAR SWORDS AND KNIVES. IN PRISON, HE WAS SAID TO HAVE EXPLAINED, "EACH OF MY VICTIMS' SCREAMS AND FACIAL EXPRESSIONS INSPIRED MY WORK." HE HAD A CULT FOLLOWING EVEN IN HIS DAY.

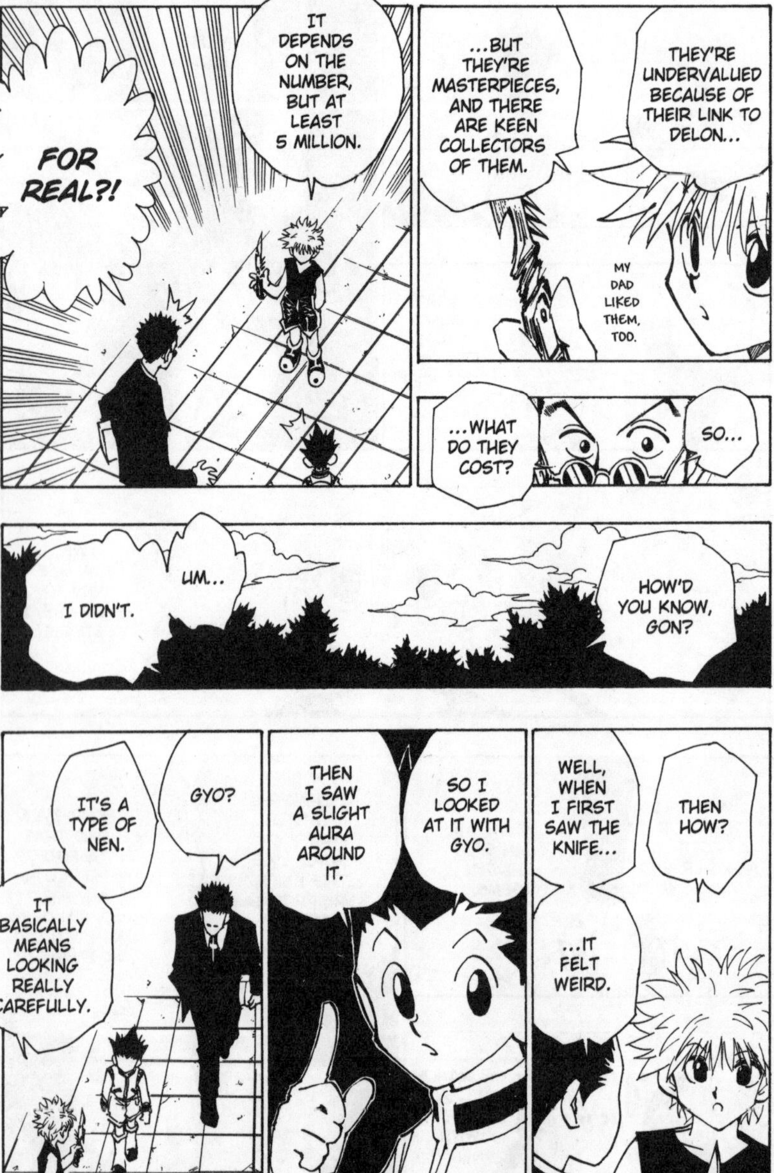
THEY'RE UNDERVALUED BECAUSE OF THEIR LINK TO DELON...
...BUT THEY'RE MASTERPIECES, AND THERE ARE KEEN COLLECTORS OF THEM.
MY DAD LIKED THEM, TOO.
SO...
...WHAT DO THEY COST?
IT DEPENDS ON THE NUMBER, BUT AT LEAST 5 MILLION.
FOR REAL?!
HOW'D YOU KNOW, GON?
UM...
I DIDN'T.
THEN HOW?
WELL, WHEN I FIRST SAW THE KNIFE...
...IT FELT WEIRD.
SO I LOOKED AT IT WITH GYO.
THEN I SAW A SLIGHT AURA AROUND IT.
GYO?
IT'S A TYPE OF NEN.
IT BASICALLY MEANS LOOKING REALLY CAREFULLY.

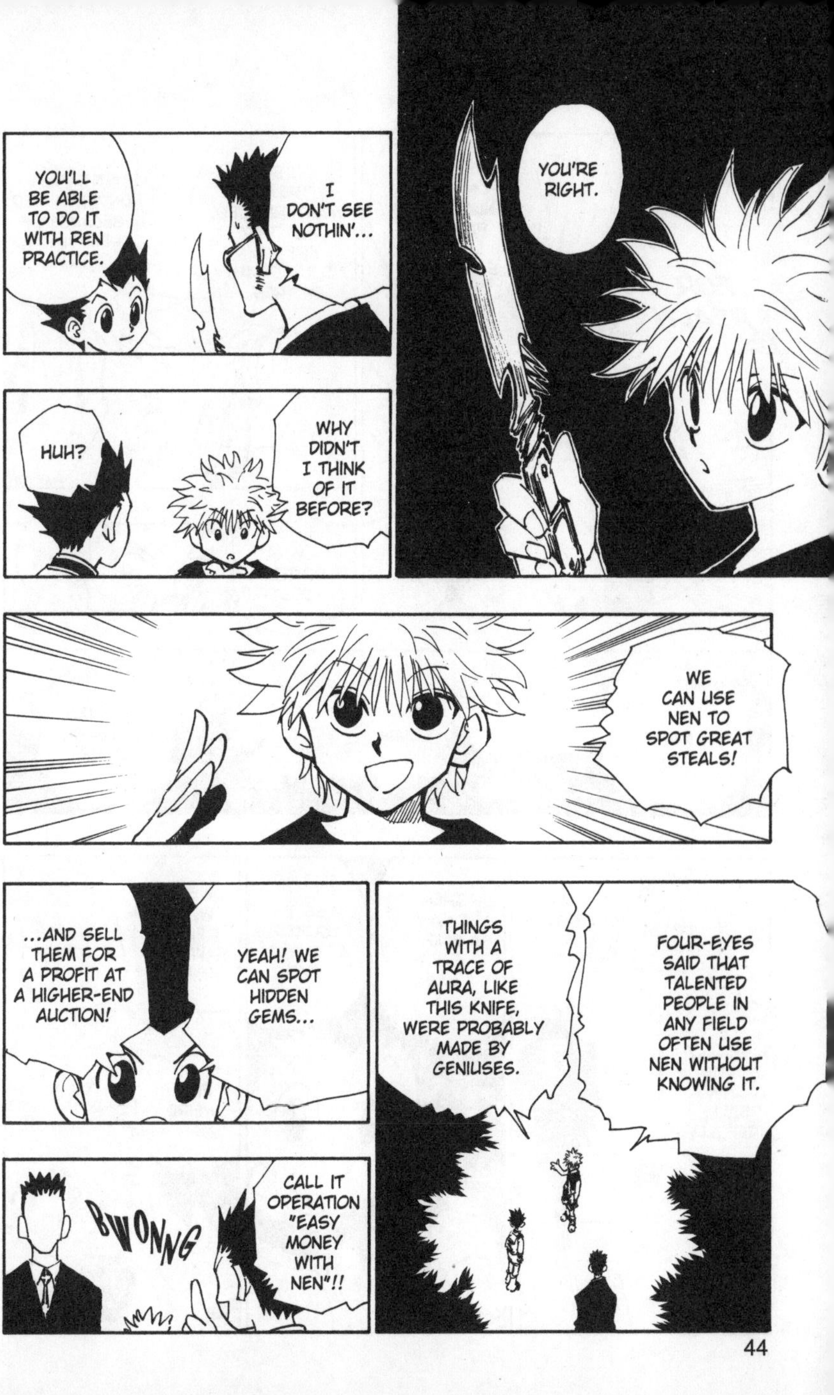
YOU'RE RIGHT.
I DON'T SEE NOTHIN'...
YOU'LL BE ABLE TO DO IT WITH REN PRACTICE.
WHY DIDN'T I THINK OF IT BEFORE?
HUH?
WE CAN USE NEN TO SPOT GREAT STEALS!
FOUR-EYES SAID THAT TALENTED PEOPLE IN ANY FIELD OFTEN USE NEN WITHOUT KNOWING IT.
THINGS WITH A TRACE OF AURA, LIKE THIS KNIFE, WERE PROBABLY MADE BY GENIUSES.
YEAH! WE CAN SPOT HIDDEN GEMS...
...AND SELL THEM FOR A PROFIT AT A HIGHER-END AUCTION!
CALL IT OPERATION "EASY MONEY WITH NEN"!!
BWONNG

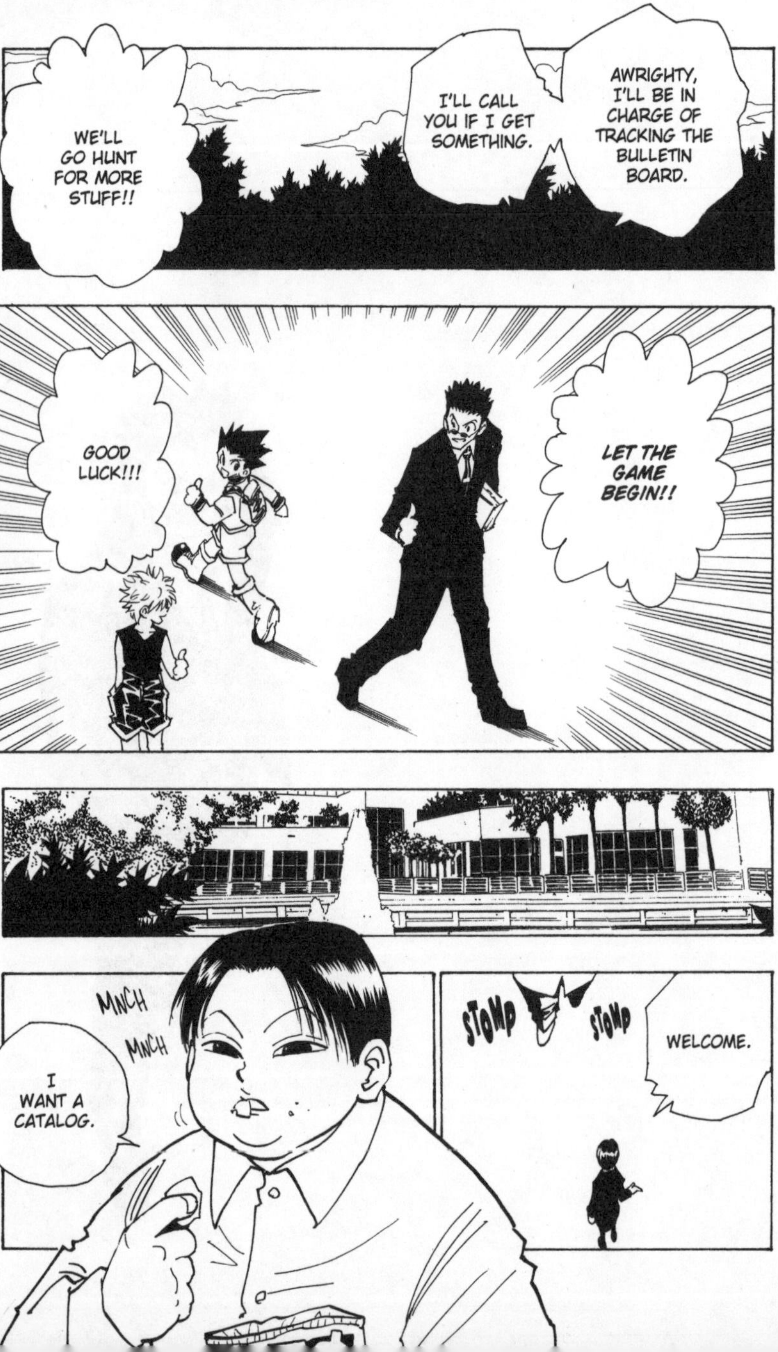
AWRIGHTY, I'LL BE IN CHARGE OF TRACKING THE BULLETIN BOARD.
I'LL CALL YOU IF I GET SOMETHING.
WE'LL GO HUNT FOR MORE STUFF!!
LET THE GAME BEGIN!!
GOOD LUCK!!!
STOMP
STOMP
WELCOME.
MNCH
MNCH
I WANT A CATALOG.

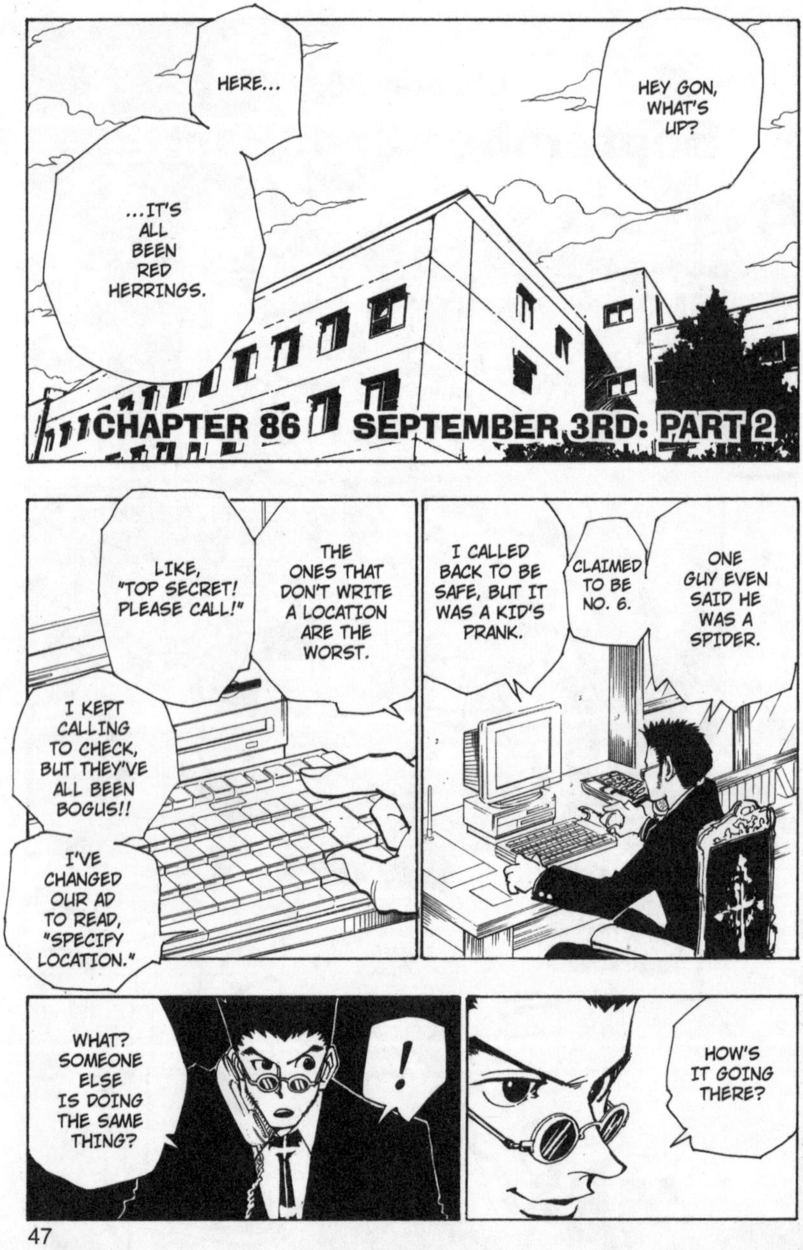
HEY GON, WHAT'S UP?
HERE...
...IT'S ALL BEEN RED HERRINGS.
CHAPTER 86 SEPTEMBER 3RD: PART 2
ONE GUY EVEN SAID HE WAS A SPIDER.
CLAIMED TO BE NO. 6.
I CALLED BACK TO BE SAFE, BUT IT WAS A KID'S PRANK.
THE ONES THAT DON'T WRITE A LOCATION ARE THE WORST.
LIKE, "TOP SECRET! PLEASE CALL!"
I KEPT CALLING TO CHECK, BUT THEY'VE ALL BEEN BOGUS!!
I'VE CHANGED OUR AD TO READ, "SPECIFY LOCATION."
HOW'S IT GOING THERE?
!
WHAT? SOMEONE ELSE IS DOING THE SAME THING?

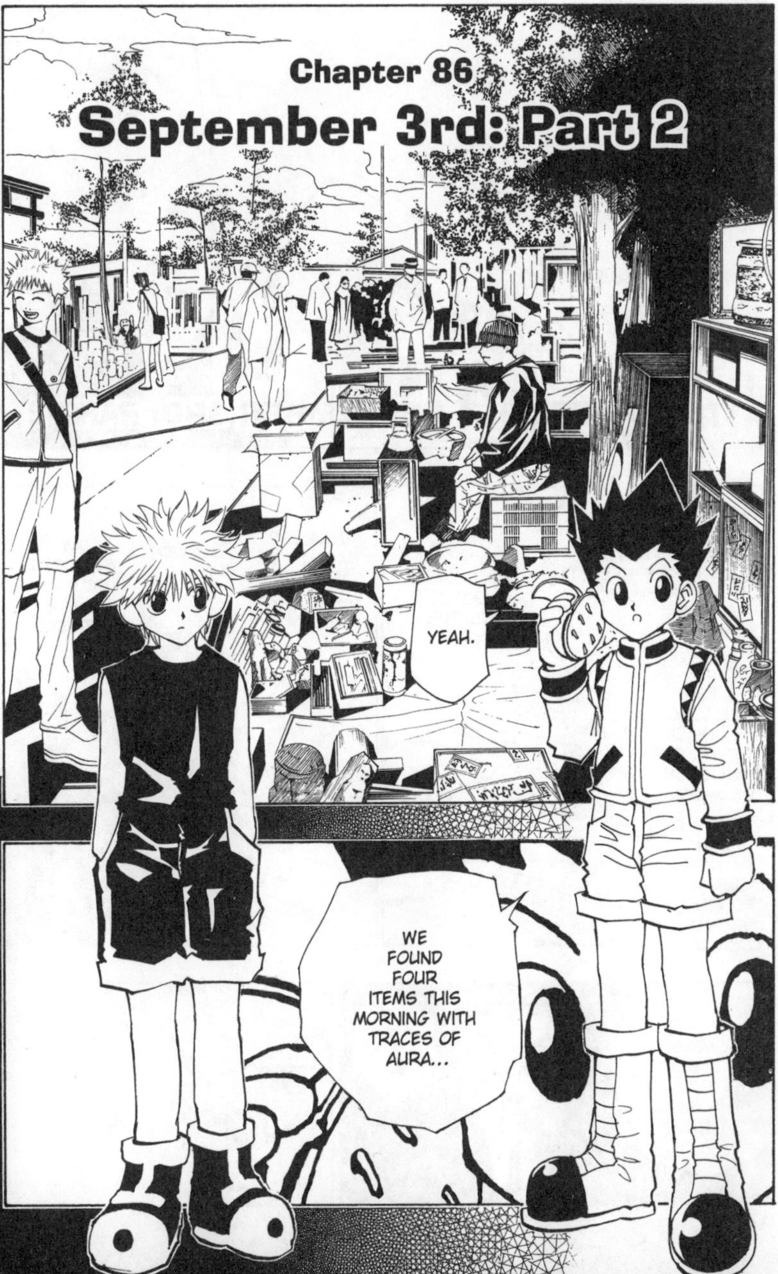
Chapter 86
September 3rd: Part 2
YEAH.
WE FOUND FOUR ITEMS THIS MORNING WITH TRACES OF AURA...

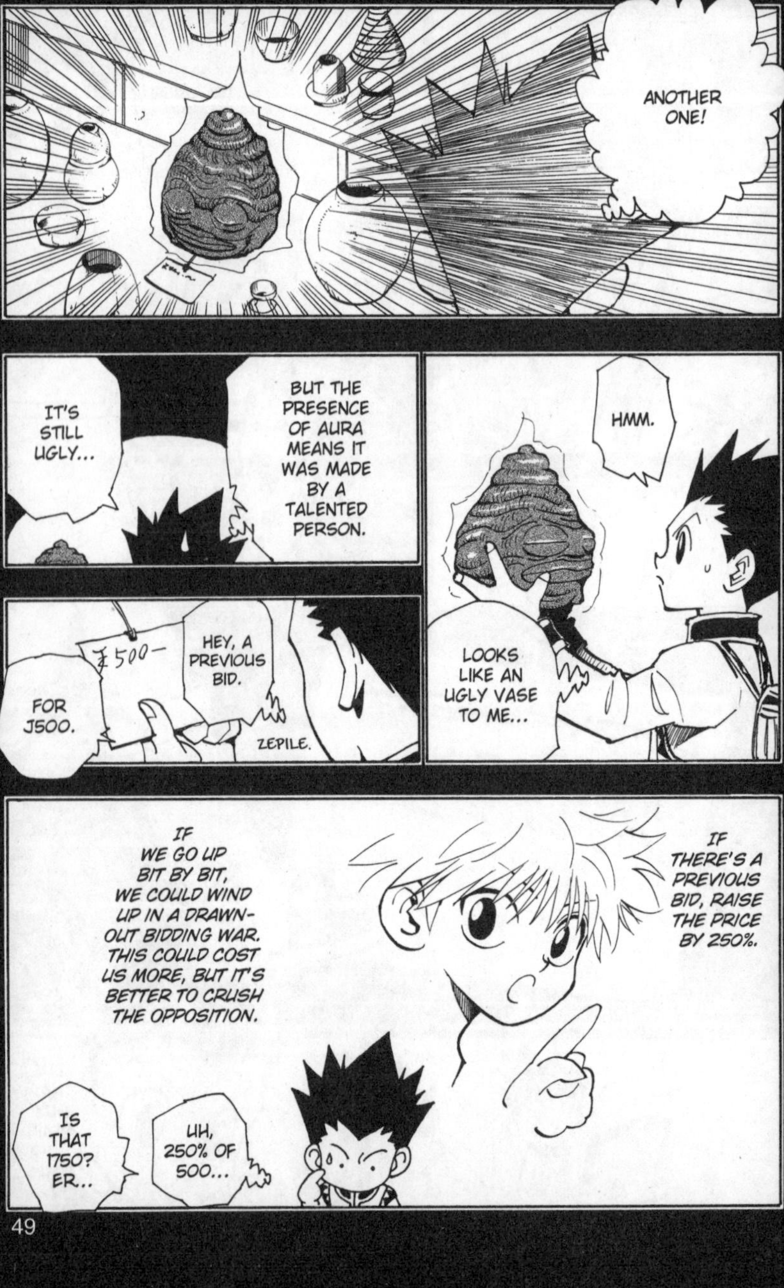
ANOTHER ONE!
HMM.
LOOKS LIKE AN UGLY VASE TO ME...
BUT THE PRESENCE OF AURA MEANS IT WAS MADE BY A TALENTED PERSON.
IT'S STILL UGLY...
HEY, A PREVIOUS BID.
ZEPILE.
J500—
FOR J500.
IF THERE'S A PREVIOUS BID, RAISE THE PRICE BY 250%.
IF WE GO UP BIT BY BIT, WE COULD WIND UP IN A DRAWN-OUT BIDDING WAR. THIS COULD COST US MORE, BUT IT'S BETTER TO CRUSH THE OPPOSITION.
UH, 250% OF 500...
IS THAT 1750? ER...

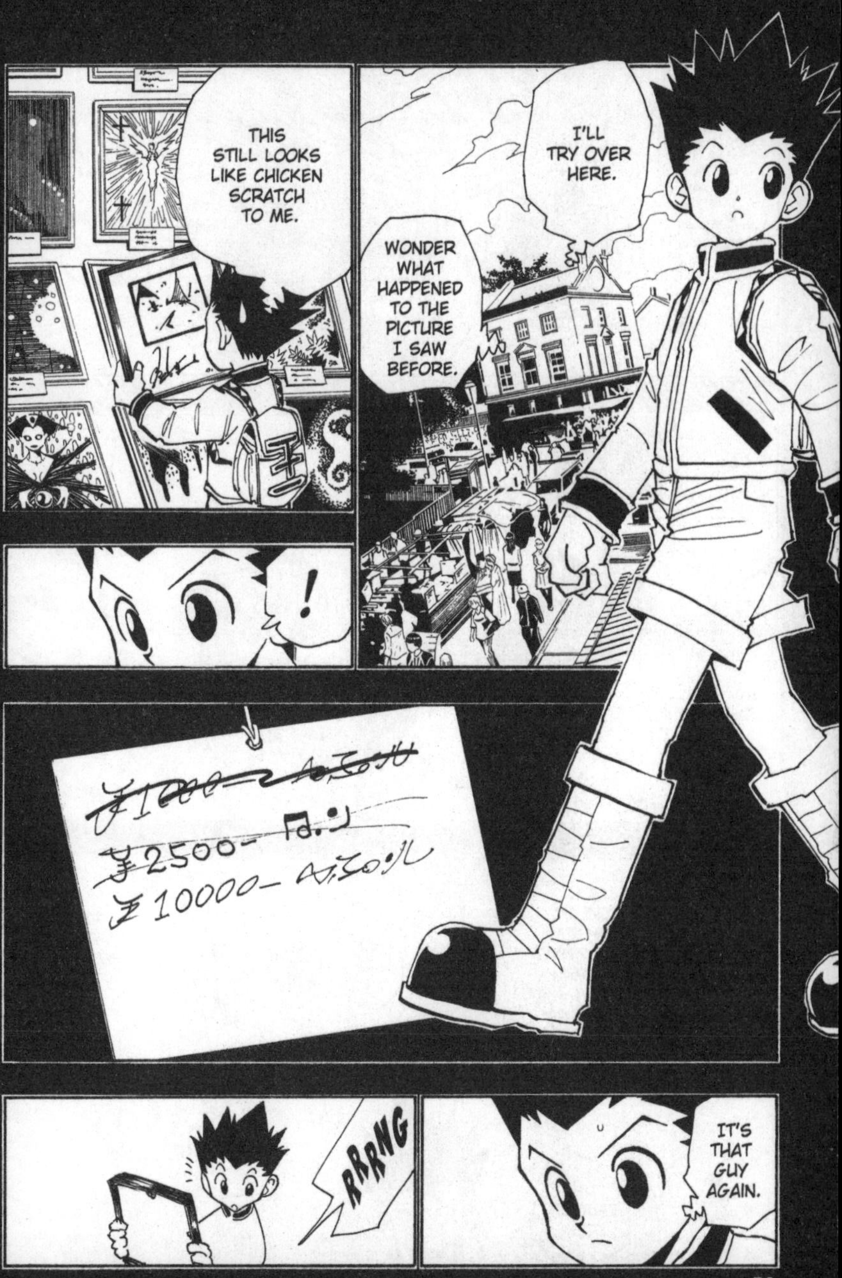

I'LL TRY OVER HERE.
WONDER WHAT HAPPENED TO THE PICTURE I SAW BEFORE.
THIS STILL LOOKS LIKE CHICKEN SCRATCH TO ME.
!
¥1000-
¥2500-
¥10000-
IT'S THAT GUY AGAIN.
RRRNG

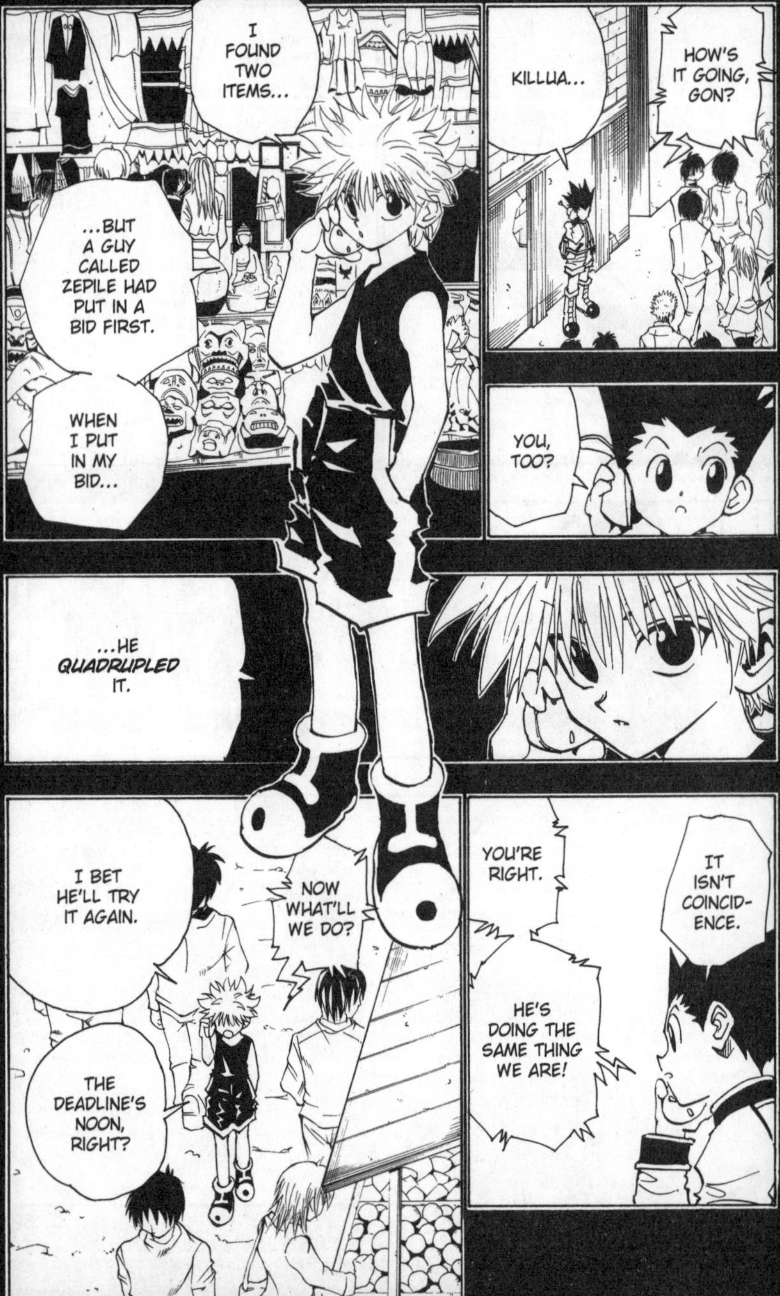
KILLUA...
HOW'S IT GOING, GON?
I FOUND TWO ITEMS...
...BUT A GUY CALLED ZEPILE HAD PUT IN A BID FIRST.
WHEN I PUT IN MY BID...
YOU, TOO?
...HE *QUADRUPLED* IT.
I BET HE'LL TRY IT AGAIN.
NOW WHAT'LL WE DO?
THE DEADLINE'S NOON, RIGHT?
IT ISN'T COINCID-ENCE.
YOU'RE RIGHT.
HE'S DOING THE SAME THING WE ARE!

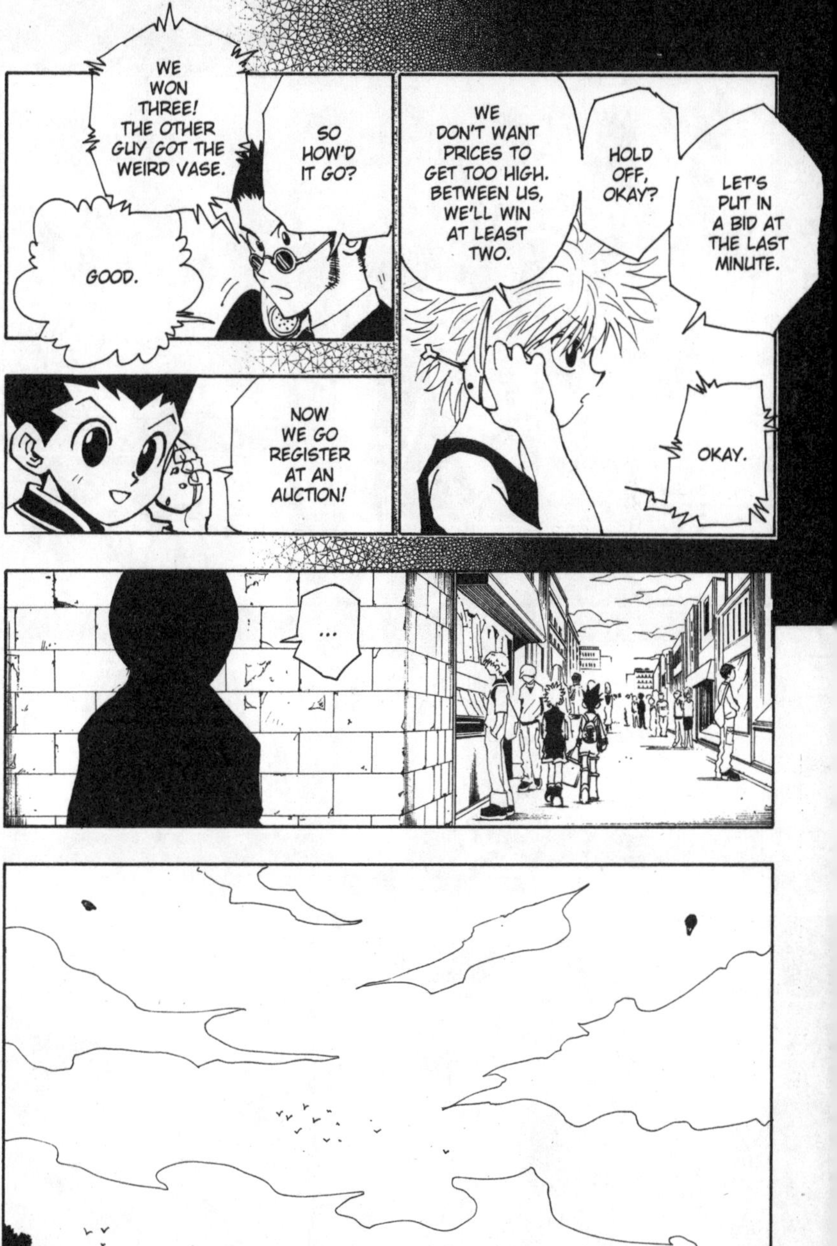
LET'S PUT IN A BID AT THE LAST MINUTE.
HOLD OFF, OKAY?
WE DON'T WANT PRICES TO GET TOO HIGH. BETWEEN US, WE'LL WIN AT LEAST TWO.
OKAY.
SO HOW'D IT GO?
WE WON THREE! THE OTHER GUY GOT THE WEIRD VASE.
GOOD.
NOW WE GO REGISTER AT AN AUCTION!
...

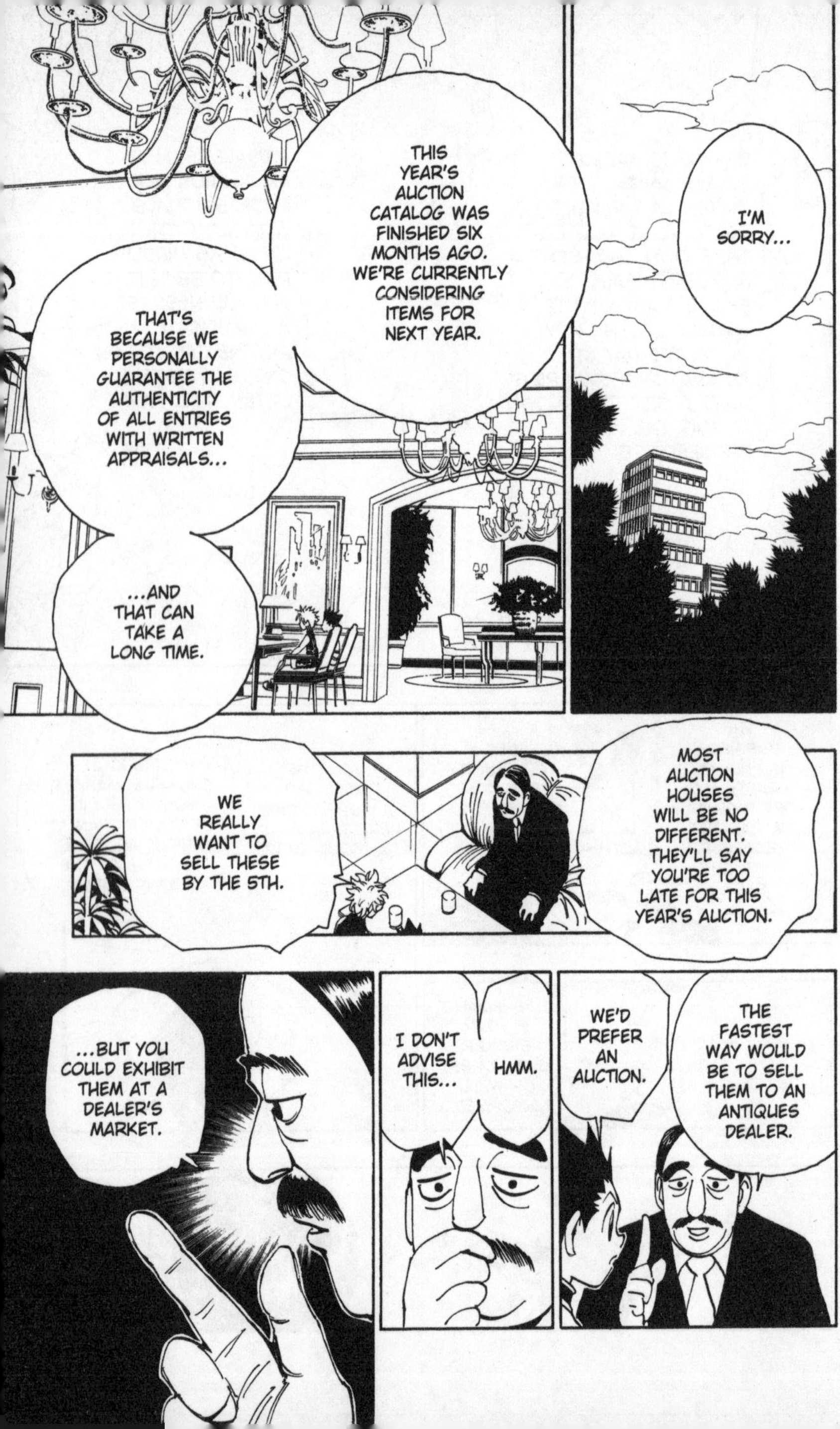
I'M SORRY...
THIS YEAR'S AUCTION CATALOG WAS FINISHED SIX MONTHS AGO. WE'RE CURRENTLY CONSIDERING ITEMS FOR NEXT YEAR.
THAT'S BECAUSE WE PERSONALLY GUARANTEE THE AUTHENTICITY OF ALL ENTRIES WITH WRITTEN APPRAISALS...
...AND THAT CAN TAKE A LONG TIME.
MOST AUCTION HOUSES WILL BE NO DIFFERENT. THEY'LL SAY YOU'RE TOO LATE FOR THIS YEAR'S AUCTION.
WE REALLY WANT TO SELL THESE BY THE 5TH.
THE FASTEST WAY WOULD BE TO SELL THEM TO AN ANTIQUES DEALER.
WE'D PREFER AN AUCTION.
HMM.
I DON'T ADVISE THIS...
...BUT YOU COULD EXHIBIT THEM AT A DEALER'S MARKET.

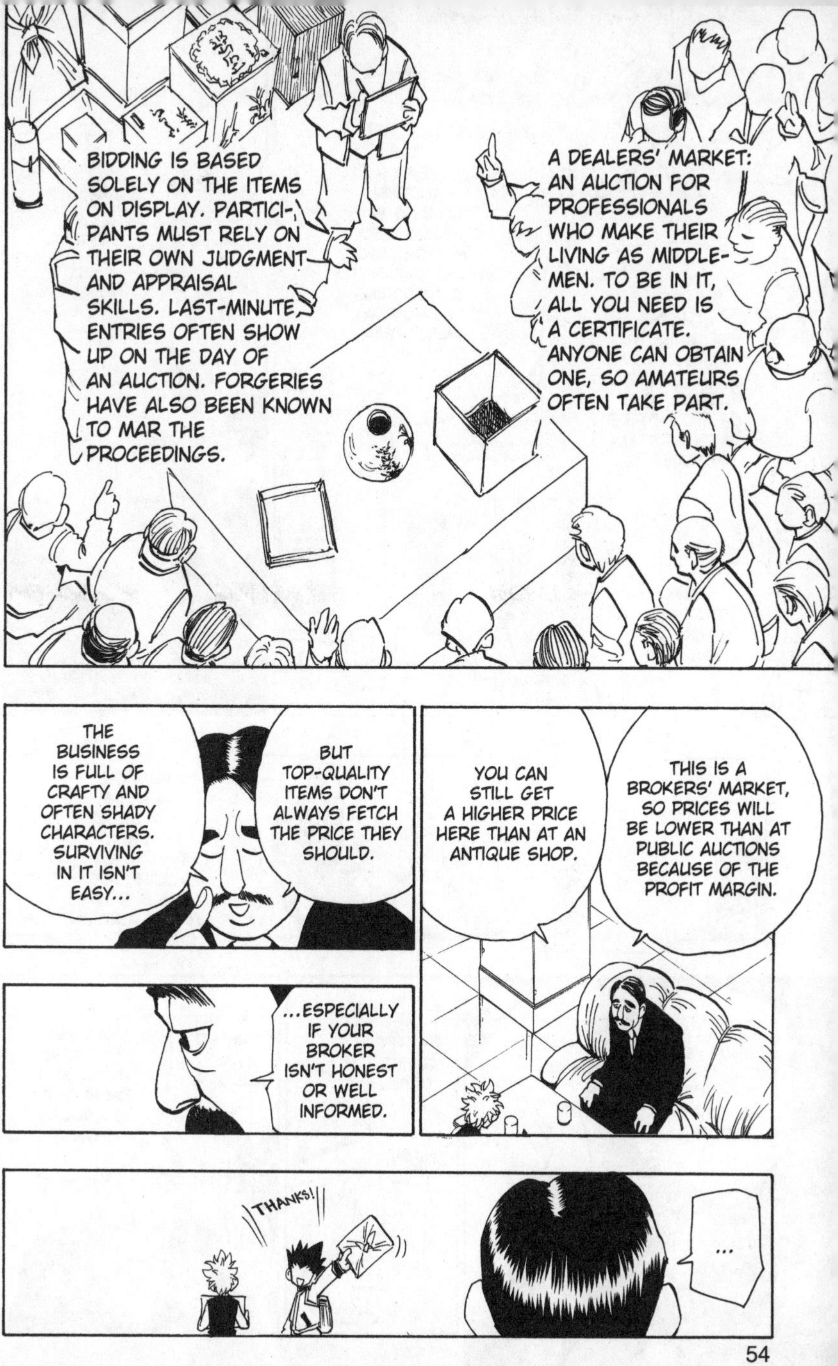
A DEALERS' MARKET: AN AUCTION FOR PROFESSIONALS WHO MAKE THEIR LIVING AS MIDDLE-MEN. TO BE IN IT, ALL YOU NEED IS A CERTIFICATE. ANYONE CAN OBTAIN ONE, SO AMATEURS OFTEN TAKE PART.
BIDDING IS BASED SOLELY ON THE ITEMS ON DISPLAY. PARTICI-PANTS MUST RELY ON THEIR OWN JUDGMENT AND APPRAISAL SKILLS. LAST-MINUTE ENTRIES OFTEN SHOW UP ON THE DAY OF AN AUCTION. FORGERIES HAVE ALSO BEEN KNOWN TO MAR THE PROCEEDINGS.
THIS IS A BROKERS' MARKET, SO PRICES WILL BE LOWER THAN AT PUBLIC AUCTIONS BECAUSE OF THE PROFIT MARGIN.
YOU CAN STILL GET A HIGHER PRICE HERE THAN AT AN ANTIQUE SHOP.
BUT TOP-QUALITY ITEMS DON'T ALWAYS FETCH THE PRICE THEY SHOULD.
THE BUSINESS IS FULL OF CRAFTY AND OFTEN SHADY CHARACTERS. SURVIVING IN IT ISN'T EASY...
...ESPECIALLY IF YOUR BROKER ISN'T HONEST OR WELL INFORMED.
...
THANKS!

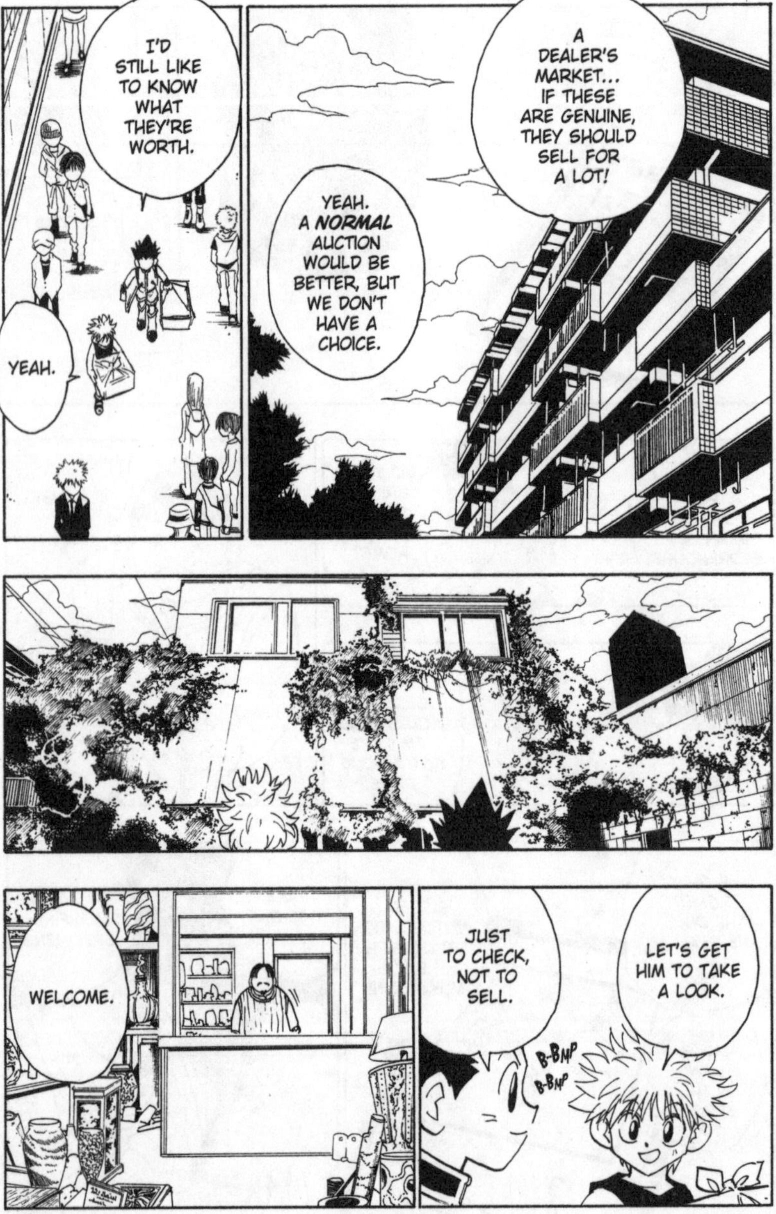
A DEALER'S MARKET... IF THESE ARE GENUINE, THEY SHOULD SELL FOR A LOT!
YEAH. A NORMAL AUCTION WOULD BE BETTER, BUT WE DON'T HAVE A CHOICE.
I'D STILL LIKE TO KNOW WHAT THEY'RE WORTH.
YEAH.
LET'S GET HIM TO TAKE A LOOK.
JUST TO CHECK, NOT TO SELL.
B-BMP
B-BMP
WELCOME.

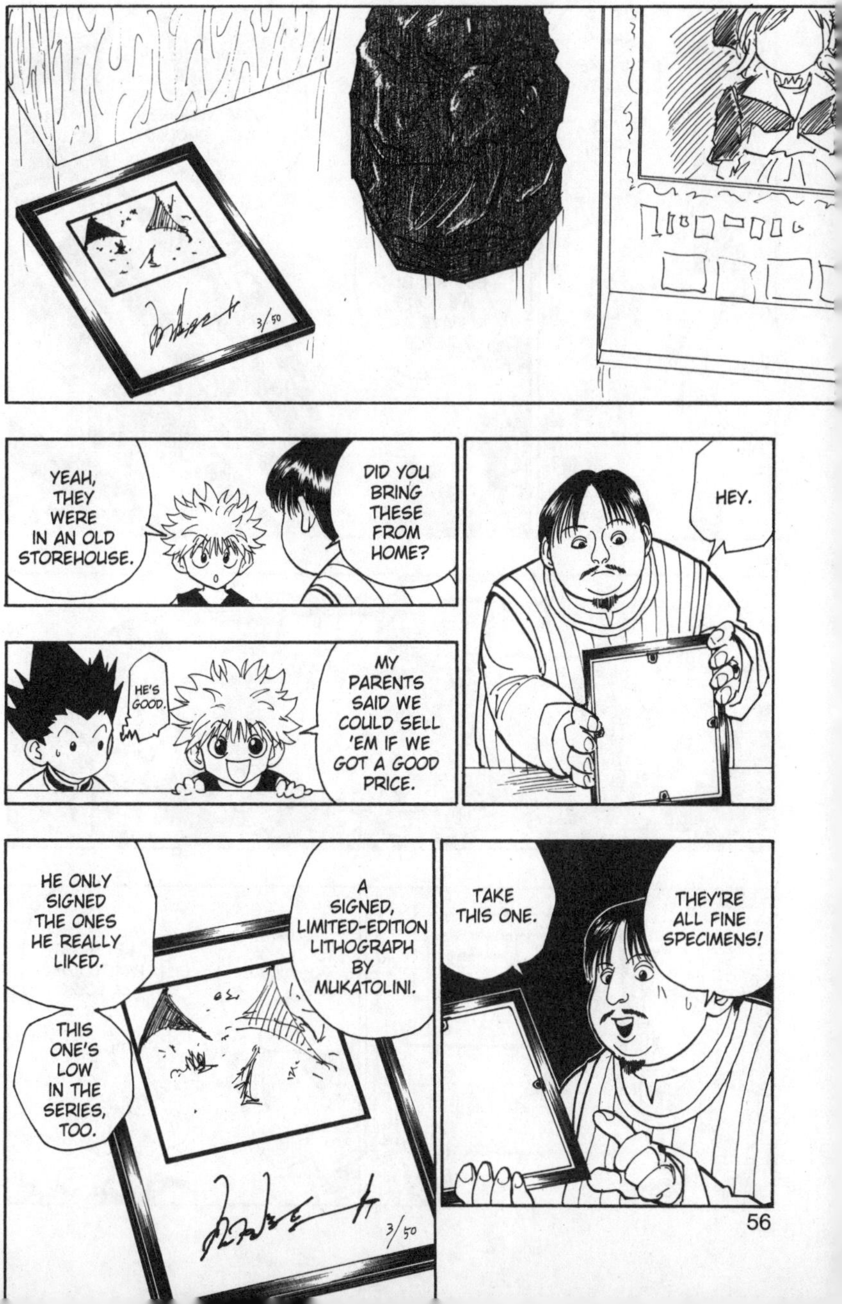

HEY.
DID YOU BRING THESE FROM HOME?
YEAH, THEY WERE IN AN OLD STOREHOUSE.
MY PARENTS SAID WE COULD SELL 'EM IF WE GOT A GOOD PRICE.
HE'S GOOD.
THEY'RE ALL FINE SPECIMENS!
TAKE THIS ONE.
A SIGNED, LIMITED-EDITION LITHOGRAPH BY MUKATOLINI.
HE ONLY SIGNED THE ONES HE REALLY LIKED.
THIS ONE'S LOW IN THE SERIES, TOO.
3/50

READ THIS WAY

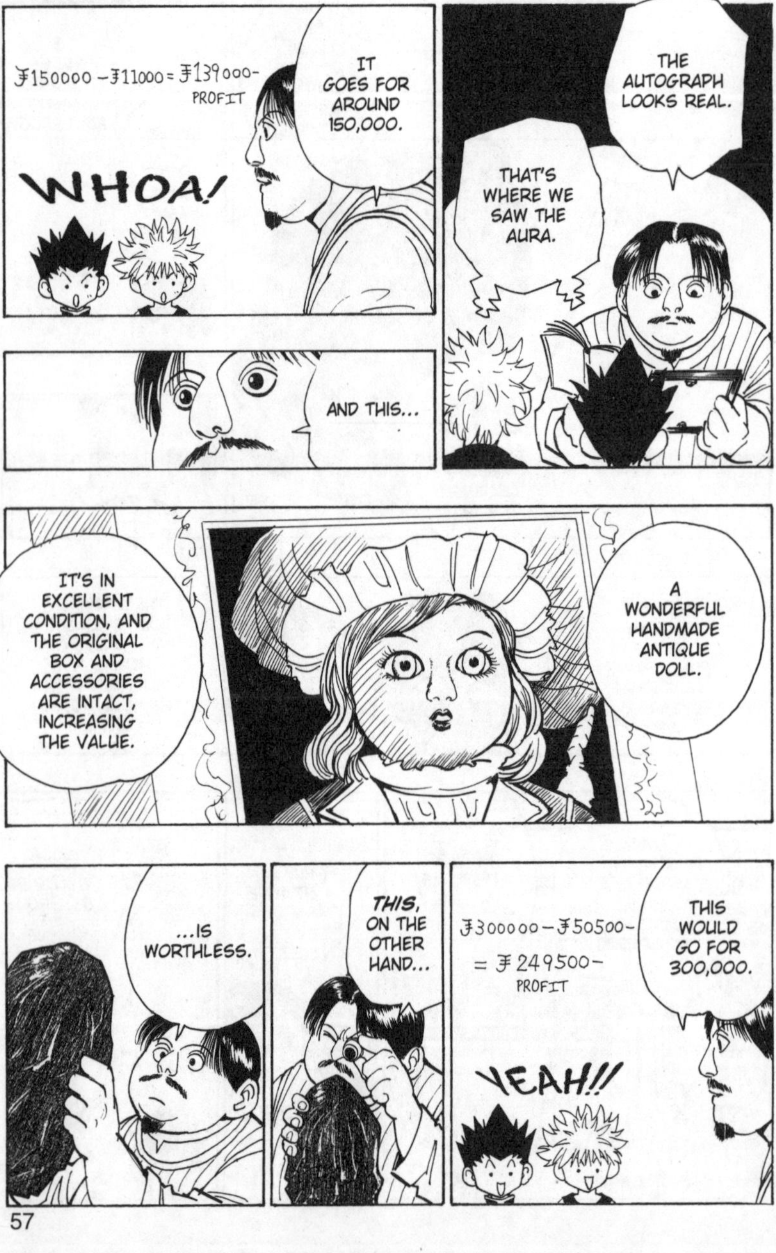

THE AUTOGRAPH LOOKS REAL.
THAT'S WHERE WE SAW THE AURA.
IT GOES FOR AROUND 150,000.
J150000 – J11000 = J139000–
PROFIT
WHOA!
AND THIS...
A WONDERFUL HANDMADE ANTIQUE DOLL.
IT'S IN EXCELLENT CONDITION, AND THE ORIGINAL BOX AND ACCESSORIES ARE INTACT, INCREASING THE VALUE.
THIS WOULD GO FOR 300,000.
J300000 – J50500 –
= J249500 –
PROFIT
YEAH!!
THIS, ON THE OTHER HAND...
...IS WORTHLESS.

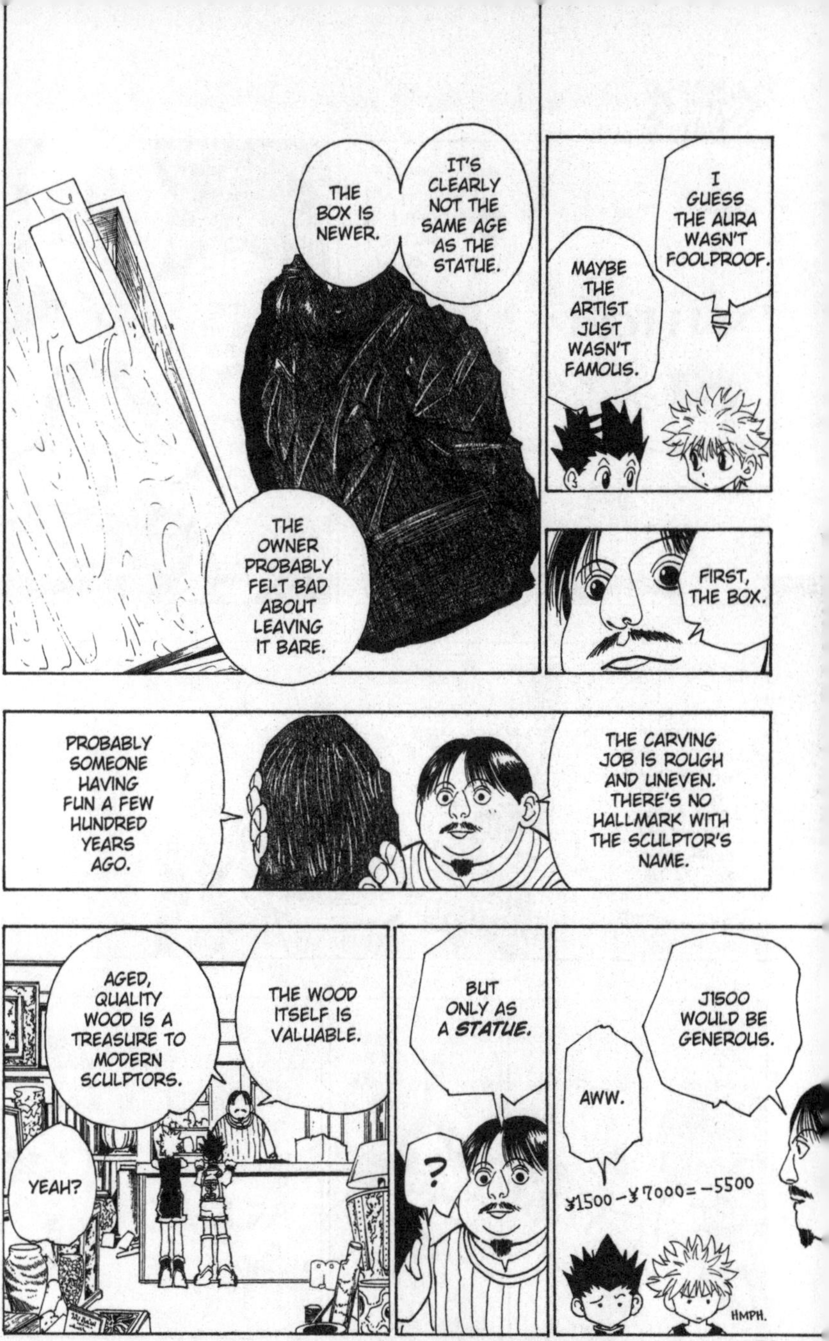
I GUESS THE AURA WASN'T FOOLPROOF.
MAYBE THE ARTIST JUST WASN'T FAMOUS.
FIRST, THE BOX.
IT'S CLEARLY NOT THE SAME AGE AS THE STATUE.
THE BOX IS NEWER.
THE OWNER PROBABLY FELT BAD ABOUT LEAVING IT BARE.
THE CARVING JOB IS ROUGH AND UNEVEN. THERE'S NO HALLMARK WITH THE SCULPTOR'S NAME.
PROBABLY SOMEONE HAVING FUN A FEW HUNDRED YEARS AGO.
J1500 WOULD BE GENEROUS.
AWW.
¥1500 – ¥7000 = –5500
HMPH.
BUT ONLY AS A *STATUE.*
?
THE WOOD ITSELF IS VALUABLE.
AGED, QUALITY WOOD IS A TREASURE TO MODERN SCULPTORS.
YEAH?

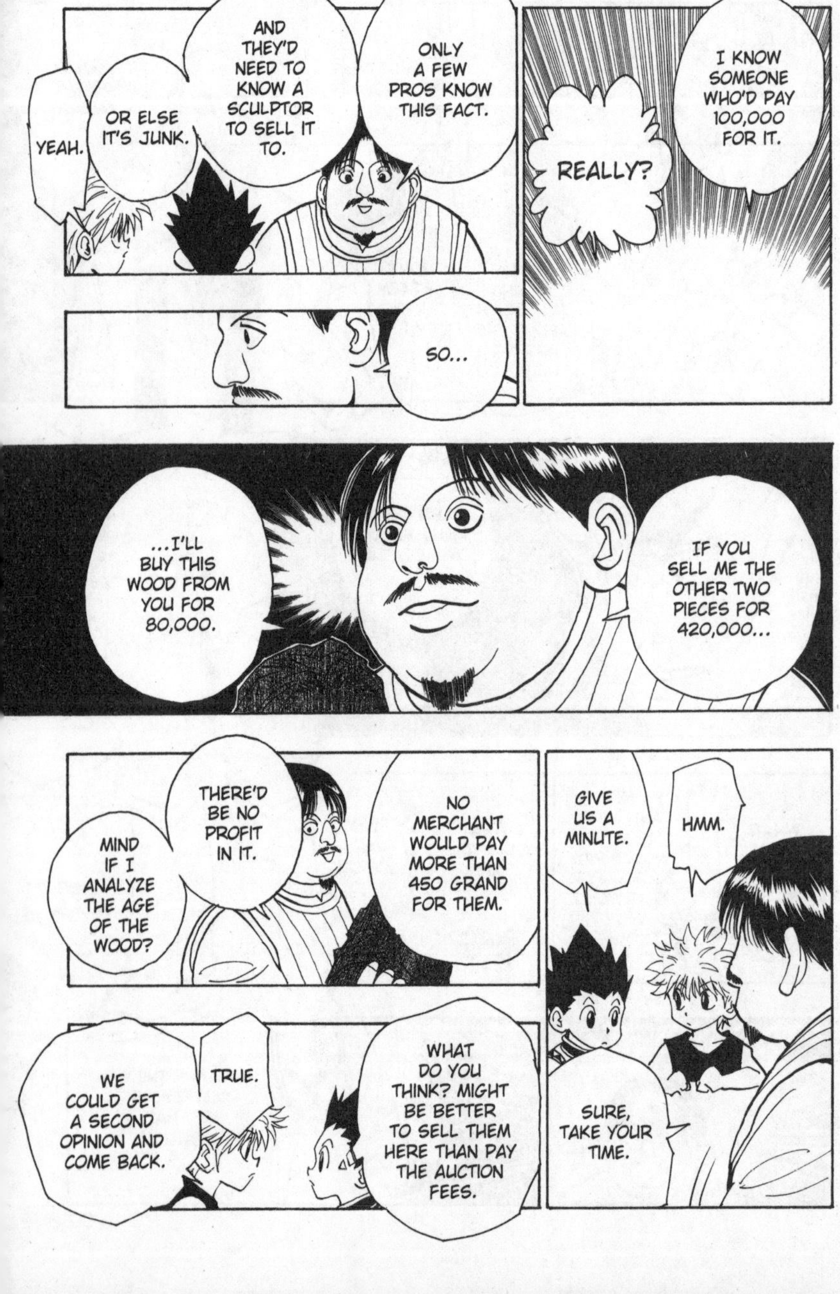
I KNOW SOMEONE WHO'D PAY 100,000 FOR IT.
REALLY?
ONLY A FEW PROS KNOW THIS FACT.
AND THEY'D NEED TO KNOW A SCULPTOR TO SELL IT TO.
OR ELSE IT'S JUNK.
YEAH.
SO...
IF YOU SELL ME THE OTHER TWO PIECES FOR 420,000...
...I'LL BUY THIS WOOD FROM YOU FOR 80,000.
HMM.
GIVE US A MINUTE.
SURE, TAKE YOUR TIME.
NO MERCHANT WOULD PAY MORE THAN 450 GRAND FOR THEM.
THERE'D BE NO PROFIT IN IT.
MIND IF I ANALYZE THE AGE OF THE WOOD?
WHAT DO YOU THINK? MIGHT BE BETTER TO SELL THEM HERE THAN PAY THE AUCTION FEES.
TRUE.
WE COULD GET A SECOND OPINION AND COME BACK.

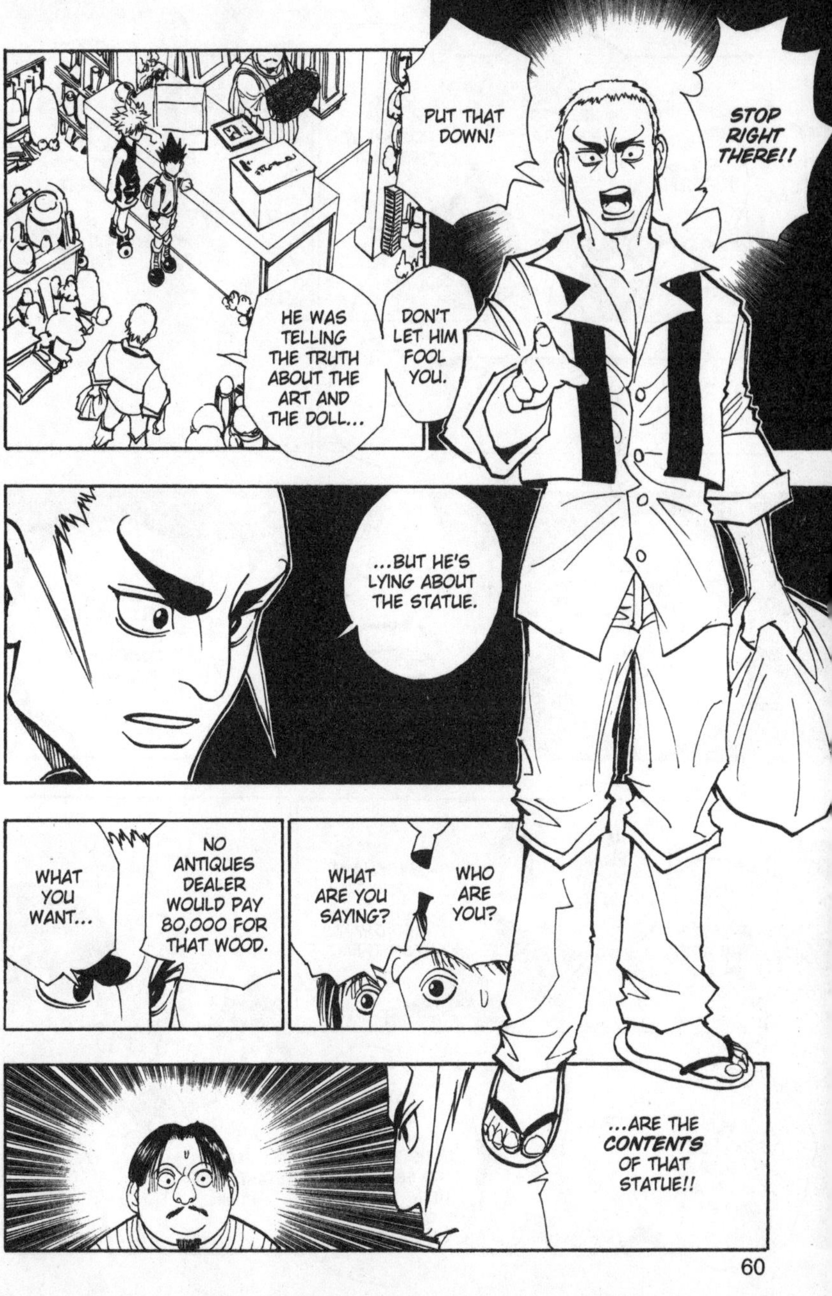
STOP RIGHT THERE!!
PUT THAT DOWN!
DON'T LET HIM FOOL YOU.
HE WAS TELLING THE TRUTH ABOUT THE ART AND THE DOLL...
...BUT HE'S LYING ABOUT THE STATUE.
WHO ARE YOU?
WHAT ARE YOU SAYING?
NO ANTIQUES DEALER WOULD PAY 80,000 FOR THAT WOOD.
WHAT YOU WANT...
...ARE THE *CONTENTS* OF THAT STATUE!!

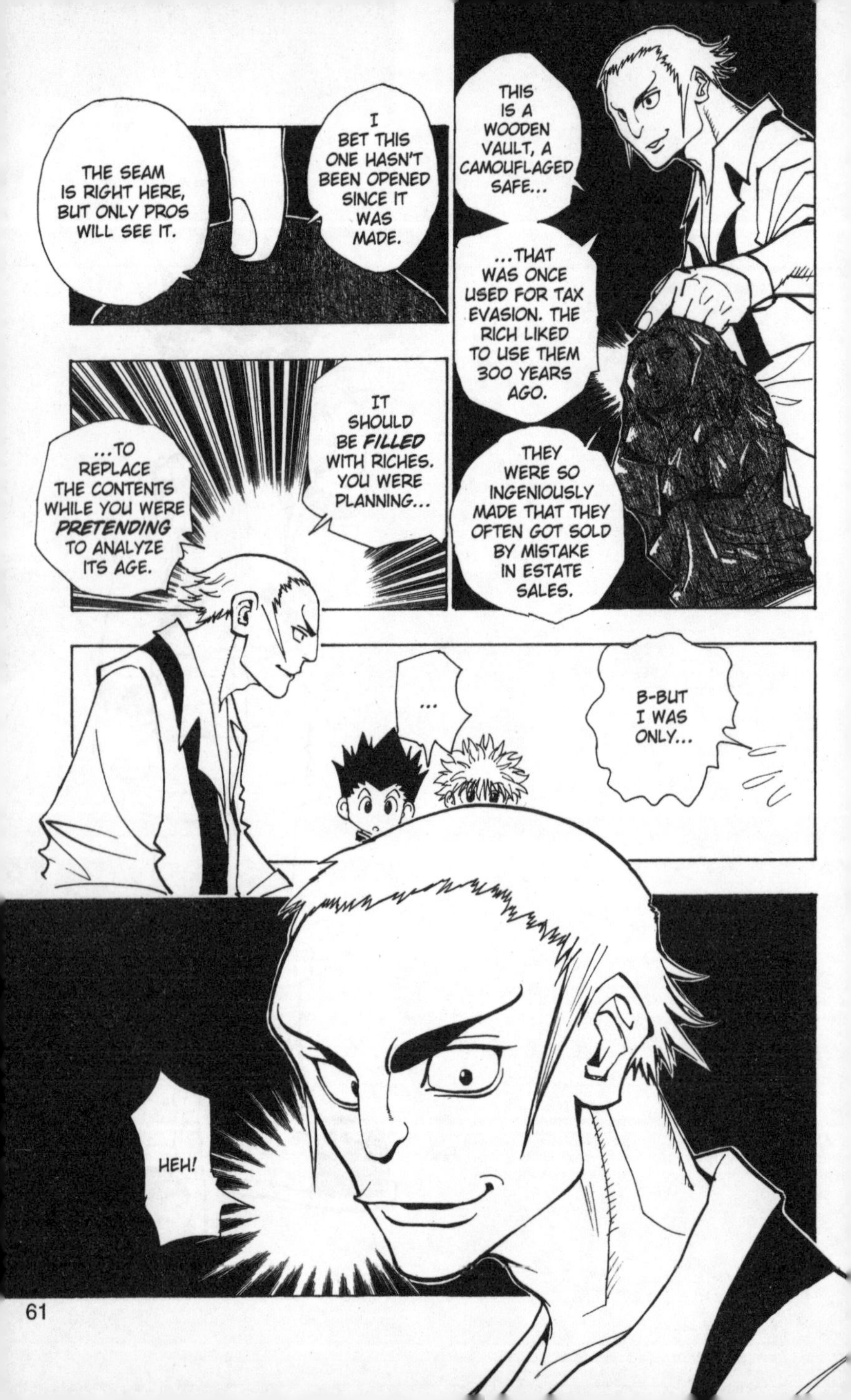
THIS IS A WOODEN VAULT, A CAMOUFLAGED SAFE...
...THAT WAS ONCE USED FOR TAX EVASION. THE RICH LIKED TO USE THEM 300 YEARS AGO.
THEY WERE SO INGENIOUSLY MADE THAT THEY OFTEN GOT SOLD BY MISTAKE IN ESTATE SALES.
I BET THIS ONE HASN'T BEEN OPENED SINCE IT WAS MADE.
THE SEAM IS RIGHT HERE, BUT ONLY PROS WILL SEE IT.
IT SHOULD BE FILLED WITH RICHES. YOU WERE PLANNING...
...TO REPLACE THE CONTENTS WHILE YOU WERE PRETENDING TO ANALYZE ITS AGE.
B-BUT I WAS ONLY...
...
HEH!

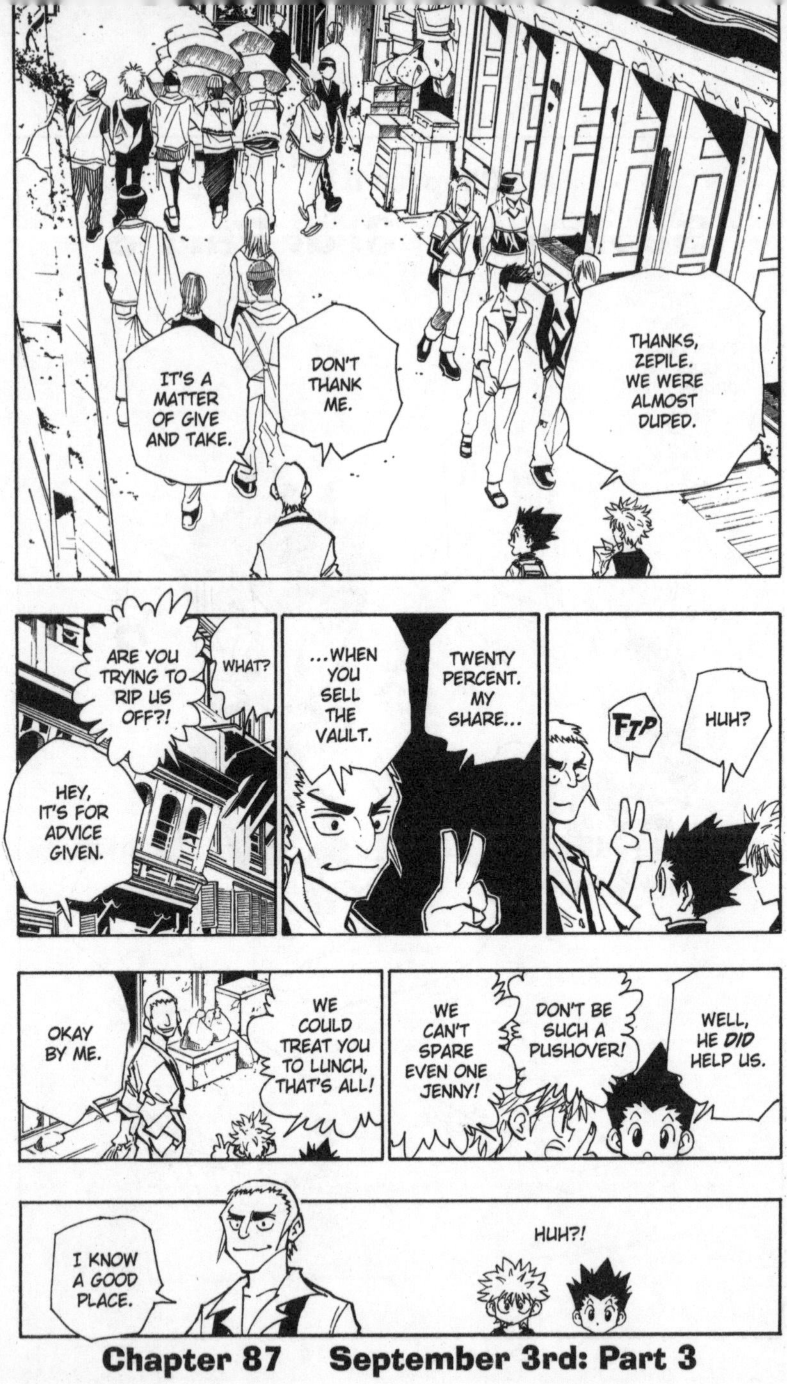
THANKS, ZEPILE. WE WERE ALMOST DUPED.
DON'T THANK ME.
IT'S A MATTER OF GIVE AND TAKE.
HUH?
FIP
TWENTY PERCENT. MY SHARE...
...WHEN YOU SELL THE VAULT.
WHAT?
ARE YOU TRYING TO RIP US OFF?!
HEY, IT'S FOR ADVICE GIVEN.
WELL, HE *DID* HELP US.
DON'T BE SUCH A PUSHOVER!
WE CAN'T SPARE EVEN ONE JENNY!
WE COULD TREAT YOU TO LUNCH, THAT'S ALL!
OKAY BY ME.
HUH?!
I KNOW A GOOD PLACE.

Chapter 87 September 3rd: Part 3

Chapter 87

September 3rd: Part 3

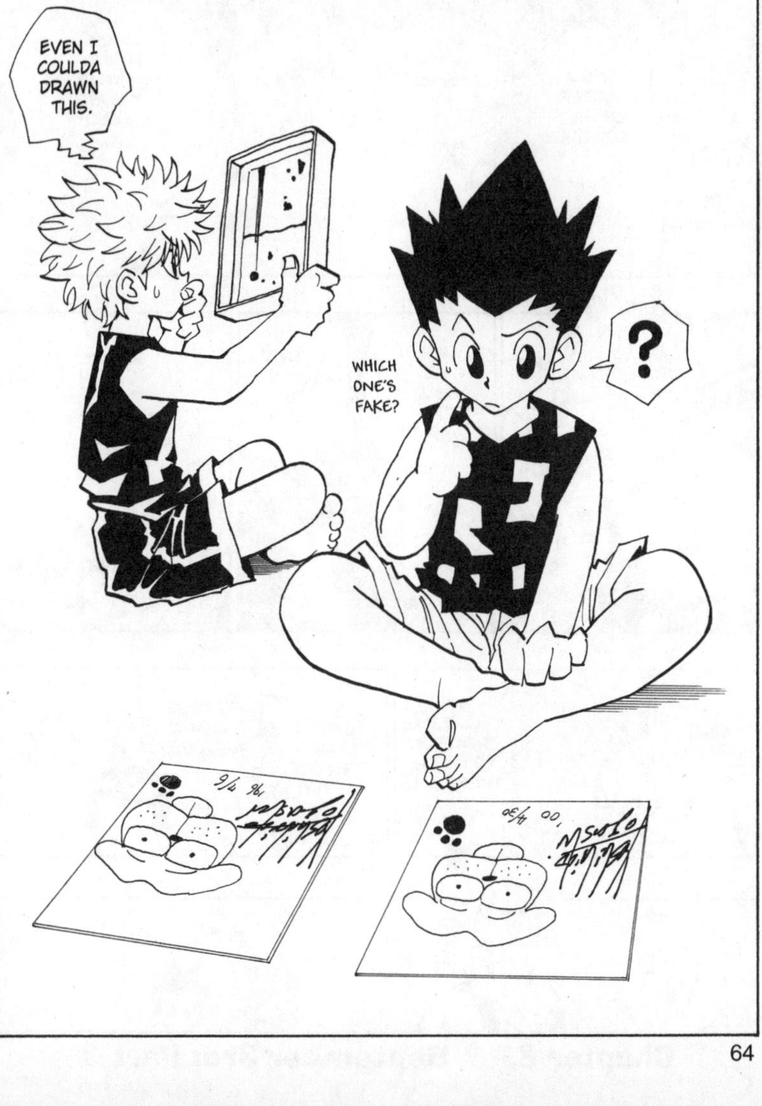
?
WHICH ONE'S FAKE?
EVEN I COULDA DRAWN THIS.

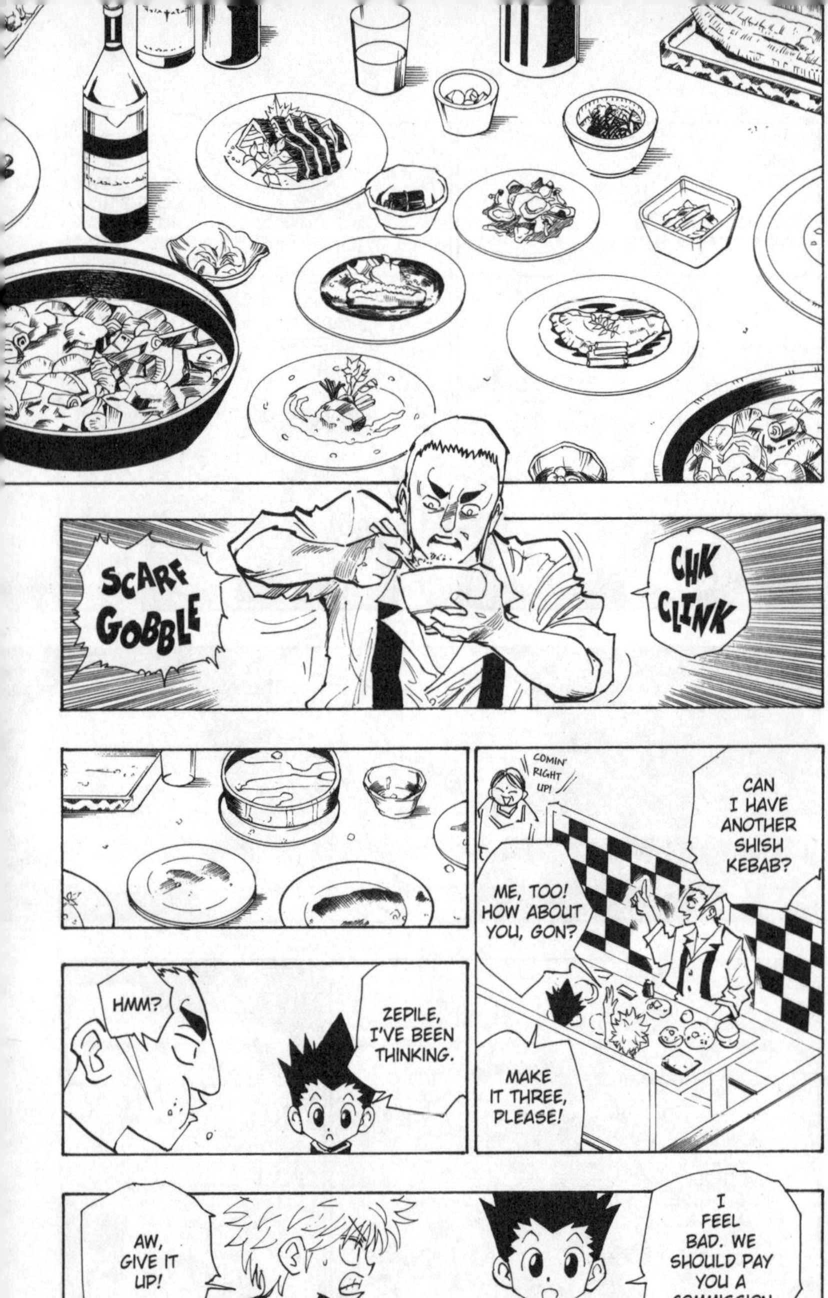

CHK CLINK
SCARF GOBBLE
CAN I HAVE ANOTHER SHISH KEBAB?
ME, TOO! HOW ABOUT YOU, GON?
MAKE IT THREE, PLEASE!
COMIN' RIGHT UP!
ZEPILE, I'VE BEEN THINKING.
HMM?
I FEEL BAD. WE SHOULD PAY YOU A COMMISSION.
AW, GIVE IT UP!

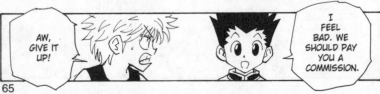

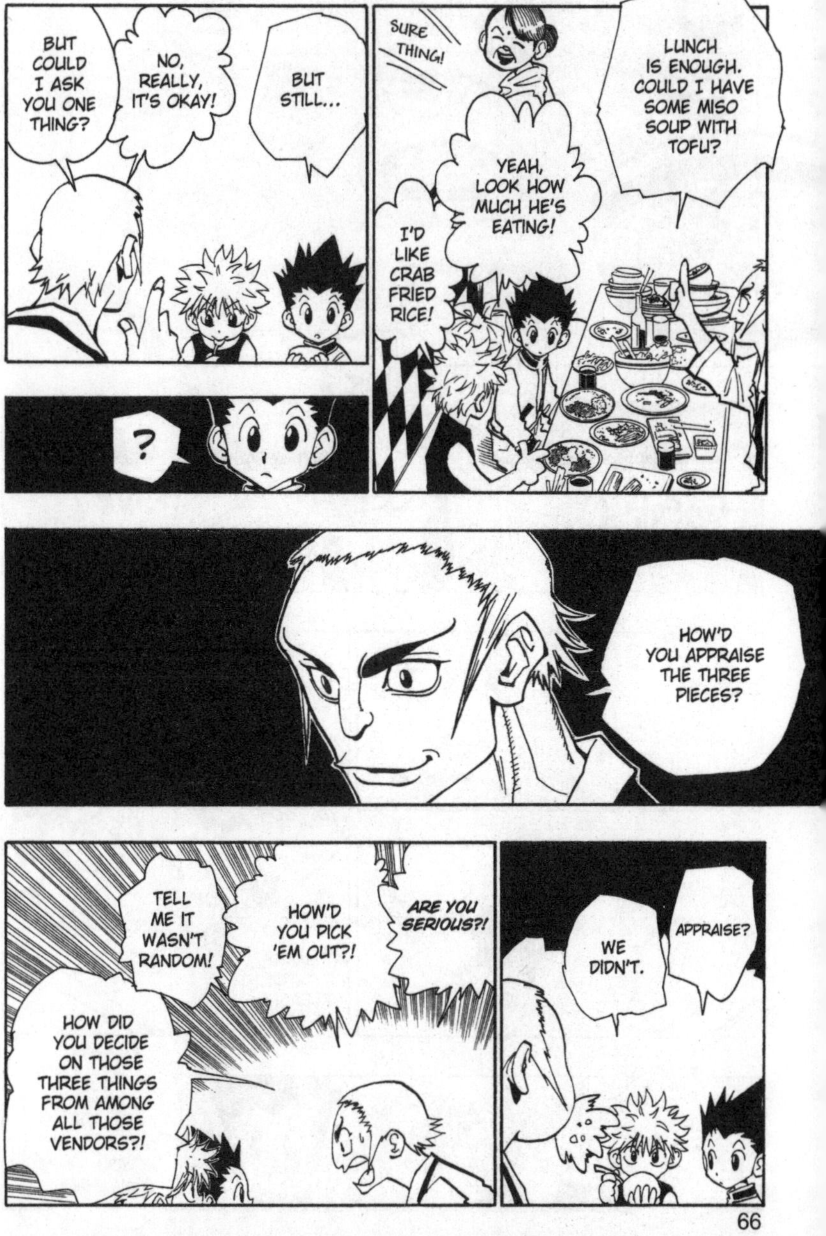
LUNCH IS ENOUGH. COULD I HAVE SOME MISO SOUP WITH TOFU?
SURE THING!
YEAH, LOOK HOW MUCH HE'S EATING!
I'D LIKE CRAB FRIED RICE!
BUT STILL...
NO, REALLY, IT'S OKAY!
BUT COULD I ASK YOU ONE THING?
?
HOW'D YOU APPRAISE THE THREE PIECES?
APPRAISE?
WE DIDN'T.
ARE YOU SERIOUS?!
HOW'D YOU PICK 'EM OUT?!
TELL ME IT WASN'T RANDOM!
HOW DID YOU DECIDE ON THOSE THREE THINGS FROM AMONG ALL THOSE VENDORS?!

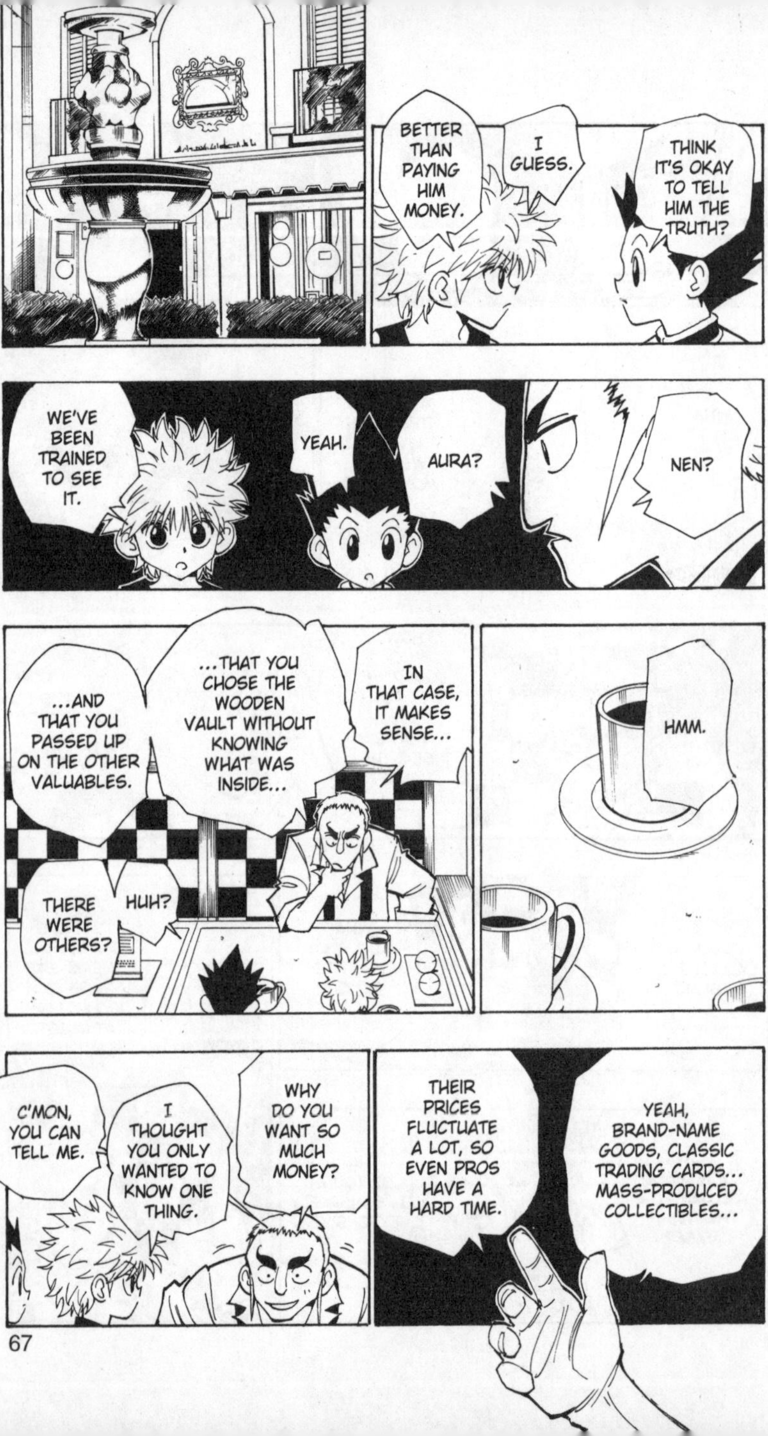

THINK IT'S OKAY TO TELL HIM THE TRUTH?
I GUESS.
BETTER THAN PAYING HIM MONEY.
NEN?
AURA?
YEAH.
WE'VE BEEN TRAINED TO SEE IT.
HMM.
IN THAT CASE, IT MAKES SENSE...
...THAT YOU CHOSE THE WOODEN VAULT WITHOUT KNOWING WHAT WAS INSIDE...
...AND THAT YOU PASSED UP ON THE OTHER VALUABLES.
HUH?
THERE WERE OTHERS?
YEAH, BRAND-NAME GOODS, CLASSIC TRADING CARDS... MASS-PRODUCED COLLECTIBLES...
THEIR PRICES FLUCTUATE A LOT, SO EVEN PROS HAVE A HARD TIME.
WHY DO YOU WANT SO MUCH MONEY?
I THOUGHT YOU ONLY WANTED TO KNOW ONE THING.
C'MON, YOU CAN TELL ME.

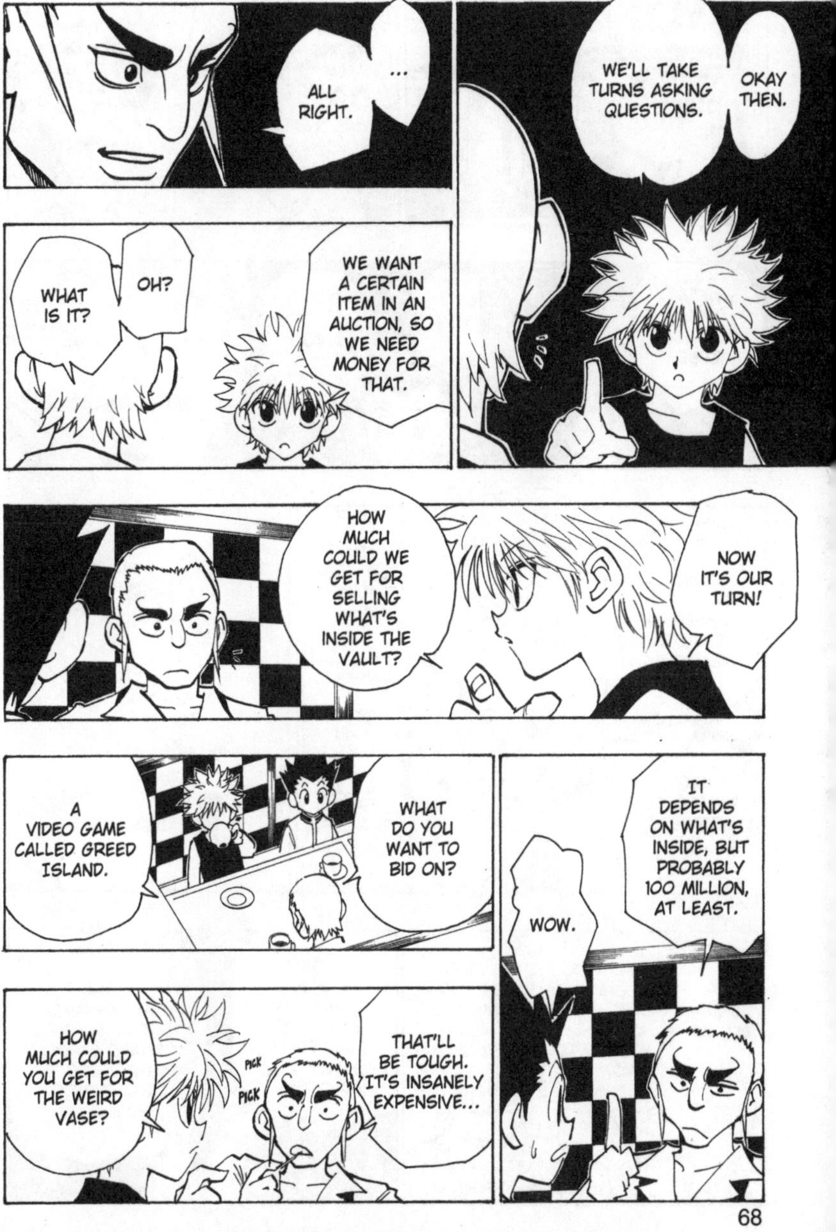
OKAY THEN.
WE'LL TAKE TURNS ASKING QUESTIONS.
...
ALL RIGHT.
WE WANT A CERTAIN ITEM IN AN AUCTION, SO WE NEED MONEY FOR THAT.
OH?
WHAT IS IT?
NOW IT'S OUR TURN!
HOW MUCH COULD WE GET FOR SELLING WHAT'S INSIDE THE VAULT?
IT DEPENDS ON WHAT'S INSIDE, BUT PROBABLY 100 MILLION, AT LEAST.
WOW.
WHAT DO YOU WANT TO BID ON?
A VIDEO GAME CALLED GREED ISLAND.
THAT'LL BE TOUGH. IT'S INSANELY EXPENSIVE...
PICK
PICK
HOW MUCH COULD YOU GET FOR THE WEIRD VASE?

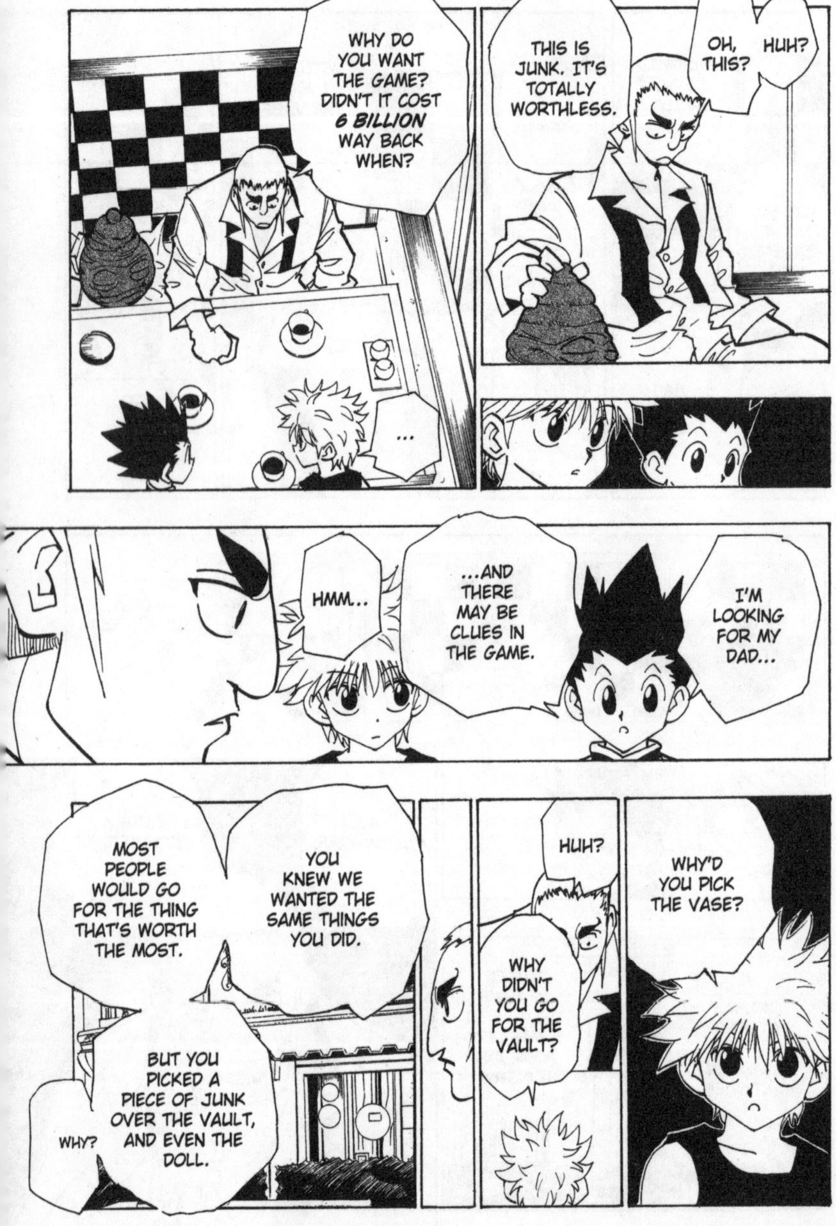
HUH?
OH, THIS?
THIS IS JUNK. IT'S TOTALLY WORTHLESS.
WHY DO YOU WANT THE GAME? DIDN'T IT COST ***6 BILLION*** WAY BACK WHEN?
...
I'M LOOKING FOR MY DAD...
...AND THERE MAY BE CLUES IN THE GAME.
HMM...
WHY'D YOU PICK THE VASE?
HUH?
WHY DIDN'T YOU GO FOR THE VAULT?
YOU KNEW WE WANTED THE SAME THINGS YOU DID.
MOST PEOPLE WOULD GO FOR THE THING THAT'S WORTH THE MOST.
BUT YOU PICKED A PIECE OF JUNK OVER THE VAULT, AND EVEN THE DOLL.
WHY?

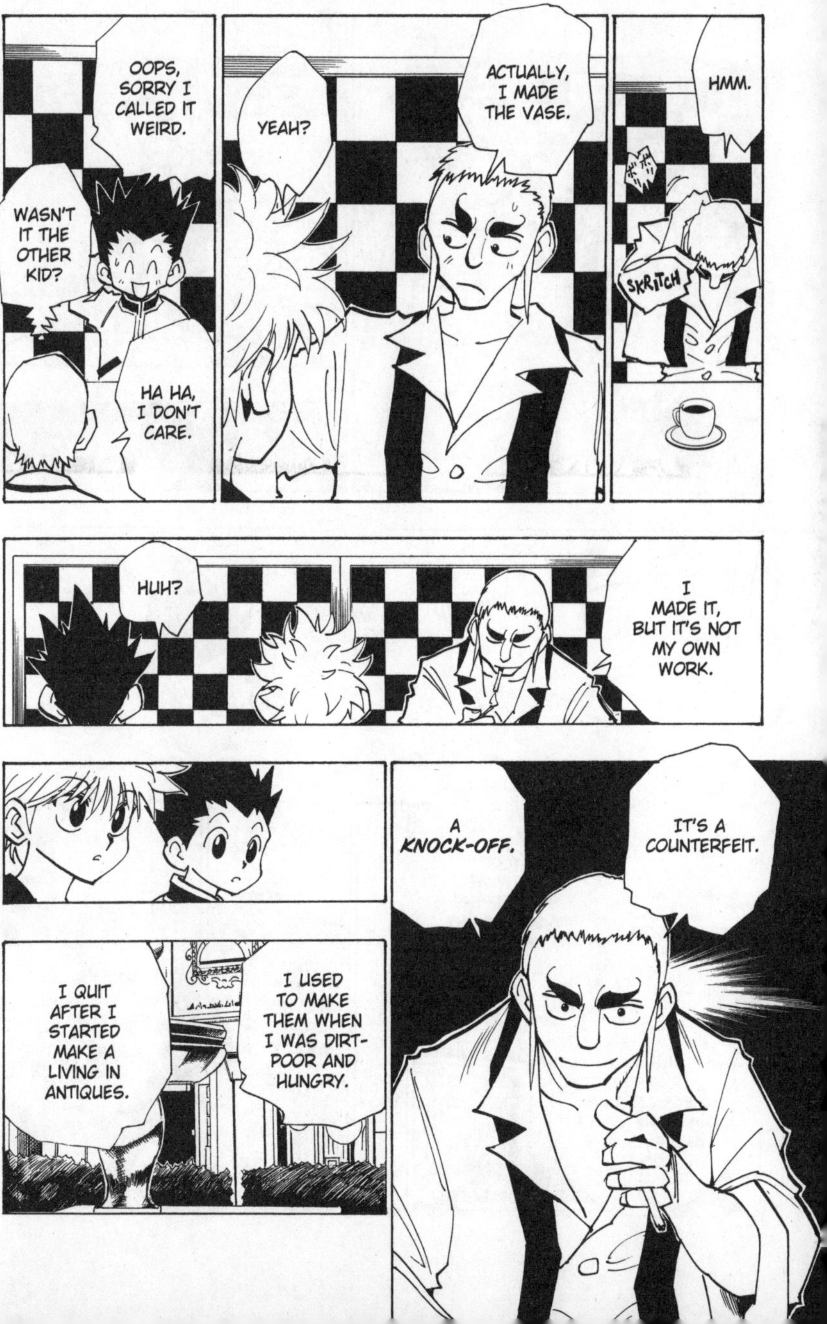
HMM.
SKRITCH
ACTUALLY, I MADE THE VASE.
YEAH?
OOPS, SORRY I CALLED IT WEIRD.
WASN'T IT THE OTHER KID?
HA HA, I DON'T CARE.
I MADE IT, BUT IT'S NOT MY OWN WORK.
HUH?
IT'S A COUNTERFEIT.
A KNOCK-OFF.
I USED TO MAKE THEM WHEN I WAS DIRT-POOR AND HUNGRY.
I QUIT AFTER I STARTED MAKE A LIVING IN ANTIQUES.

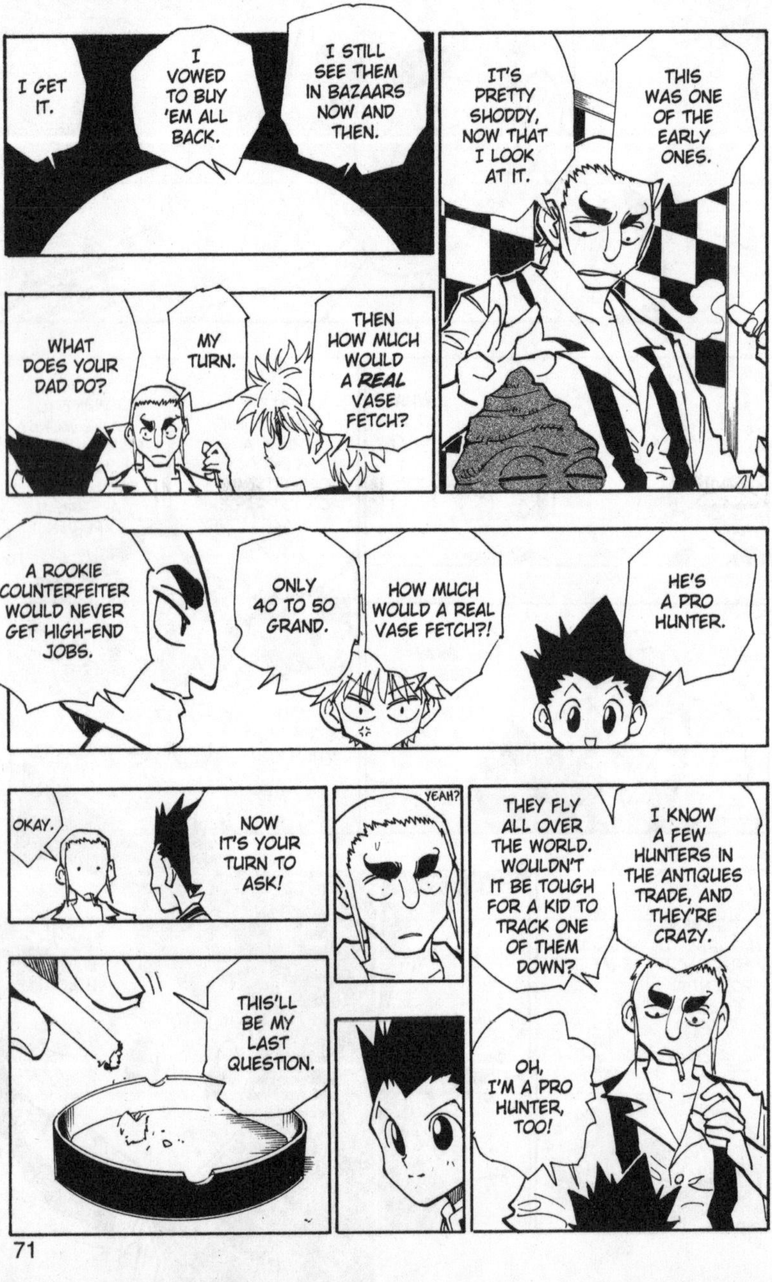
THIS WAS ONE OF THE EARLY ONES.
IT'S PRETTY SHODDY, NOW THAT I LOOK AT IT.
I STILL SEE THEM IN BAZAARS NOW AND THEN.
I VOWED TO BUY 'EM ALL BACK.
I GET IT.
THEN HOW MUCH WOULD A *REAL* VASE FETCH?
MY TURN.
WHAT DOES YOUR DAD DO?
HE'S A PRO HUNTER.
HOW MUCH WOULD A REAL VASE FETCH?!
ONLY 40 TO 50 GRAND.
A ROOKIE COUNTERFEITER WOULD NEVER GET HIGH-END JOBS.
I KNOW A FEW HUNTERS IN THE ANTIQUES TRADE, AND THEY'RE CRAZY.
THEY FLY ALL OVER THE WORLD. WOULDN'T IT BE TOUGH FOR A KID TO TRACK ONE OF THEM DOWN?
OH, I'M A PRO HUNTER, TOO!
YEAH?
NOW IT'S YOUR TURN TO ASK!
OKAY.
THIS'LL BE MY LAST QUESTION.

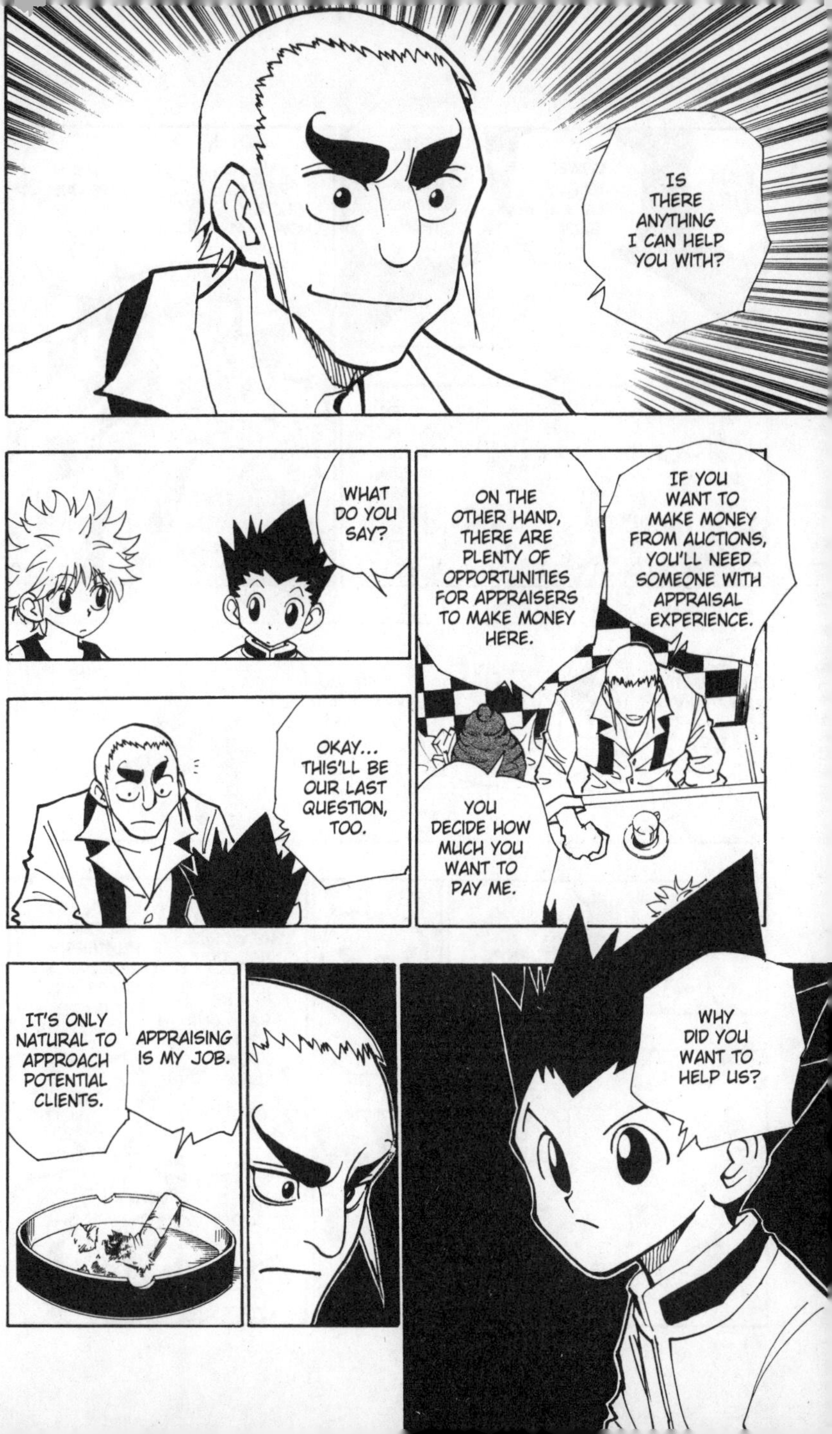
IS THERE ANYTHING I CAN HELP YOU WITH?
IF YOU WANT TO MAKE MONEY FROM AUCTIONS, YOU'LL NEED SOMEONE WITH APPRAISAL EXPERIENCE.
ON THE OTHER HAND, THERE ARE PLENTY OF OPPORTUNITIES FOR APPRAISERS TO MAKE MONEY HERE.
YOU DECIDE HOW MUCH YOU WANT TO PAY ME.
WHAT DO YOU SAY?
OKAY... THIS'LL BE OUR LAST QUESTION, TOO.
WHY DID YOU WANT TO HELP US?
APPRAISING IS MY JOB.
IT'S ONLY NATURAL TO APPROACH POTENTIAL CLIENTS.

READ THIS WAY

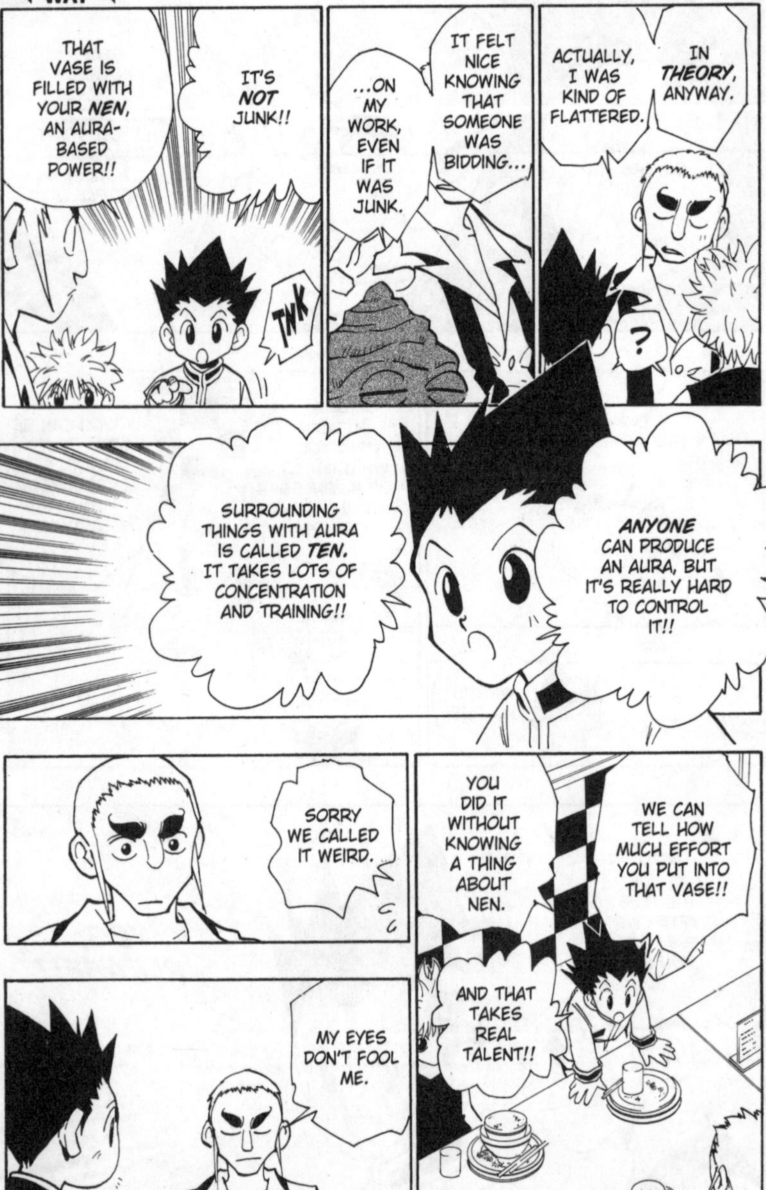

IN THEORY, ANYWAY.
ACTUALLY, I WAS KIND OF FLATTERED.
IT FELT NICE KNOWING THAT SOMEONE WAS BIDDING...
...ON MY WORK, EVEN IF IT WAS JUNK.
IT'S NOT JUNK!!
TNK
THAT VASE IS FILLED WITH YOUR NEN, AN AURA-BASED POWER!!
ANYONE CAN PRODUCE AN AURA, BUT IT'S REALLY HARD TO CONTROL IT!!
SURROUNDING THINGS WITH AURA IS CALLED TEN. IT TAKES LOTS OF CONCENTRATION AND TRAINING!!
WE CAN TELL HOW MUCH EFFORT YOU PUT INTO THAT VASE!!
YOU DID IT WITHOUT KNOWING A THING ABOUT NEN.
AND THAT TAKES REAL TALENT!!
SORRY WE CALLED IT WEIRD.
MY EYES DON'T FOOL ME.

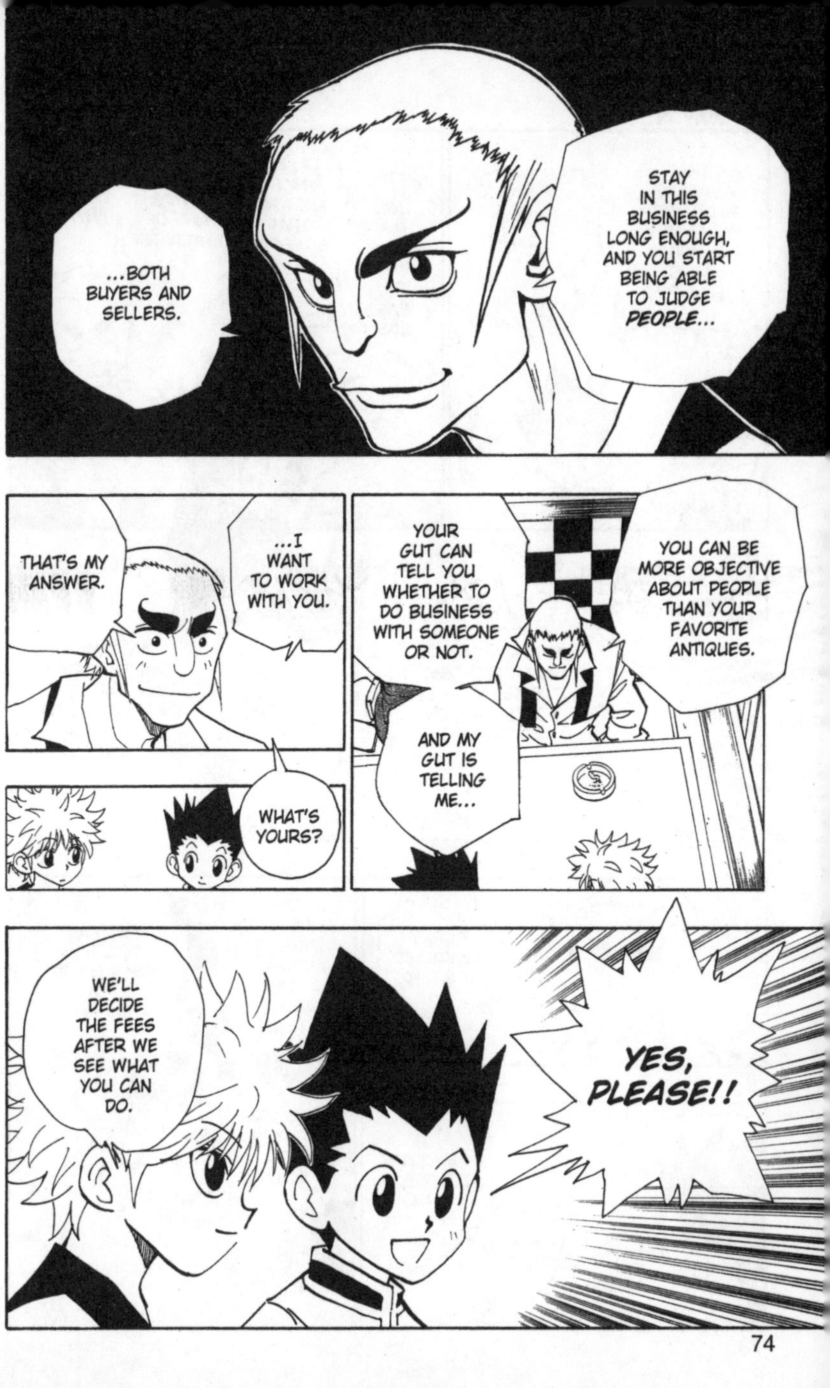
STAY IN THIS BUSINESS LONG ENOUGH, AND YOU START BEING ABLE TO JUDGE *PEOPLE...*
...BOTH BUYERS AND SELLERS.
YOU CAN BE MORE OBJECTIVE ABOUT PEOPLE THAN YOUR FAVORITE ANTIQUES.
YOUR GUT CAN TELL YOU WHETHER TO DO BUSINESS WITH SOMEONE OR NOT.
AND MY GUT IS TELLING ME...
...I WANT TO WORK WITH YOU.
THAT'S MY ANSWER.
WHAT'S YOURS?
YES, PLEASE!!
WE'LL DECIDE THE FEES AFTER WE SEE WHAT YOU CAN DO.

READ THIS WAY

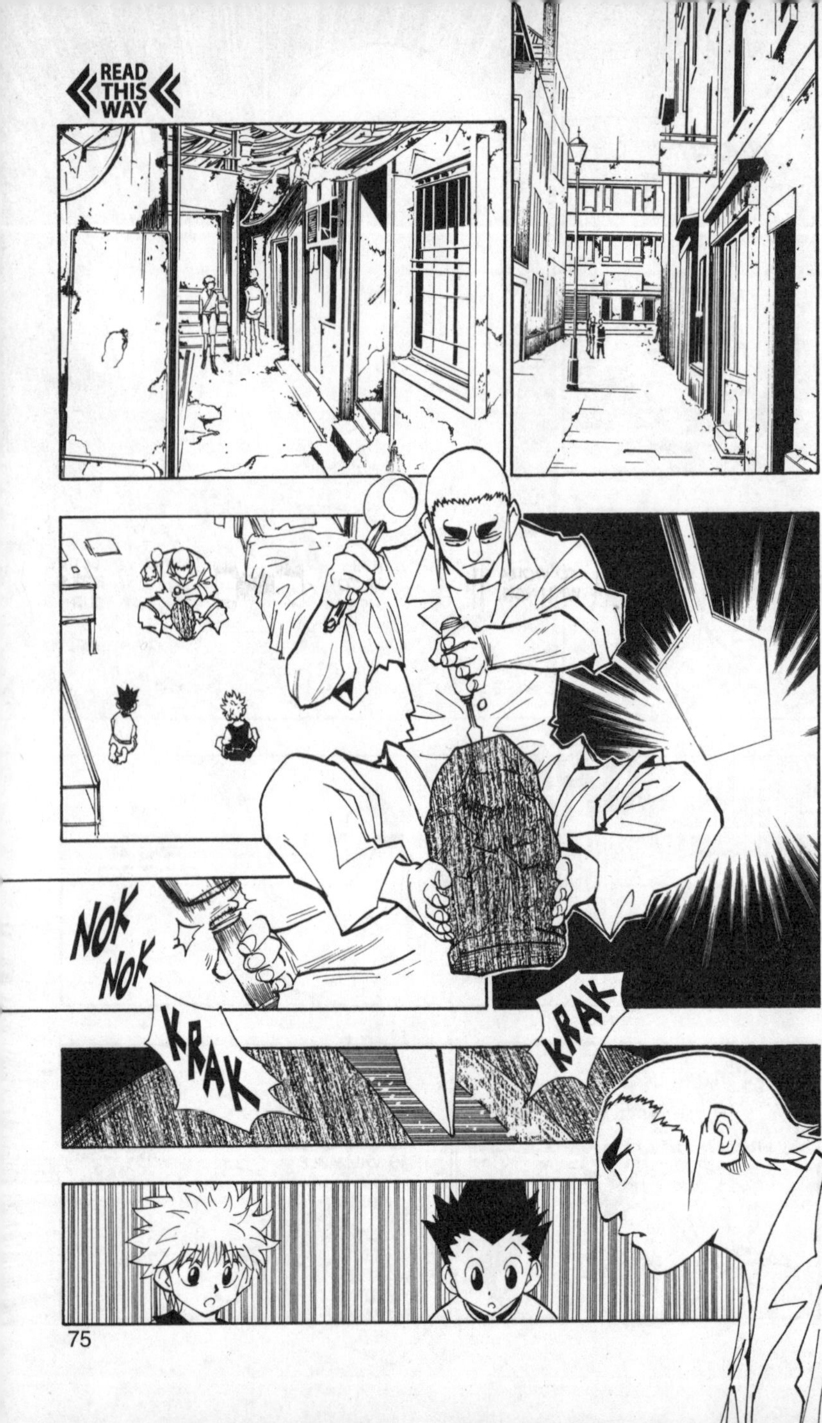
NOK NOK
KRAK
KRAK

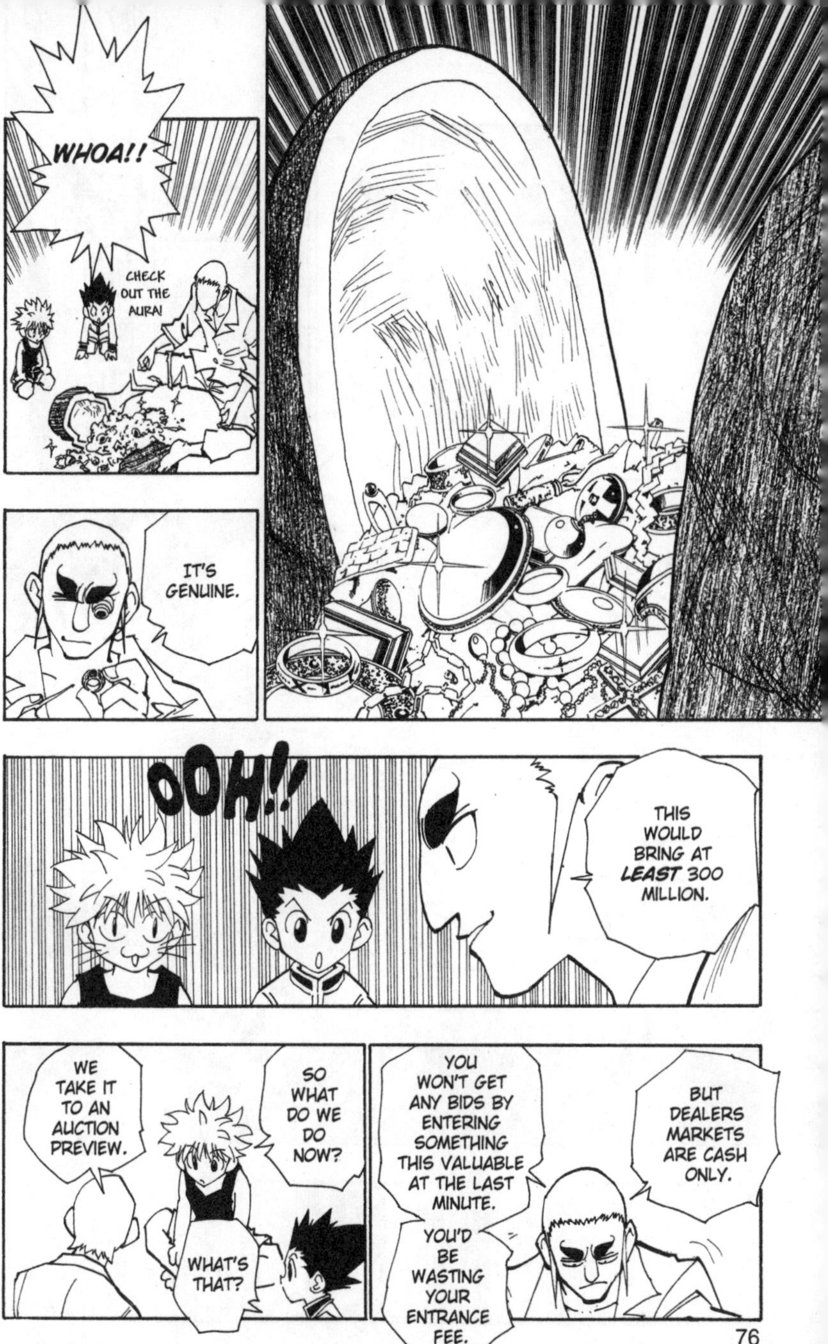
WHOA!!
CHECK OUT THE AURA!
IT'S GENUINE.
THIS WOULD BRING AT LEAST 300 MILLION.
OOH!!
BUT DEALERS MARKETS ARE CASH ONLY.
YOU WON'T GET ANY BIDS BY ENTERING SOMETHING THIS VALUABLE AT THE LAST MINUTE.
YOU'D BE WASTING YOUR ENTRANCE FEE.
SO WHAT DO WE DO NOW?
WE TAKE IT TO AN AUCTION PREVIEW.
WHAT'S THAT?

READ THIS WAY

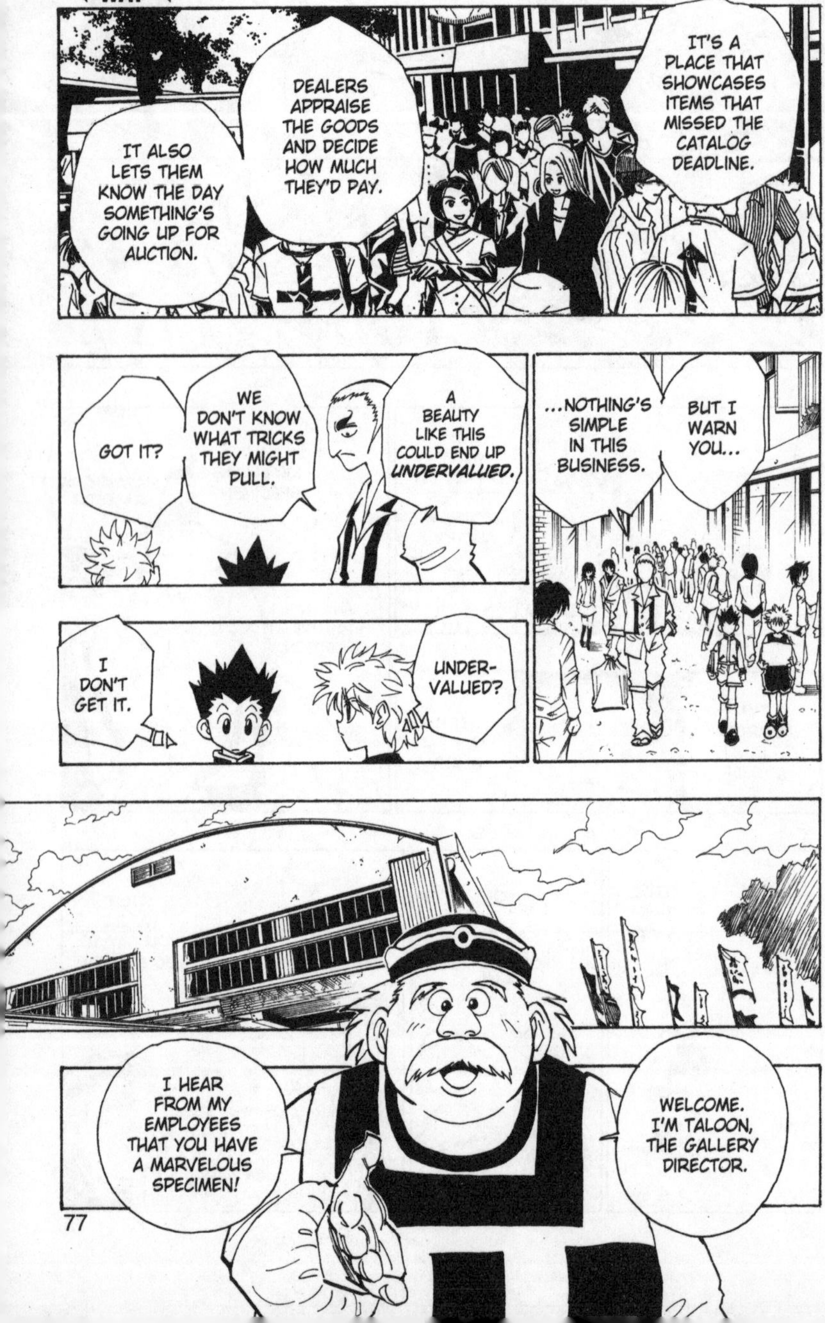

IT'S A PLACE THAT SHOWCASES ITEMS THAT MISSED THE CATALOG DEADLINE.
DEALERS APPRAISE THE GOODS AND DECIDE HOW MUCH THEY'D PAY.
IT ALSO LETS THEM KNOW THE DAY SOMETHING'S GOING UP FOR AUCTION.
BUT I WARN YOU...
...NOTHING'S SIMPLE IN THIS BUSINESS.
A BEAUTY LIKE THIS COULD END UP *UNDERVALUED.*
WE DON'T KNOW WHAT TRICKS THEY MIGHT PULL.
GOT IT?
UNDER-VALUED?
I DON'T GET IT.
WELCOME. I'M TALOON, THE GALLERY DIRECTOR.
I HEAR FROM MY EMPLOYEES THAT YOU HAVE A MARVELOUS SPECIMEN!

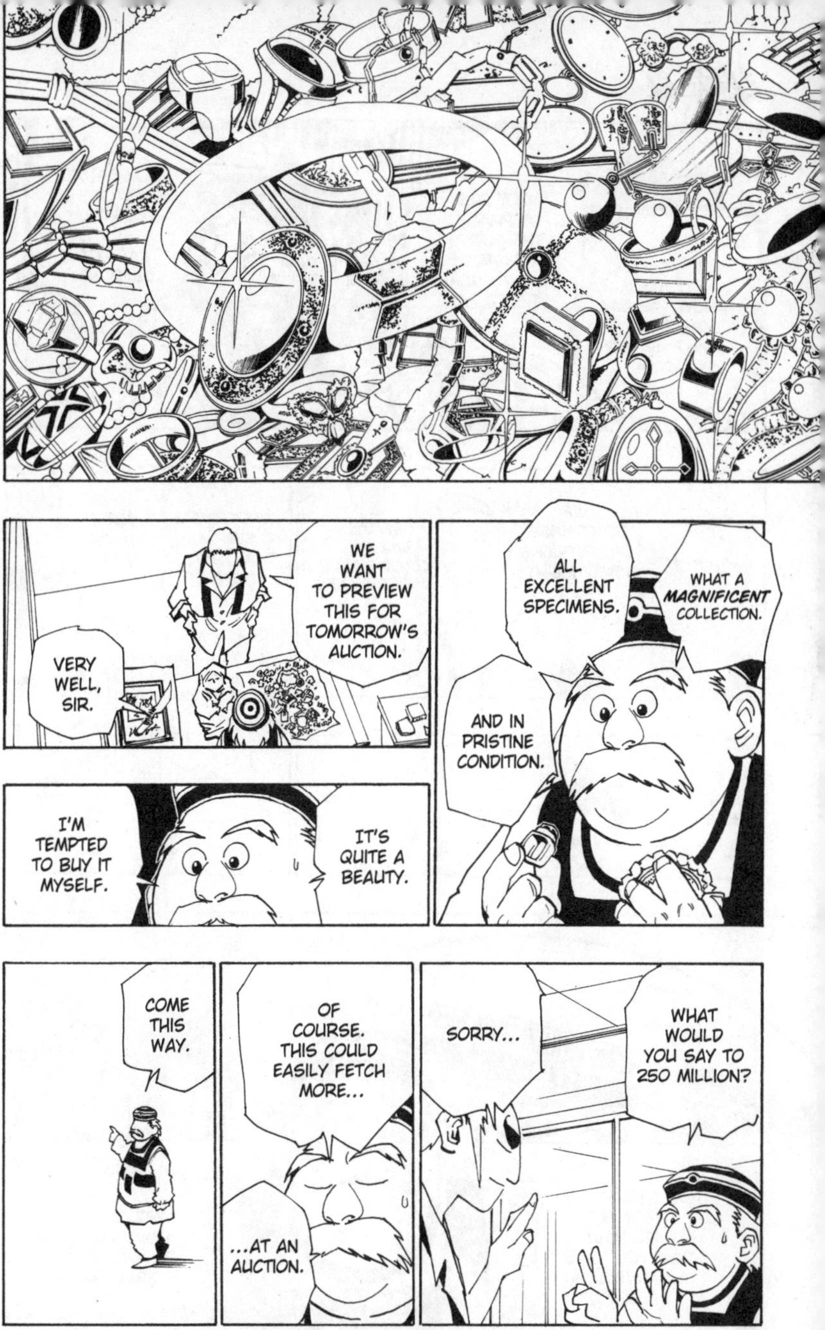
WHAT A *MAGNIFICENT* COLLECTION.
ALL EXCELLENT SPECIMENS.
AND IN PRISTINE CONDITION.
WE WANT TO PREVIEW THIS FOR TOMORROW'S AUCTION.
VERY WELL, SIR.
IT'S QUITE A BEAUTY.
I'M TEMPTED TO BUY IT MYSELF.
WHAT WOULD YOU SAY TO 250 MILLION?
SORRY...
OF COURSE. THIS COULD EASILY FETCH MORE...
...AT AN AUCTION.
COME THIS WAY.

READ THIS WAY

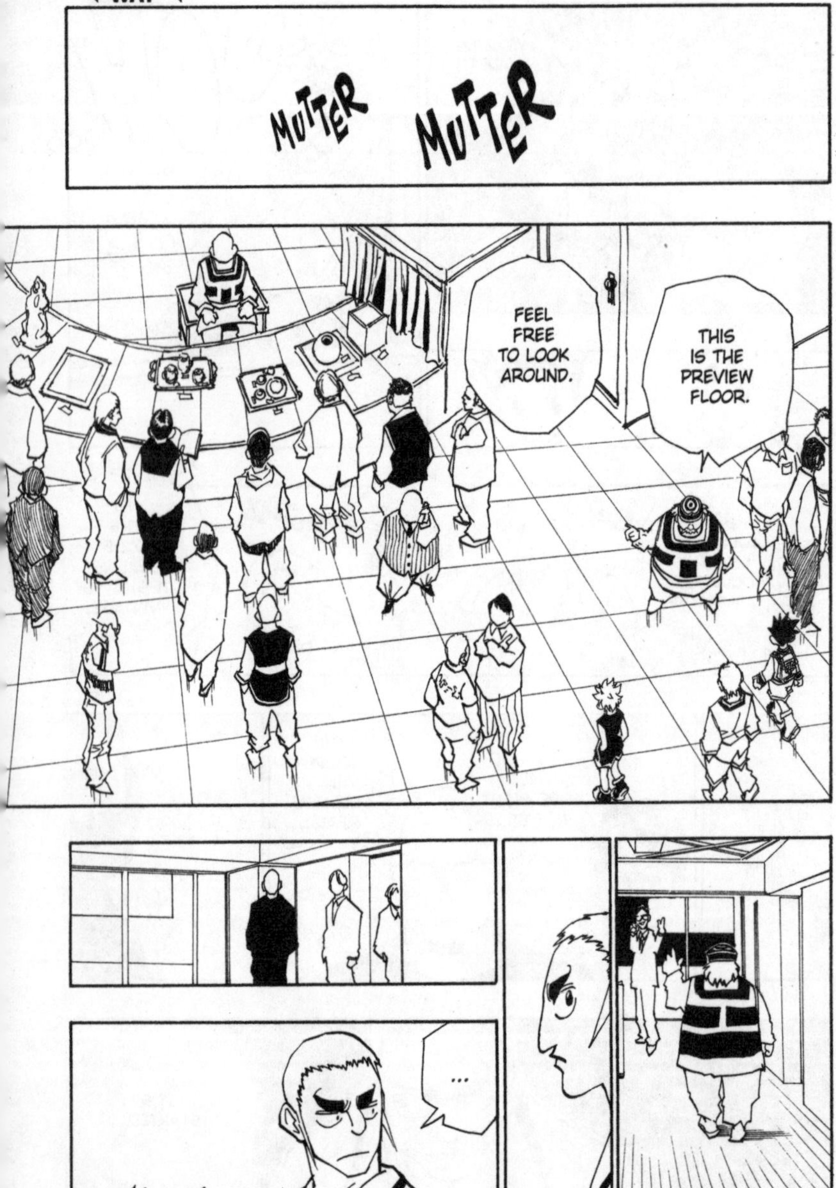
MUTTER MUTTER
THIS IS THE PREVIEW FLOOR.
FEEL FREE TO LOOK AROUND.
...

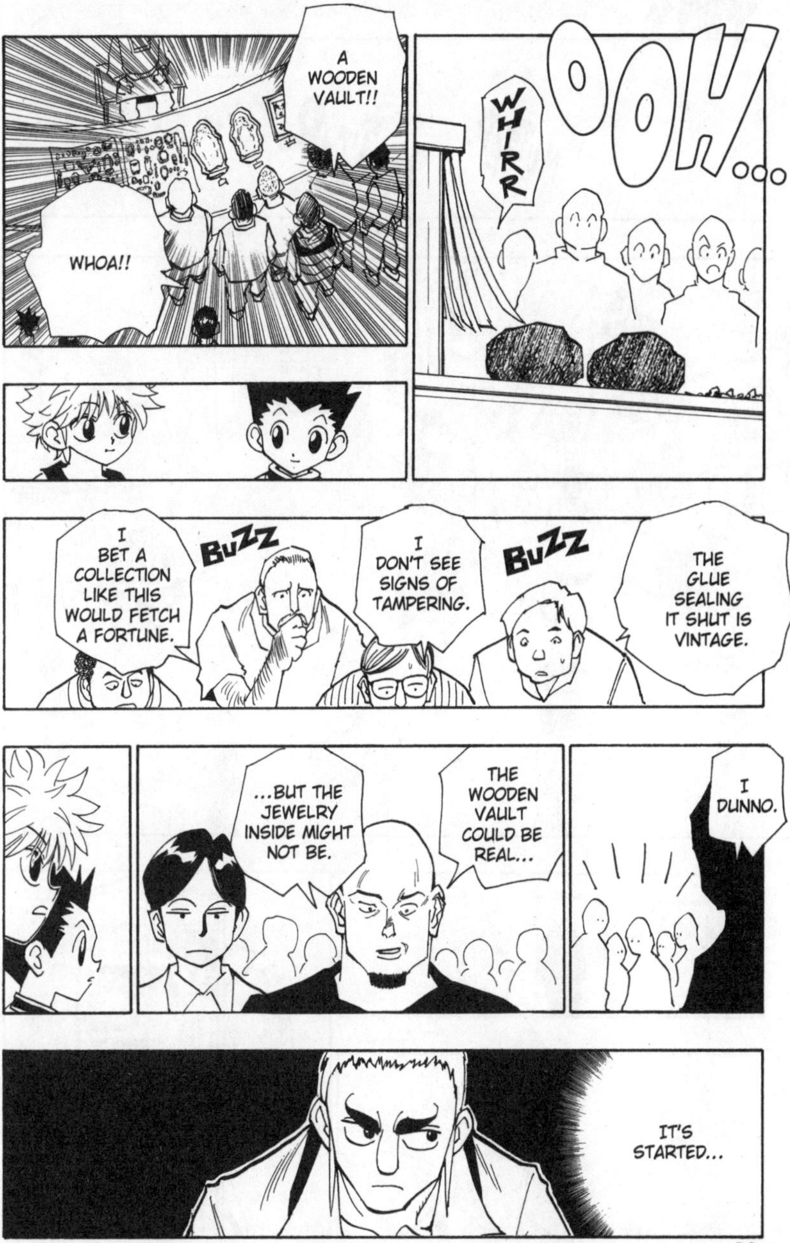
OOH...
WHIRR
A WOODEN VAULT!!
WHOA!!
THE GLUE SEALING IT SHUT IS VINTAGE.
BUZZ
I DON'T SEE SIGNS OF TAMPERING.
BUZZ
I BET A COLLECTION LIKE THIS WOULD FETCH A FORTUNE.
I DUNNO.
THE WOODEN VAULT COULD BE REAL...
...BUT THE JEWELRY INSIDE MIGHT NOT BE.
IT'S STARTED...

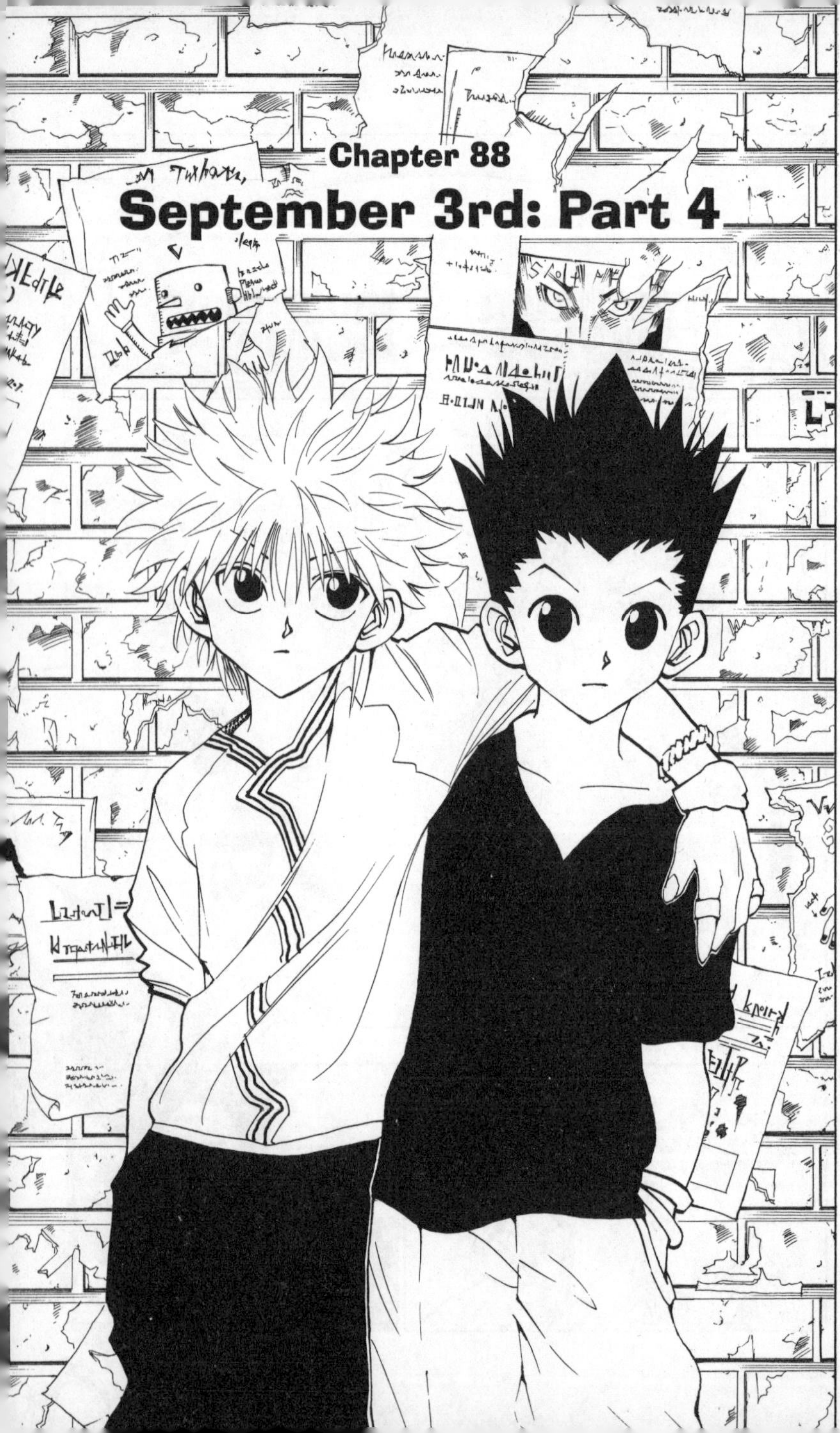

Chapter 88
September 3rd: Part 4

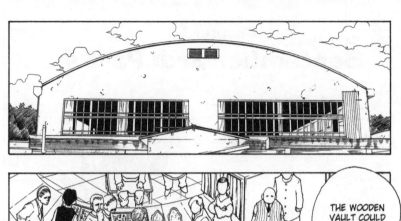

THE WOODEN VAULT COULD BE REAL...

...BUT THE JEWELRY INSIDE MIGHT NOT BE.

...THE JEWELS ARE REAL.

YEAH, BUT...

IT'S STARTED.

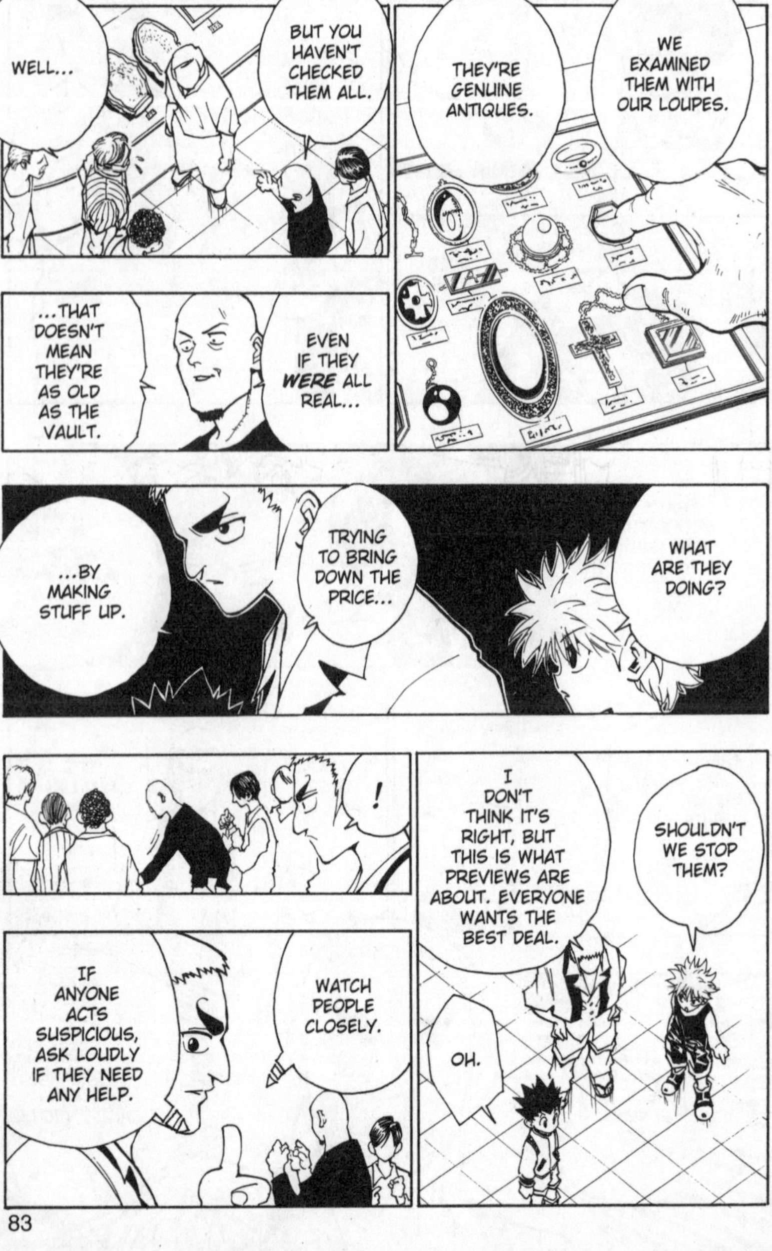
WE EXAMINED THEM WITH OUR LOUPES.
THEY'RE GENUINE ANTIQUES.
BUT YOU HAVEN'T CHECKED THEM ALL.
WELL...
EVEN IF THEY *WERE* ALL REAL...
...THAT DOESN'T MEAN THEY'RE AS OLD AS THE VAULT.
WHAT ARE THEY DOING?
TRYING TO BRING DOWN THE PRICE...
...BY MAKING STUFF UP.
SHOULDN'T WE STOP THEM?
I DON'T THINK IT'S RIGHT, BUT THIS IS WHAT PREVIEWS ARE ABOUT. EVERYONE WANTS THE BEST DEAL.
OH.
!
WATCH PEOPLE CLOSELY.
IF ANYONE ACTS SUSPICIOUS, ASK LOUDLY IF THEY NEED ANY HELP.

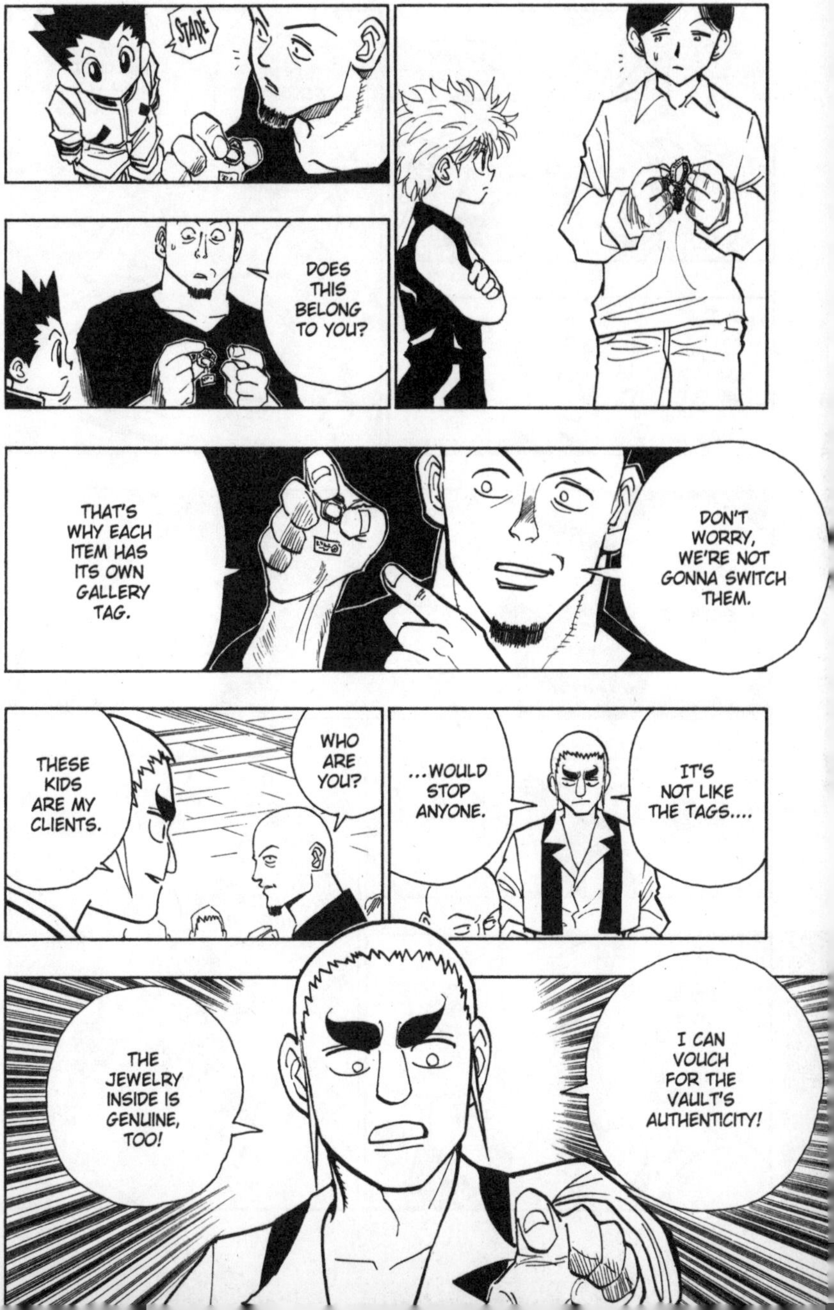
STARE
DOES THIS BELONG TO YOU?
DON'T WORRY, WE'RE NOT GONNA SWITCH THEM.
THAT'S WHY EACH ITEM HAS ITS OWN GALLERY TAG.
IT'S NOT LIKE THE TAGS....
...WOULD STOP ANYONE.
WHO ARE YOU?
THESE KIDS ARE MY CLIENTS.
I CAN VOUCH FOR THE VAULT'S AUTHENTICITY!
THE JEWELRY INSIDE IS GENUINE, TOO!

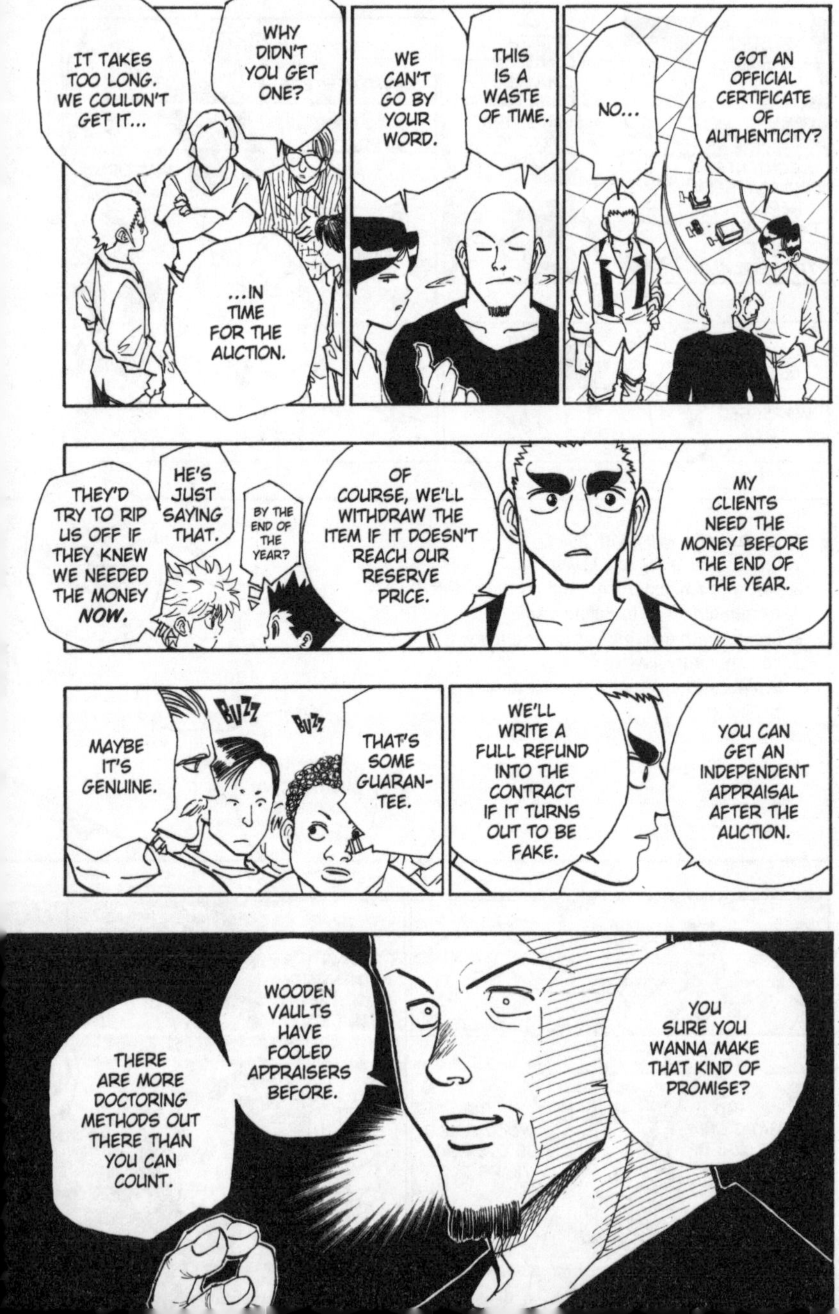
GOT AN OFFICIAL CERTIFICATE OF AUTHENTICITY?
NO...
THIS IS A WASTE OF TIME.
WE CAN'T GO BY YOUR WORD.
WHY DIDN'T YOU GET ONE?
IT TAKES TOO LONG. WE COULDN'T GET IT...
...IN TIME FOR THE AUCTION.
MY CLIENTS NEED THE MONEY BEFORE THE END OF THE YEAR.
OF COURSE, WE'LL WITHDRAW THE ITEM IF IT DOESN'T REACH OUR RESERVE PRICE.
BY THE END OF THE YEAR?
HE'S JUST SAYING THAT.
THEY'D TRY TO RIP US OFF IF THEY KNEW WE NEEDED THE MONEY *NOW.*
YOU CAN GET AN INDEPENDENT APPRAISAL AFTER THE AUCTION.
WE'LL WRITE A FULL REFUND INTO THE CONTRACT IF IT TURNS OUT TO BE FAKE.
THAT'S SOME GUARAN-TEE.
BUZZ
BUZZ
MAYBE IT'S GENUINE.
YOU SURE YOU WANNA MAKE THAT KIND OF PROMISE?
WOODEN VAULTS HAVE FOOLED APPRAISERS BEFORE.
THERE ARE MORE DOCTORING METHODS OUT THERE THAN YOU CAN COUNT.

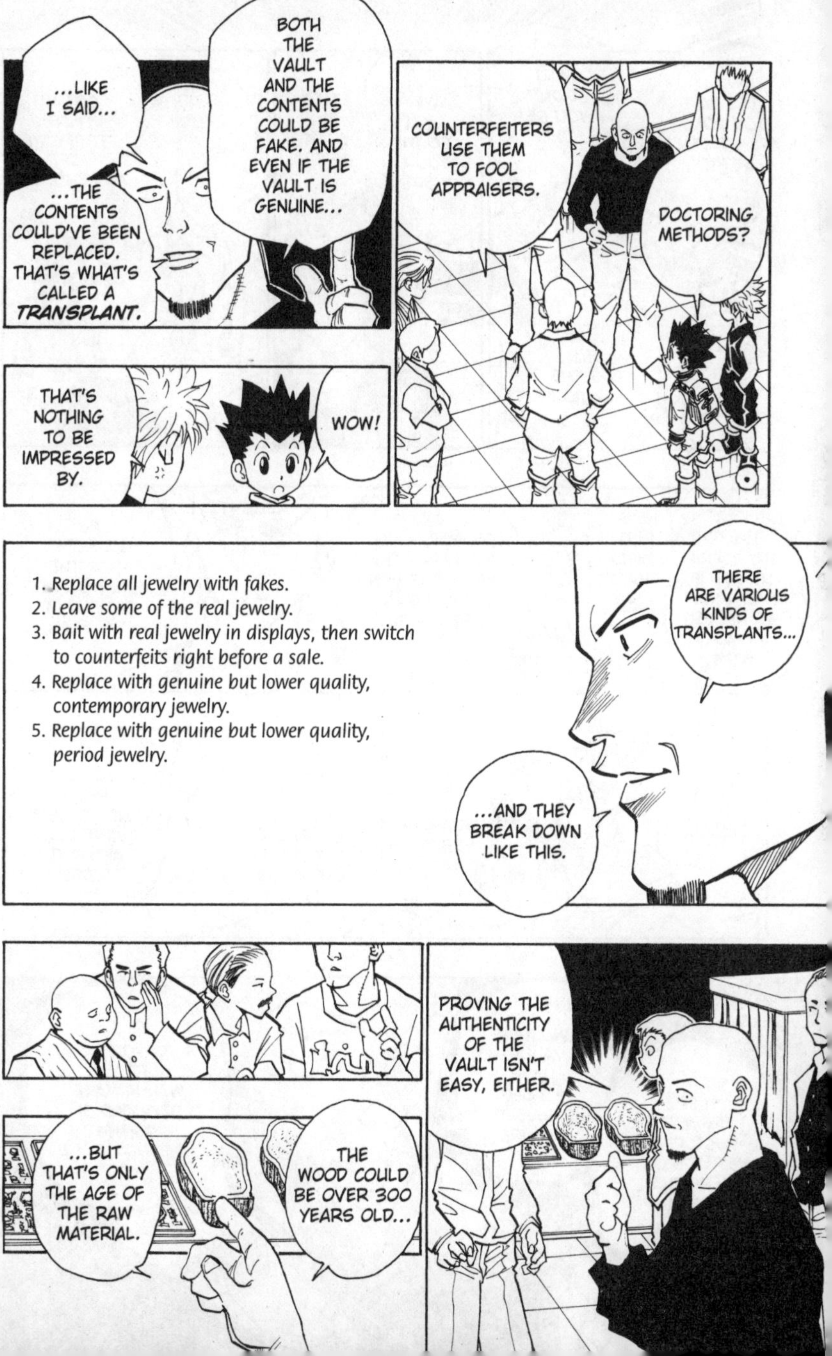
DOCTORING METHODS?
COUNTERFEITERS USE THEM TO FOOL APPRAISERS.
BOTH THE VAULT AND THE CONTENTS COULD BE FAKE. AND EVEN IF THE VAULT IS GENUINE...
...LIKE I SAID...
...THE CONTENTS COULD'VE BEEN REPLACED. THAT'S WHAT'S CALLED A *TRANSPLANT.*
WOW!
THAT'S NOTHING TO BE IMPRESSED BY.
THERE ARE VARIOUS KINDS OF TRANSPLANTS...
...AND THEY BREAK DOWN LIKE THIS.
1. Replace all jewelry with fakes.
2. Leave some of the real jewelry.
3. Bait with real jewelry in displays, then switch to counterfeits right before a sale.
4. Replace with genuine but lower quality, contemporary jewelry.
5. Replace with genuine but lower quality, period jewelry.
PROVING THE AUTHENTICITY OF THE VAULT ISN'T EASY, EITHER.
THE WOOD COULD BE OVER 300 YEARS OLD...
...BUT THAT'S ONLY THE AGE OF THE RAW MATERIAL.

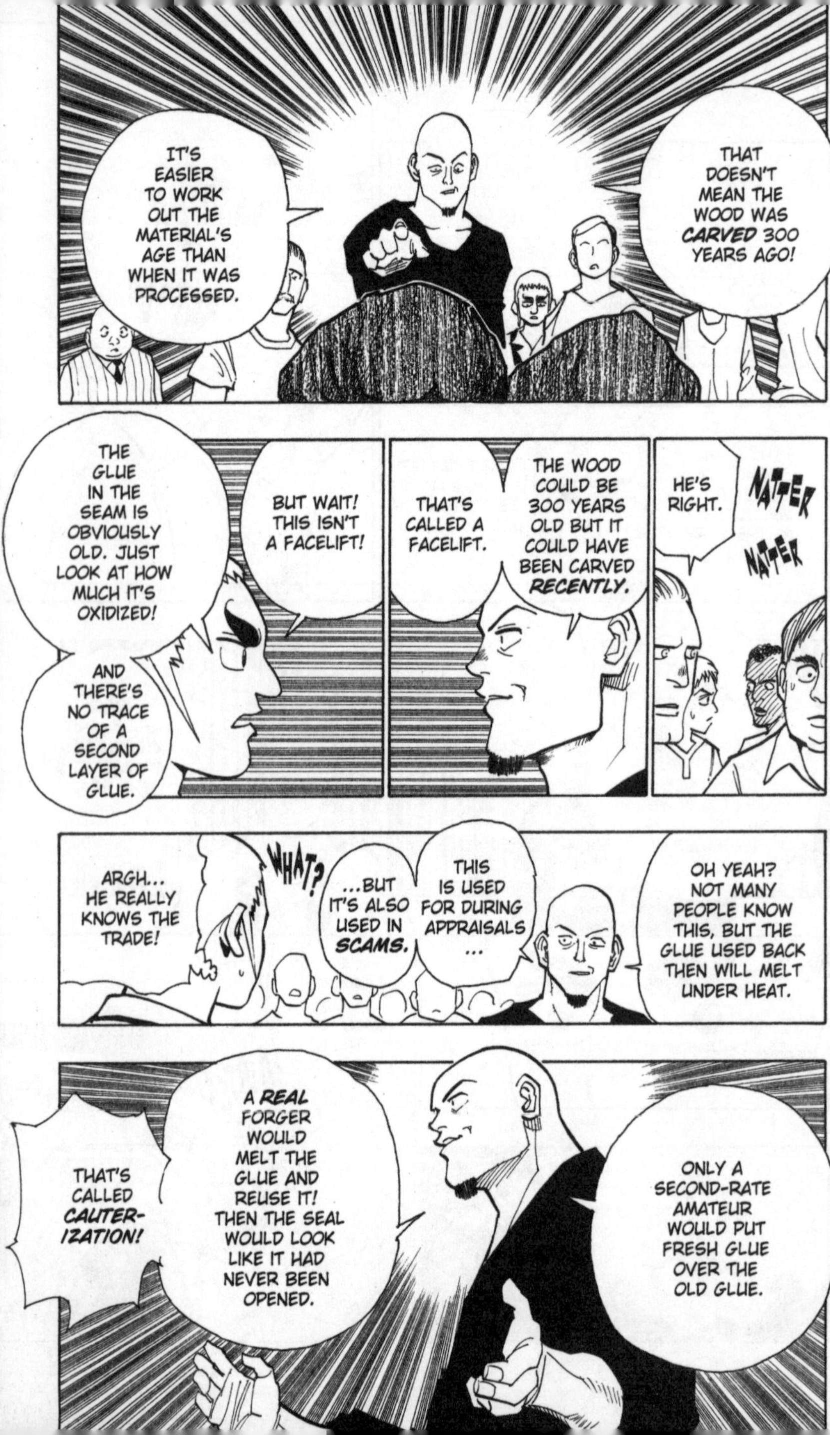
THAT DOESN'T MEAN THE WOOD WAS CARVED 300 YEARS AGO!
IT'S EASIER TO WORK OUT THE MATERIAL'S AGE THAN WHEN IT WAS PROCESSED.
HE'S RIGHT.
NATTER
NATTER
THE WOOD COULD BE 300 YEARS OLD BUT IT COULD HAVE BEEN CARVED RECENTLY.
THAT'S CALLED A FACELIFT.
BUT WAIT! THIS ISN'T A FACELIFT!
THE GLUE IN THE SEAM IS OBVIOUSLY OLD. JUST LOOK AT HOW MUCH IT'S OXIDIZED!
AND THERE'S NO TRACE OF A SECOND LAYER OF GLUE.
OH YEAH? NOT MANY PEOPLE KNOW THIS, BUT THE GLUE USED BACK THEN WILL MELT UNDER HEAT.
THIS IS USED FOR DURING APPRAISALS ...
...BUT IT'S ALSO USED IN SCAMS.
WHAT?
ARGH... HE REALLY KNOWS THE TRADE!
ONLY A SECOND-RATE AMATEUR WOULD PUT FRESH GLUE OVER THE OLD GLUE.
A REAL FORGER WOULD MELT THE GLUE AND REUSE IT! THEN THE SEAL WOULD LOOK LIKE IT HAD NEVER BEEN OPENED.
THAT'S CALLED CAUTERIZATION!

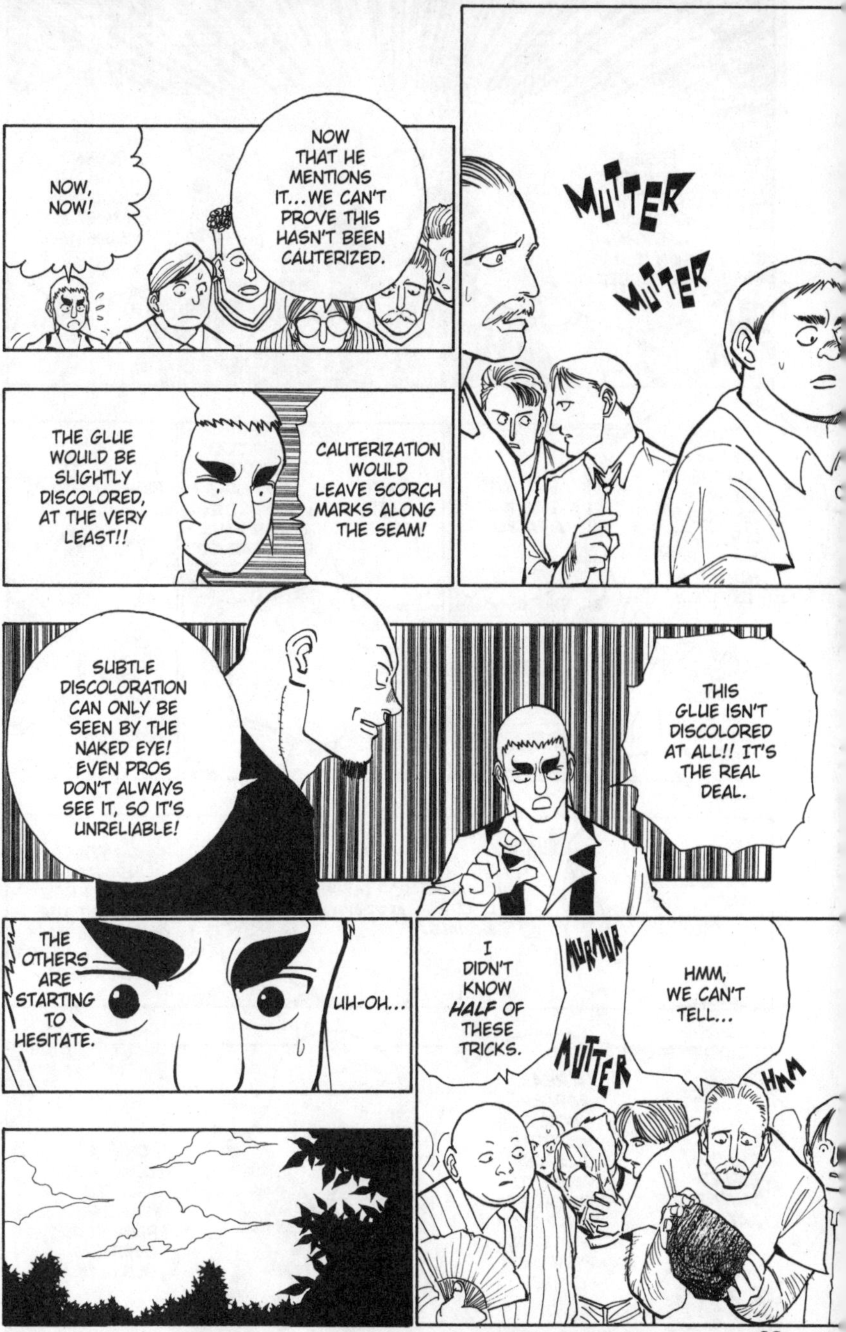
MUTTER
MUTTER
NOW THAT HE MENTIONS IT...WE CAN'T PROVE THIS HASN'T BEEN CAUTERIZED.
NOW, NOW!
CAUTERIZATION WOULD LEAVE SCORCH MARKS ALONG THE SEAM!
THE GLUE WOULD BE SLIGHTLY DISCOLORED, AT THE VERY LEAST!!
THIS GLUE ISN'T DISCOLORED AT ALL!! IT'S THE REAL DEAL.
SUBTLE DISCOLORATION CAN ONLY BE SEEN BY THE NAKED EYE! EVEN PROS DON'T ALWAYS SEE IT, SO IT'S UNRELIABLE!
HMM, WE CAN'T TELL...
MURMUR
I DIDN'T KNOW *HALF* OF THESE TRICKS.
MUTTER
HMM
UH-OH...
THE OTHERS ARE STARTING TO HESITATE.

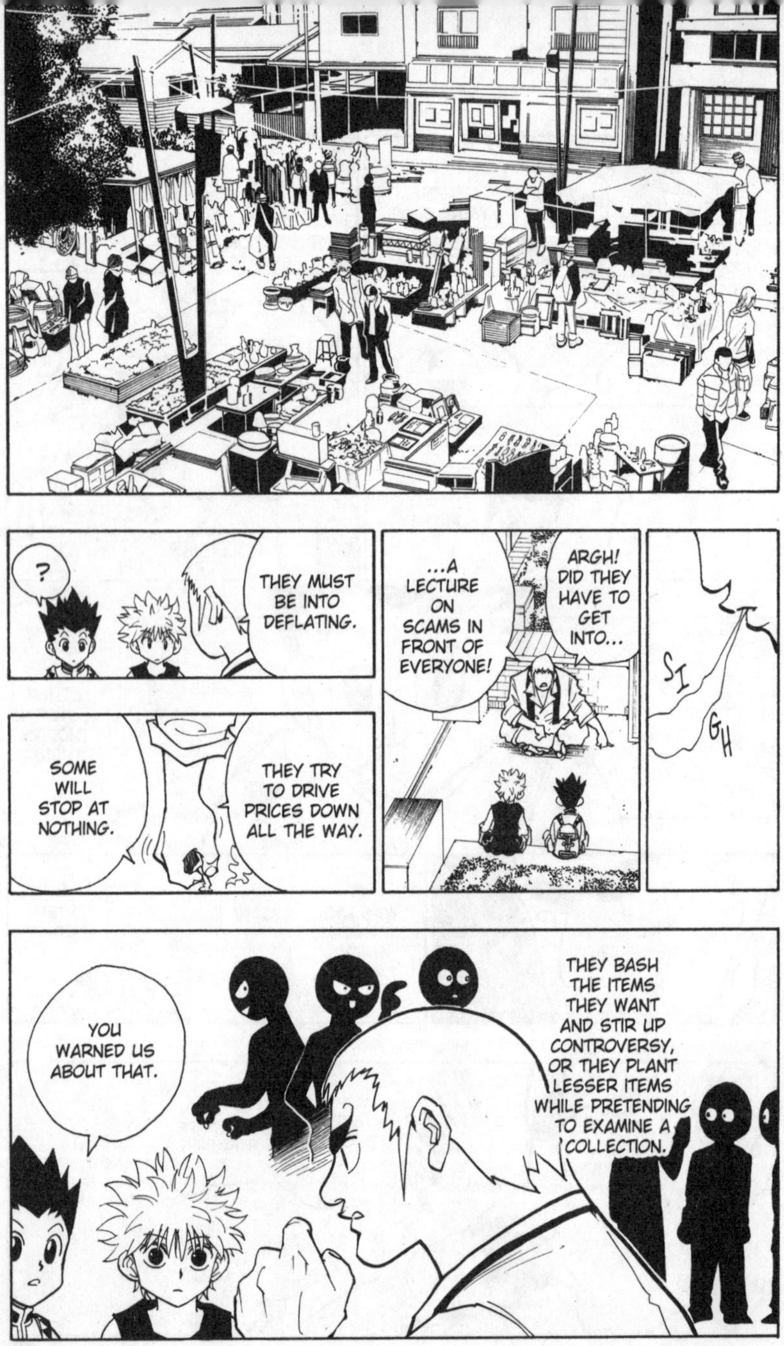
SIGH
ARGH! DID THEY HAVE TO GET INTO...
...A LECTURE ON SCAMS IN FRONT OF EVERYONE!
THEY MUST BE INTO DEFLATING.
?
THEY TRY TO DRIVE PRICES DOWN ALL THE WAY.
SOME WILL STOP AT NOTHING.
THEY BASH THE ITEMS THEY WANT AND STIR UP CONTROVERSY, OR THEY PLANT LESSER ITEMS WHILE PRETENDING TO EXAMINE A COLLECTION.
YOU WARNED US ABOUT THAT.

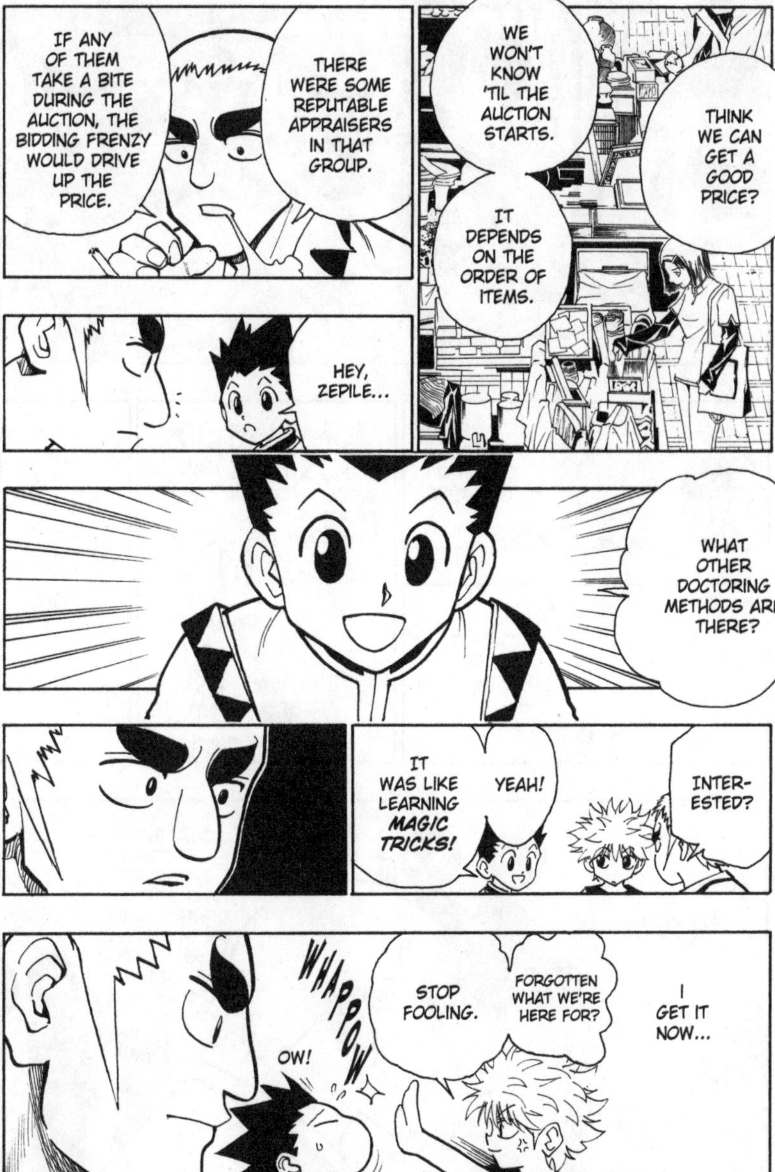
THINK WE CAN GET A GOOD PRICE?
WE WON'T KNOW 'TIL THE AUCTION STARTS.
IT DEPENDS ON THE ORDER OF ITEMS.
THERE WERE SOME REPUTABLE APPRAISERS IN THAT GROUP.
IF ANY OF THEM TAKE A BITE DURING THE AUCTION, THE BIDDING FRENZY WOULD DRIVE UP THE PRICE.
HEY, ZEPILE...
WHAT OTHER DOCTORING METHODS ARE THERE?
INTER-ESTED?
YEAH!
IT WAS LIKE LEARNING *MAGIC TRICKS!*
I GET IT NOW...
FORGOTTEN WHAT WE'RE HERE FOR?
STOP FOOLING.
WHAPPOW
OW!

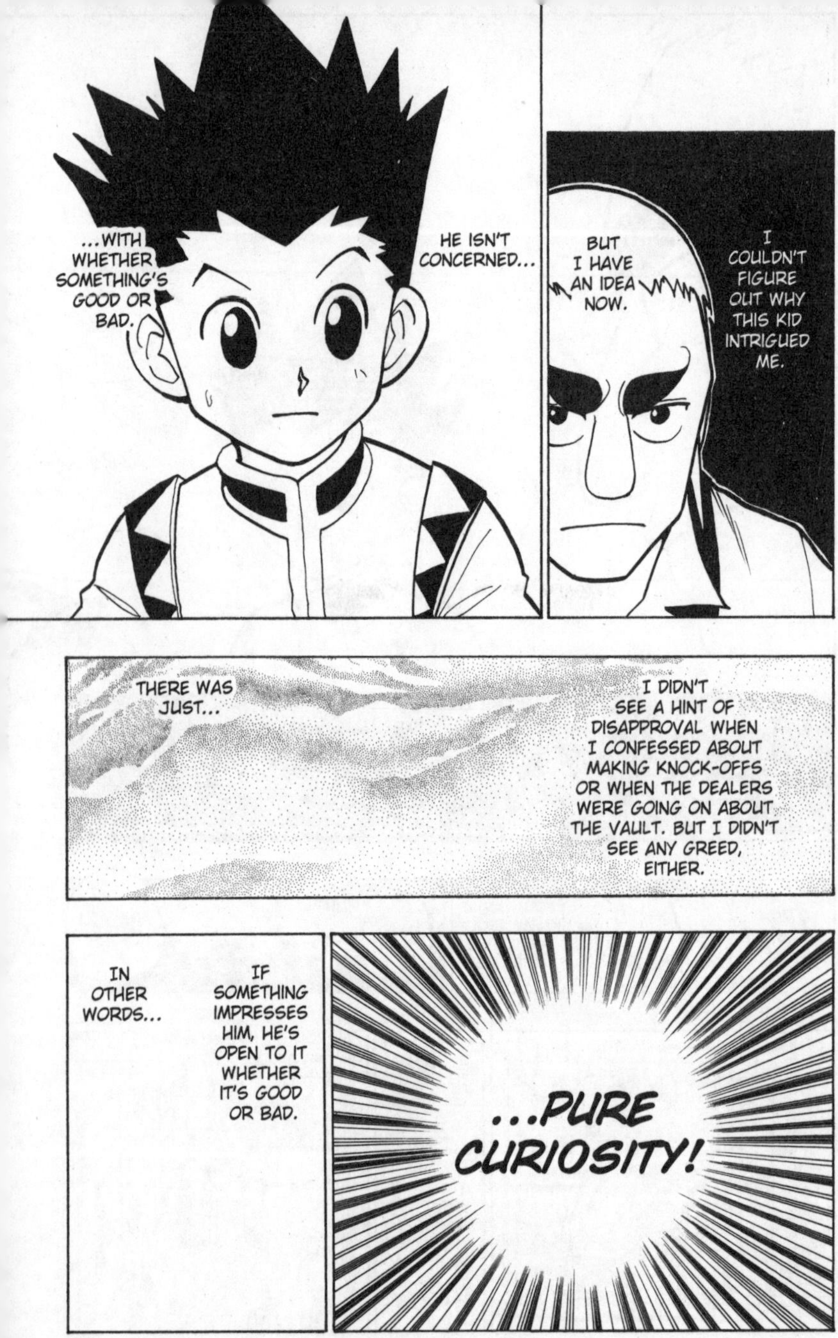
I COULDN'T FIGURE OUT WHY THIS KID INTRIGUED ME.
BUT I HAVE AN IDEA NOW.
HE ISN'T CONCERNED...
...WITH WHETHER SOMETHING'S GOOD OR BAD.
I DIDN'T SEE A HINT OF DISAPPROVAL WHEN I CONFESSED ABOUT MAKING KNOCK-OFFS OR WHEN THE DEALERS WERE GOING ON ABOUT THE VAULT. BUT I DIDN'T SEE ANY GREED, EITHER.
THERE WAS JUST...
...PURE CURIOSITY!
IF SOMETHING IMPRESSES HIM, HE'S OPEN TO IT WHETHER IT'S GOOD OR BAD.
IN OTHER WORDS...

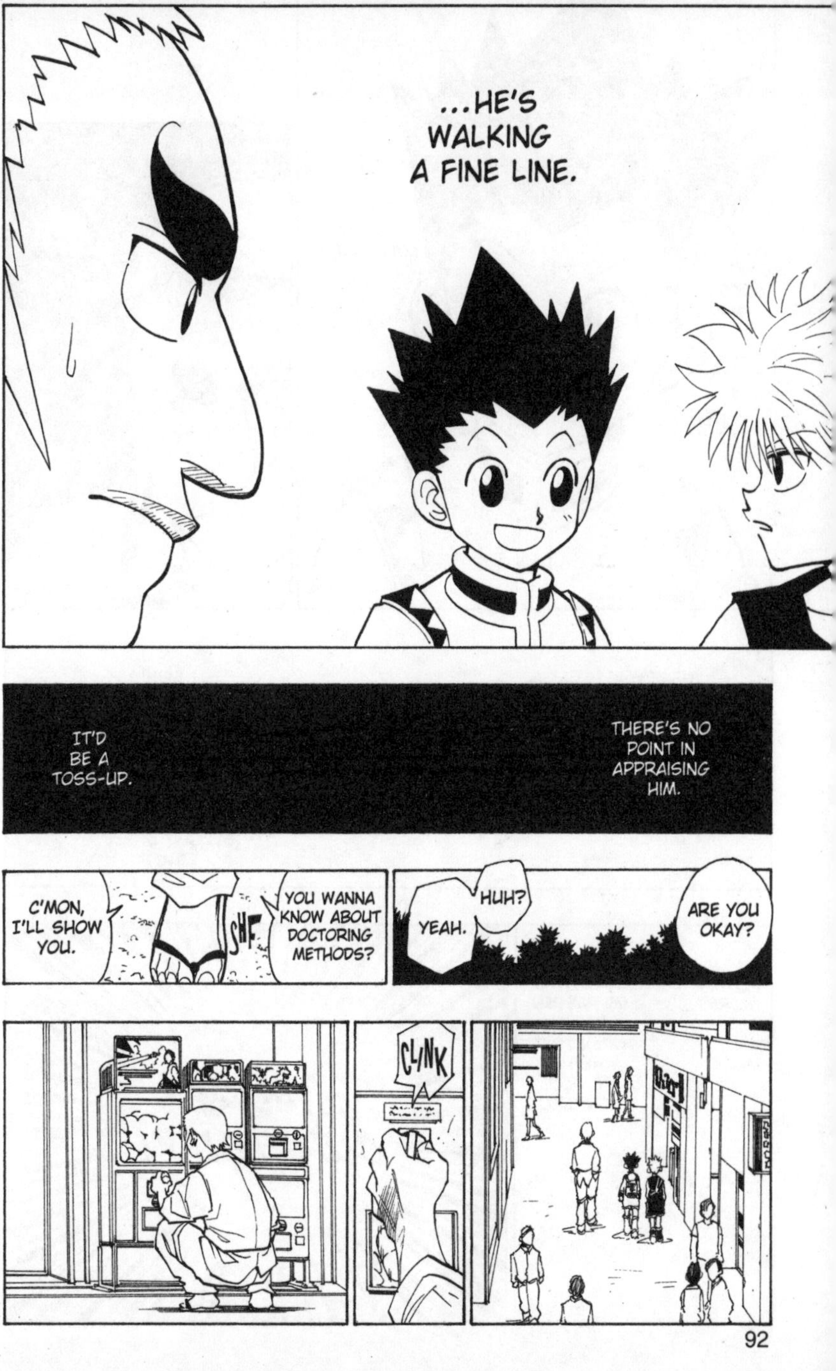
...HE'S WALKING A FINE LINE.
THERE'S NO POINT IN APPRAISING HIM.
IT'D BE A TOSS-UP.
ARE YOU OKAY?
HUH?
YEAH.
YOU WANNA KNOW ABOUT DOCTORING METHODS?
SHF
C'MON, I'LL SHOW YOU.
CLINK

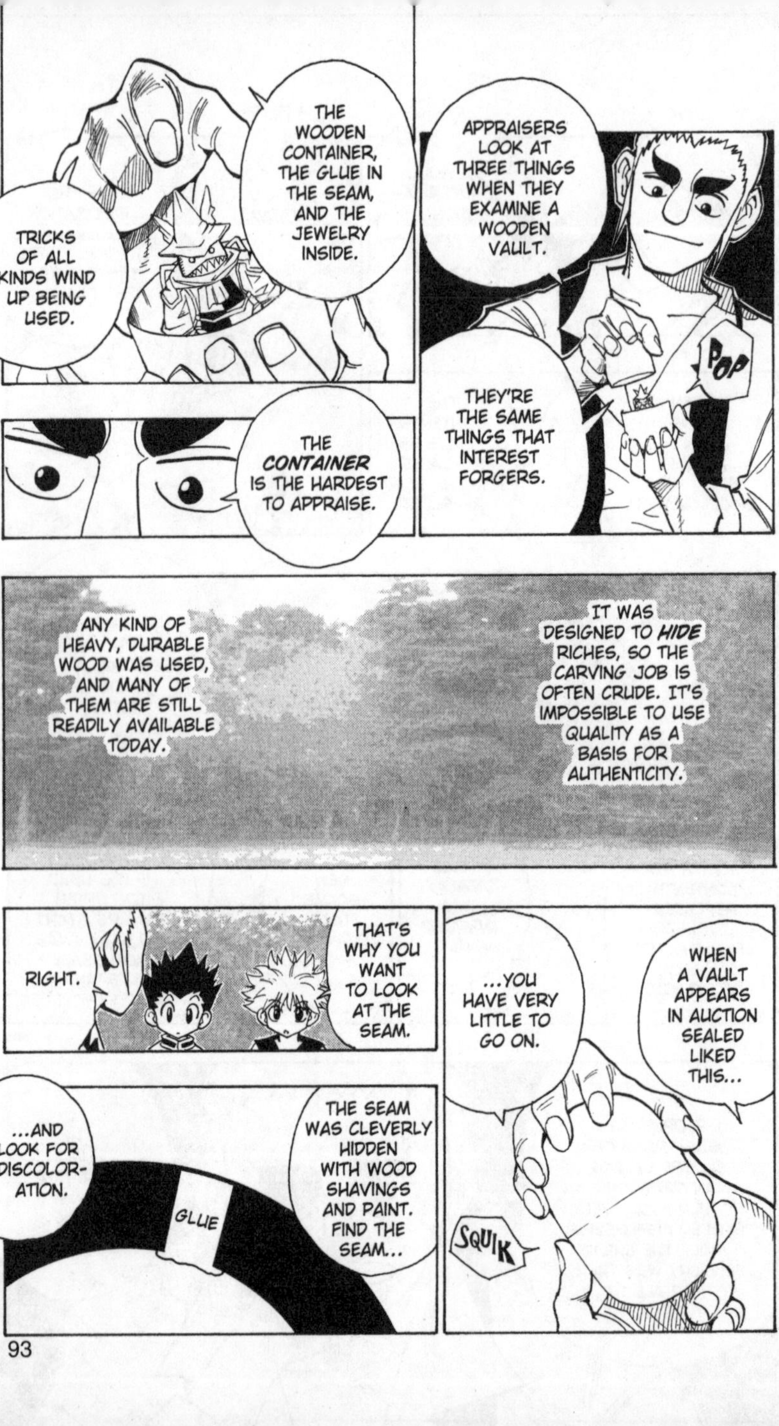
APPRAISERS LOOK AT THREE THINGS WHEN THEY EXAMINE A WOODEN VAULT.
POP
THEY'RE THE SAME THINGS THAT INTEREST FORGERS.
THE WOODEN CONTAINER, THE GLUE IN THE SEAM, AND THE JEWELRY INSIDE.
TRICKS OF ALL KINDS WIND UP BEING USED.
THE *CONTAINER* IS THE HARDEST TO APPRAISE.
IT WAS DESIGNED TO *HIDE* RICHES, SO THE CARVING JOB IS OFTEN CRUDE. IT'S IMPOSSIBLE TO USE QUALITY AS A BASIS FOR AUTHENTICITY.
ANY KIND OF HEAVY, DURABLE WOOD WAS USED, AND MANY OF THEM ARE STILL READILY AVAILABLE TODAY.
WHEN A VAULT APPEARS IN AUCTION SEALED LIKED THIS...
...YOU HAVE VERY LITTLE TO GO ON.
SQUIK
THAT'S WHY YOU WANT TO LOOK AT THE SEAM.
RIGHT.
THE SEAM WAS CLEVERLY HIDDEN WITH WOOD SHAVINGS AND PAINT. FIND THE SEAM...
GLUE
...AND LOOK FOR DISCOLOR-ATION.

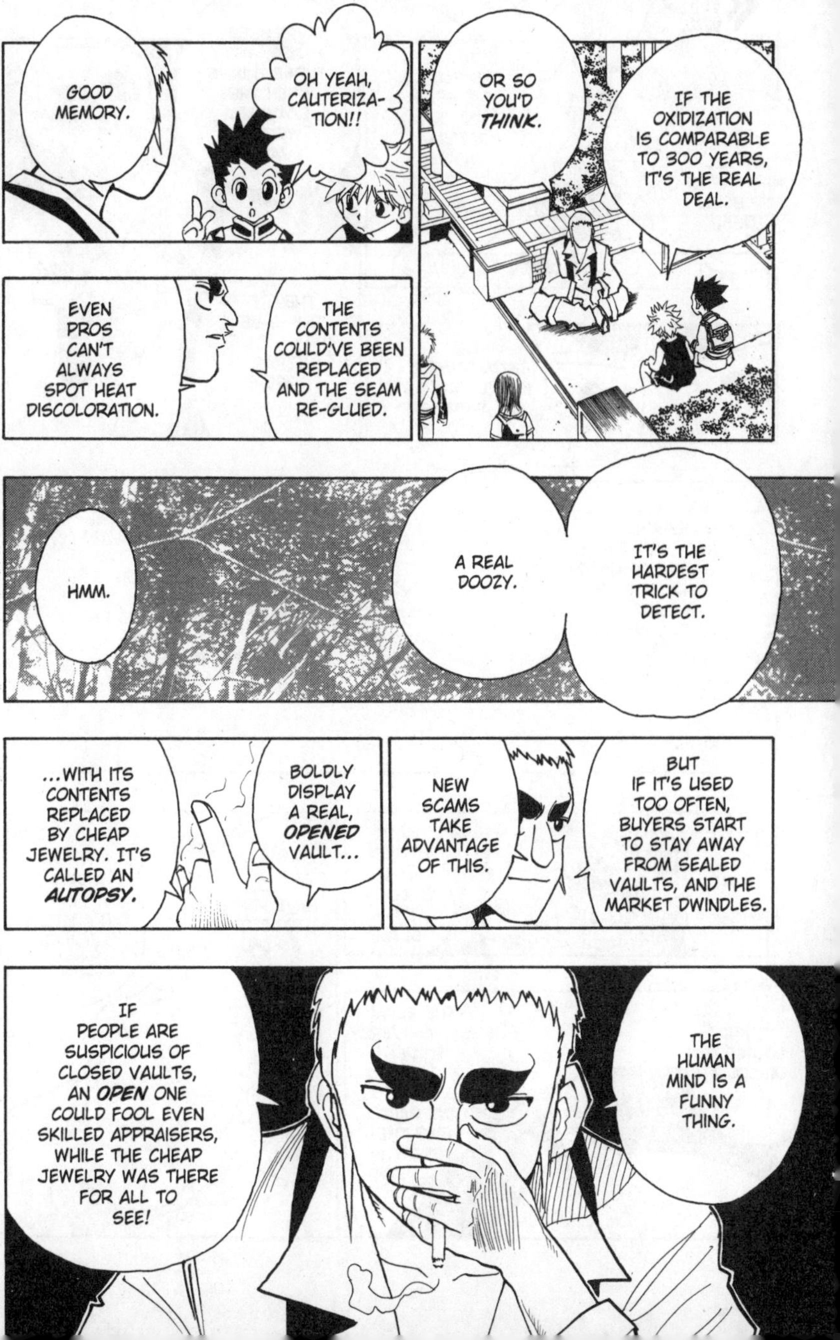
IF THE OXIDIZATION IS COMPARABLE TO 300 YEARS, IT'S THE REAL DEAL.
OR SO YOU'D *THINK.*
OH YEAH, CAUTERIZA-TION!!
GOOD MEMORY.
THE CONTENTS COULD'VE BEEN REPLACED AND THE SEAM RE-GLUED.
EVEN PROS CAN'T ALWAYS SPOT HEAT DISCOLORATION.
IT'S THE HARDEST TRICK TO DETECT.
A REAL DOOZY.
HMM.
BUT IF IT'S USED TOO OFTEN, BUYERS START TO STAY AWAY FROM SEALED VAULTS, AND THE MARKET DWINDLES.
NEW SCAMS TAKE ADVANTAGE OF THIS.
BOLDLY DISPLAY A REAL, *OPENED* VAULT...
...WITH ITS CONTENTS REPLACED BY CHEAP JEWELRY. IT'S CALLED AN *AUTOPSY.*
THE HUMAN MIND IS A FUNNY THING.
IF PEOPLE ARE SUSPICIOUS OF CLOSED VAULTS, AN *OPEN* ONE COULD FOOL EVEN SKILLED APPRAISERS, WHILE THE CHEAP JEWELRY WAS THERE FOR ALL TO SEE!

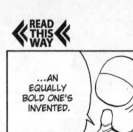

READ THIS WAY

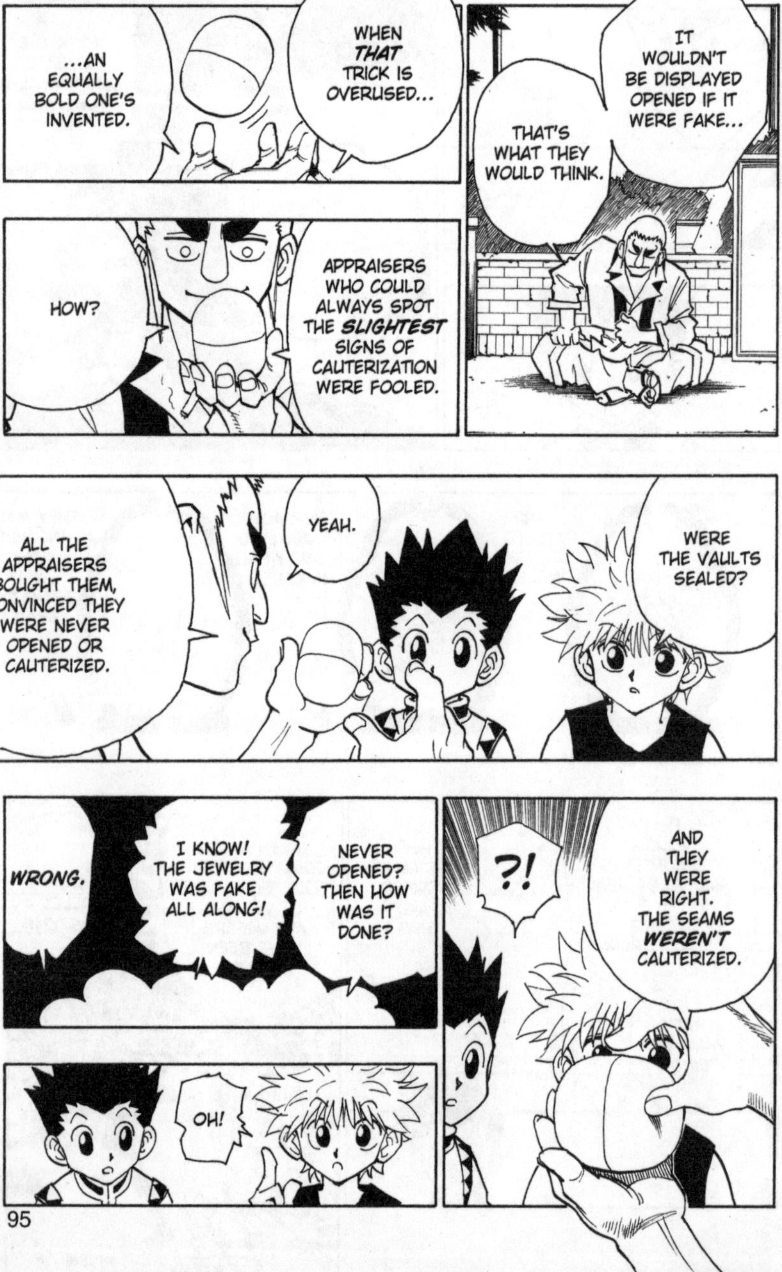
IT WOULDN'T BE DISPLAYED OPENED IF IT WERE FAKE...
THAT'S WHAT THEY WOULD THINK.
WHEN *THAT* TRICK IS OVERUSED...
...AN EQUALLY BOLD ONE'S INVENTED.
APPRAISERS WHO COULD ALWAYS SPOT THE ***SLIGHTEST*** SIGNS OF CAUTERIZATION WERE FOOLED.
HOW?
WERE THE VAULTS SEALED?
YEAH.
ALL THE APPRAISERS BOUGHT THEM, CONVINCED THEY WERE NEVER OPENED OR CAUTERIZED.
AND THEY WERE RIGHT. THE SEAMS ***WEREN'T*** CAUTERIZED.
?!
NEVER OPENED? THEN HOW WAS IT DONE?
I KNOW! THE JEWELRY WAS FAKE ALL ALONG!
WRONG.
OH!

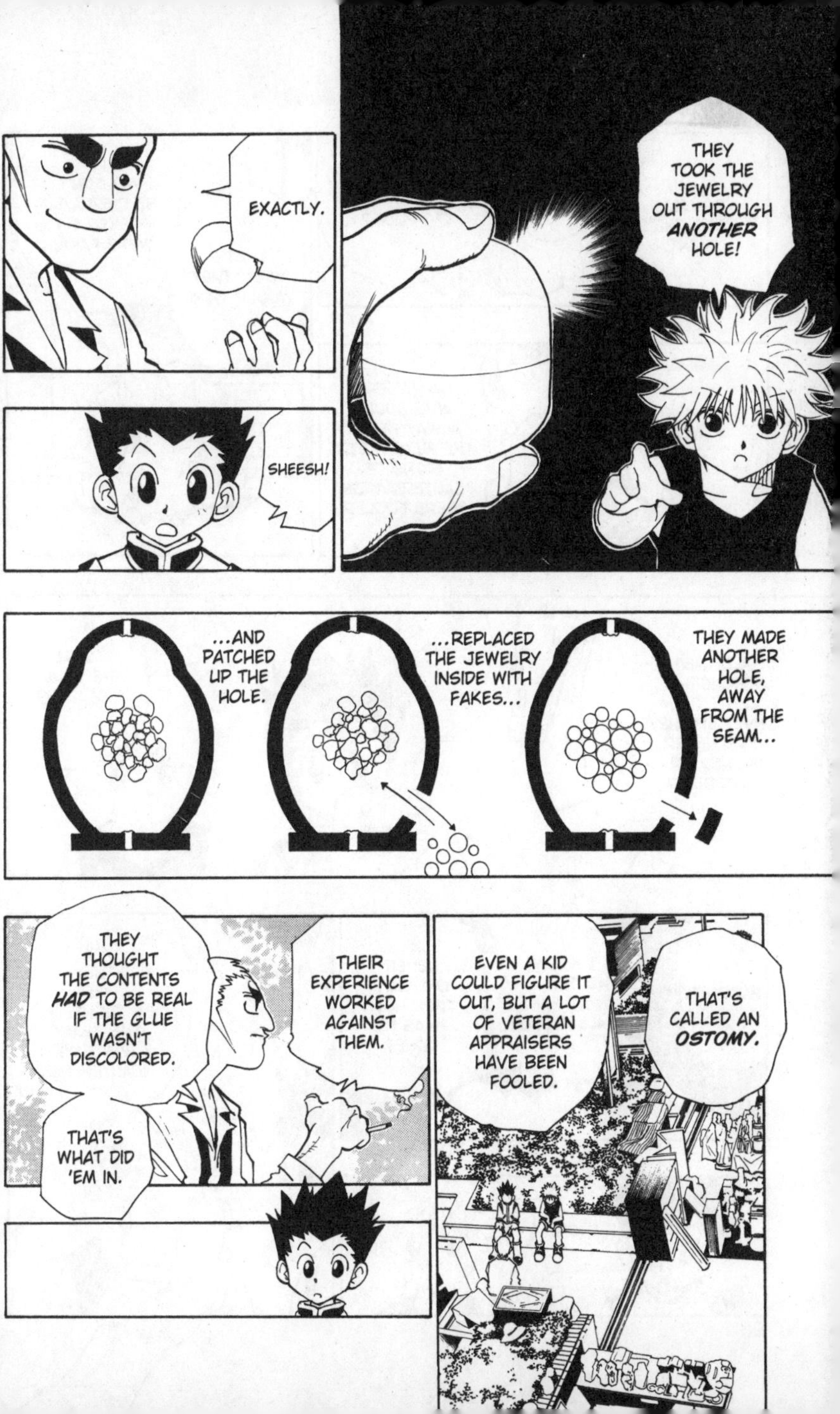
THEY TOOK THE JEWELRY OUT THROUGH ANOTHER HOLE!
EXACTLY.
SHEESH!
THEY MADE ANOTHER HOLE, AWAY FROM THE SEAM...
...REPLACED THE JEWELRY INSIDE WITH FAKES...
...AND PATCHED UP THE HOLE.
THAT'S CALLED AN OSTOMY.
EVEN A KID COULD FIGURE IT OUT, BUT A LOT OF VETERAN APPRAISERS HAVE BEEN FOOLED.
THEIR EXPERIENCE WORKED AGAINST THEM.
THEY THOUGHT THE CONTENTS HAD TO BE REAL IF THE GLUE WASN'T DISCOLORED.
THAT'S WHAT DID 'EM IN.

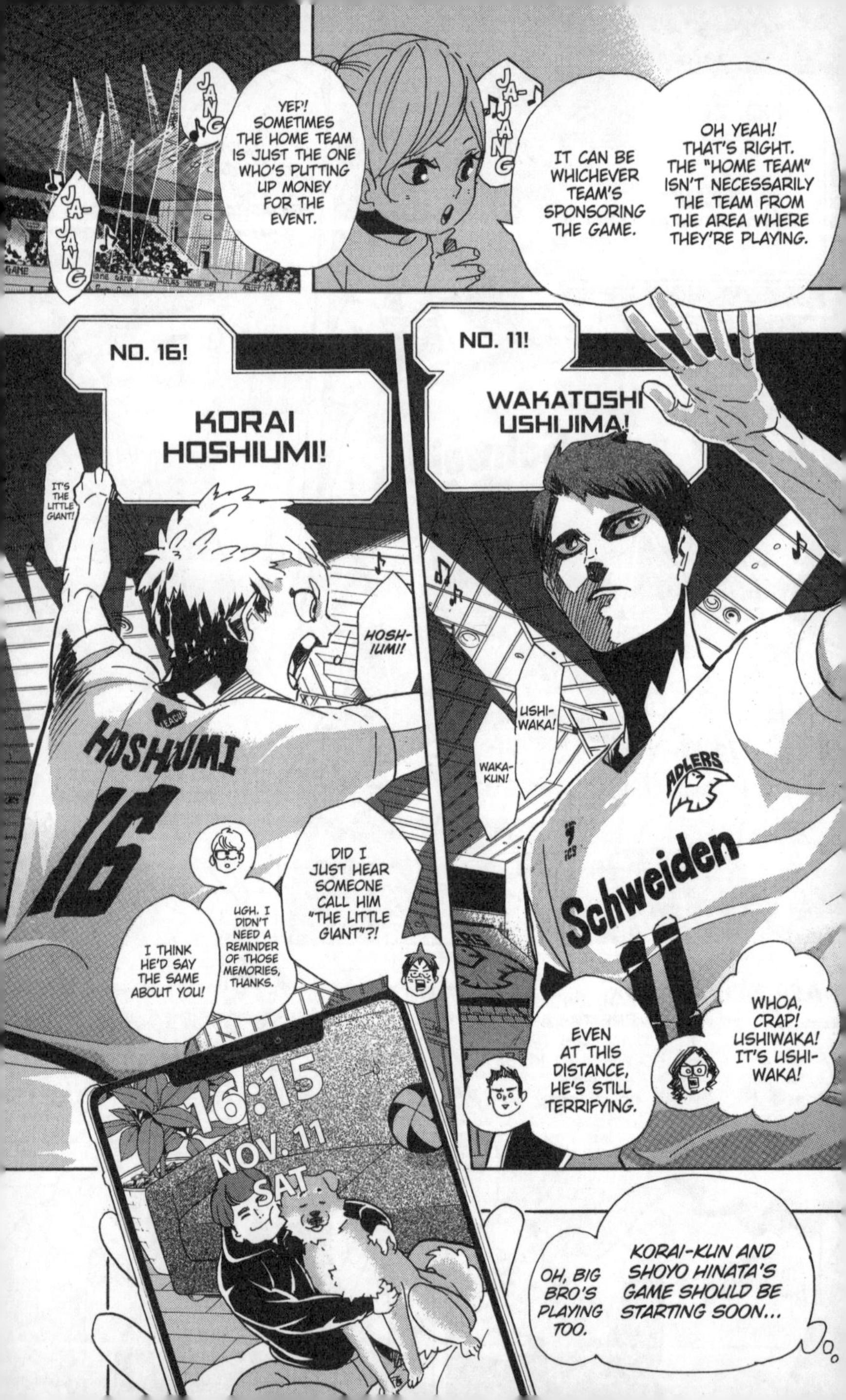

JA-JANG
OH YEAH! THAT'S RIGHT. THE "HOME TEAM" ISN'T NECESSARILY THE TEAM FROM THE AREA WHERE THEY'RE PLAYING.
IT CAN BE WHICHEVER TEAM'S SPONSORING THE GAME.
YEP! SOMETIMES THE HOME TEAM IS JUST THE ONE WHO'S PUTTING UP MONEY FOR THE EVENT.
JANG
JA-JANG
NO. 11!
WAKATOSHI USHIJIMA!
USHI-WAKA!
WAKA-KUN!
ADLERS
Schweiden
WHOA, CRAP! USHIWAKA! IT'S USHI-WAKA!
EVEN AT THIS DISTANCE, HE'S STILL TERRIFYING.
NO. 16!
KORAI HOSHIUMI!
IT'S THE LITTLE GIANT!
HOSH-IUMI!
HOSHIUMI
16
DID I JUST HEAR SOMEONE CALL HIM "THE LITTLE GIANT"?!
UGH. I DIDN'T NEED A REMINDER OF THOSE MEMORIES, THANKS.
I THINK HE'D SAY THE SAME ABOUT YOU!
16:15
NOV. 11
SAT
KORAI-KUN AND SHOYO HINATA'S GAME SHOULD BE STARTING SOON...
OH, BIG BRO'S PLAYING TOO.

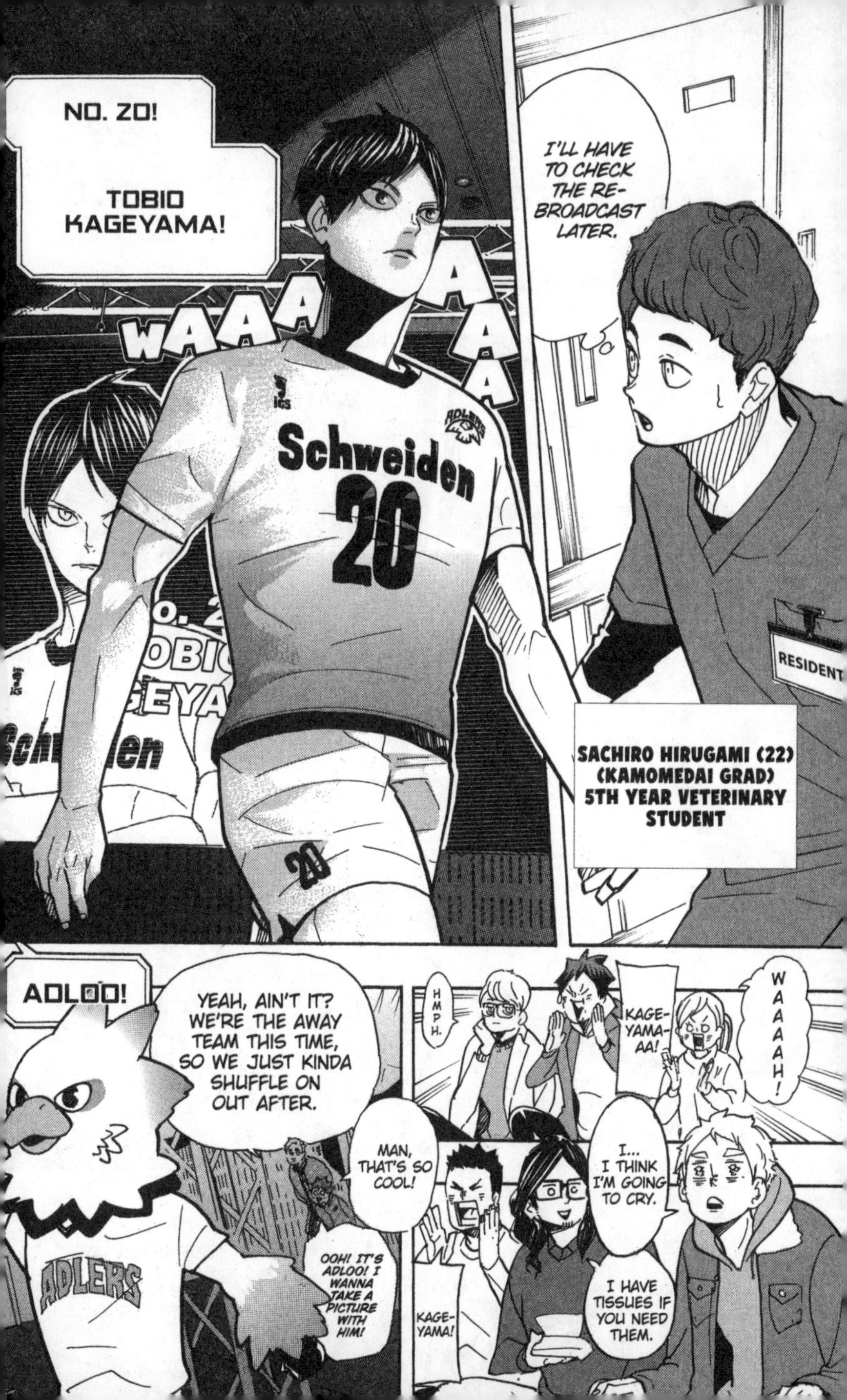
I'LL HAVE TO CHECK THE RE-BROADCAST LATER.
RESIDENT
SACHIRO HIRUGAMI (22) (KAMOMEDAI GRAD) 5TH YEAR VETERINARY STUDENT
NO. 20!
TOBIO KAGEYAMA!
WAAAAAAA
Schweiden
20
WAAAAAH!
KAGE-YAMAAA!
HMPH.
I... I THINK I'M GOING TO CRY.
I HAVE TISSUES IF YOU NEED THEM.
MAN, THAT'S SO COOL!
KAGE-YAMA!
YEAH, AIN'T IT? WE'RE THE AWAY TEAM THIS TIME, SO WE JUST KINDA SHUFFLE ON OUT AFTER.
ADLOO!
OOH! IT'S ADLOO! I WANNA TAKE A PICTURE WITH HIM!
ADLERS

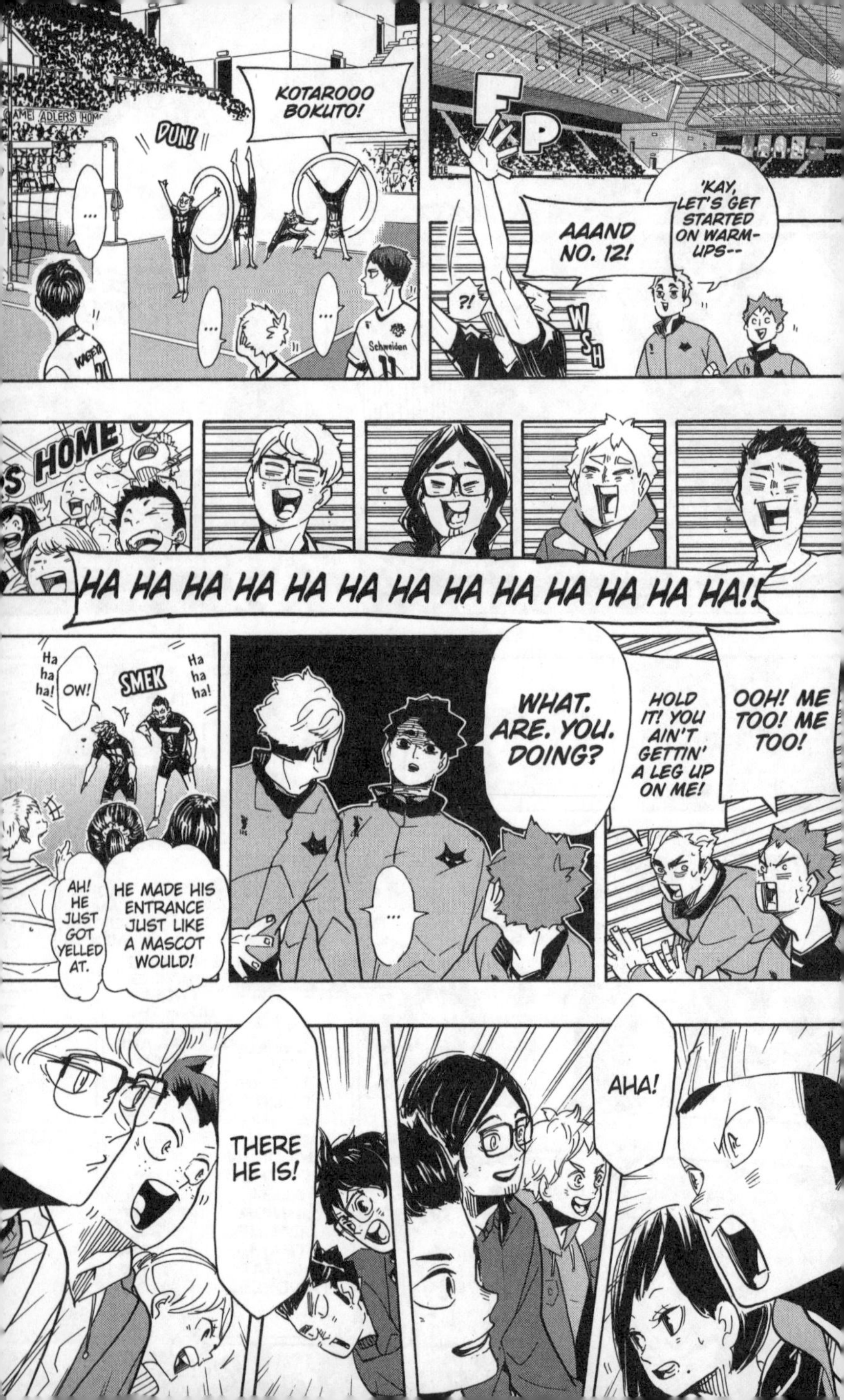
'KAY, LET'S GET STARTED ON WARM-UPS--
FP
AAAND NO. 12!
?!
WSH
KOTAROOO BOKUTO!
DUN!
...
...
...
...
HA HA HA HA HA HA HA HA HA HA HA HA HA!!
OOH! ME TOO! ME TOO!
HOLD IT! YOU AIN'T GETTIN' A LEG UP ON ME!
WHAT. ARE. YOU. DOING?
...
Ha ha ha!
SMEK
OW!
Ha ha ha!
HE MADE HIS ENTRANCE JUST LIKE A MASCOT WOULD!
AH! HE JUST GOT YELLED AT.
AHA!
THERE HE IS!

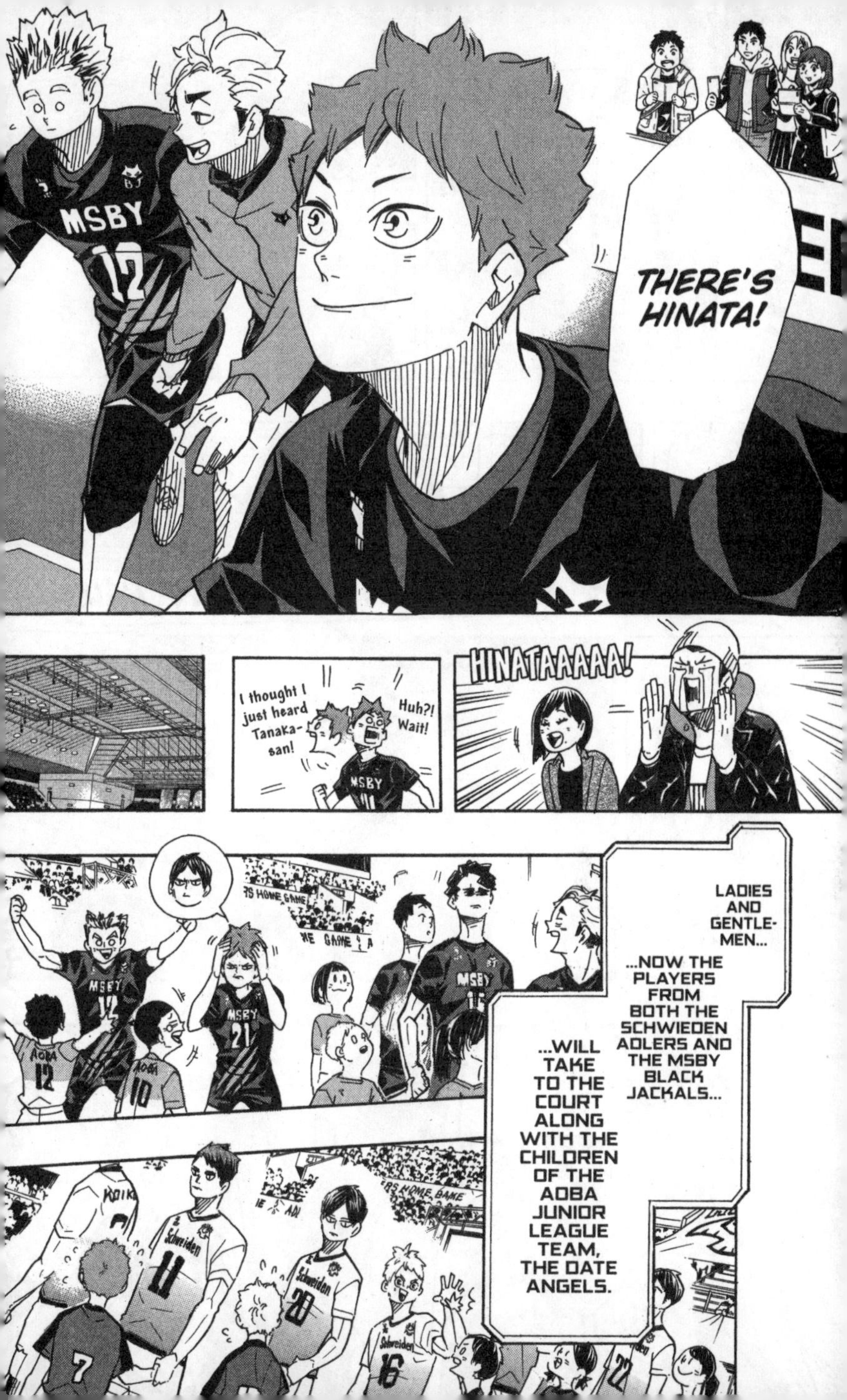
THERE'S HINATA!
HINATAAAAAA!
Huh?! Wait!
I thought I just heard Tanaka-san!
LADIES AND GENTLEMEN...
...NOW THE PLAYERS FROM BOTH THE SCHWIEDEN ADLERS AND THE MSBY BLACK JACKALS...
...WILL TAKE TO THE COURT ALONG WITH THE CHILDREN OF THE AOBA JUNIOR LEAGUE TEAM, THE DATE ANGELS.

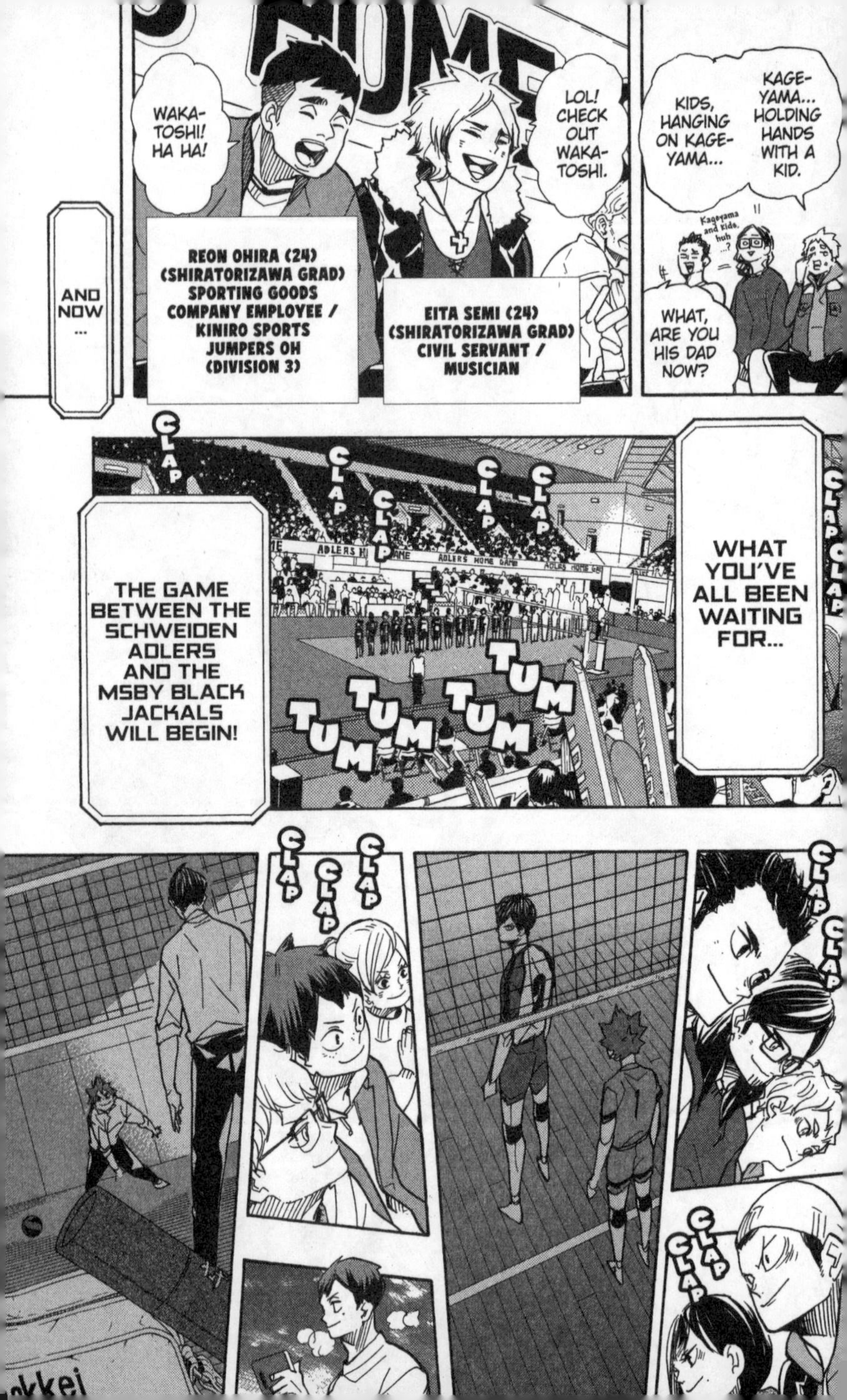
KIDS, HANGING ON KAGE-YAMA...
KAGE-YAMA... HOLDING HANDS WITH A KID.
Kageyama and kids, huh ...?
WHAT, ARE YOU HIS DAD NOW?
LOL! CHECK OUT WAKA-TOSHI.
WAKA-TOSHI! HA HA!
EITA SEMI (24) (SHIRATORIZAWA GRAD) CIVIL SERVANT / MUSICIAN
REON OHIRA (24) (SHIRATORIZAWA GRAD) SPORTING GOODS COMPANY EMPLOYEE / KINIRO SPORTS JUMPERS OH (DIVISION 3)
AND NOW...
WHAT YOU'VE ALL BEEN WAITING FOR...
CLAP CLAP
CLAP CLAP CLAP CLAP CLAP
ADLERS HOME GAME
TUM TUM TUM TUM
THE GAME BETWEEN THE SCHWEIDEN ADLERS AND THE MSBY BLACK JACKALS WILL BEGIN!
CLAP CLAP
CLAP CLAP
CLAP CLAP CLAP

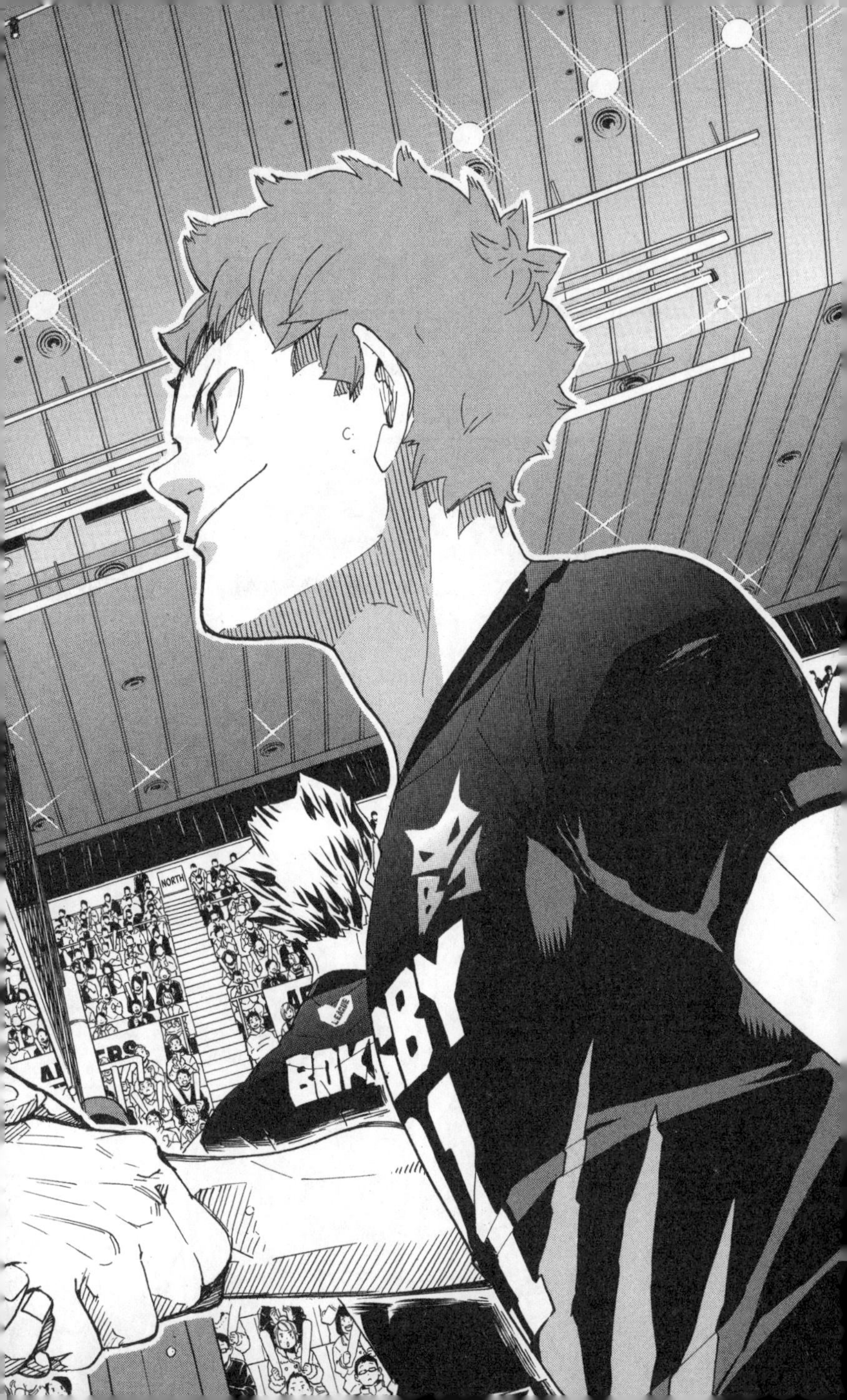
NORTH

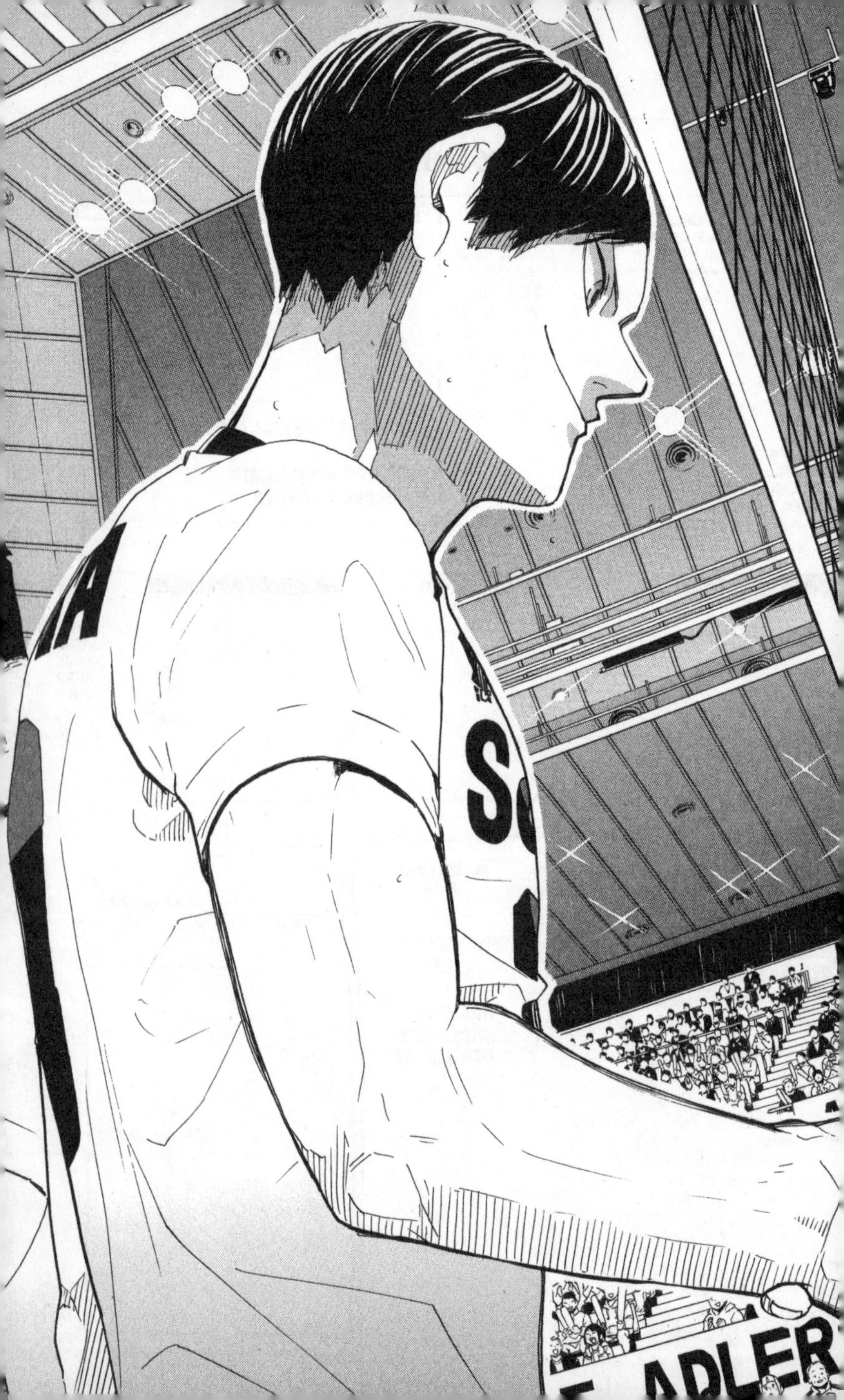
ADLER

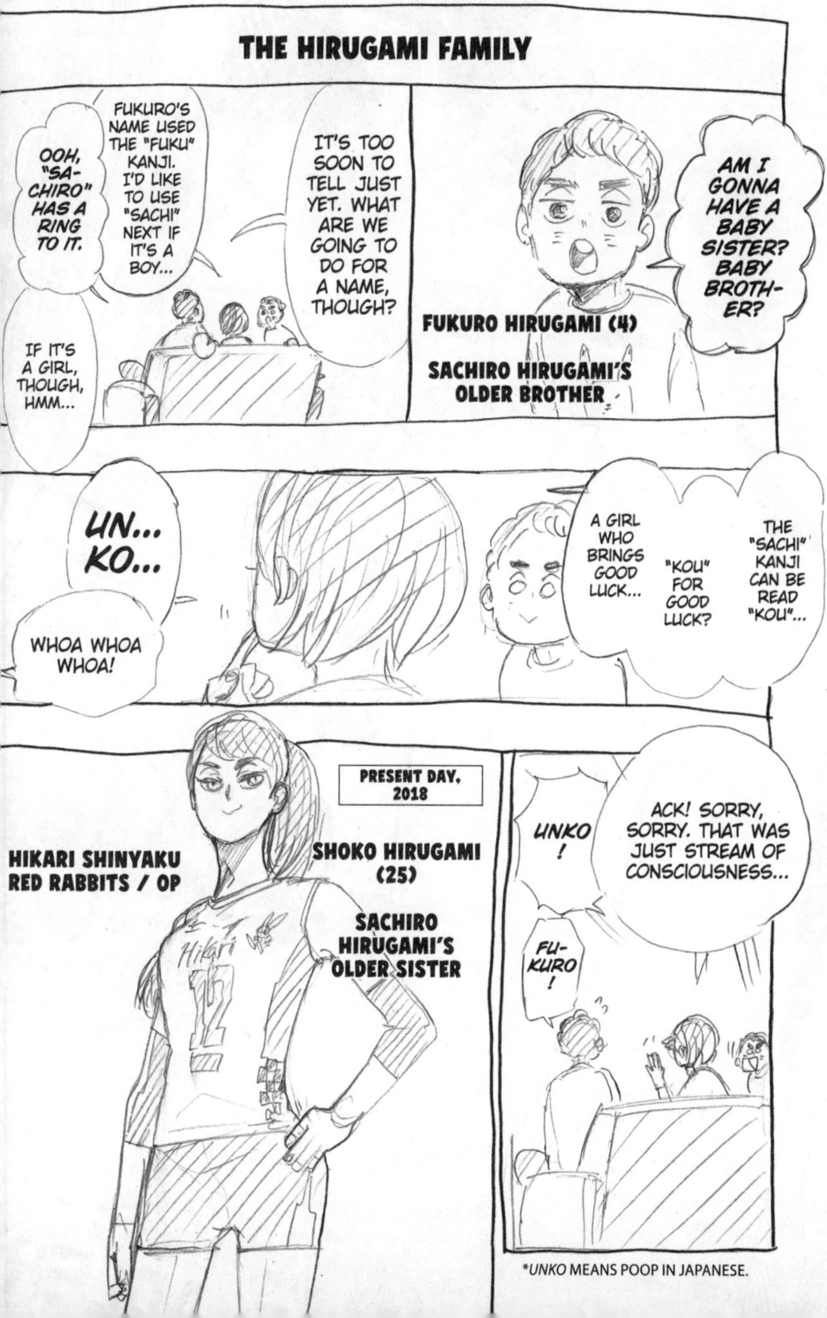
THE HIRUGAMI FAMILY
AM I GONNA HAVE A BABY SISTER? BABY BROTHER?
FUKURO HIRUGAMI (4)
SACHIRO HIRUGAMI'S OLDER BROTHER
IT'S TOO SOON TO TELL JUST YET. WHAT ARE WE GOING TO DO FOR A NAME, THOUGH?
FUKURO'S NAME USED THE "FUKU" KANJI. I'D LIKE TO USE "SACHI" NEXT IF IT'S A BOY...
OOH, "SA-CHIRO" HAS A RING TO IT.
IF IT'S A GIRL, THOUGH, HMM...
THE "SACHI" KANJI CAN BE READ "KOU"...
"KOU" FOR GOOD LUCK?
A GIRL WHO BRINGS GOOD LUCK...
UN... KO...
WHOA WHOA WHOA!
ACK! SORRY, SORRY. THAT WAS JUST STREAM OF CONSCIOUSNESS...
UNKO!
FU-KURO!
PRESENT DAY, 2018
SHOKO HIRUGAMI (25)
SACHIRO HIRUGAMI'S OLDER SISTER
HIKARI SHINYAKU RED RABBITS / OP
Hikari 12

**UNKO* MEANS POOP IN JAPANESE.

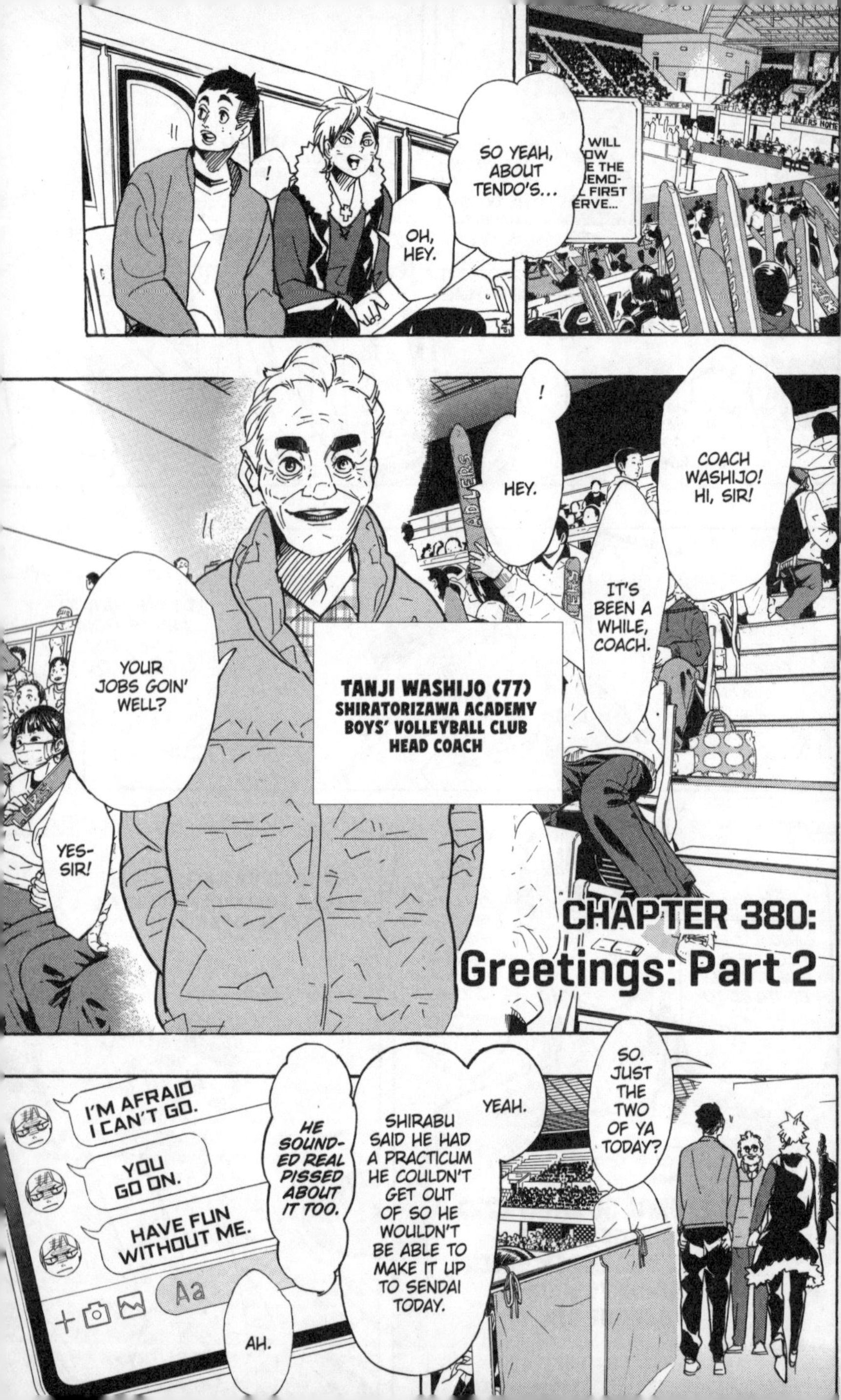
SO YEAH, ABOUT TENDO'S...
!
OH, HEY.
COACH WASHIJO! HI, SIR!
!
HEY.
IT'S BEEN A WHILE, COACH.
TANJI WASHIJO (77)
SHIRATORIZAWA ACADEMY BOYS' VOLLEYBALL CLUB HEAD COACH
YOUR JOBS GOIN' WELL?
YES-SIR!
CHAPTER 380:
Greetings: Part 2
SO. JUST THE TWO OF YA TODAY?
YEAH.
SHIRABU SAID HE HAD A PRACTICUM HE COULDN'T GET OUT OF SO HE WOULDN'T BE ABLE TO MAKE IT UP TO SENDAI TODAY.
HE SOUNDED REAL PISSED ABOUT IT TOO.
AH.
I'M AFRAID I CAN'T GO.
YOU GO ON.
HAVE FUN WITHOUT ME.
Aa

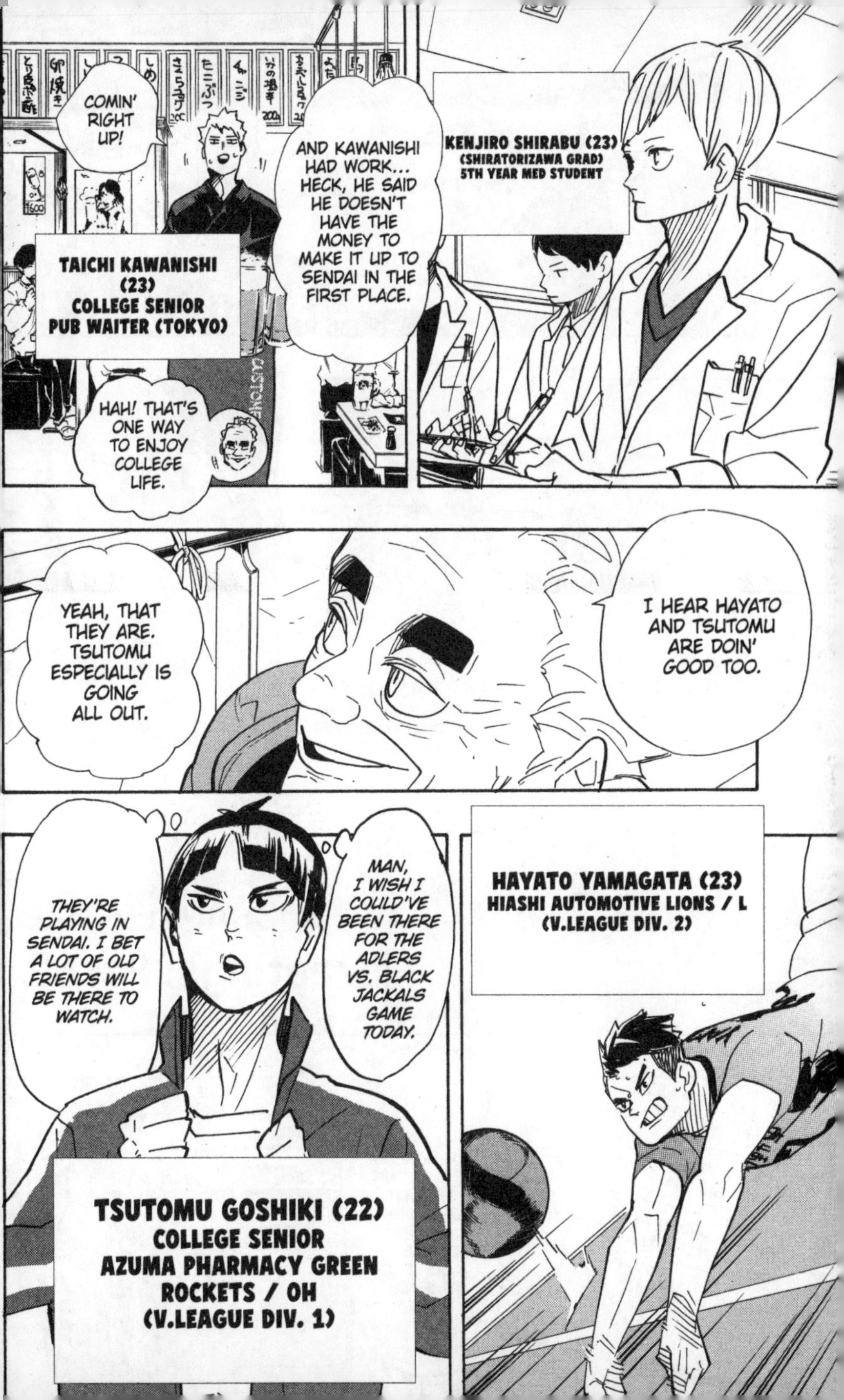
KENJIRO SHIRABU (23)
(SHIRATORIZAWA GRAD)
5TH YEAR MED STUDENT
AND KAWANISHI HAD WORK... HECK, HE SAID HE DOESN'T HAVE THE MONEY TO MAKE IT UP TO SENDAI IN THE FIRST PLACE.
COMIN' RIGHT UP!
TAICHI KAWANISHI (23)
COLLEGE SENIOR
PUB WAITER (TOKYO)
HAH! THAT'S ONE WAY TO ENJOY COLLEGE LIFE.
I HEAR HAYATO AND TSUTOMU ARE DOIN' GOOD TOO.
YEAH, THAT THEY ARE. TSUTOMU ESPECIALLY IS GOING ALL OUT.
HAYATO YAMAGATA (23)
HIASHI AUTOMOTIVE LIONS / L
(V.LEAGUE DIV. 2)
MAN, I WISH I COULD'VE BEEN THERE FOR THE ADLERS VS. BLACK JACKALS GAME TODAY.
THEY'RE PLAYING IN SENDAI. I BET A LOT OF OLD FRIENDS WILL BE THERE TO WATCH.
TSUTOMU GOSHIKI (22)
COLLEGE SENIOR
AZUMA PHARMACY GREEN ROCKETS / OH
(V.LEAGUE DIV. 1)

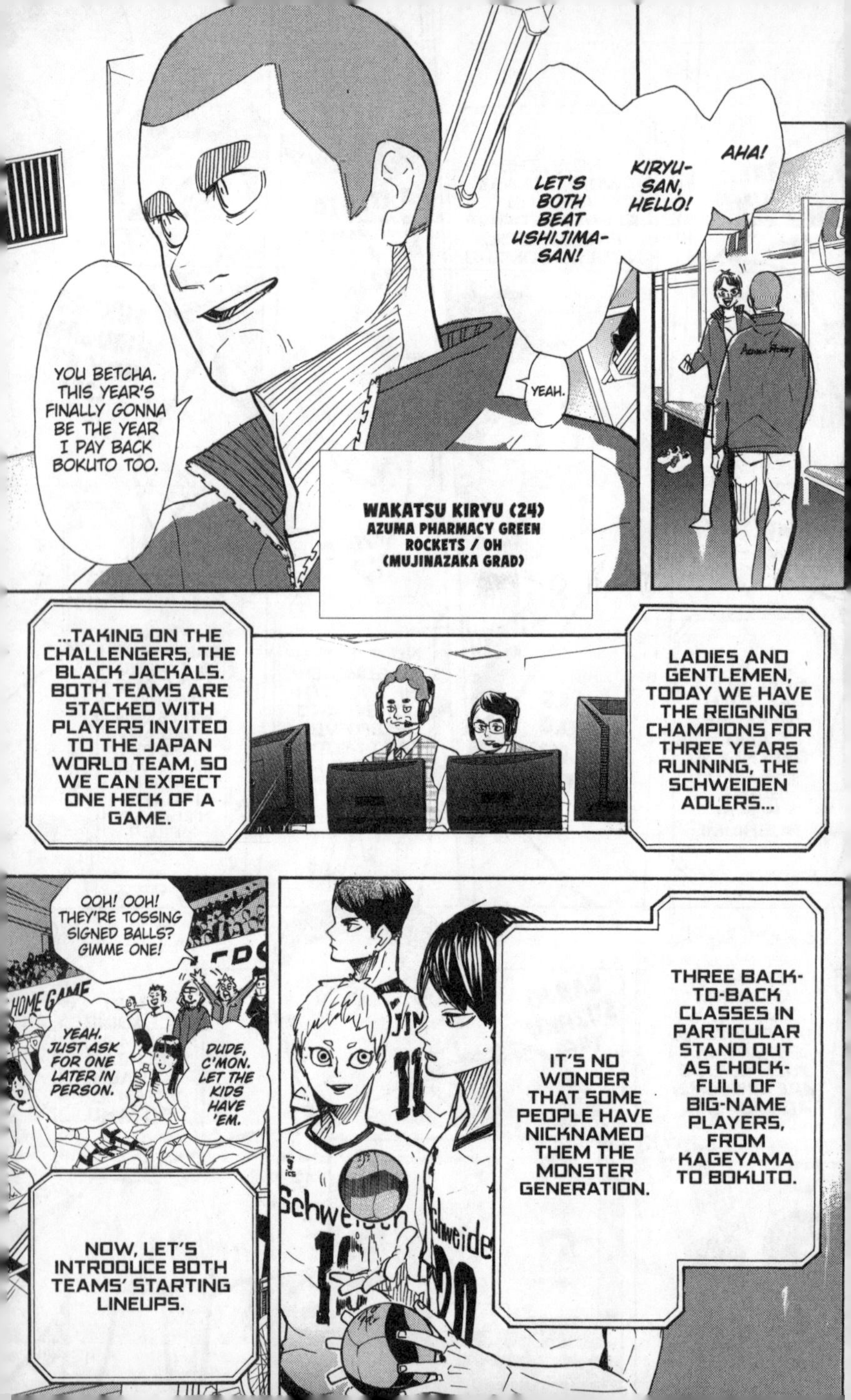
AHA!
KIRYU-SAN, HELLO!
LET'S BOTH BEAT USHIJIMA-SAN!
YEAH.
YOU BETCHA. THIS YEAR'S FINALLY GONNA BE THE YEAR I PAY BACK BOKUTO TOO.
WAKATSU KIRYU (24)
AZUMA PHARMACY GREEN ROCKETS / OH
(MUJINAZAKA GRAD)
LADIES AND GENTLEMEN, TODAY WE HAVE THE REIGNING CHAMPIONS FOR THREE YEARS RUNNING, THE SCHWEIDEN ADLERS...
...TAKING ON THE CHALLENGERS, THE BLACK JACKALS. BOTH TEAMS ARE STACKED WITH PLAYERS INVITED TO THE JAPAN WORLD TEAM, SO WE CAN EXPECT ONE HECK OF A GAME.
THREE BACK-TO-BACK CLASSES IN PARTICULAR STAND OUT AS CHOCK-FULL OF BIG-NAME PLAYERS, FROM KAGEYAMA TO BOKUTO.
IT'S NO WONDER THAT SOME PEOPLE HAVE NICKNAMED THEM THE MONSTER GENERATION.
OOH! OOH! THEY'RE TOSSING SIGNED BALLS? GIMME ONE!
DUDE, C'MON. LET THE KIDS HAVE 'EM.
YEAH. JUST ASK FOR ONE LATER IN PERSON.
HOME GAME
NOW, LET'S INTRODUCE BOTH TEAMS' STARTING LINEUPS.

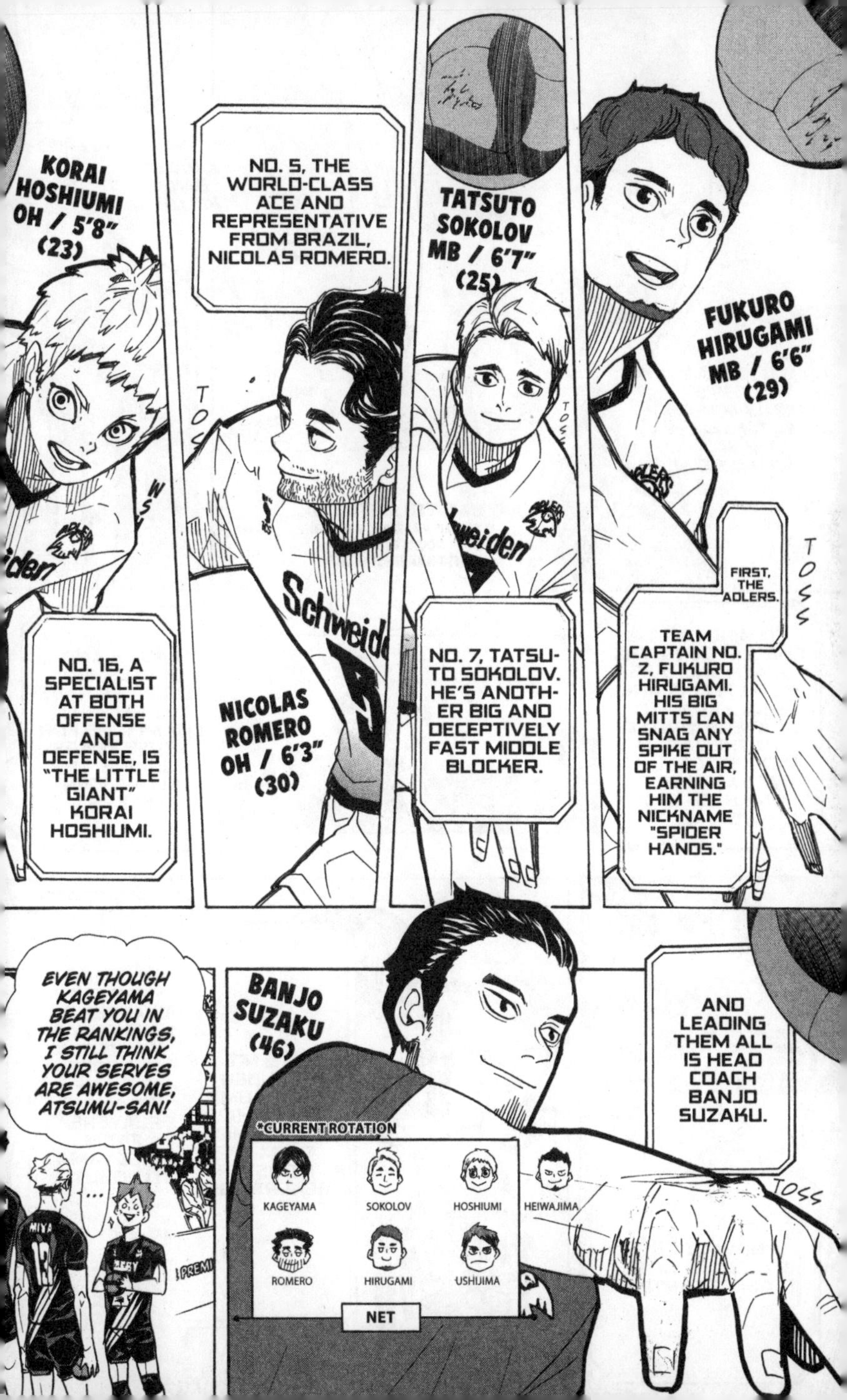
FIRST, THE ADLERS.
TOSS
FUKURO HIRUGAMI MB / 6'6" (29)
TEAM CAPTAIN NO. 2, FUKURO HIRUGAMI. HIS BIG MITTS CAN SNAG ANY SPIKE OUT OF THE AIR, EARNING HIM THE NICKNAME "SPIDER HANDS."
TATSUTO SOKOLOV MB / 6'7" (25)
TOSS
NO. 7, TATSU-TO SOKOLOV. HE'S ANOTH-ER BIG AND DECEPTIVELY FAST MIDDLE BLOCKER.
NO. 5, THE WORLD-CLASS ACE AND REPRESENTATIVE FROM BRAZIL, NICOLAS ROMERO.
TOS
NICOLAS ROMERO OH / 6'3" (30)
KORAI HOSHIUMI OH / 5'8" (23)
WS
NO. 16, A SPECIALIST AT BOTH OFFENSE AND DEFENSE, IS "THE LITTLE GIANT" KORAI HOSHIUMI.
AND LEADING THEM ALL IS HEAD COACH BANJO SUZAKU.
TOSS
BANJO SUZAKU (46)
*CURRENT ROTATION
KAGEYAMA
SOKOLOV
HOSHIUMI
HEIWAJIMA
ROMERO
HIRUGAMI
USHIJIMA
NET
EVEN THOUGH KAGEYAMA BEAT YOU IN THE RANKINGS, I STILL THINK YOUR SERVES ARE AWESOME, ATSUMU-SAN!
...

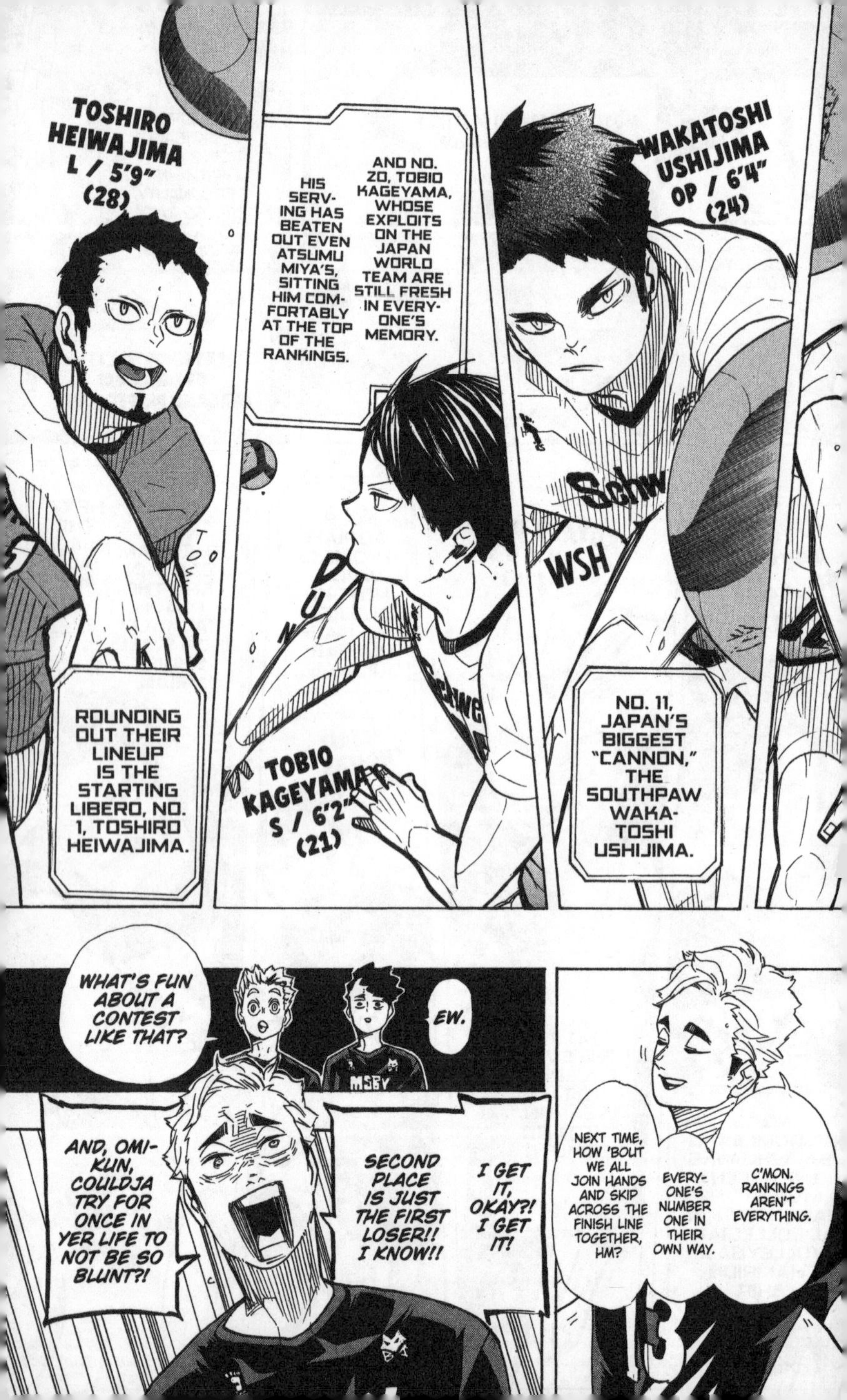
WAKATOSHI USHIJIMA OP / 6'4" (24)
WSH
NO. 11, JAPAN'S BIGGEST "CANNON," THE SOUTHPAW WAKA-TOSHI USHIJIMA.
AND NO. 20, TOBIO KAGEYAMA, WHOSE EXPLOITS ON THE JAPAN WORLD TEAM ARE STILL FRESH IN EVERY-ONE'S MEMORY.
HIS SERV-ING HAS BEATEN OUT EVEN ATSUMU MIYA'S, SITTING HIM COM-FORTABLY AT THE TOP OF THE RANKINGS.
DUN
TOBIO KAGEYAMA S / 6'2" (21)
TOSHIRO HEIWAJIMA L / 5'9" (28)
TOS
ROUNDING OUT THEIR LINEUP IS THE STARTING LIBERO, NO. 1, TOSHIRO HEIWAJIMA.
C'MON. RANKINGS AREN'T EVERYTHING.
EVERY-ONE'S NUMBER ONE IN THEIR OWN WAY.
NEXT TIME, HOW 'BOUT WE ALL JOIN HANDS AND SKIP ACROSS THE FINISH LINE TOGETHER, HM?
EW.
WHAT'S FUN ABOUT A CONTEST LIKE THAT?
I GET IT, OKAY?! I GET IT!
SECOND PLACE IS JUST THE FIRST LOSER!! I KNOW!!
AND, OMI-KUN, COULDJA TRY FOR ONCE IN YER LIFE TO NOT BE SO BLUNT?!

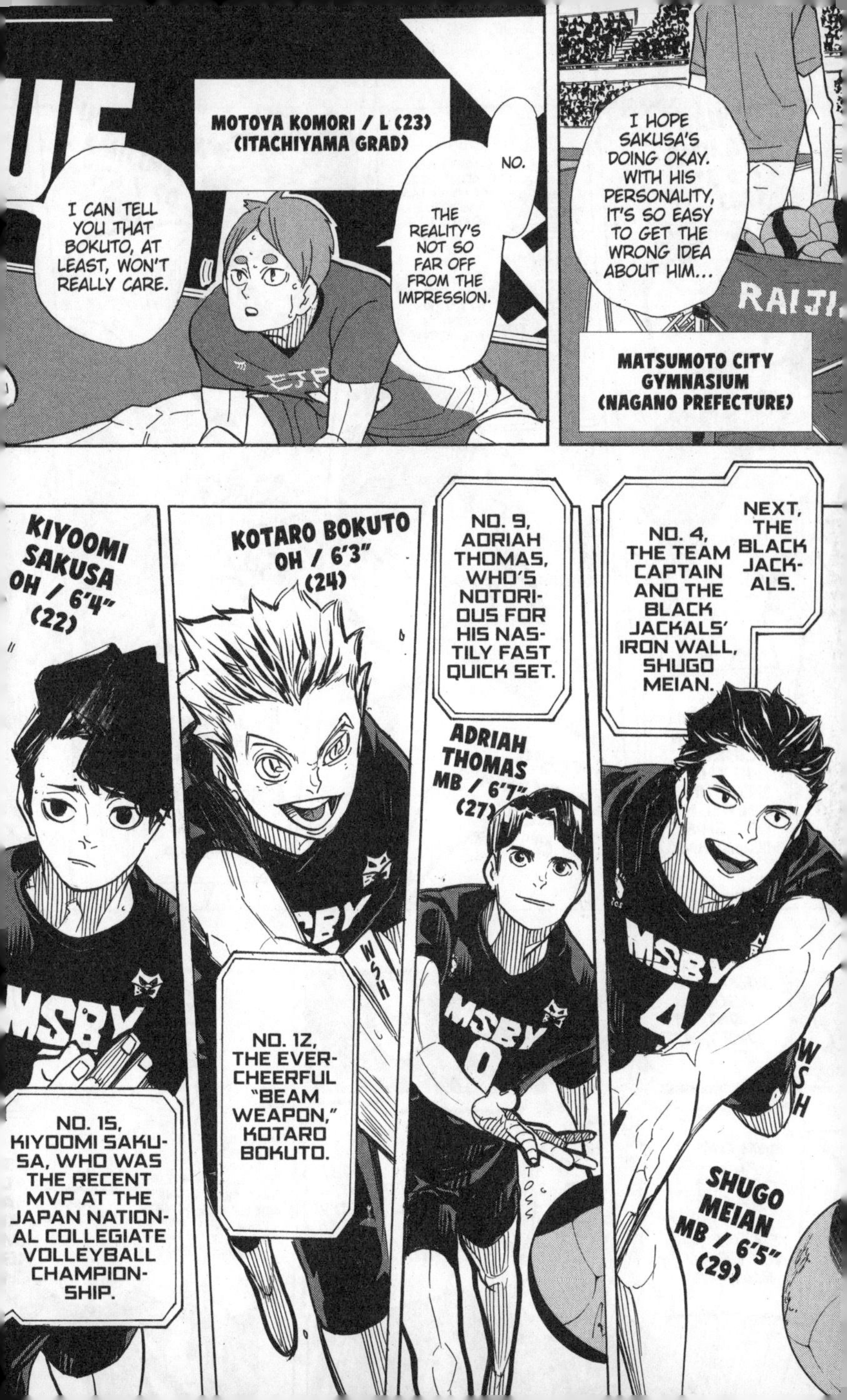
I HOPE SAKUSA'S DOING OKAY. WITH HIS PERSONALITY, IT'S SO EASY TO GET THE WRONG IDEA ABOUT HIM...
RAIJI.
MATSUMOTO CITY GYMNASIUM (NAGANO PREFECTURE)
MOTOYA KOMORI / L (23) (ITACHIYAMA GRAD)
NO.
THE REALITY'S NOT SO FAR OFF FROM THE IMPRESSION.
I CAN TELL YOU THAT BOKUTO, AT LEAST, WON'T REALLY CARE.
NEXT, THE BLACK JACKALS.
NO. 4, THE TEAM CAPTAIN AND THE BLACK JACKALS' IRON WALL, SHUGO MEIAN.
WSH
SHUGO MEIAN MB / 6'5" (29)
NO. 9, ADRIAH THOMAS, WHO'S NOTORIOUS FOR HIS NASTILY FAST QUICK SET.
ADRIAH THOMAS MB / 6'7" (27)
TOSS
KOTARO BOKUTO OH / 6'3" (24)
WSH
NO. 12, THE EVER-CHEERFUL "BEAM WEAPON," KOTARO BOKUTO.
KIYOOMI SAKUSA OH / 6'4" (22)
NO. 15, KIYOOMI SAKUSA, WHO WAS THE RECENT MVP AT THE JAPAN NATIONAL COLLEGIATE VOLLEYBALL CHAMPIONSHIP.

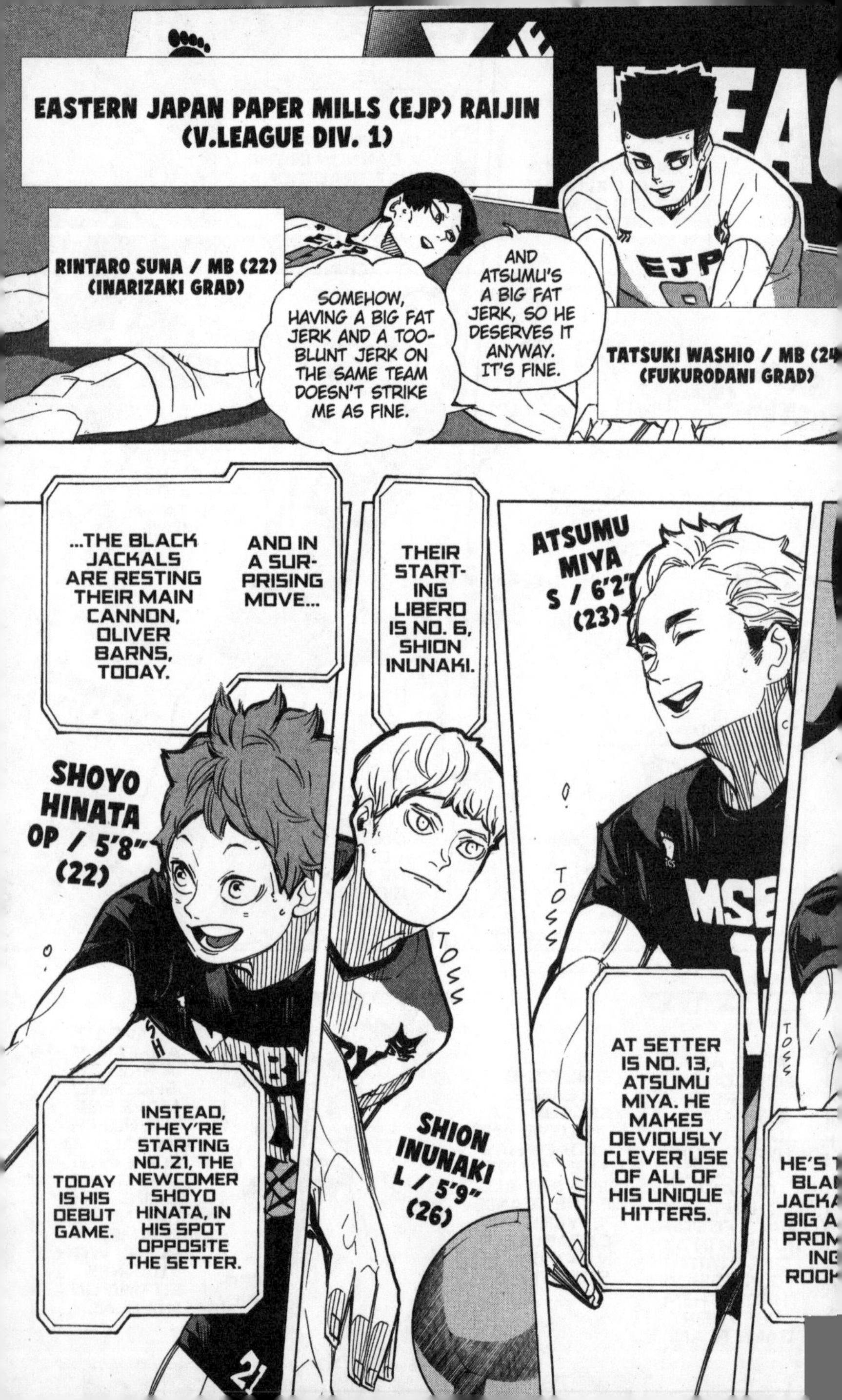

EASTERN JAPAN PAPER MILLS (EJP) RAIJIN (V.LEAGUE DIV. 1)
TATSUKI WASHIO / MB (24 (FUKURODANI GRAD)
AND ATSUMU'S A BIG FAT JERK, SO HE DESERVES IT ANYWAY. IT'S FINE.
SOMEHOW, HAVING A BIG FAT JERK AND A TOO-BLUNT JERK ON THE SAME TEAM DOESN'T STRIKE ME AS FINE.
RINTARO SUNA / MB (22) (INARIZAKI GRAD)
ATSUMU MIYA S / 6'2" (23)
TOSS
TOSS
AT SETTER IS NO. 13, ATSUMU MIYA. HE MAKES DEVIOUSLY CLEVER USE OF ALL OF HIS UNIQUE HITTERS.
THEIR STARTING LIBERO IS NO. 6, SHION INUNAKI.
TOSS
SHION INUNAKI L / 5'9" (26)
AND IN A SURPRISING MOVE...
...THE BLACK JACKALS ARE RESTING THEIR MAIN CANNON, OLIVER BARNS, TODAY.
SHOYO HINATA OP / 5'8" (22)
INSTEAD, THEY'RE STARTING NO. 21, THE NEWCOMER SHOYO HINATA, IN HIS SPOT OPPOSITE THE SETTER.
TODAY IS HIS DEBUT GAME.

IN CONTROL OF IT ALL IS HEAD COACH SAMSON FOSTER.

SAMSON FOSTER (43)

OLIVER BARNS IS A CANNON IN THE MOST TRADITIONAL SENSE, STAYING CLEAR OF THE SERVE RECEIVE TO FOCUS ON ATTACKING ONLY.

I EXPECT THEY'VE PUT SHOYO HINATA IN AS MORE OF AN ALL-ROUNDER.

THOUGH THEY BOTH PLAY THE SAME POSITION, THEIR ROLES ON THE COURT ARE VERY DIFFERENT.

OLIVER BARNES OP / 6'10" (31)

*CURRENT ROTATION

THOMAS	SAKUSA	HINATA	INUNAKI
MIYA	BOKUTO	MEIAN	

NET

ALSO, AS A NEWCOMER, THERE IS ZERO DATA ON SHOYO HINATA FOR THE ADLERS TO WORK WITH. I FIGURE COACH FOSTER PUT HIM IN AT THE START TO POSSIBLY THROW THEM OFF THEIR GAME PLAN.

BUT THE LEAGUE SEASON IS A LONG ONE, AND A COACH HAS TO GET AN IDEA OF WHAT ALL OF THE TEAM'S PLAYERS ARE CAPABLE OF IN GAME-TIME SITUATIONS.

IT CERTAINLY IS.

I HAVE TO ADMIT, IT'S A PRETTY SHOCKING MOVE FOR THE BLACK JACKALS TO COME INTO THIS GAME AGAINST THE PERENNIAL-CHAMPION ADLERS WITH BARNES SITTING ON THE BENCH.

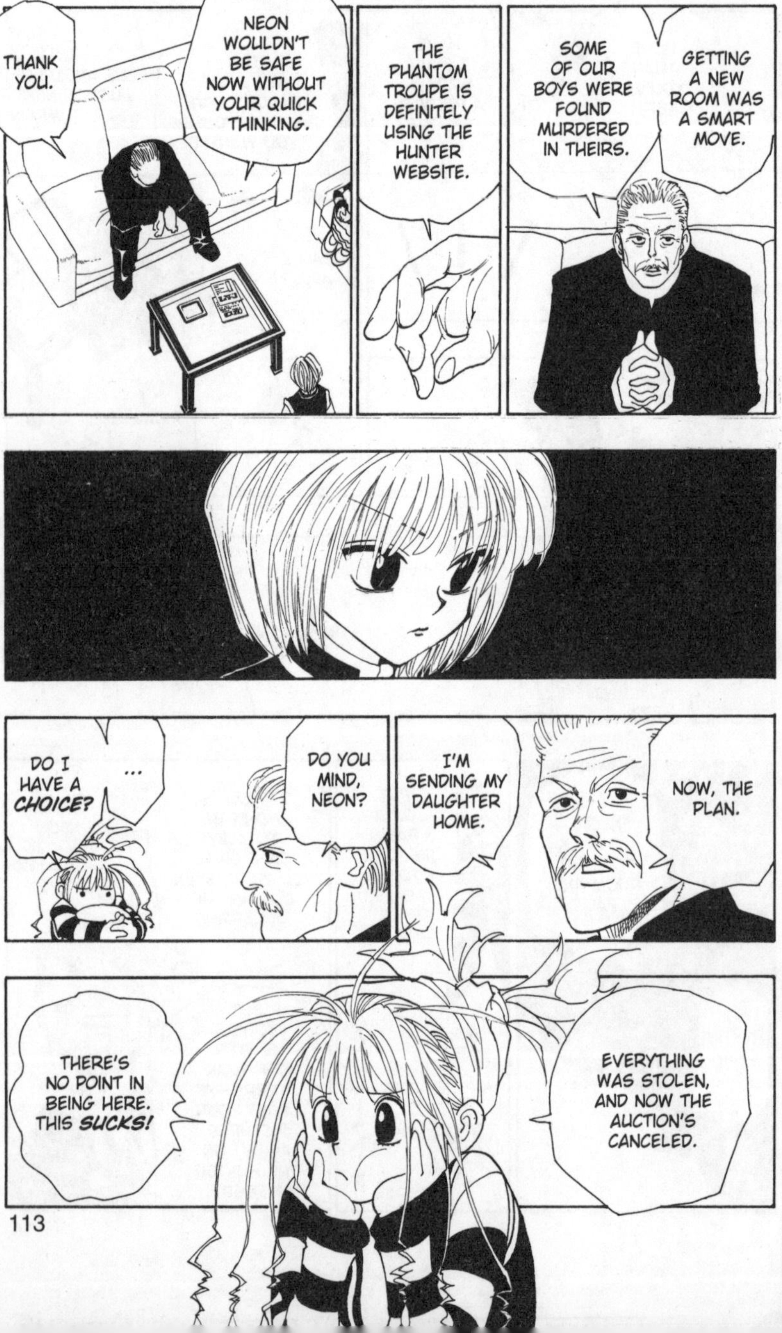
GETTING A NEW ROOM WAS A SMART MOVE.
SOME OF OUR BOYS WERE FOUND MURDERED IN THEIRS.
THE PHANTOM TROUPE IS DEFINITELY USING THE HUNTER WEBSITE.
NEON WOULDN'T BE SAFE NOW WITHOUT YOUR QUICK THINKING.
THANK YOU.
NOW, THE PLAN.
I'M SENDING MY DAUGHTER HOME.
DO YOU MIND, NEON?
...
DO I HAVE A *CHOICE?*
EVERYTHING WAS STOLEN, AND NOW THE AUCTION'S CANCELED.
THERE'S NO POINT IN BEING HERE. THIS *SUCKS!*

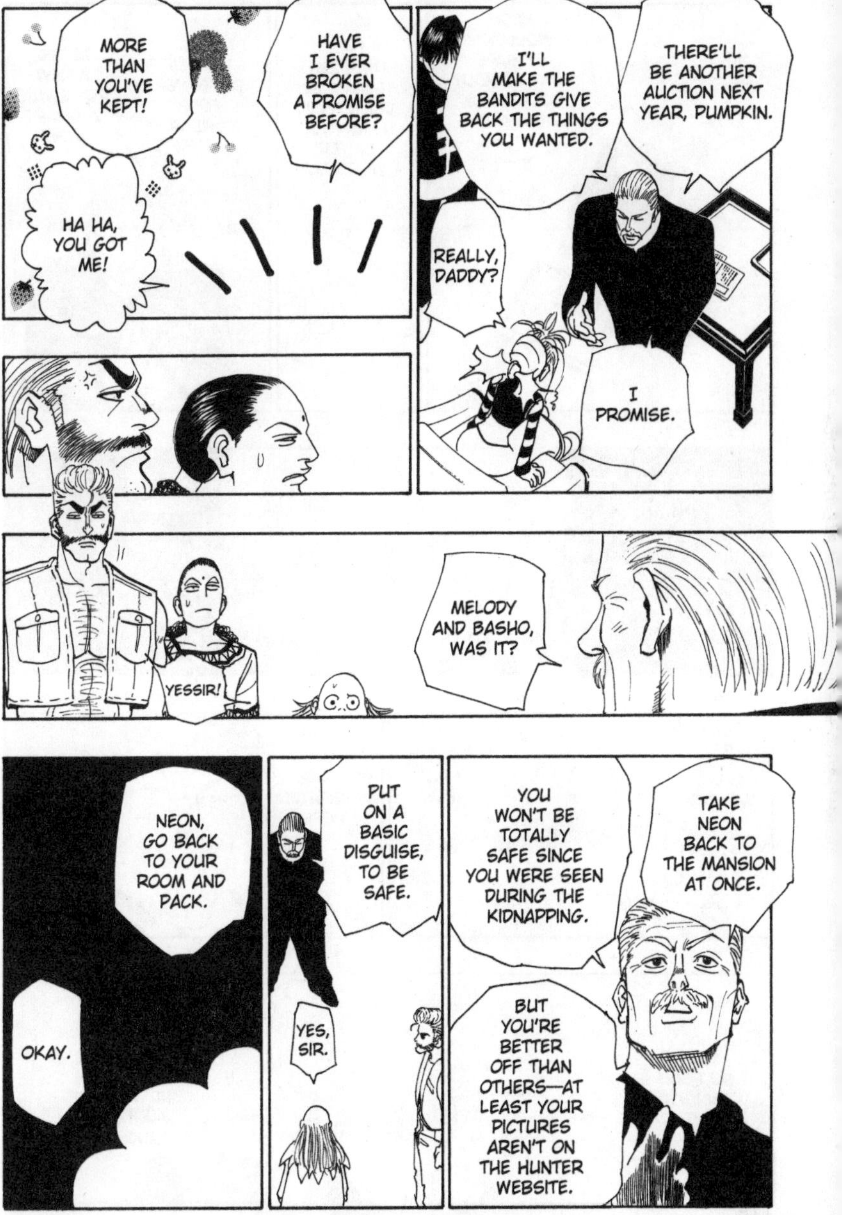
THERE'LL BE ANOTHER AUCTION NEXT YEAR, PUMPKIN.
I'LL MAKE THE BANDITS GIVE BACK THE THINGS YOU WANTED.
REALLY, DADDY?
I PROMISE.
HAVE I EVER BROKEN A PROMISE BEFORE?
MORE THAN YOU'VE KEPT!
HA HA, YOU GOT ME!
MELODY AND BASHO, WAS IT?
YESSIR!
TAKE NEON BACK TO THE MANSION AT ONCE.
YOU WON'T BE TOTALLY SAFE SINCE YOU WERE SEEN DURING THE KIDNAPPING.
BUT YOU'RE BETTER OFF THAN OTHERS—AT LEAST YOUR PICTURES AREN'T ON THE HUNTER WEBSITE.
PUT ON A BASIC DISGUISE, TO BE SAFE.
YES, SIR.
NEON, GO BACK TO YOUR ROOM AND PACK.
OKAY.

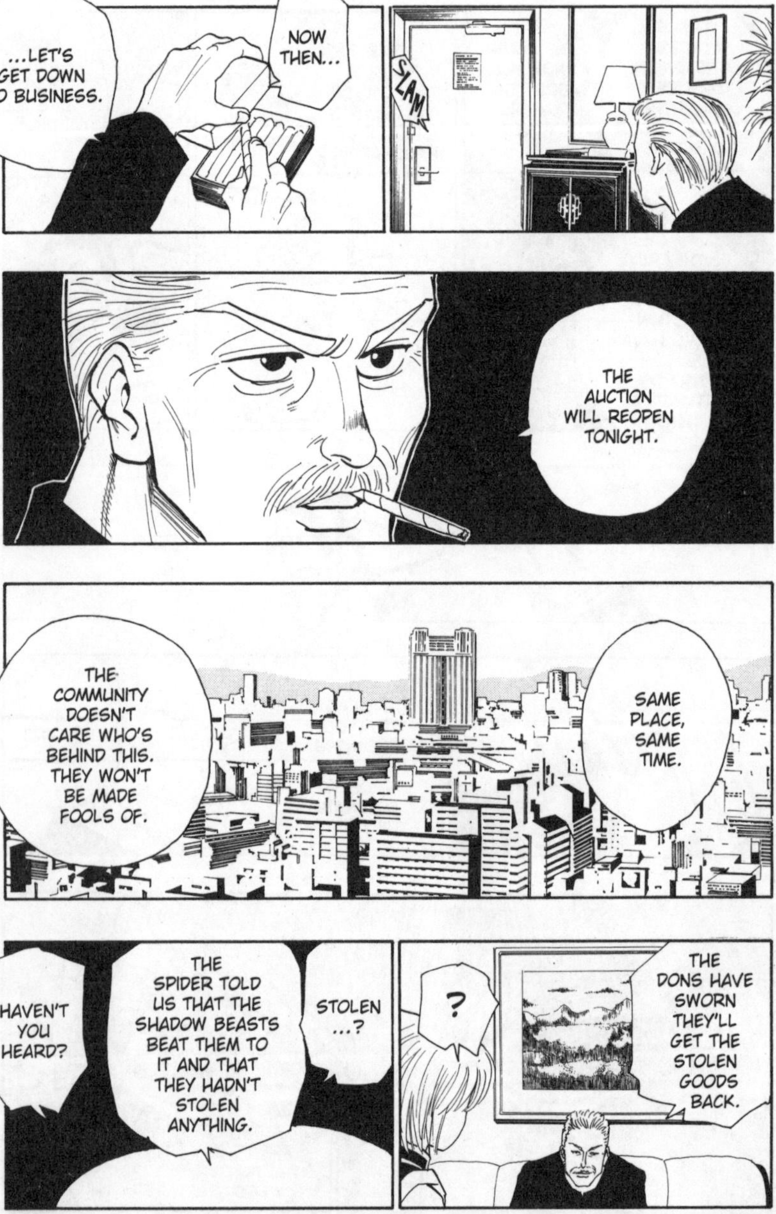
SLAM
NOW THEN...
...LET'S GET DOWN TO BUSINESS.
THE AUCTION WILL REOPEN TONIGHT.
SAME PLACE, SAME TIME.
THE COMMUNITY DOESN'T CARE WHO'S BEHIND THIS. THEY WON'T BE MADE FOOLS OF.
THE DONS HAVE SWORN THEY'LL GET THE STOLEN GOODS BACK.
?
STOLEN ...?
THE SPIDER TOLD US THAT THE SHADOW BEASTS BEAT THEM TO IT AND THAT THEY HADN'T STOLEN ANYTHING.
HAVEN'T YOU HEARD?

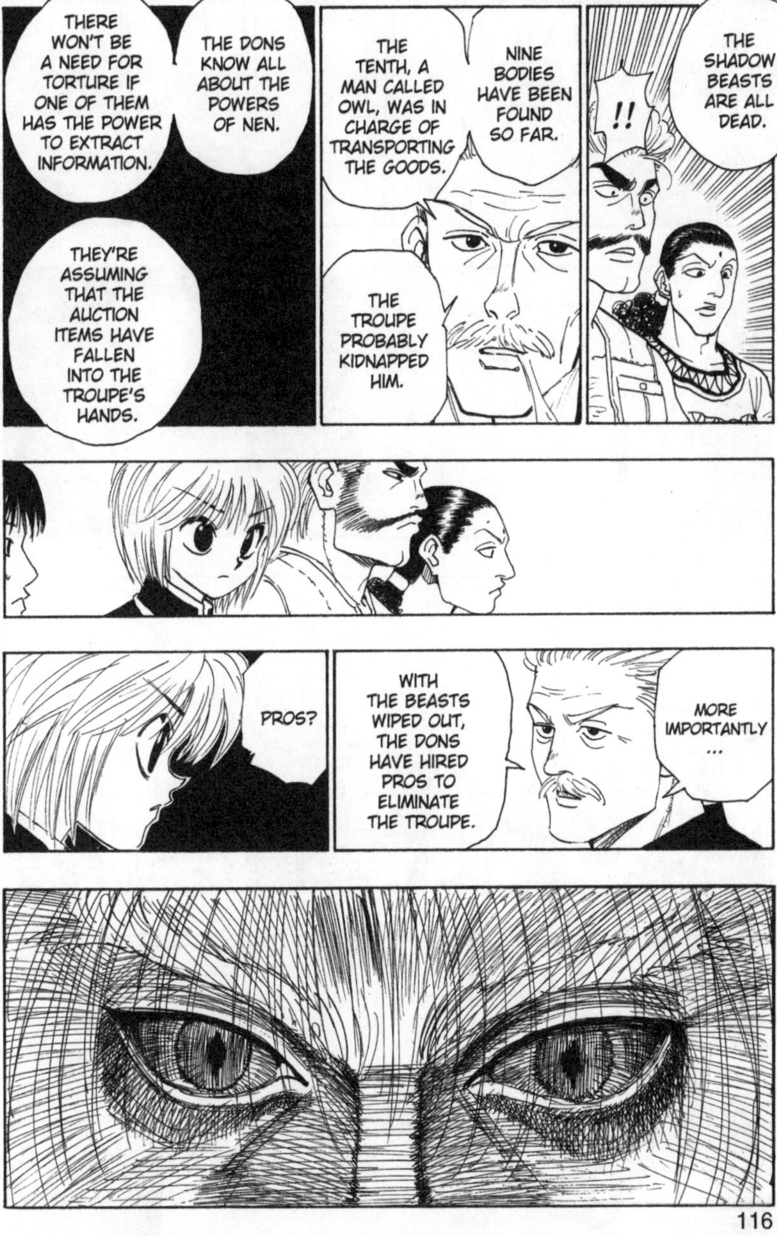
THE SHADOW BEASTS ARE ALL DEAD.
!!
NINE BODIES HAVE BEEN FOUND SO FAR.
THE TENTH, A MAN CALLED OWL, WAS IN CHARGE OF TRANSPORTING THE GOODS.
THE TROUPE PROBABLY KIDNAPPED HIM.
THE DONS KNOW ALL ABOUT THE POWERS OF NEN.
THERE WON'T BE A NEED FOR TORTURE IF ONE OF THEM HAS THE POWER TO EXTRACT INFORMATION.
THEY'RE ASSUMING THAT THE AUCTION ITEMS HAVE FALLEN INTO THE TROUPE'S HANDS.
MORE IMPORTANTLY ...
WITH THE BEASTS WIPED OUT, THE DONS HAVE HIRED PROS TO ELIMINATE THE TROUPE.
PROS?

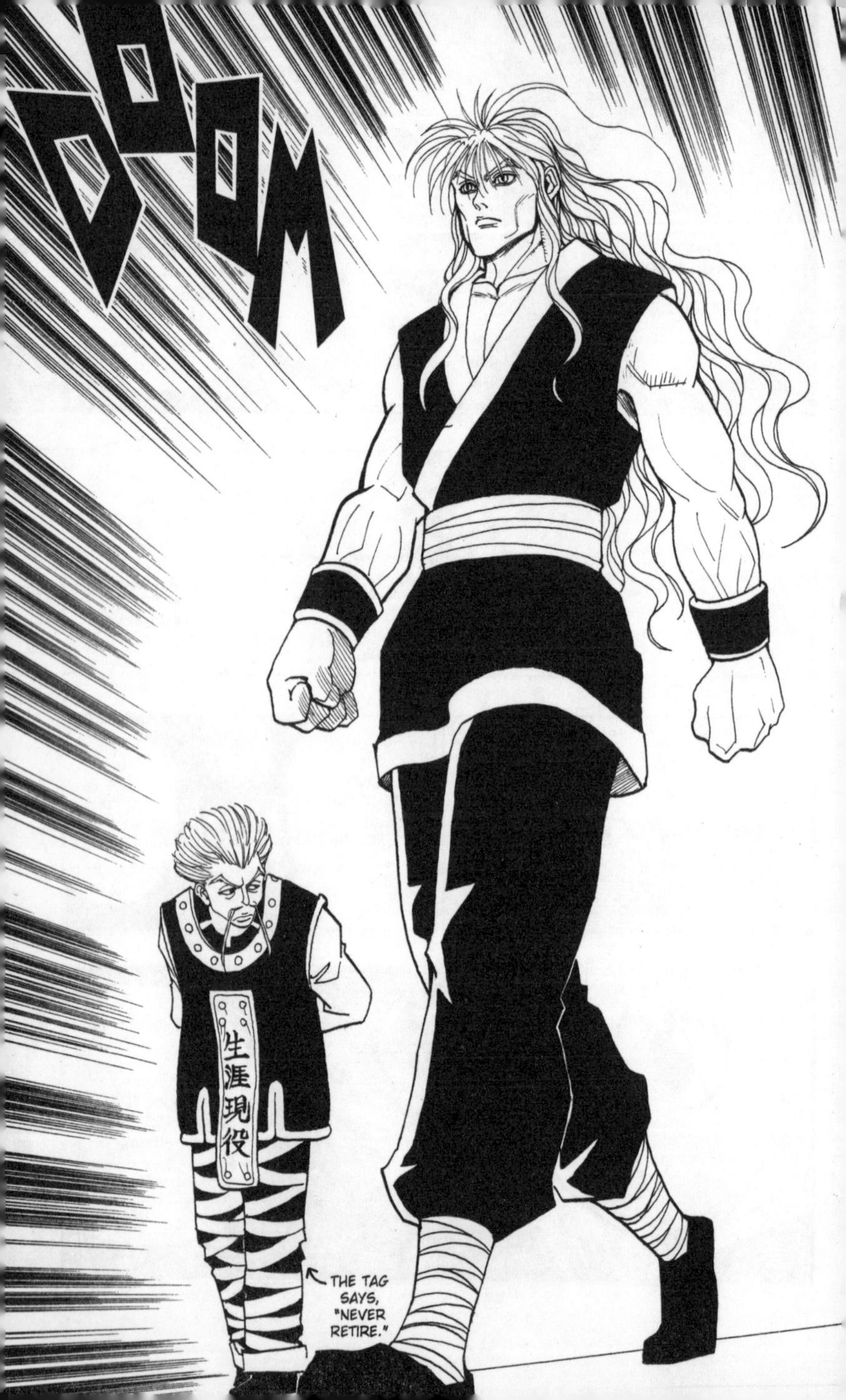
DO-OOM
生涯現役
THE TAG SAYS, "NEVER RETIRE."

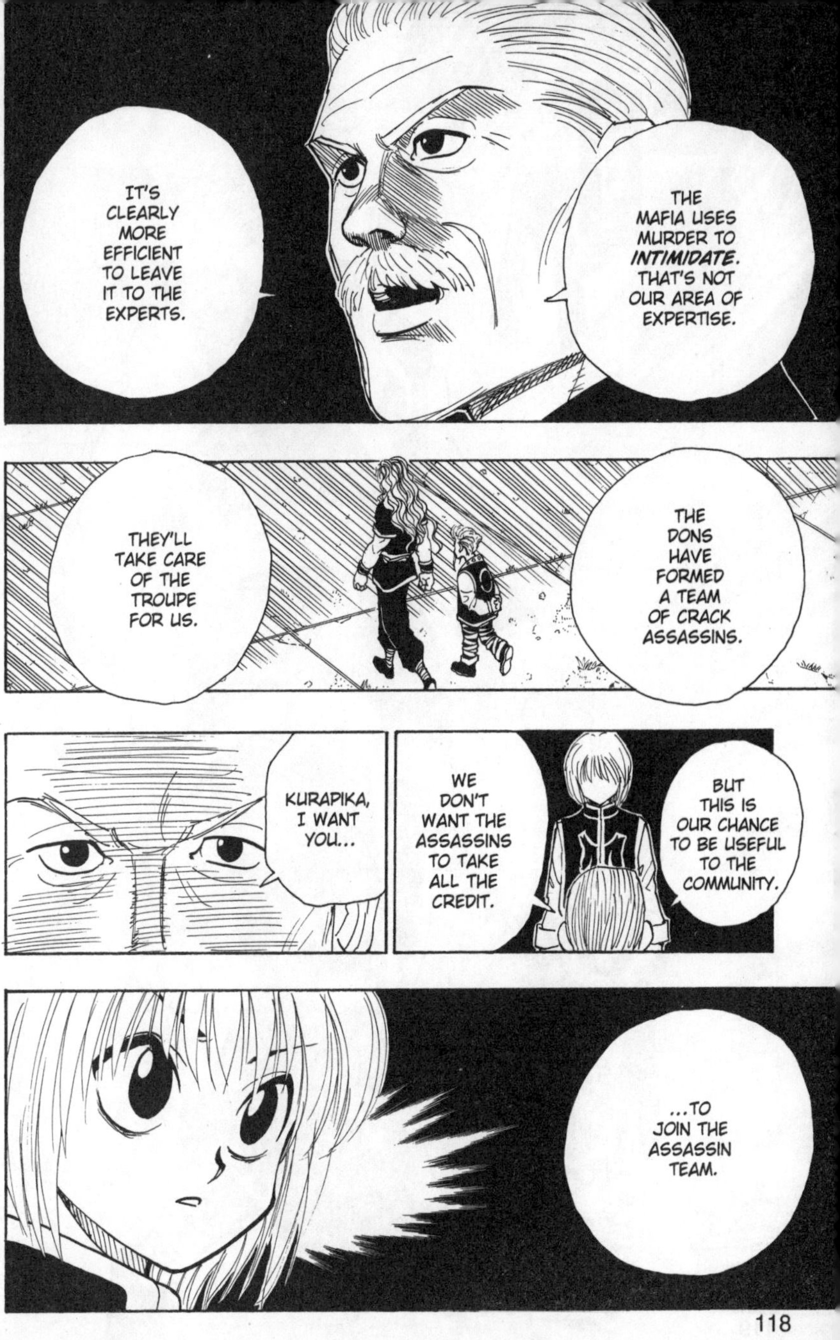
THE MAFIA USES MURDER TO ***INTIMIDATE***. THAT'S NOT OUR AREA OF EXPERTISE.
IT'S CLEARLY MORE EFFICIENT TO LEAVE IT TO THE EXPERTS.
THE DONS HAVE FORMED A TEAM OF CRACK ASSASSINS.
THEY'LL TAKE CARE OF THE TROUPE FOR US.
BUT THIS IS OUR CHANCE TO BE USEFUL TO THE COMMUNITY.
WE DON'T WANT THE ASSASSINS TO TAKE ALL THE CREDIT.
KURAPIKA, I WANT YOU...
...TO JOIN THE ASSASSIN TEAM.

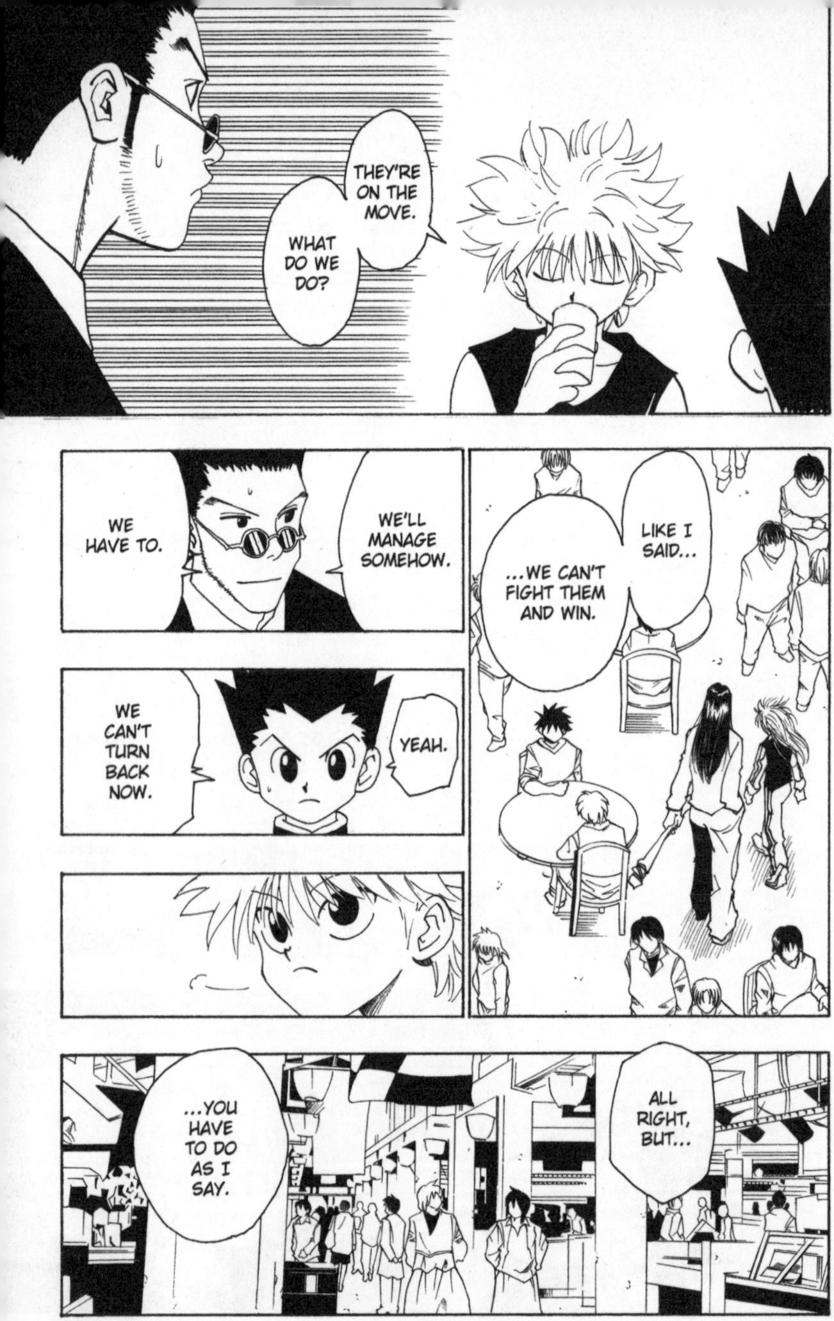
THEY'RE ON THE MOVE.
WHAT DO WE DO?
LIKE I SAID...
...WE CAN'T FIGHT THEM AND WIN.
WE'LL MANAGE SOMEHOW.
WE HAVE TO.
YEAH.
WE CAN'T TURN BACK NOW.
ALL RIGHT, BUT...
...YOU HAVE TO DO AS I SAY.

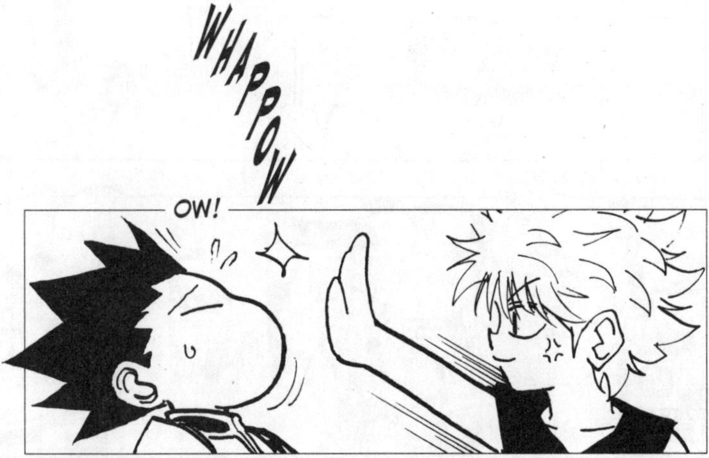
WHAPPOW
OW!

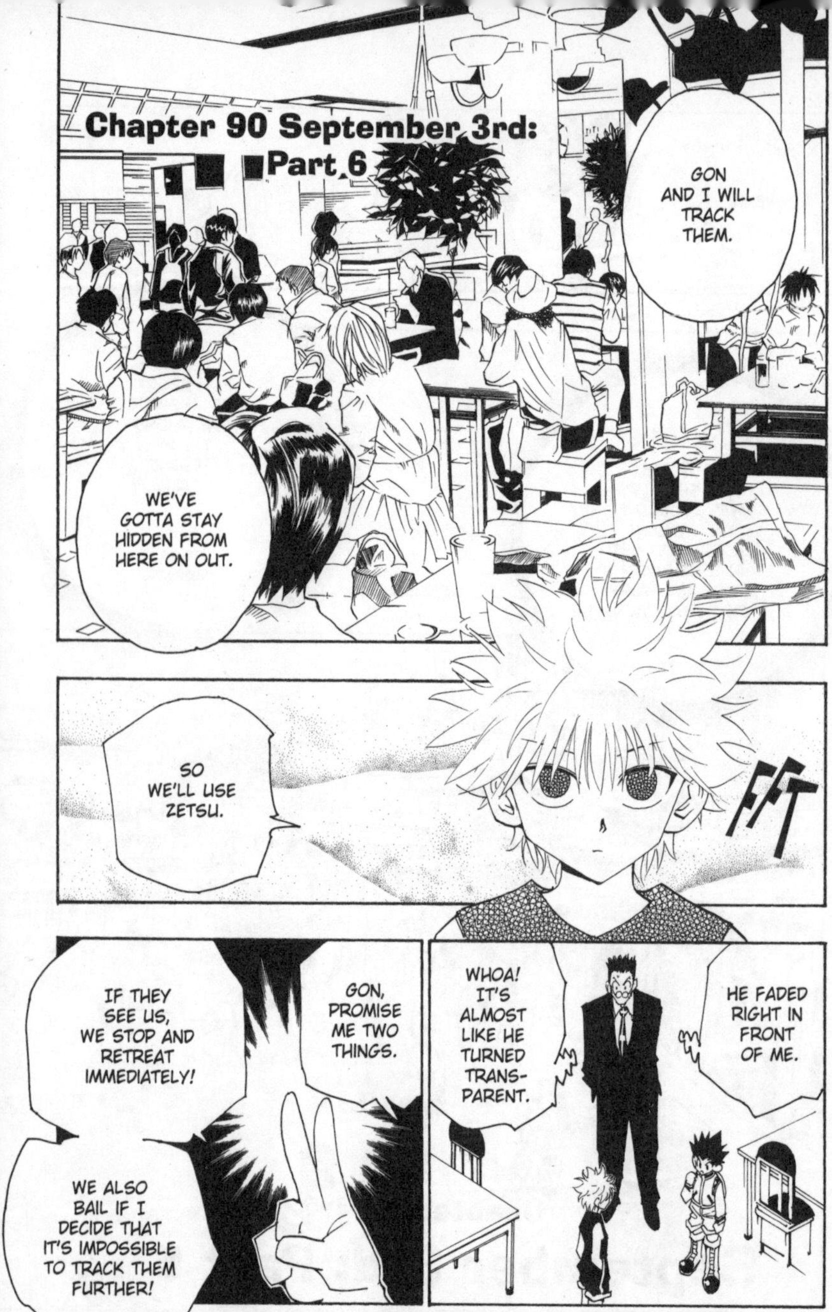
Chapter 90 September 3rd: Part 6
GON AND I WILL TRACK THEM.
WE'VE GOTTA STAY HIDDEN FROM HERE ON OUT.
SO WE'LL USE ZETSU.
FFT
HE FADED RIGHT IN FRONT OF ME.
WHOA! IT'S ALMOST LIKE HE TURNED TRANS-PARENT.
GON, PROMISE ME TWO THINGS.
IF THEY SEE US, WE STOP AND RETREAT IMMEDIATELY!
WE ALSO BAIL IF I DECIDE THAT IT'S IMPOSSIBLE TO TRACK THEM FURTHER!

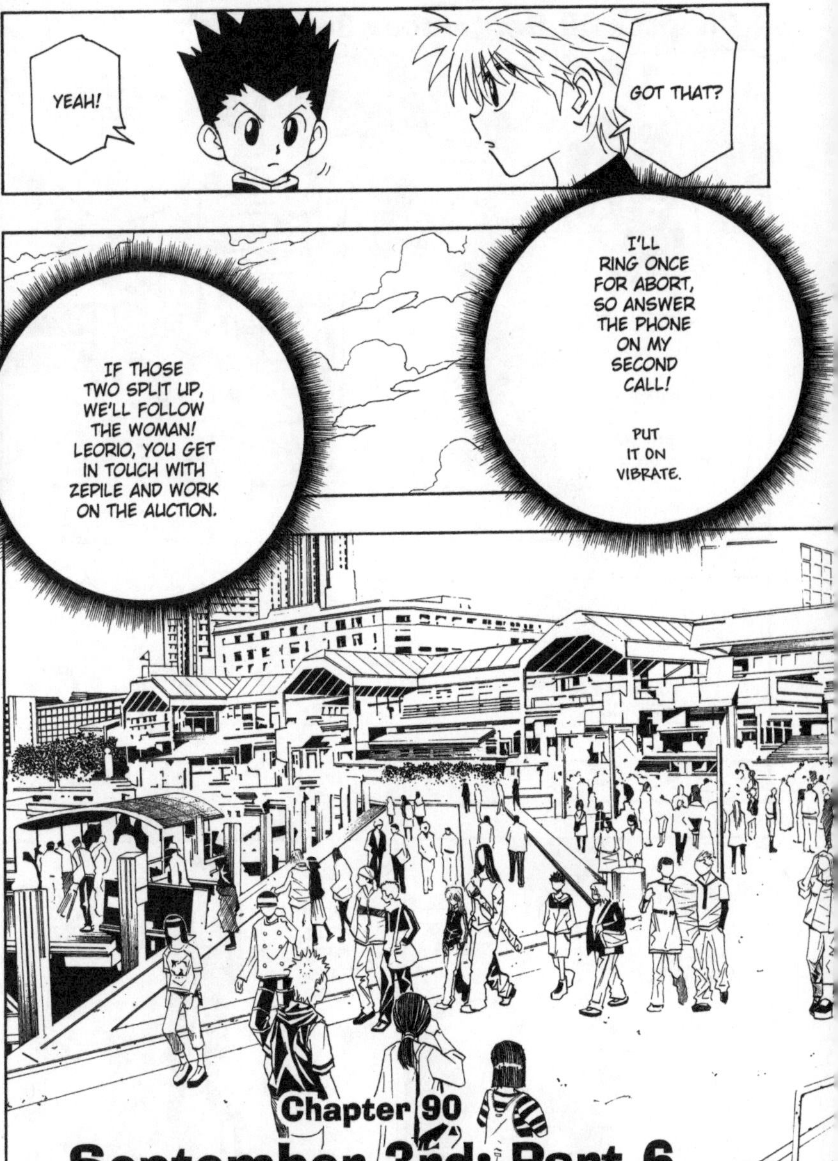
GOT THAT?
YEAH!
I'LL RING ONCE FOR ABORT, SO ANSWER THE PHONE ON MY SECOND CALL!
PUT IT ON VIBRATE.
IF THOSE TWO SPLIT UP, WE'LL FOLLOW THE WOMAN! LEORIO, YOU GET IN TOUCH WITH ZEPILE AND WORK ON THE AUCTION.

Chapter 90

September 3rd: Part 6

READ THIS WAY

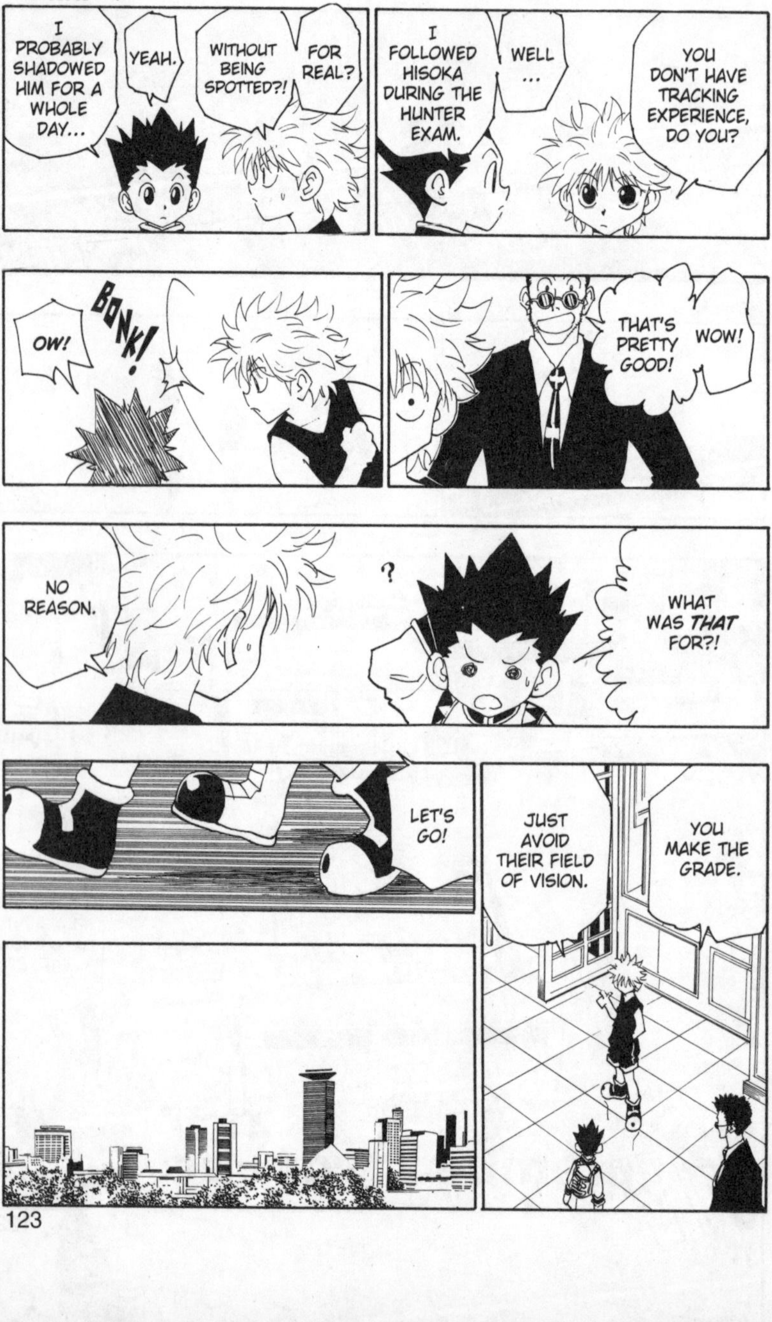
YOU DON'T HAVE TRACKING EXPERIENCE, DO YOU?
WELL ...
I FOLLOWED HISOKA DURING THE HUNTER EXAM.
FOR REAL?
WITHOUT BEING SPOTTED?!
YEAH.
I PROBABLY SHADOWED HIM FOR A WHOLE DAY...
WOW!
THAT'S PRETTY GOOD!
BONK!
OW!
WHAT WAS *THAT* FOR?!
?
NO REASON.
YOU MAKE THE GRADE.
JUST AVOID THEIR FIELD OF VISION.
LET'S GO!

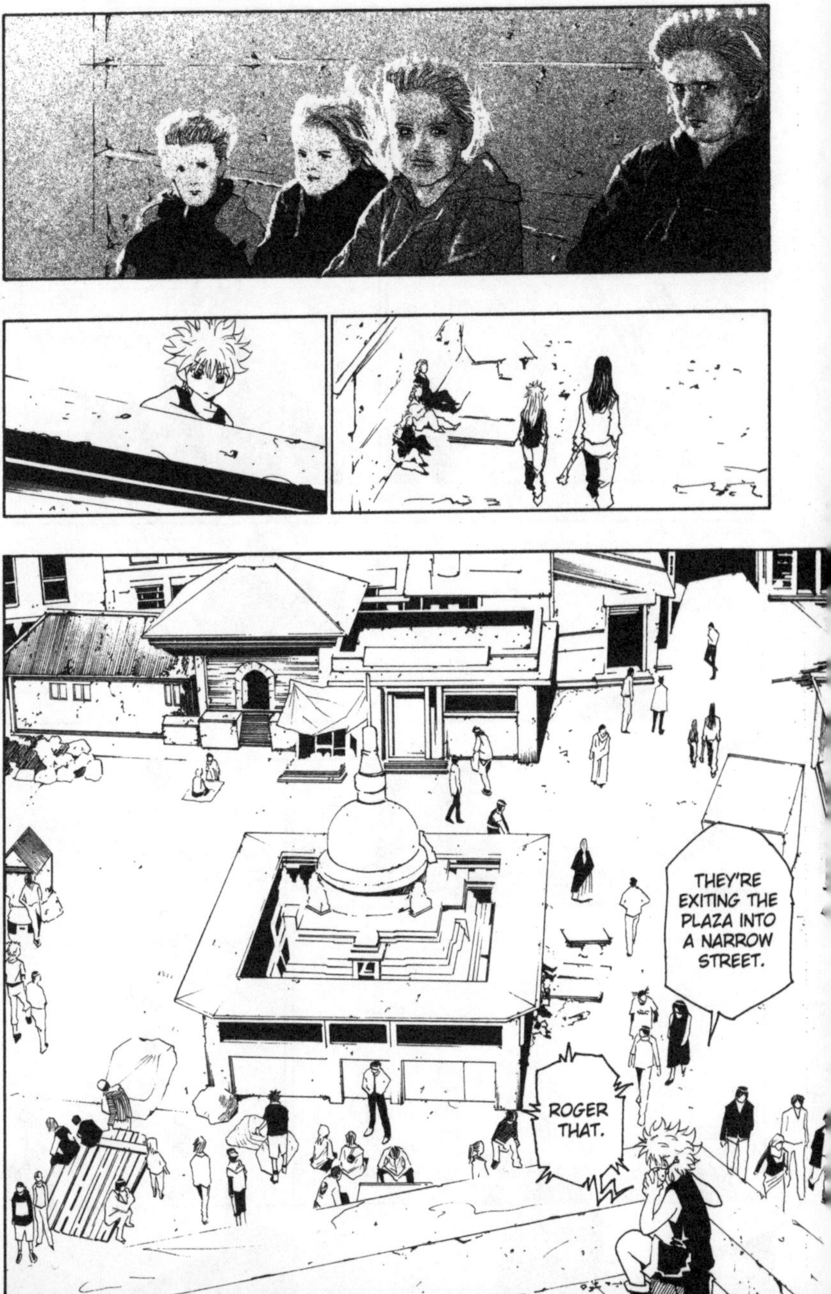
THEY'RE EXITING THE PLAZA INTO A NARROW STREET.
ROGER THAT.

READ THIS WAY

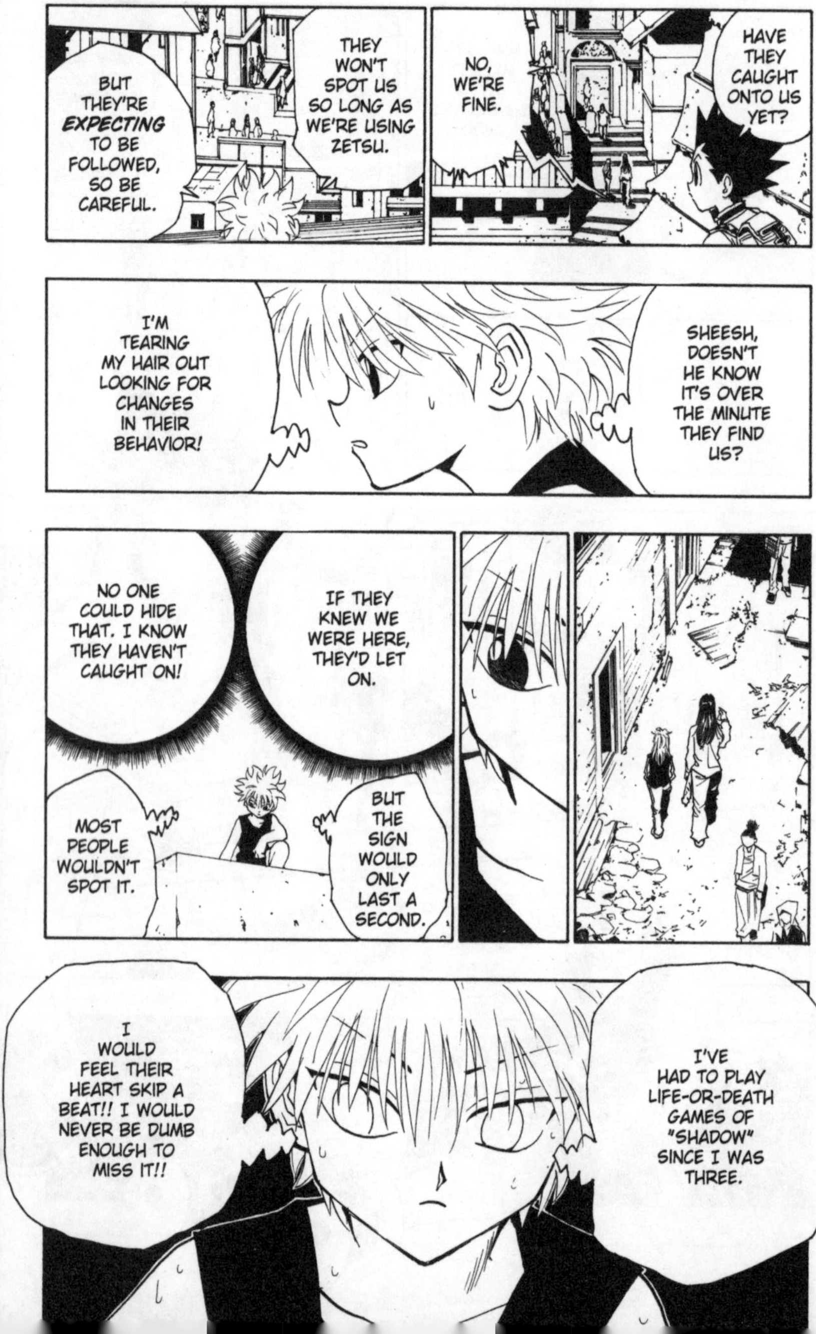
HAVE THEY CAUGHT ONTO US YET?
NO, WE'RE FINE.
THEY WON'T SPOT US SO LONG AS WE'RE USING ZETSU.
BUT THEY'RE *EXPECTING* TO BE FOLLOWED, SO BE CAREFUL.
SHEESH, DOESN'T HE KNOW IT'S OVER THE MINUTE THEY FIND US?
I'M TEARING MY HAIR OUT LOOKING FOR CHANGES IN THEIR BEHAVIOR!
IF THEY KNEW WE WERE HERE, THEY'D LET ON.
NO ONE COULD HIDE THAT. I KNOW THEY HAVEN'T CAUGHT ON!
BUT THE SIGN WOULD ONLY LAST A SECOND.
MOST PEOPLE WOULDN'T SPOT IT.
I'VE HAD TO PLAY LIFE-OR-DEATH GAMES OF "SHADOW" SINCE I WAS THREE.
I WOULD FEEL THEIR HEART SKIP A BEAT!! I WOULD NEVER BE DUMB ENOUGH TO MISS IT!!

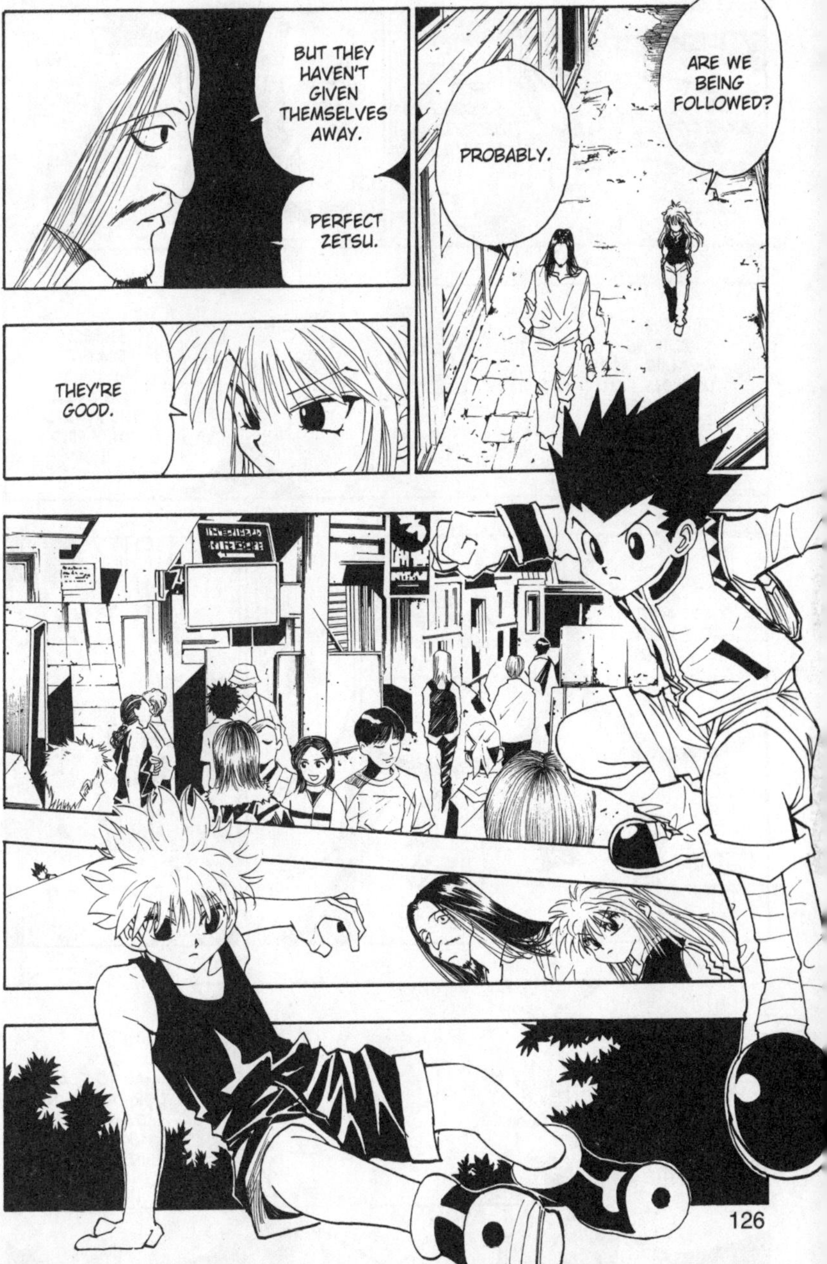
ARE WE BEING FOLLOWED?
PROBABLY.
BUT THEY HAVEN'T GIVEN THEMSELVES AWAY.
PERFECT ZETSU.
THEY'RE GOOD.

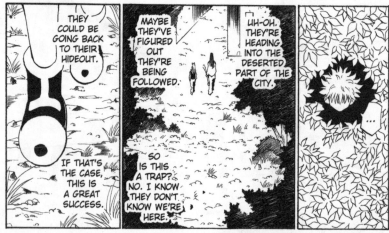

READ THIS WAY

...
UH-OH. THEY'RE HEADING INTO THE DESERTED PART OF THE CITY.
MAYBE THEY'VE FIGURED OUT THEY'RE BEING FOLLOWED.
SO IS THIS A TRAP? NO. I KNOW THEY DON'T KNOW WE'RE HERE.
THEY COULD BE GOING BACK TO THEIR HIDEOUT.
IF THAT'S THE CASE, THIS IS A GREAT SUCCESS.
IF IT'S A TRAP, WE BAIL. IF IT'S THEIR HIDEOUT, WE FOLLOW THEM...
...A WHILE LONGER.
IS THIS A TRAP OR THEIR HIDEOUT?
I DON'T SENSE ANYTHING UNNATURAL IN THEIR BEHAVIOR.
WE KEEP GOING!!
WHOOOOO

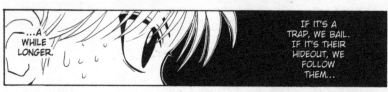

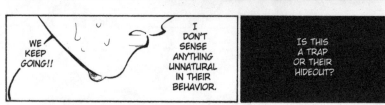

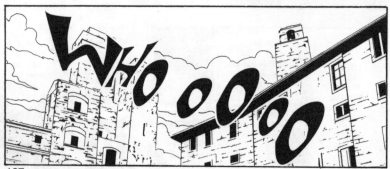

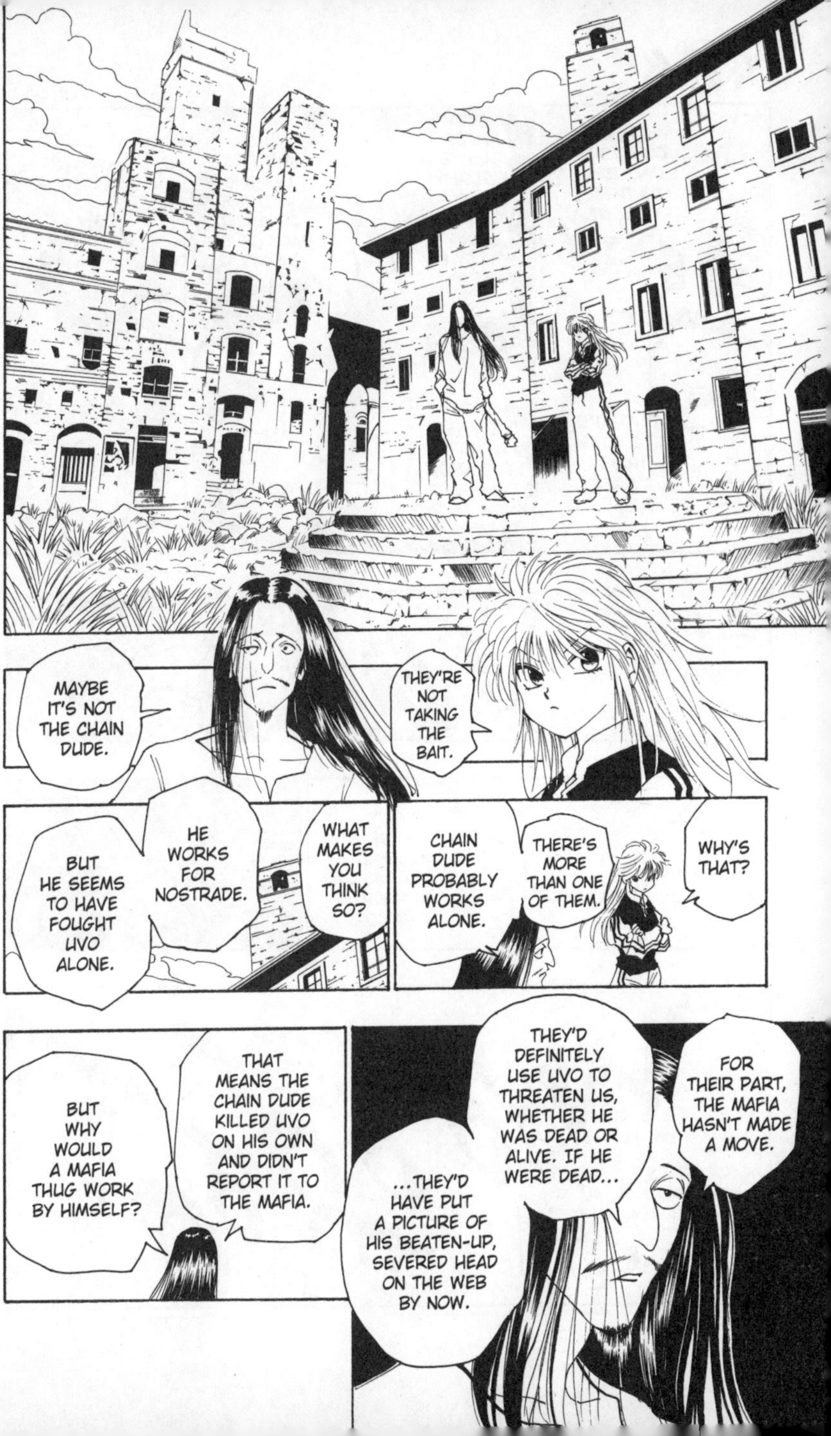
THEY'RE NOT TAKING THE BAIT.
MAYBE IT'S NOT THE CHAIN DUDE.
WHY'S THAT?
THERE'S MORE THAN ONE OF THEM.
CHAIN DUDE PROBABLY WORKS ALONE.
WHAT MAKES YOU THINK SO?
HE WORKS FOR NOSTRADE.
BUT HE SEEMS TO HAVE FOUGHT UVO ALONE.
FOR THEIR PART, THE MAFIA HASN'T MADE A MOVE.
THEY'D DEFINITELY USE UVO TO THREATEN US, WHETHER HE WAS DEAD OR ALIVE. IF HE WERE DEAD...
...THEY'D HAVE PUT A PICTURE OF HIS BEATEN-UP, SEVERED HEAD ON THE WEB BY NOW.
THAT MEANS THE CHAIN DUDE KILLED UVO ON HIS OWN AND DIDN'T REPORT IT TO THE MAFIA.
BUT WHY WOULD A MAFIA THUG WORK BY HIMSELF?

IT'S PROBABLY A PERSONAL GRUDGE.
YOU'RE GUESSING AN AWFUL LOT.
QUIET.
I CAN'T IMAGINE A GUY LIKE THAT WOULD TEAM UP WITH ANYONE.
SO CHAIN DUDE WORKS ALONE...
...AND THESE GUYS ARE UNRELATED.
YOUR LOGIC'S FULL OF HOLES.
THEN WHAT DO *YOU* THINK?!
WELL...
...I THINK THEY'RE STILL SOMEHOW RELATED TO THE CHAIN DUDE.
IS THAT A HUNCH?
YEAH.
GEEZ...
THAT'S GOT NOTHING TO DO WITH LOGIC.
...
WHAT DO YOU THINK, KILLUA?
THEY'RE EITHER GOING TO MEET UP WITH OTHERS... OR THEY'RE TRYING TO DRAW US OUT.

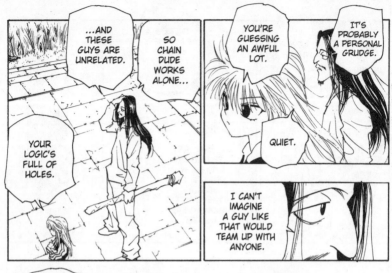

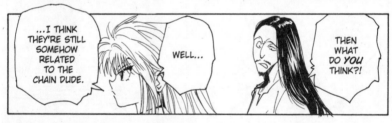

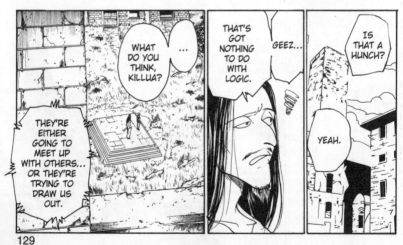

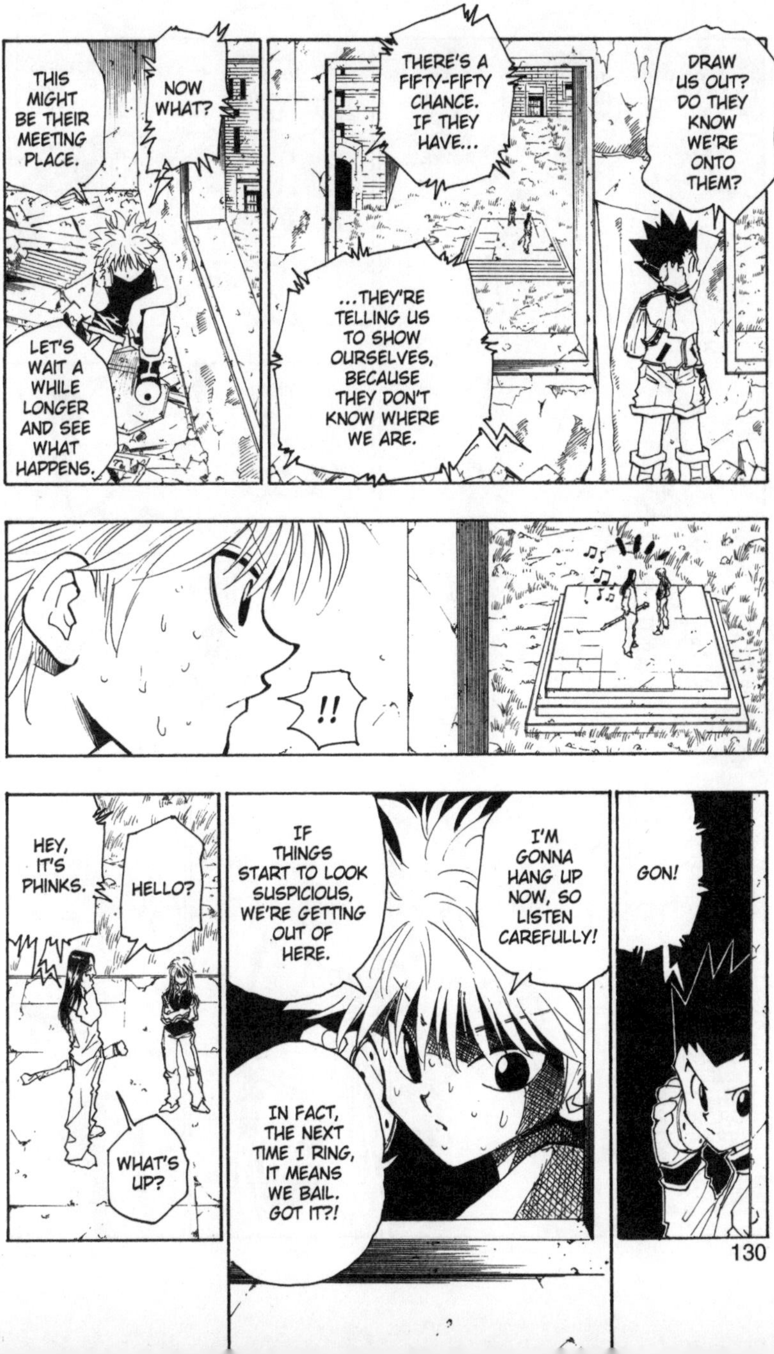
DRAW US OUT? DO THEY KNOW WE'RE ONTO THEM?
THERE'S A FIFTY-FIFTY CHANCE. IF THEY HAVE...
...THEY'RE TELLING US TO SHOW OURSELVES, BECAUSE THEY DON'T KNOW WHERE WE ARE.
NOW WHAT?
THIS MIGHT BE THEIR MEETING PLACE.
LET'S WAIT A WHILE LONGER AND SEE WHAT HAPPENS.
!!
GON!
I'M GONNA HANG UP NOW, SO LISTEN CAREFULLY!
IF THINGS START TO LOOK SUSPICIOUS, WE'RE GETTING OUT OF HERE.
IN FACT, THE NEXT TIME I RING, IT MEANS WE BAIL. GOT IT?!
HELLO?
HEY, IT'S PHINKS.
WHAT'S UP?

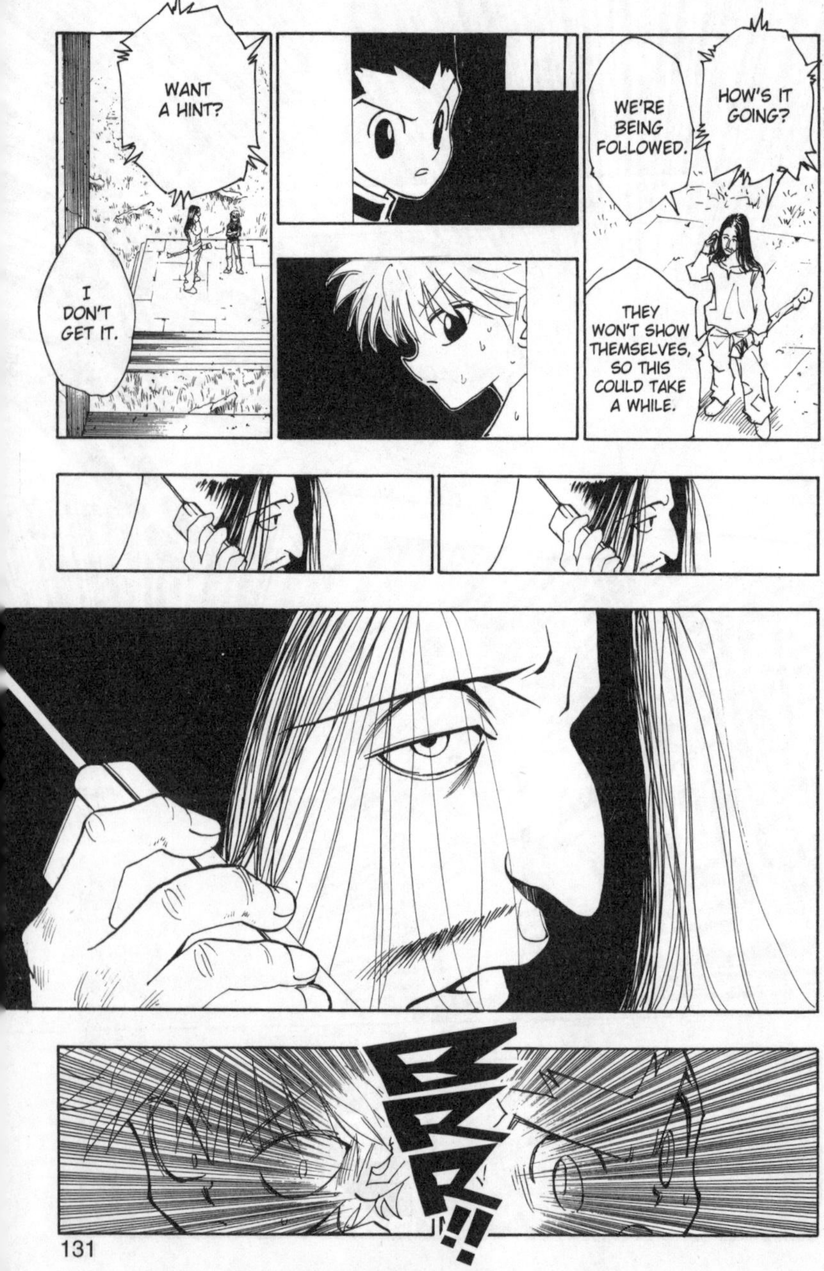
HOW'S IT GOING?
WE'RE BEING FOLLOWED.
THEY WON'T SHOW THEMSELVES, SO THIS COULD TAKE A WHILE.
WANT A HINT?
I DON'T GET IT.

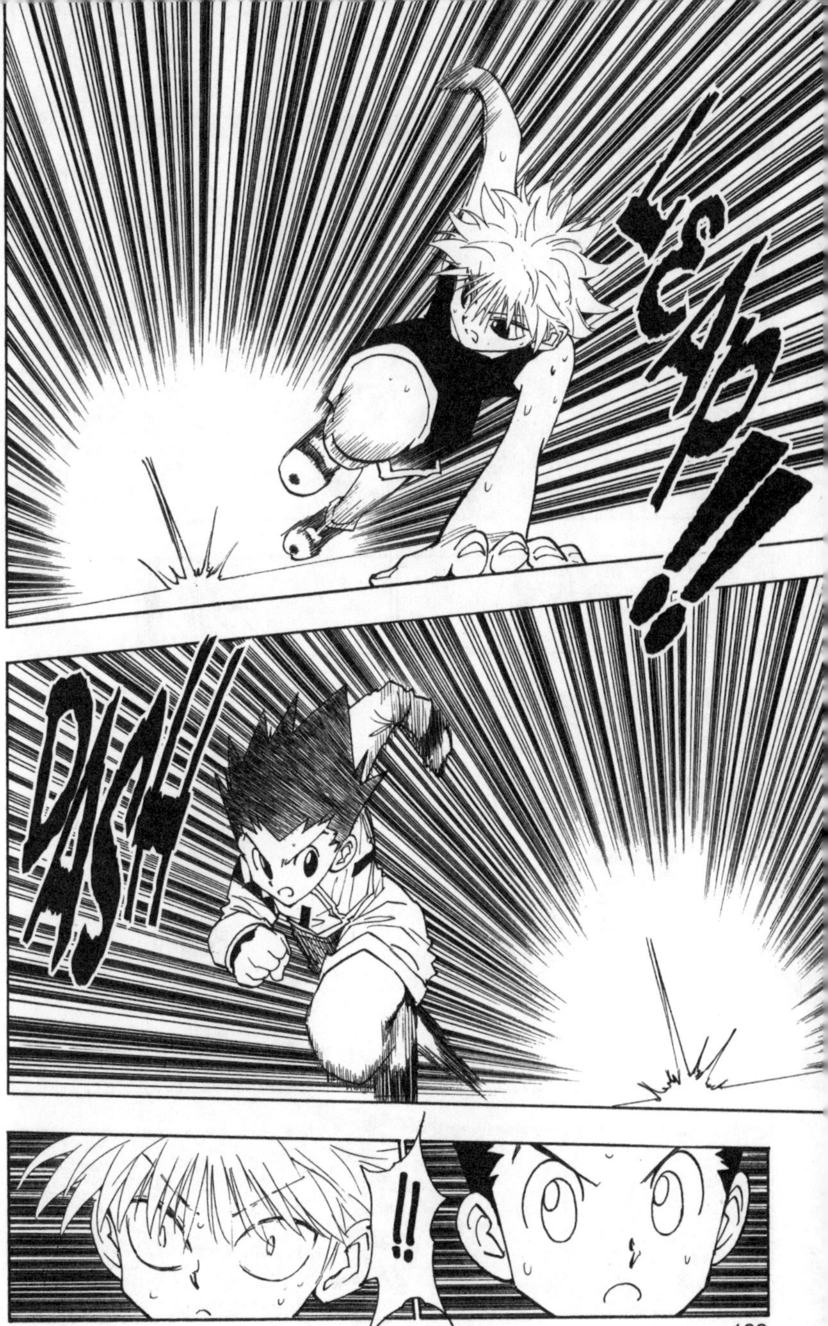

!!

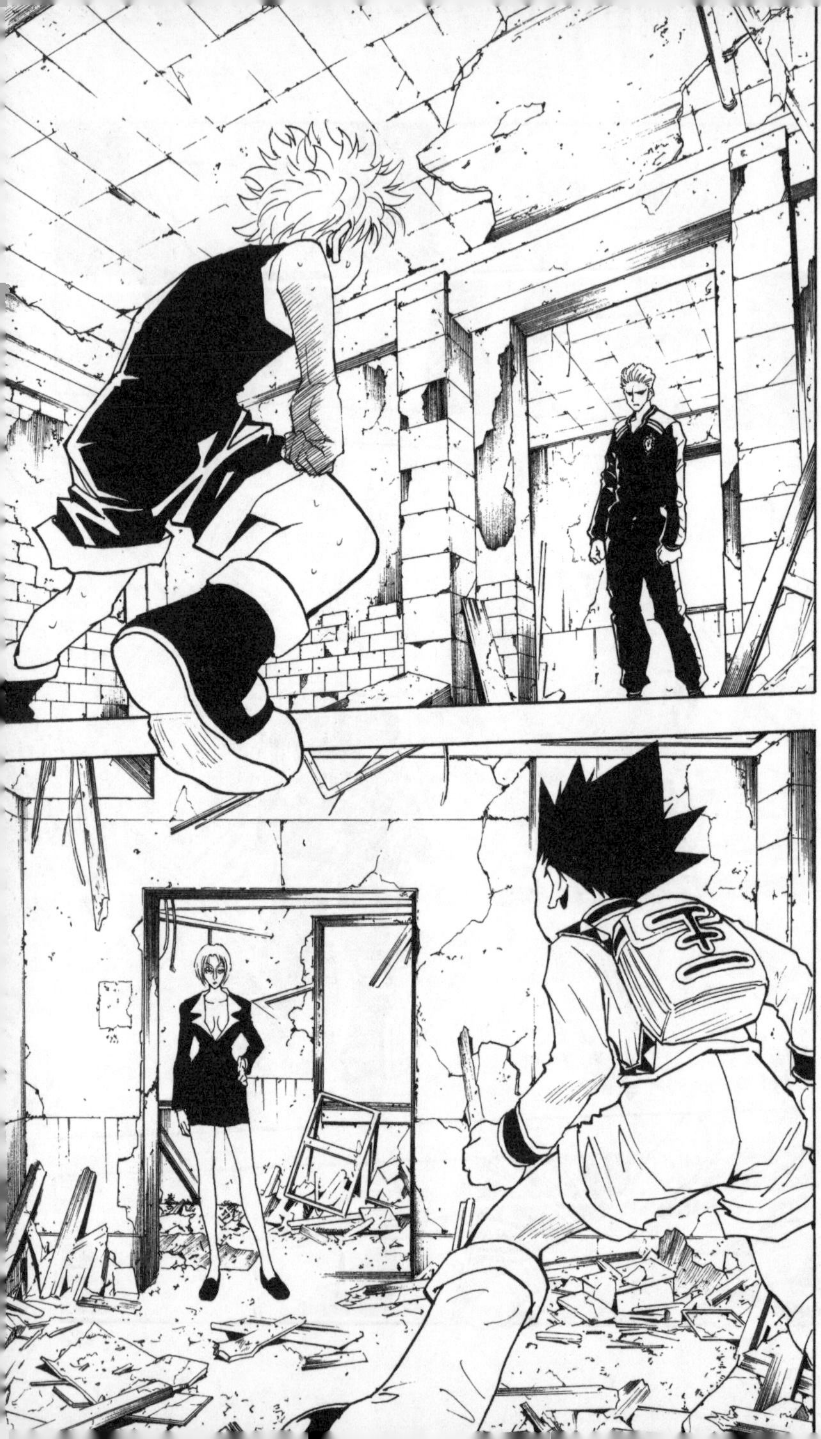

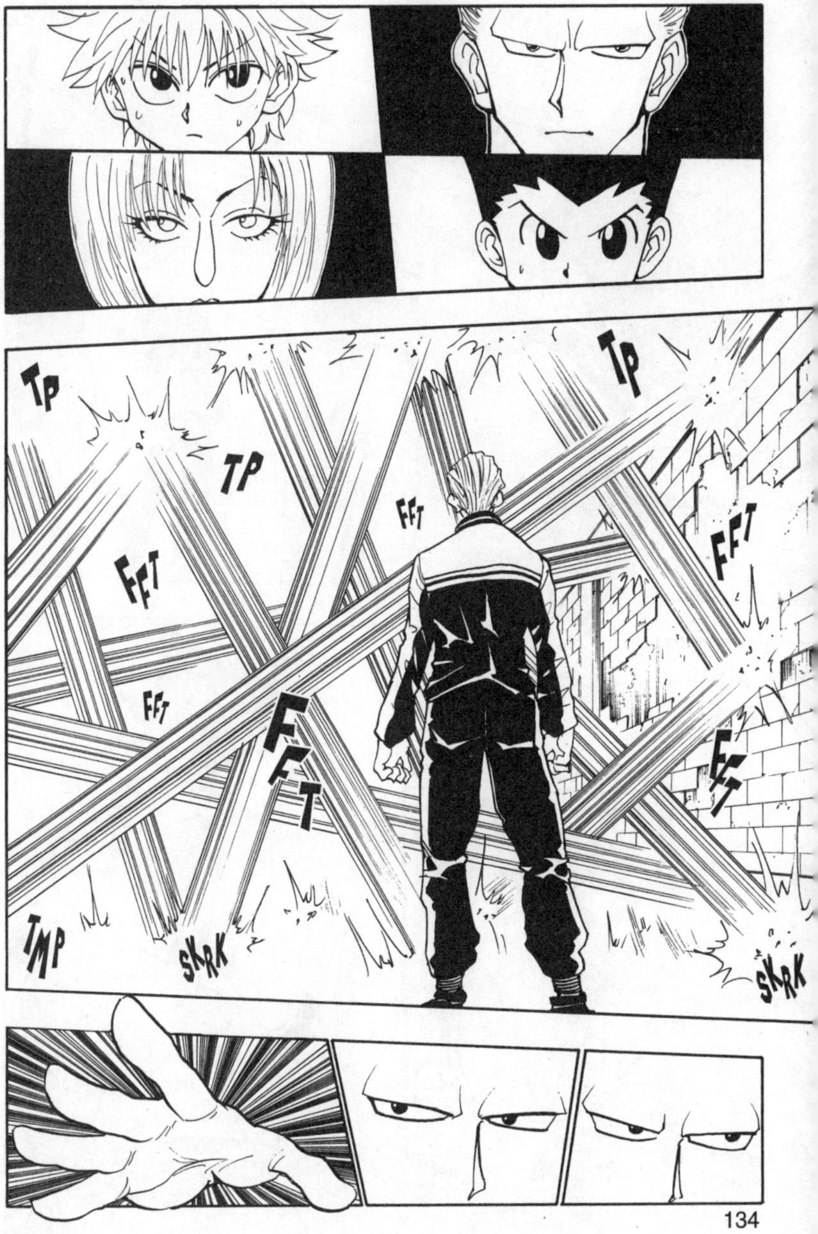
TP
TP
TP
FFT
FFT
FFT
FFT
FFT
FFT
SKRK
SKRK
TMP

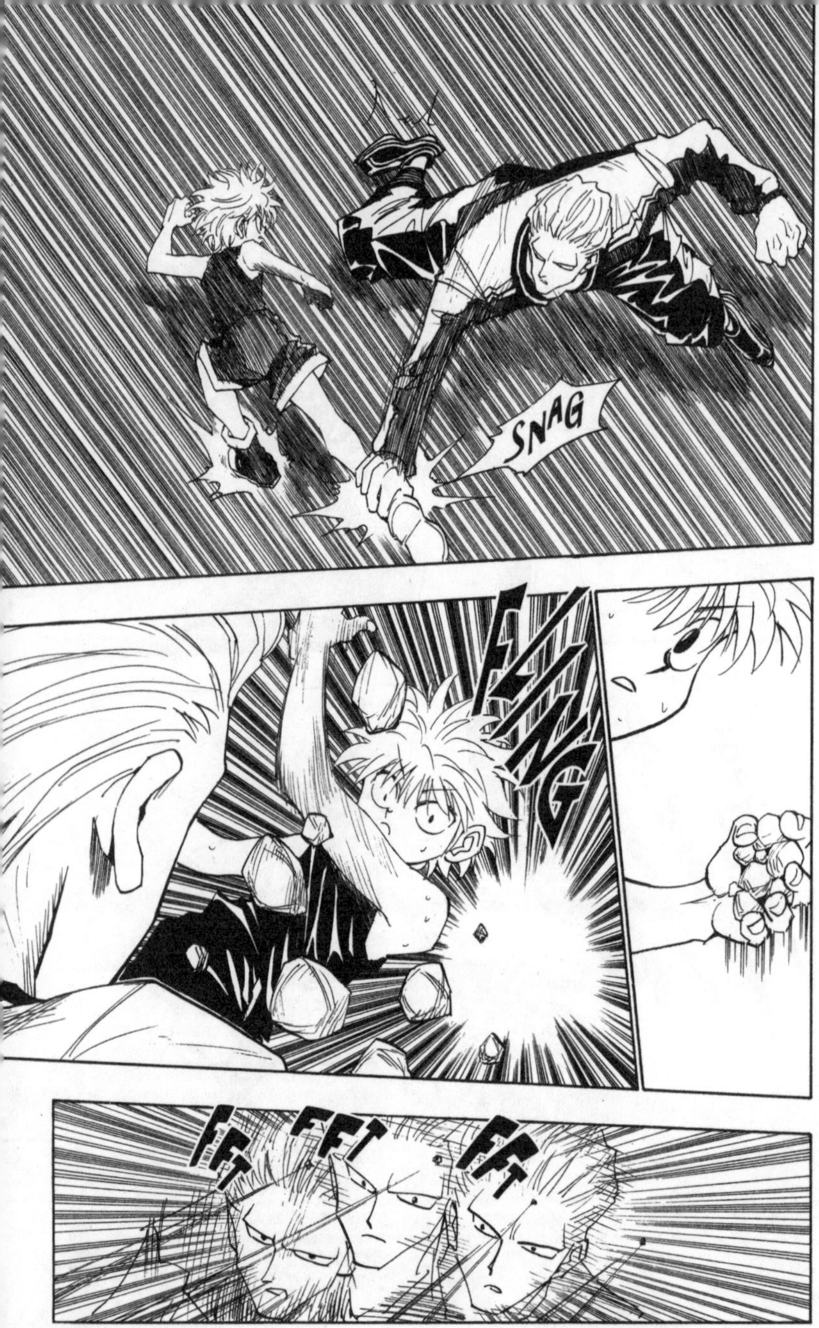
SNAG
FWING
FFT
FFT
FFT

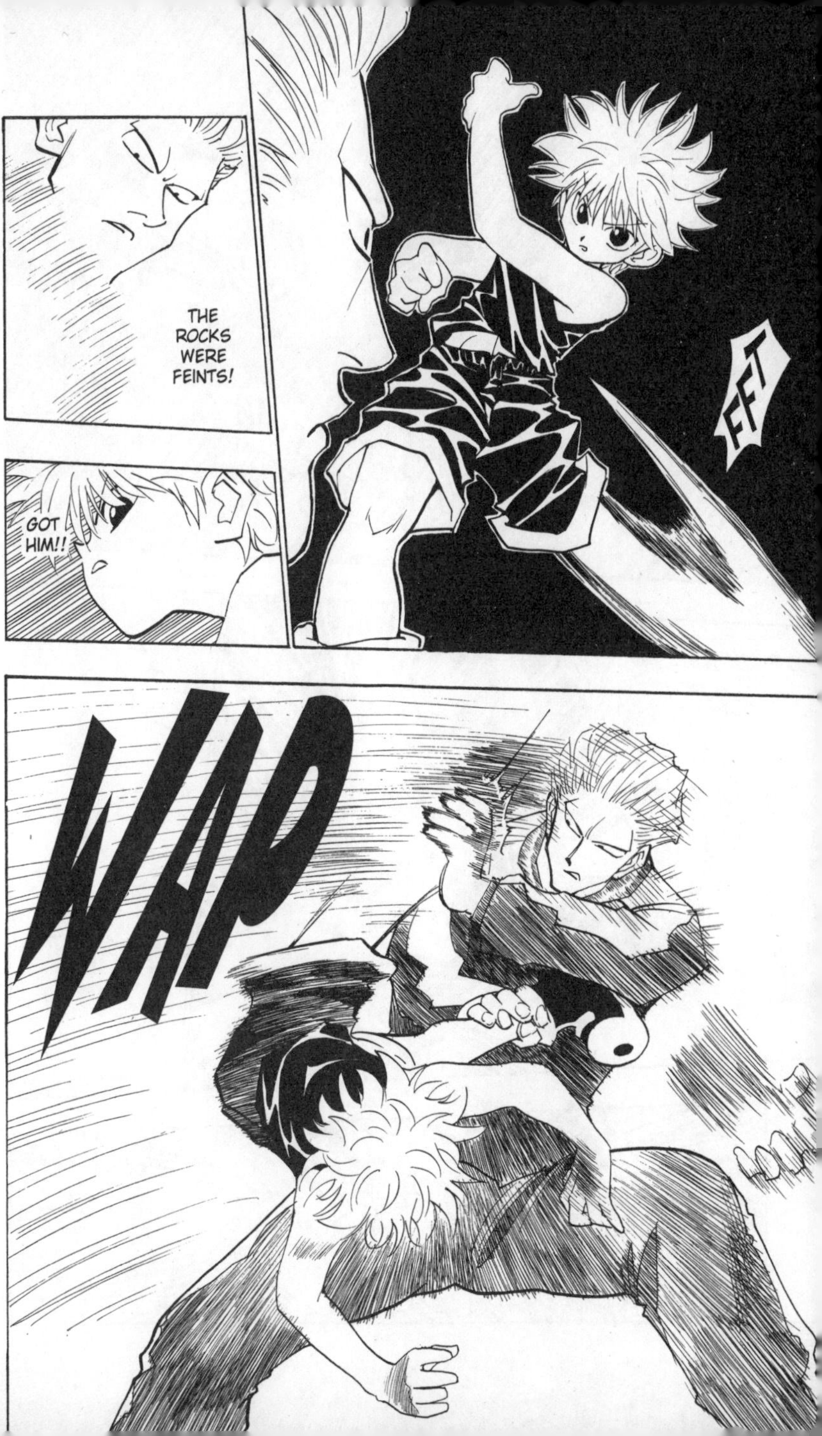
FFT
THE ROCKS WERE FEINTS!
GOT HIM!!
WAP

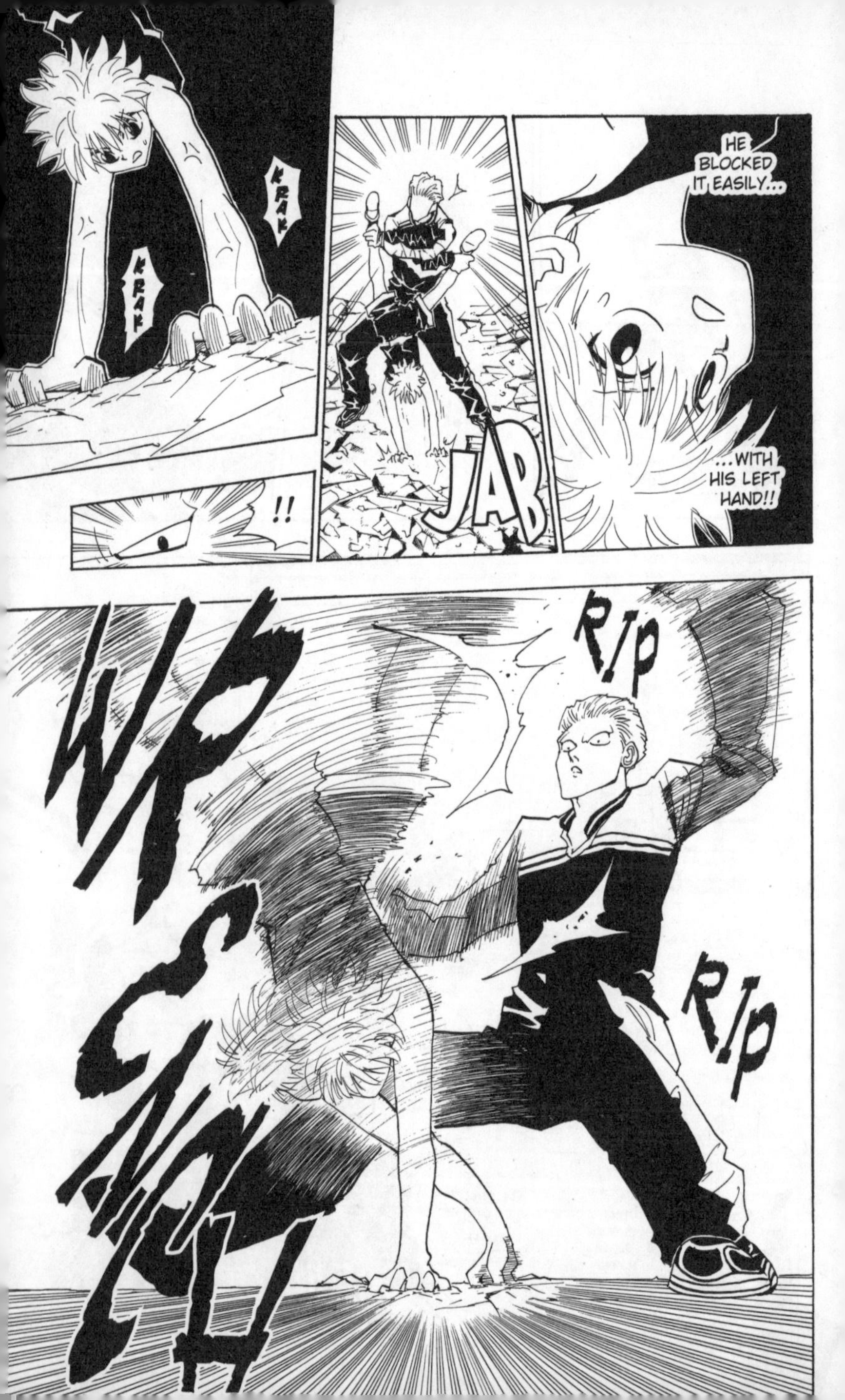
HE BLOCKED IT EASILY...
...WITH HIS LEFT HAND!!
JAB
KRAK
KRAK
!!
RIP
RIP

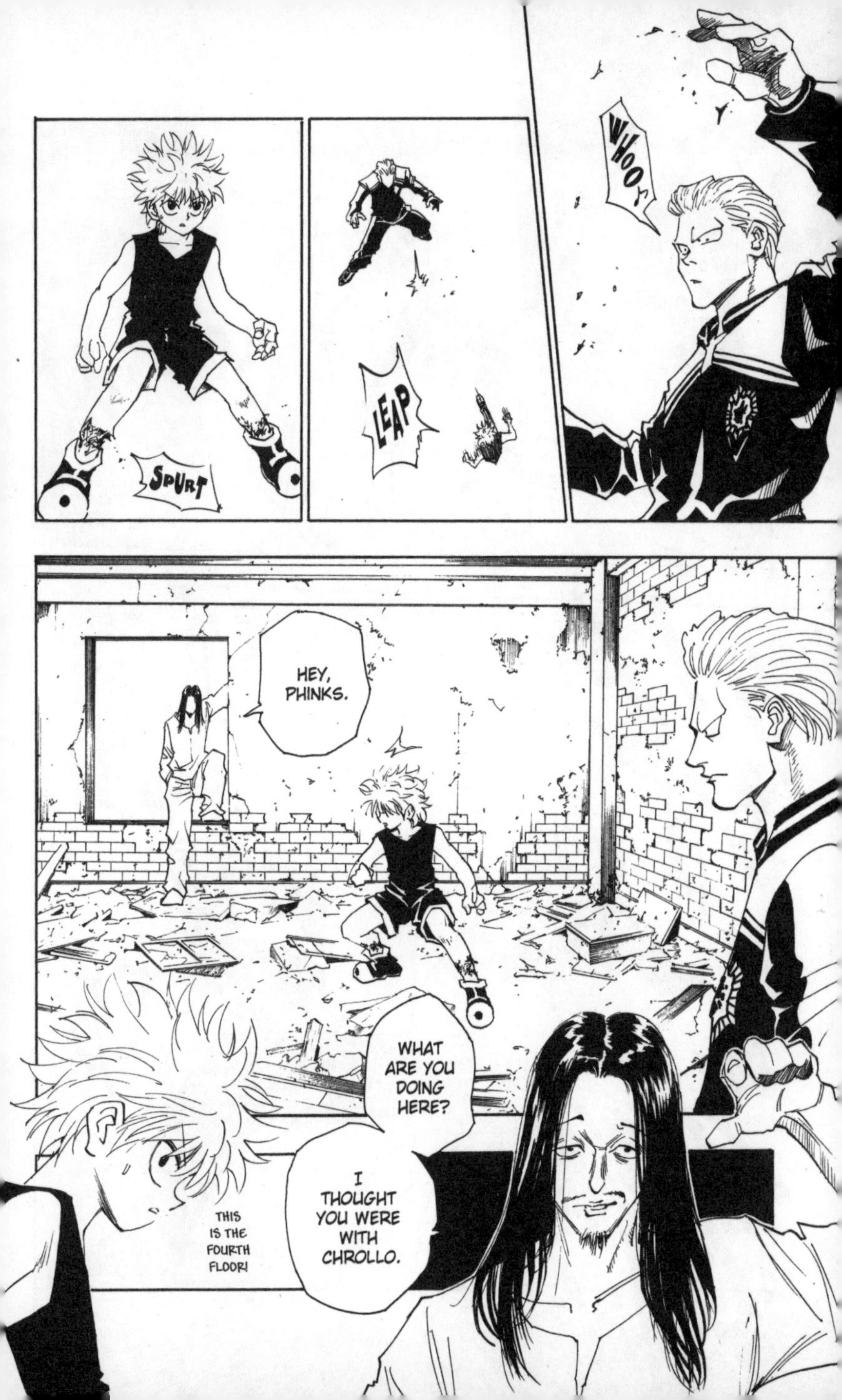
WHOOO
LEAP
SPURT
HEY, PHINKS.
WHAT ARE YOU DOING HERE?
I THOUGHT YOU WERE WITH CHROLLO.
THIS IS THE FOURTH FLOOR!

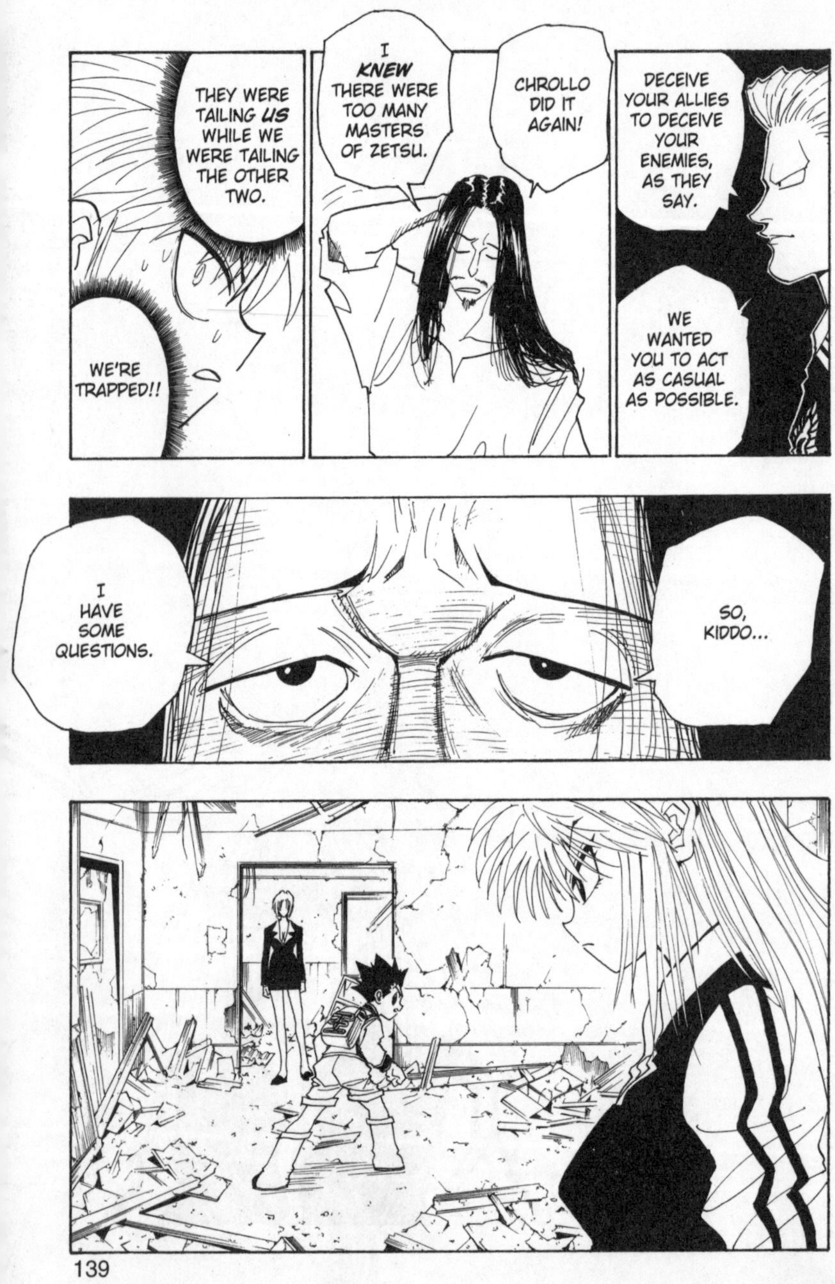

DECEIVE YOUR ALLIES TO DECEIVE YOUR ENEMIES, AS THEY SAY.
WE WANTED YOU TO ACT AS CASUAL AS POSSIBLE.
CHROLLO DID IT AGAIN!
I *KNEW* THERE WERE TOO MANY MASTERS OF ZETSU.
THEY WERE TAILING *US* WHILE WE WERE TAILING THE OTHER TWO.
WE'RE TRAPPED!!
SO, KIDDO...
I HAVE SOME QUESTIONS.

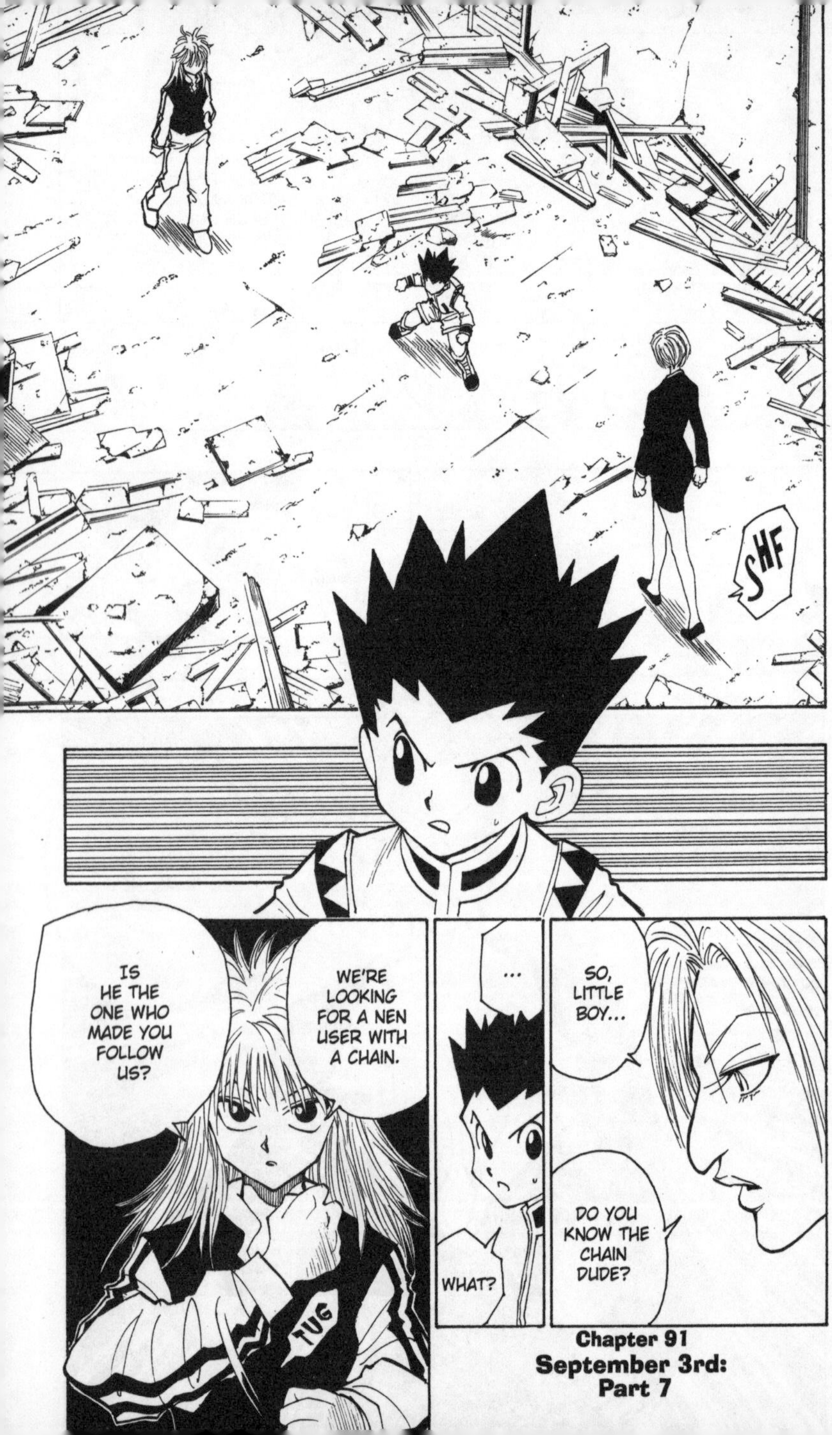
SHF
SO, LITTLE BOY...
DO YOU KNOW THE CHAIN DUDE?
...
WHAT?
WE'RE LOOKING FOR A NEN USER WITH A CHAIN.
IS HE THE ONE WHO MADE YOU FOLLOW US?
TUG

Chapter 91
September 3rd: Part 7

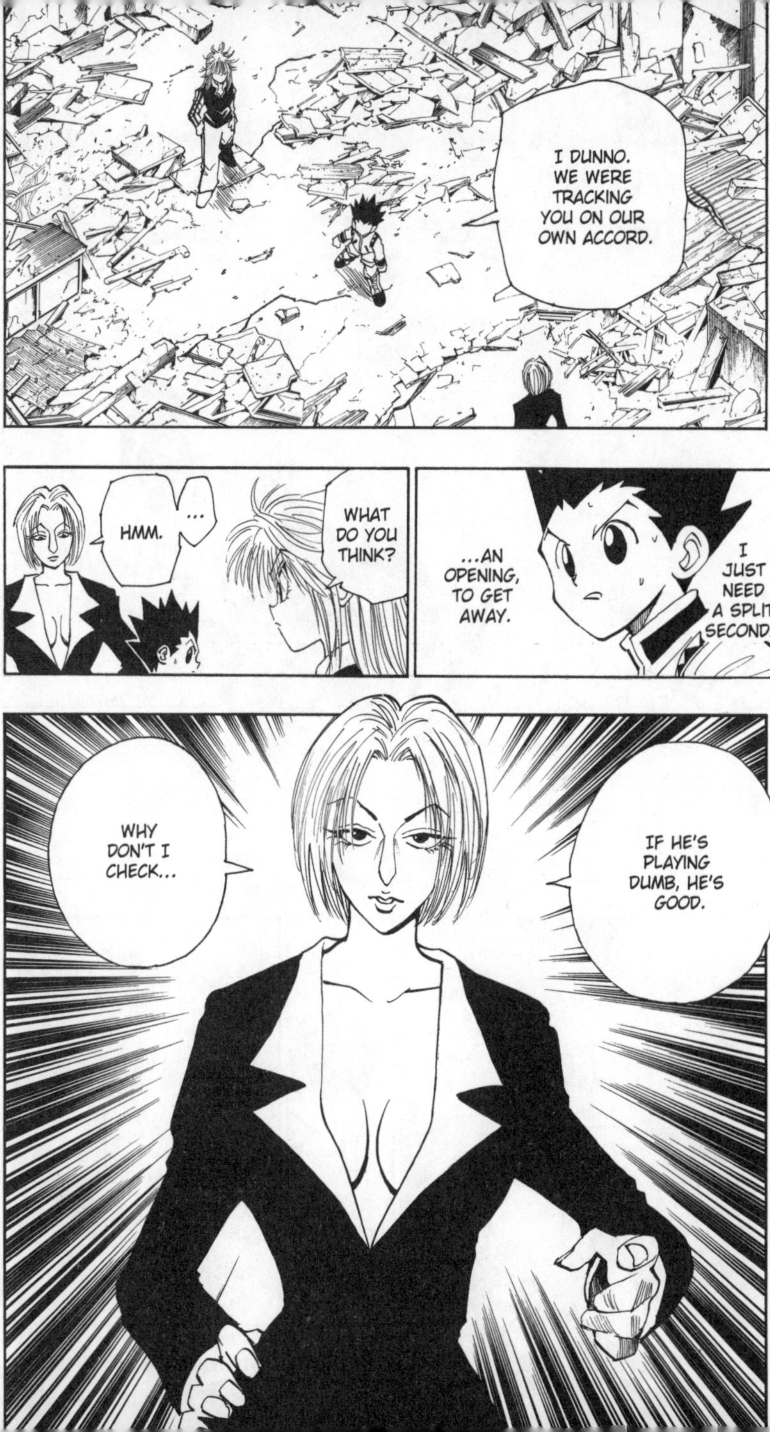
I DUNNO. WE WERE TRACKING YOU ON OUR OWN ACCORD.
I JUST NEED A SPLIT SECOND...
...AN OPENING, TO GET AWAY.
WHAT DO YOU THINK?
...
HMM.
IF HE'S PLAYING DUMB, HE'S GOOD.
WHY DON'T I CHECK...

Chapter 91
September 3rd: Part 7

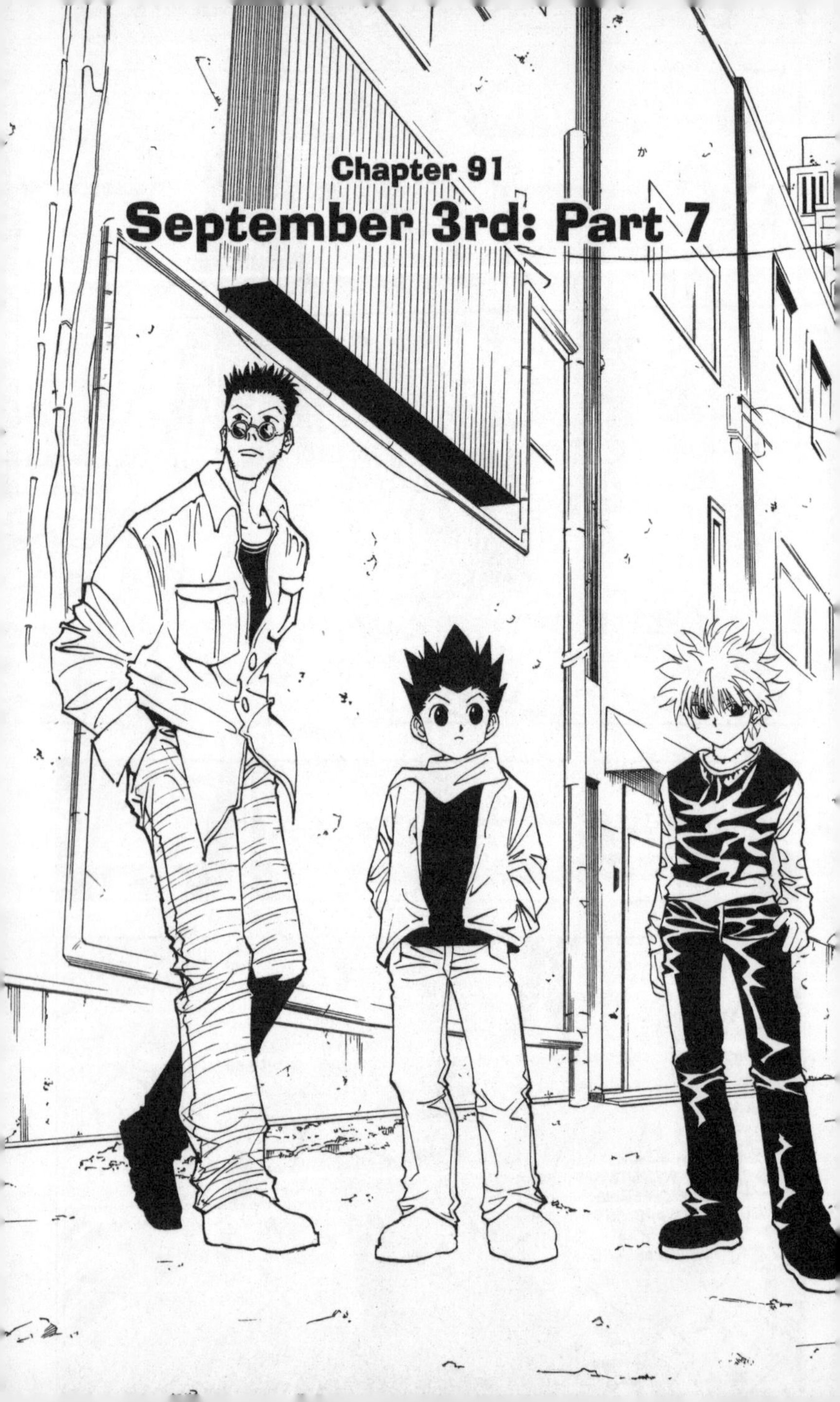

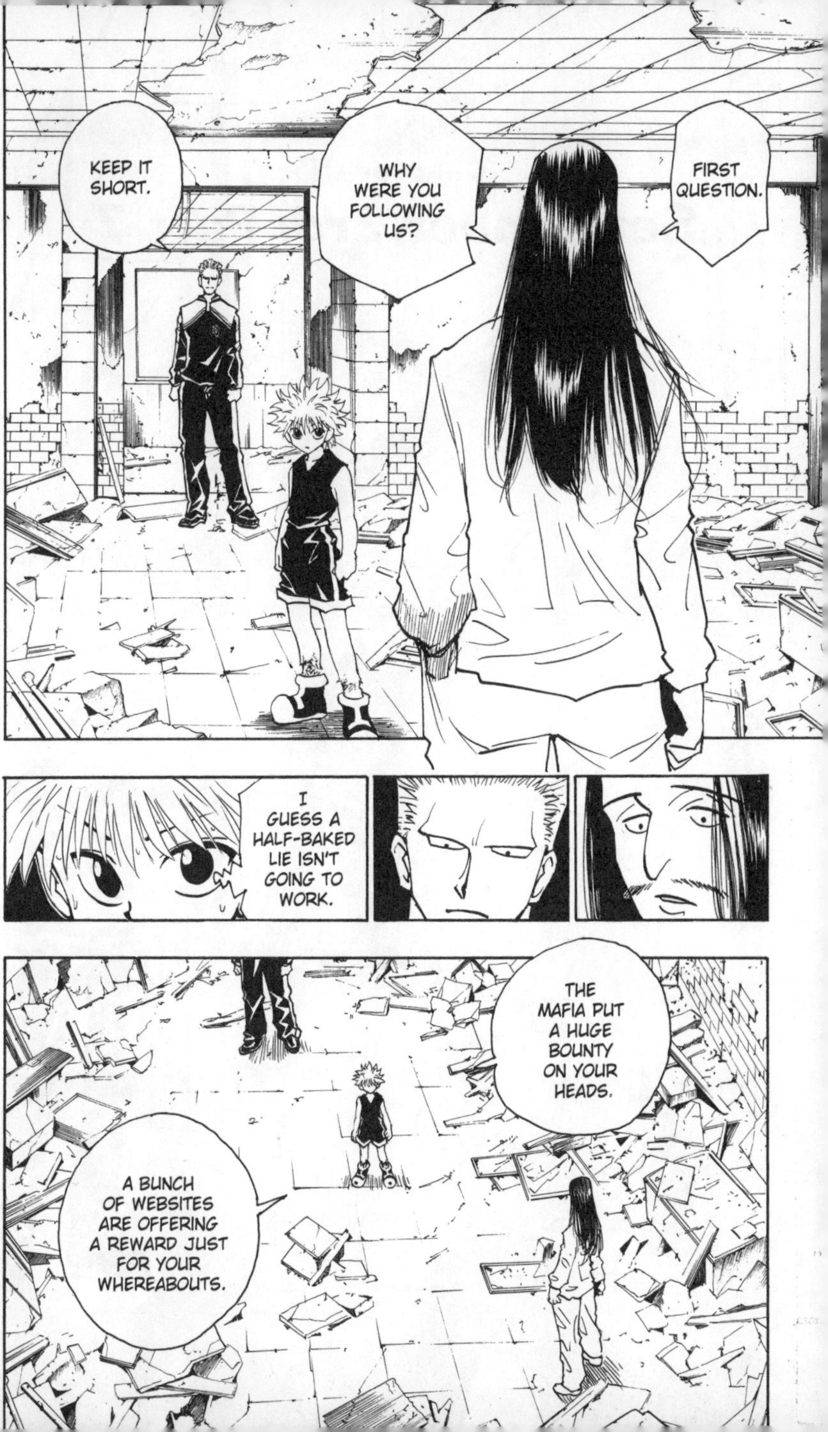
FIRST QUESTION.
WHY WERE YOU FOLLOWING US?
KEEP IT SHORT.
I GUESS A HALF-BAKED LIE ISN'T GOING TO WORK.
THE MAFIA PUT A HUGE BOUNTY ON YOUR HEADS.
A BUNCH OF WEBSITES ARE OFFERING A REWARD JUST FOR YOUR WHEREABOUTS.

READ THIS WAY

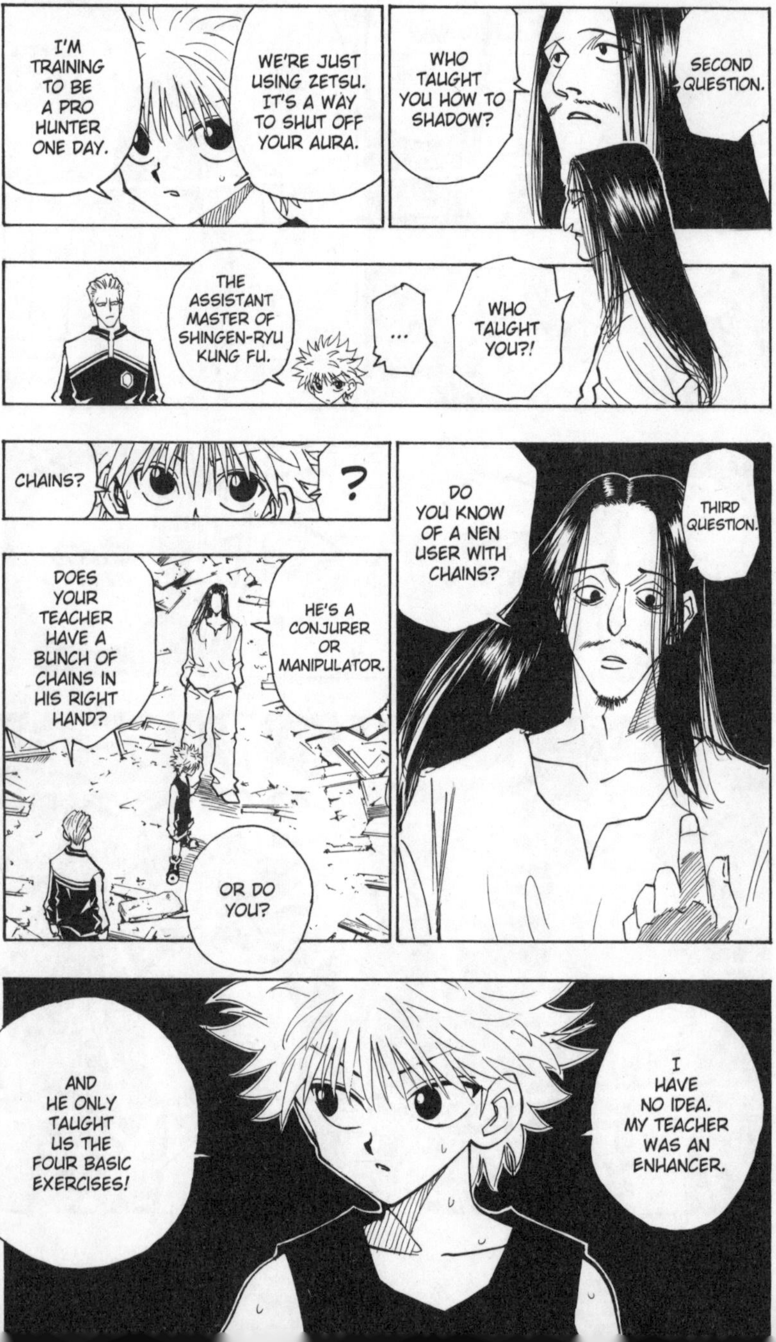
SECOND QUESTION.
WHO TAUGHT YOU HOW TO SHADOW?
WE'RE JUST USING ZETSU. IT'S A WAY TO SHUT OFF YOUR AURA.
I'M TRAINING TO BE A PRO HUNTER ONE DAY.
WHO TAUGHT YOU?!
...
THE ASSISTANT MASTER OF SHINGEN-RYU KUNG FU.
THIRD QUESTION.
DO YOU KNOW OF A NEN USER WITH CHAINS?
?
CHAINS?
HE'S A CONJURER OR MANIPULATOR.
DOES YOUR TEACHER HAVE A BUNCH OF CHAINS IN HIS RIGHT HAND?
OR DO YOU?
I HAVE NO IDEA. MY TEACHER WAS AN ENHANCER.
AND HE ONLY TAUGHT US THE FOUR BASIC EXERCISES!

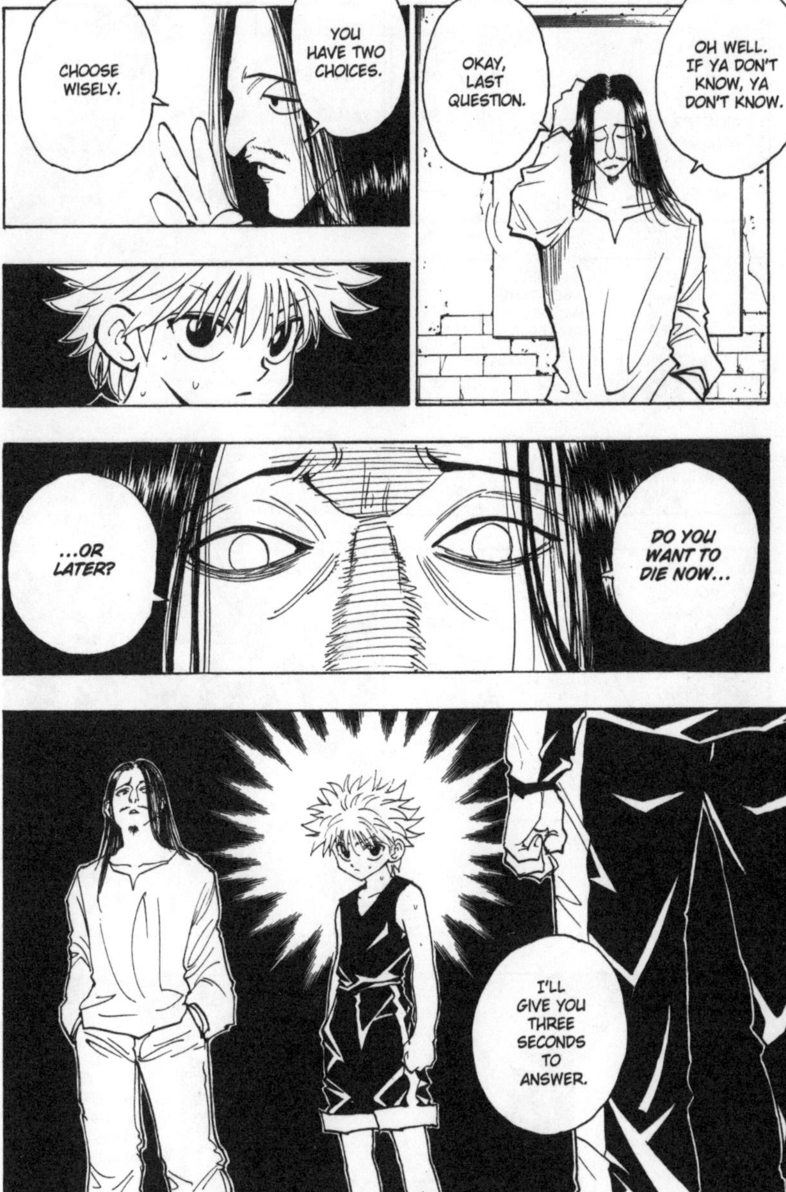
OH WELL. IF YA DON'T KNOW, YA DON'T KNOW.
OKAY, LAST QUESTION.
YOU HAVE TWO CHOICES.
CHOOSE WISELY.
DO YOU WANT TO DIE NOW...
...OR LATER?
I'LL GIVE YOU THREE SECONDS TO ANSWER.

READ THIS WAY

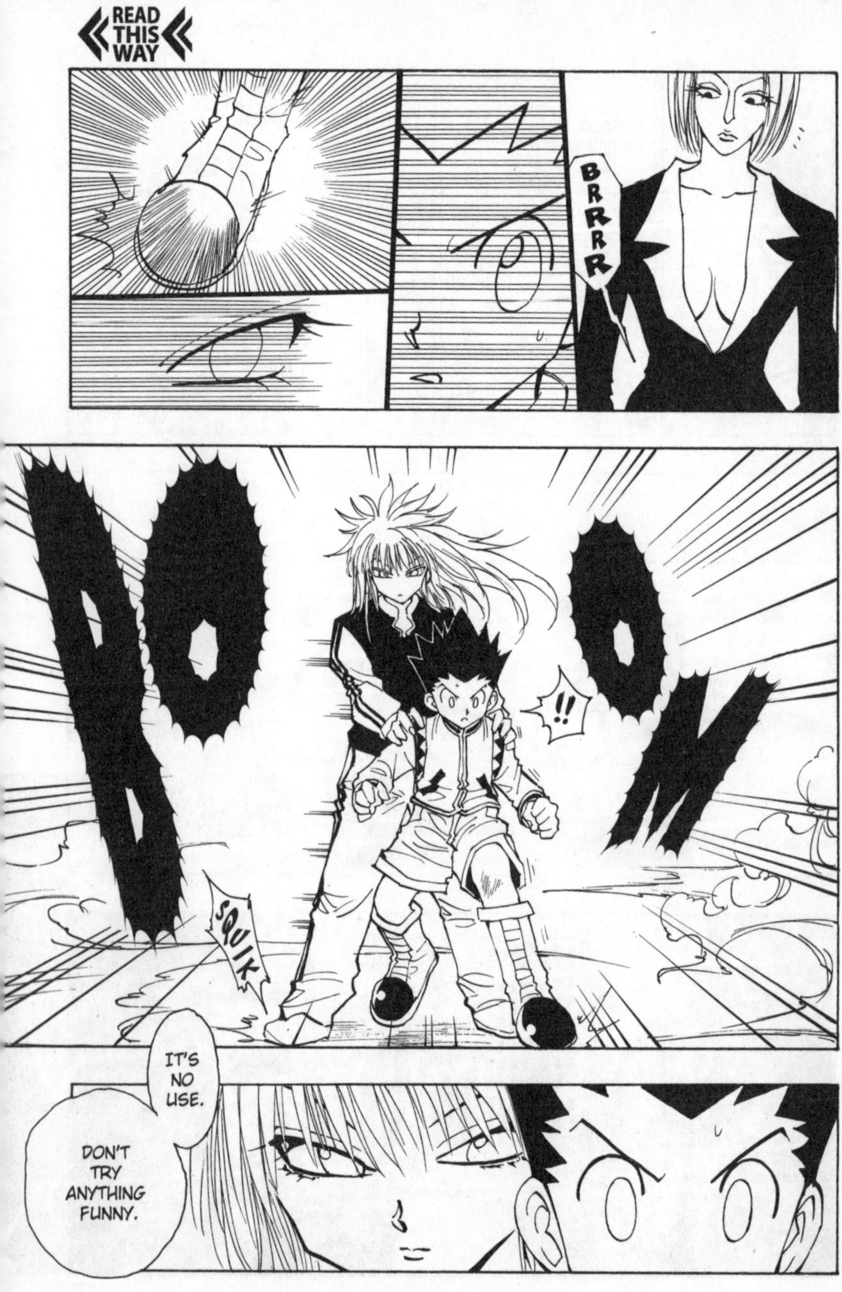

BRRRR
BOOM
!!
SQUIK
IT'S NO USE.
DON'T TRY ANYTHING FUNNY.

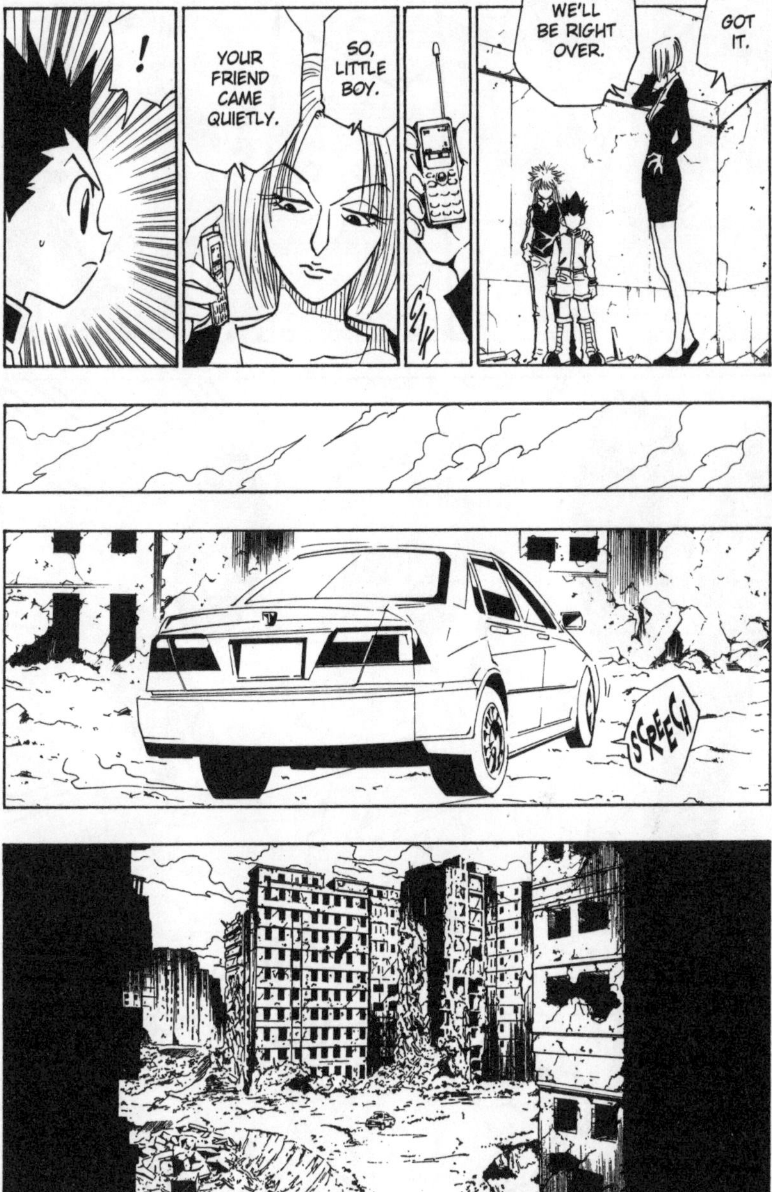
GOT IT.
WE'LL BE RIGHT OVER.
CLIK
SO, LITTLE BOY.
YOUR FRIEND CAME QUIETLY.
!
SCREECH

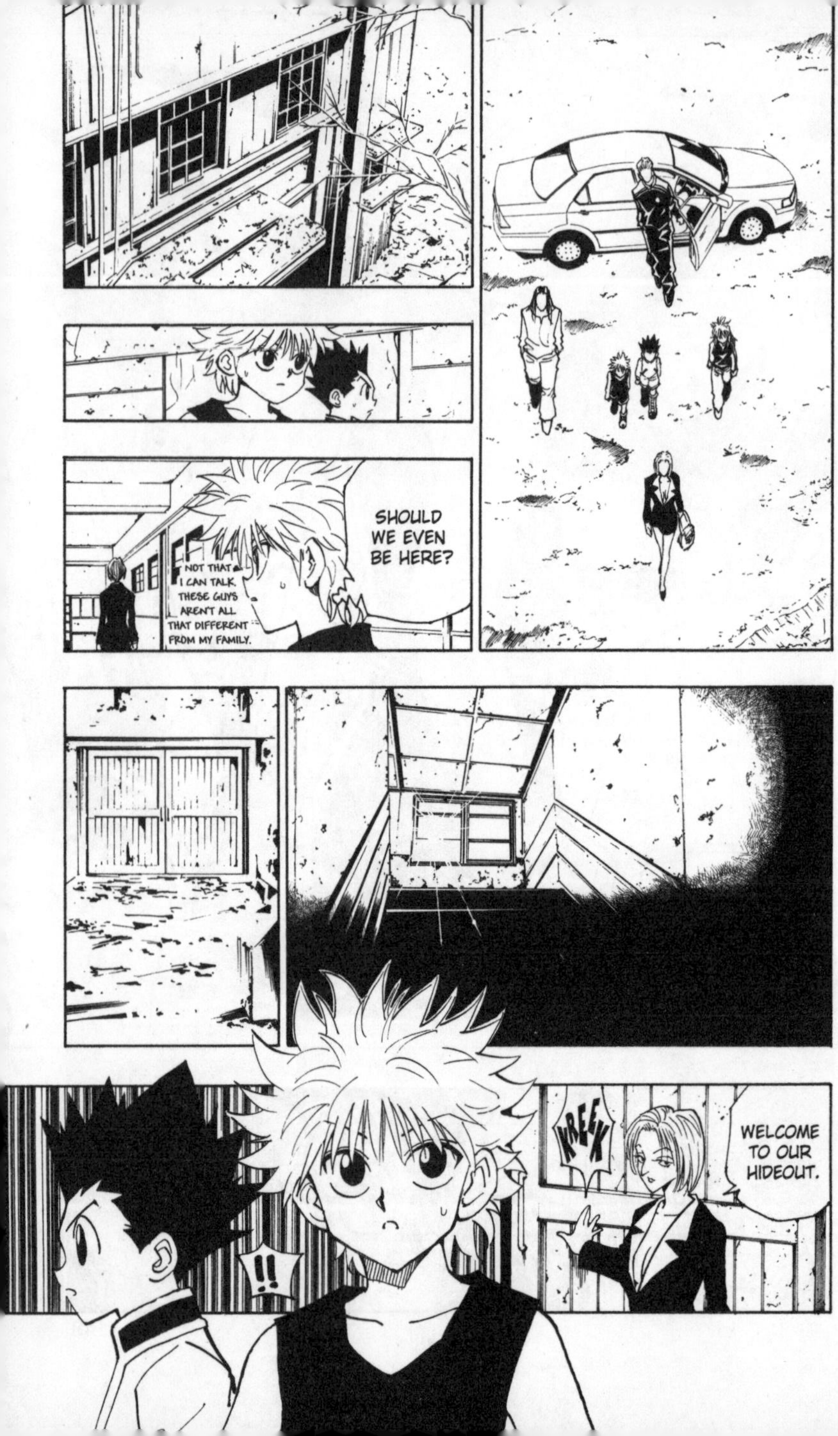
SHOULD WE EVEN BE HERE?
NOT THAT I CAN TALK. THESE GUYS AREN'T ALL THAT DIFFERENT FROM MY FAMILY.
WELCOME TO OUR HIDEOUT.
KREEK
!!

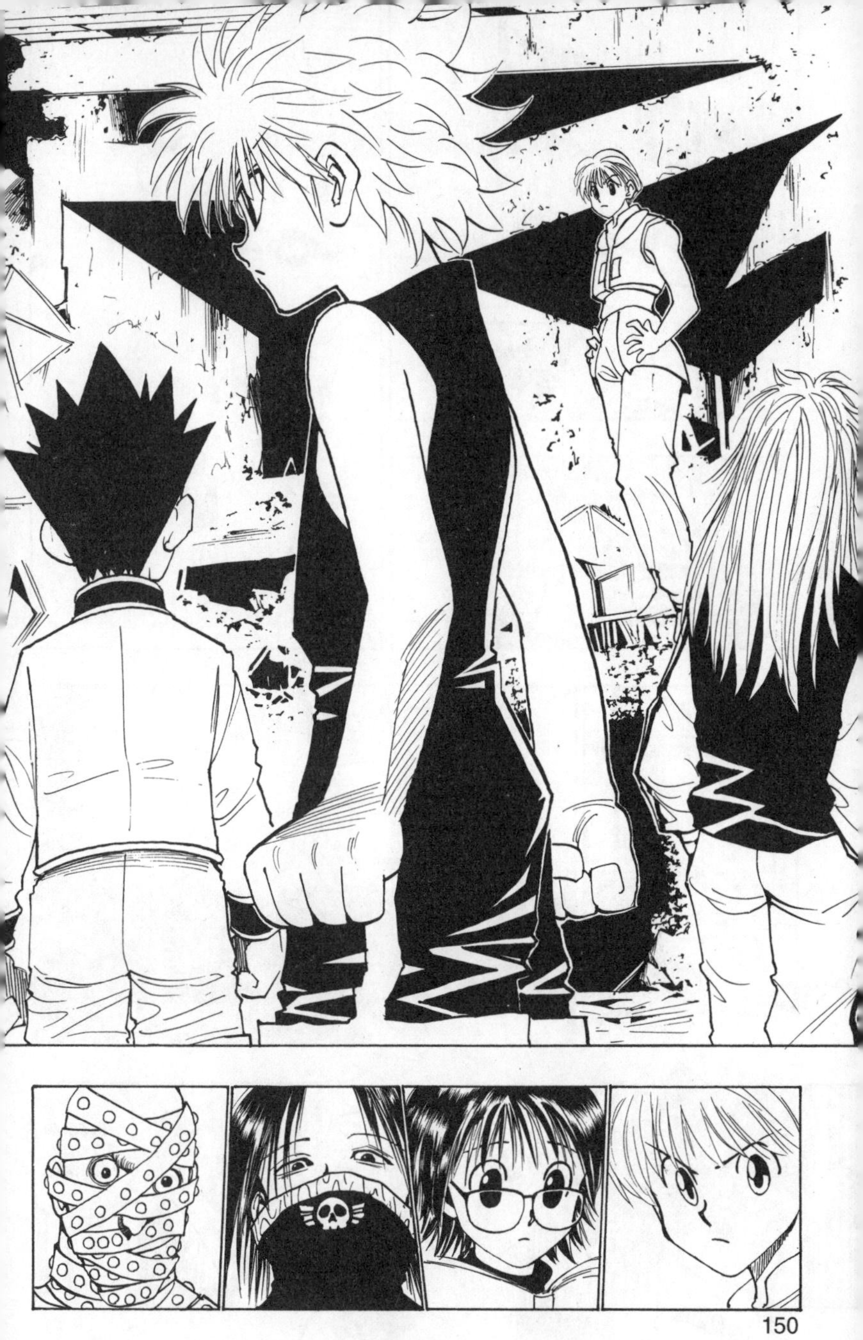

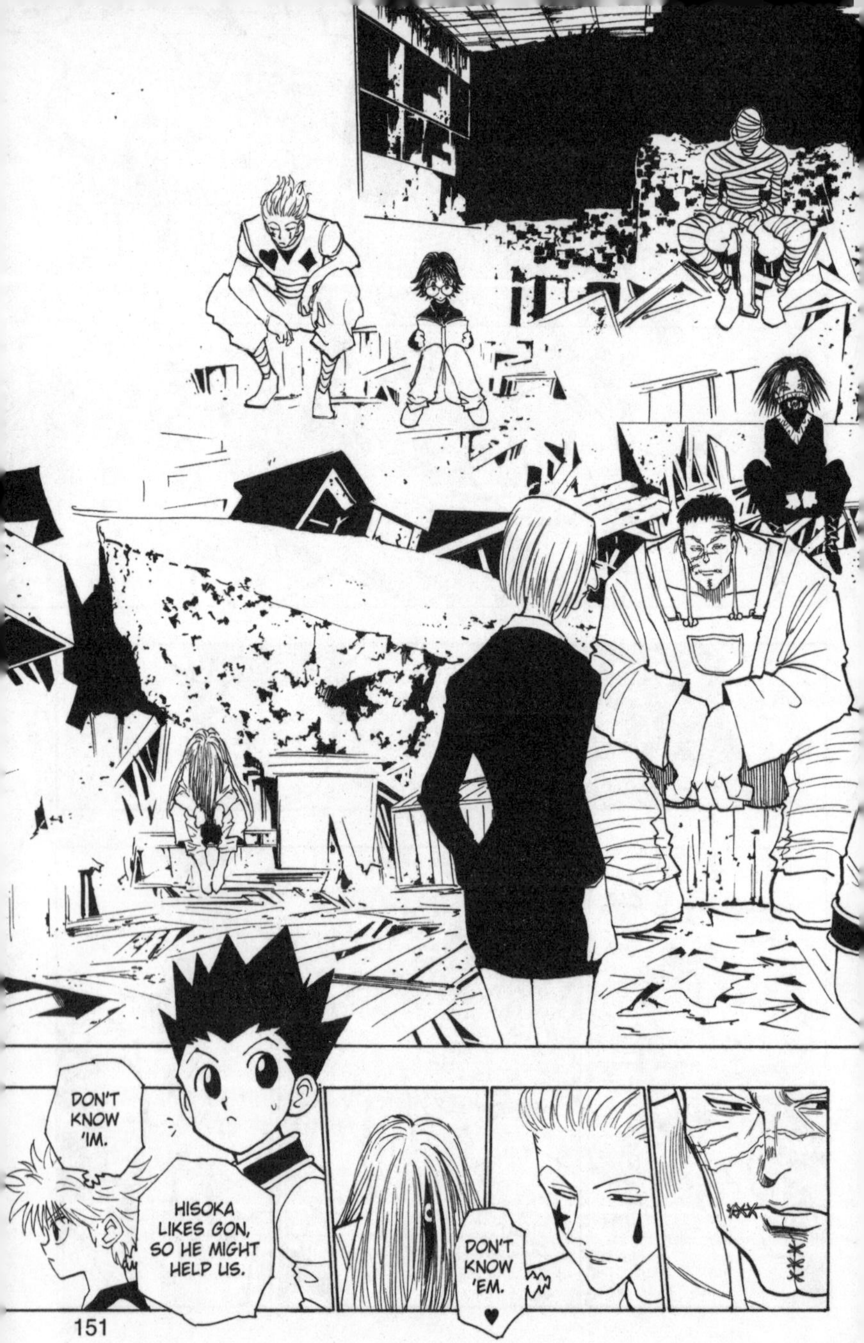
DON'T KNOW 'EM. ♥
DON'T KNOW 'IM.
HISOKA LIKES GON, SO HE MIGHT HELP US.

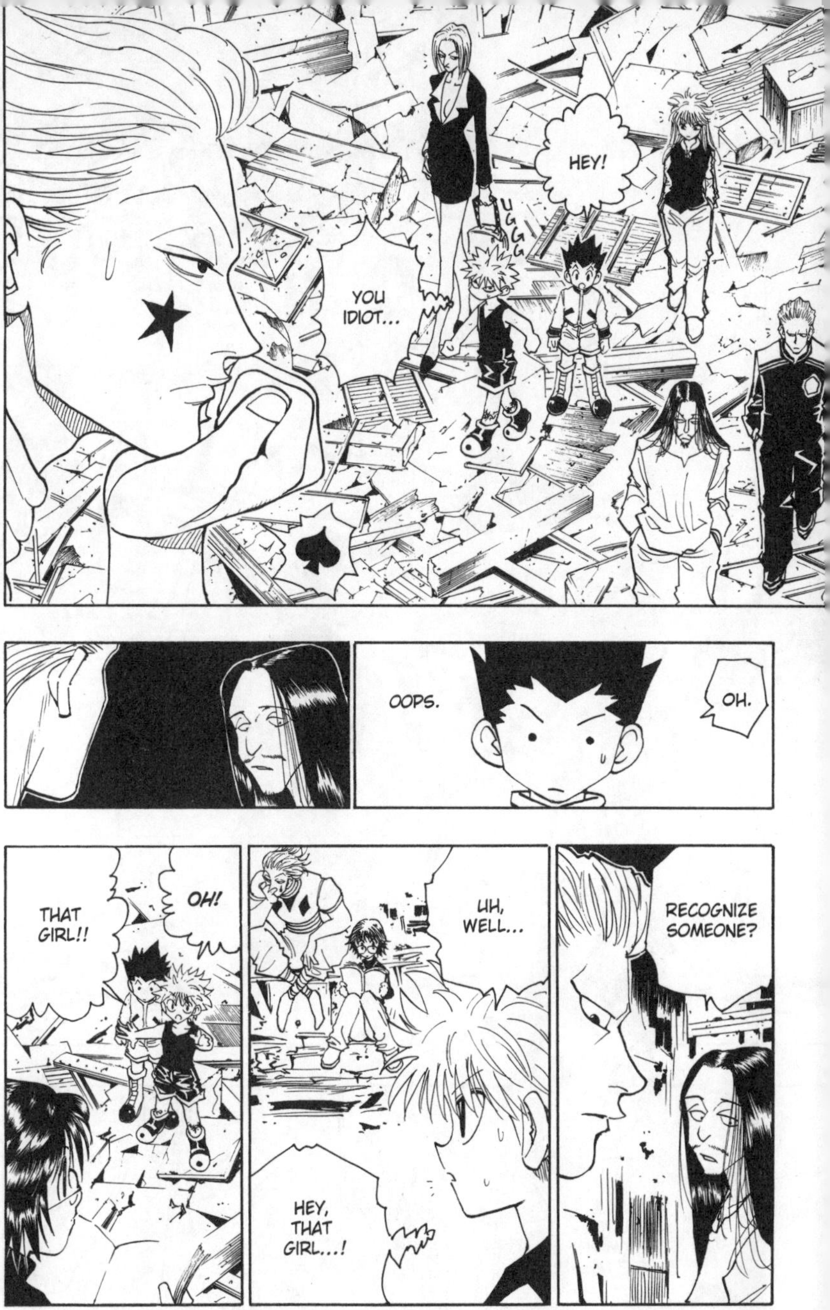
HEY!
UGGG
YOU IDIOT...
OH.
OOPS.
RECOGNIZE SOMEONE?
UH, WELL...
HEY, THAT GIRL...!
OH!
THAT GIRL!!

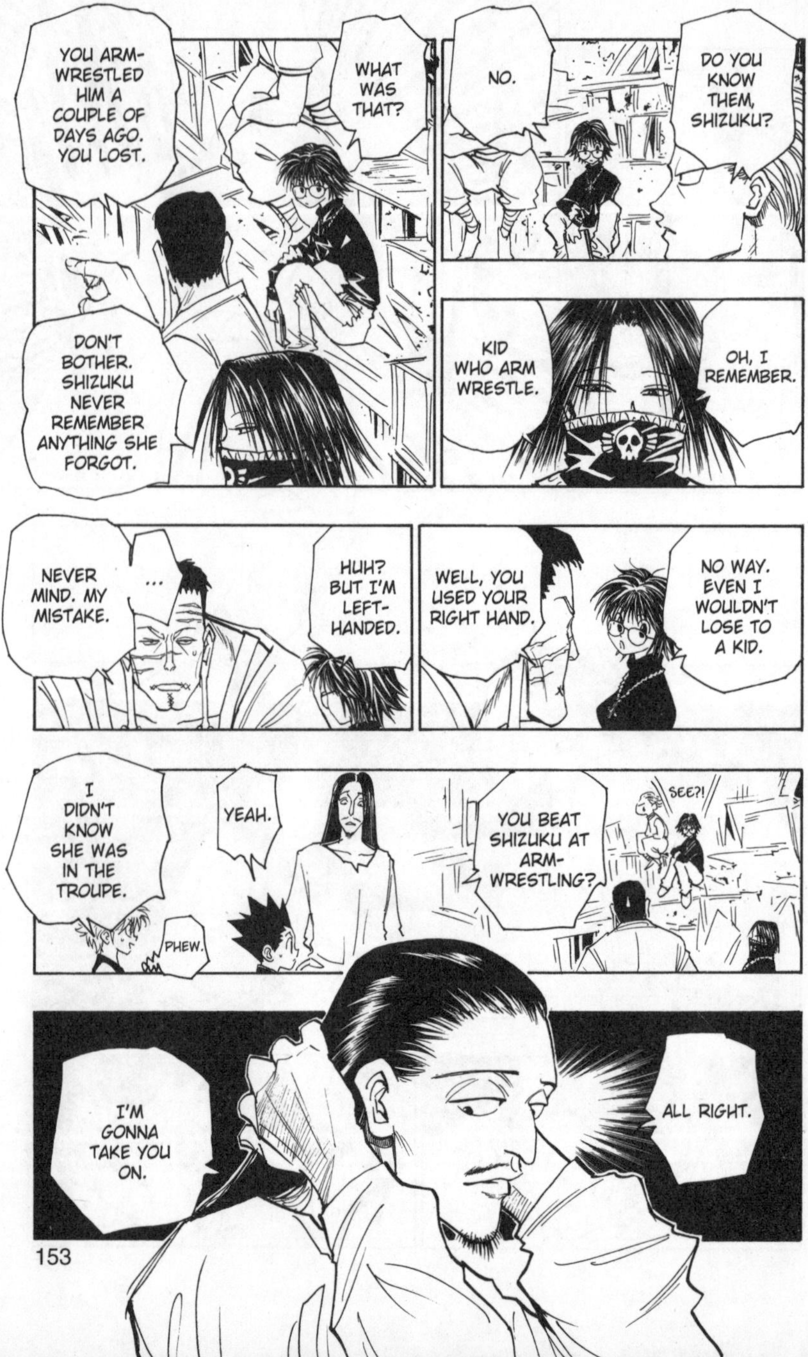

DO YOU KNOW THEM, SHIZUKU?
NO.
OH, I REMEMBER.
KID WHO ARM WRESTLE.
WHAT WAS THAT?
YOU ARM-WRESTLED HIM A COUPLE OF DAYS AGO. YOU LOST.
DON'T BOTHER. SHIZUKU NEVER REMEMBER ANYTHING SHE FORGOT.
NO WAY. EVEN I WOULDN'T LOSE TO A KID.
WELL, YOU USED YOUR RIGHT HAND.
HUH? BUT I'M LEFT-HANDED.
...
NEVER MIND. MY MISTAKE.
SEE?!
YOU BEAT SHIZUKU AT ARM-WRESTLING?
YEAH.
I DIDN'T KNOW SHE WAS IN THE TROUPE.
PHEW.
ALL RIGHT.
I'M GONNA TAKE YOU ON.

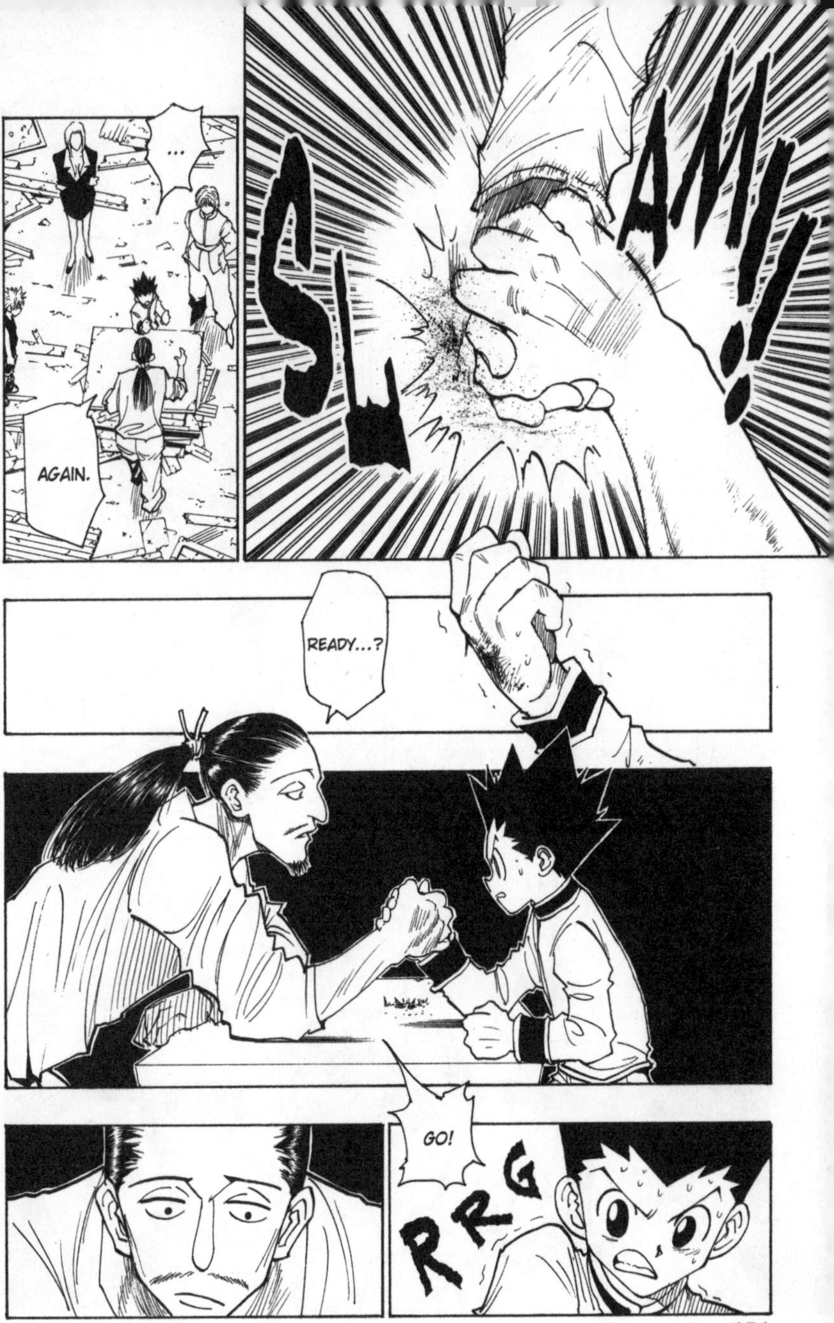
SLAM!!
...
AGAIN.
READY...?
GO!
RRG

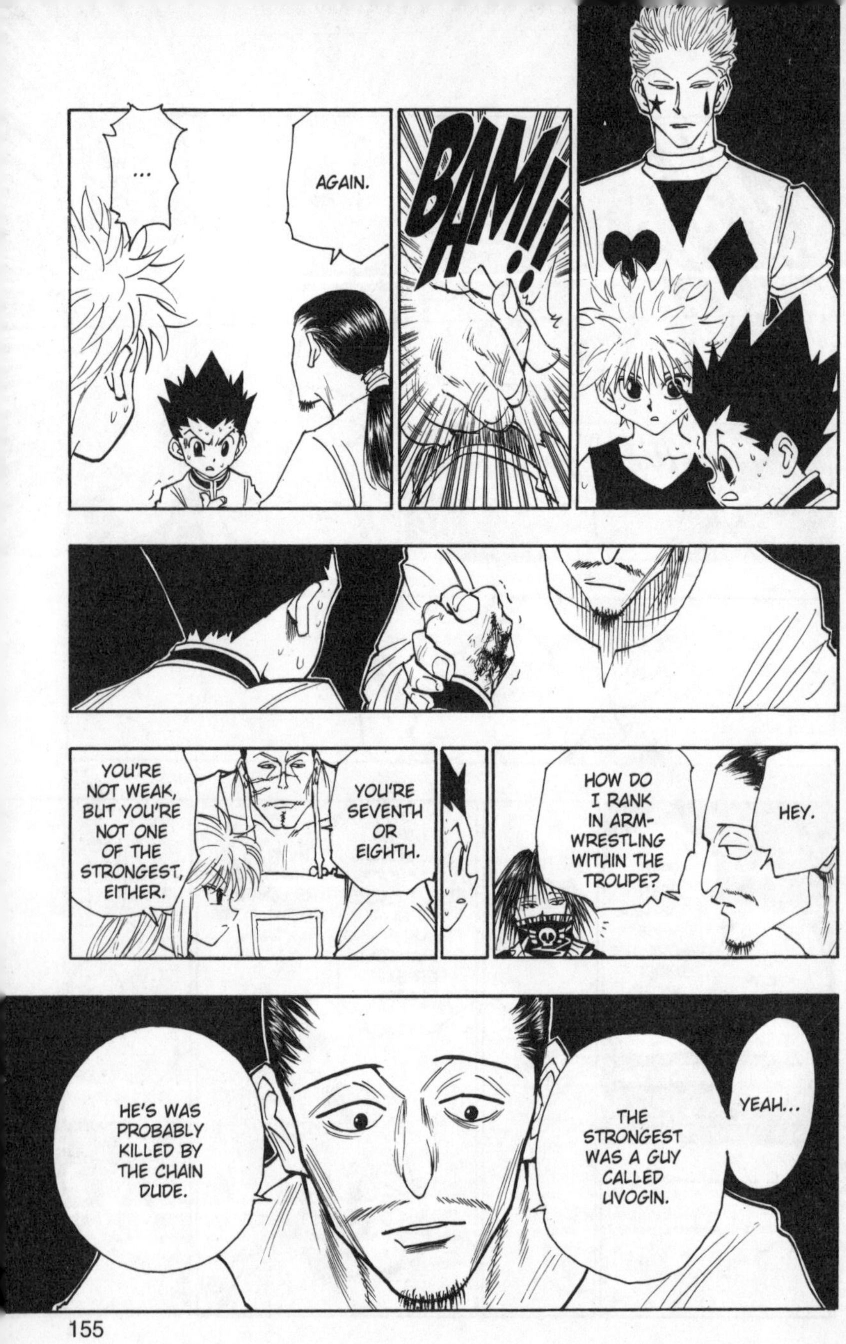
BAM!!
AGAIN.
...
HEY.
HOW DO I RANK IN ARM-WRESTLING WITHIN THE TROUPE?
YOU'RE SEVENTH OR EIGHTH.
YOU'RE NOT WEAK, BUT YOU'RE NOT ONE OF THE STRONGEST, EITHER.
YEAH...
THE STRONGEST WAS A GUY CALLED UVOGIN.
HE'S WAS PROBABLY KILLED BY THE CHAIN DUDE.

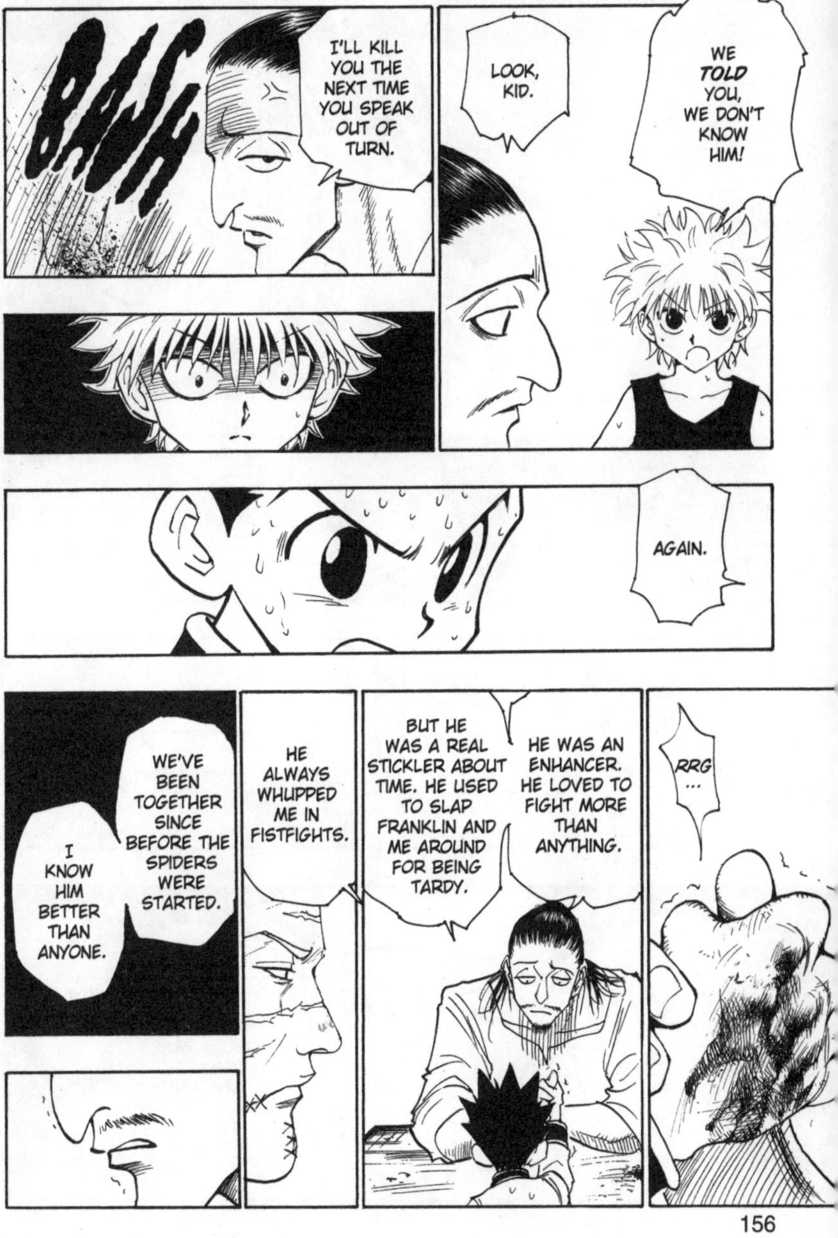
WE *TOLD* YOU, WE DON'T KNOW HIM!
LOOK, KID.
BAM
I'LL KILL YOU THE NEXT TIME YOU SPEAK OUT OF TURN.
AGAIN.
RRG ...
HE WAS AN ENHANCER. HE LOVED TO FIGHT MORE THAN ANYTHING.
BUT HE WAS A REAL STICKLER ABOUT TIME. HE USED TO SLAP FRANKLIN AND ME AROUND FOR BEING TARDY.
HE ALWAYS WHUPPED ME IN FISTFIGHTS.
WE'VE BEEN TOGETHER SINCE BEFORE THE SPIDERS WERE STARTED.
I KNOW HIM BETTER THAN ANYONE.

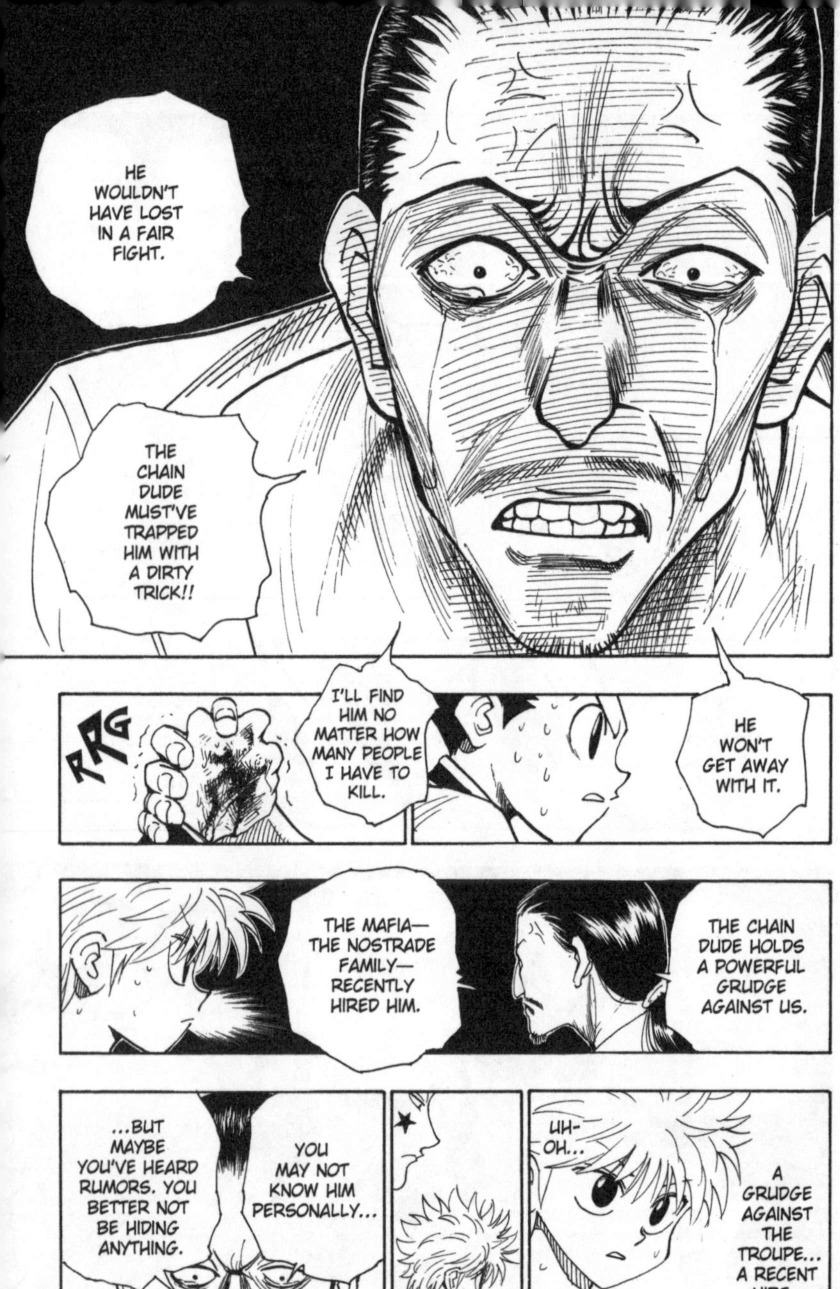
HE WOULDN'T HAVE LOST IN A FAIR FIGHT.
THE CHAIN DUDE MUST'VE TRAPPED HIM WITH A DIRTY TRICK!!
HE WON'T GET AWAY WITH IT.
I'LL FIND HIM NO MATTER HOW MANY PEOPLE I HAVE TO KILL.
RRG
THE CHAIN DUDE HOLDS A POWERFUL GRUDGE AGAINST US.
THE MAFIA— THE NOSTRADE FAMILY— RECENTLY HIRED HIM.
A GRUDGE AGAINST THE TROUPE... A RECENT HIRE...
UH-OH...
YOU MAY NOT KNOW HIM PERSONALLY...
...BUT MAYBE YOU'VE HEARD RUMORS. YOU BETTER NOT BE HIDING ANYTHING.

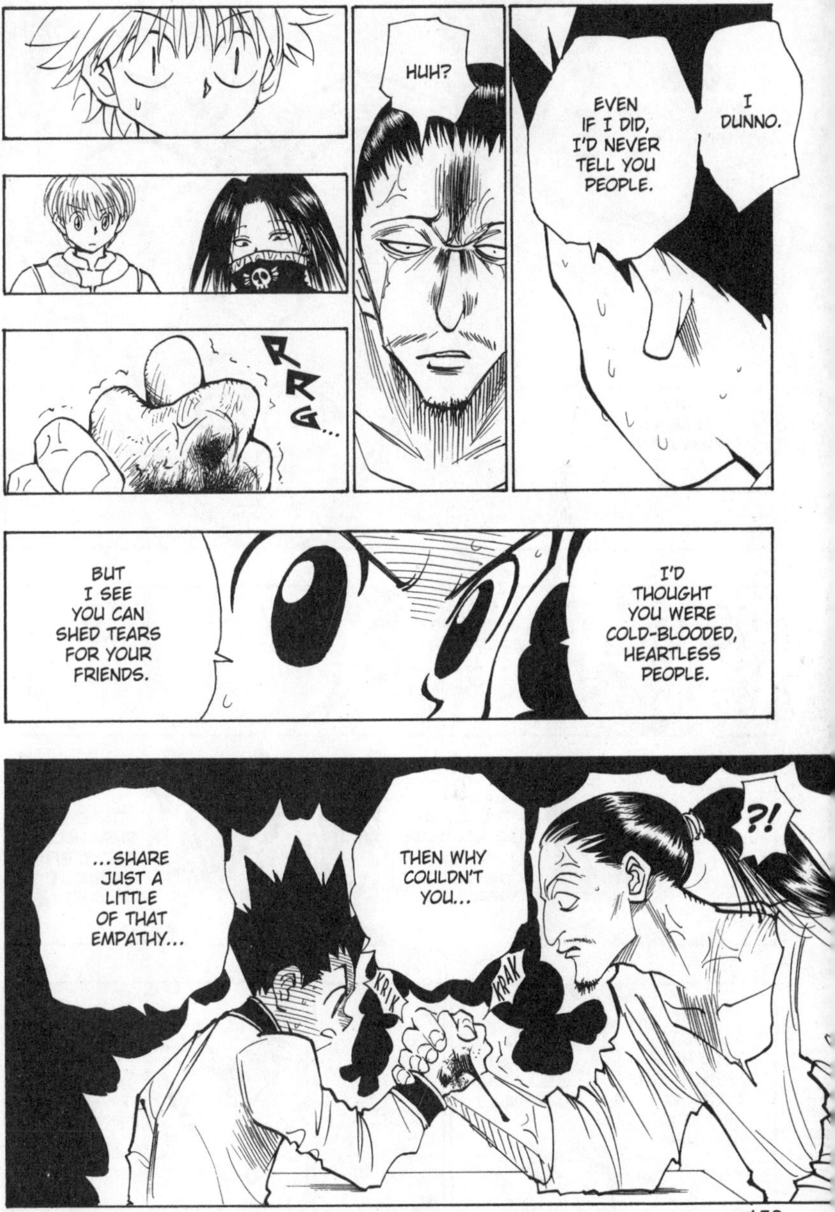
I DUNNO.
EVEN IF I DID, I'D NEVER TELL YOU PEOPLE.
HUH?
RRG...
I'D THOUGHT YOU WERE COLD-BLOODED, HEARTLESS PEOPLE.
BUT I SEE YOU CAN SHED TEARS FOR YOUR FRIENDS.
?!
THEN WHY COULDN'T YOU...
KRAK
KRIK
...SHARE JUST A LITTLE OF THAT EMPATHY...

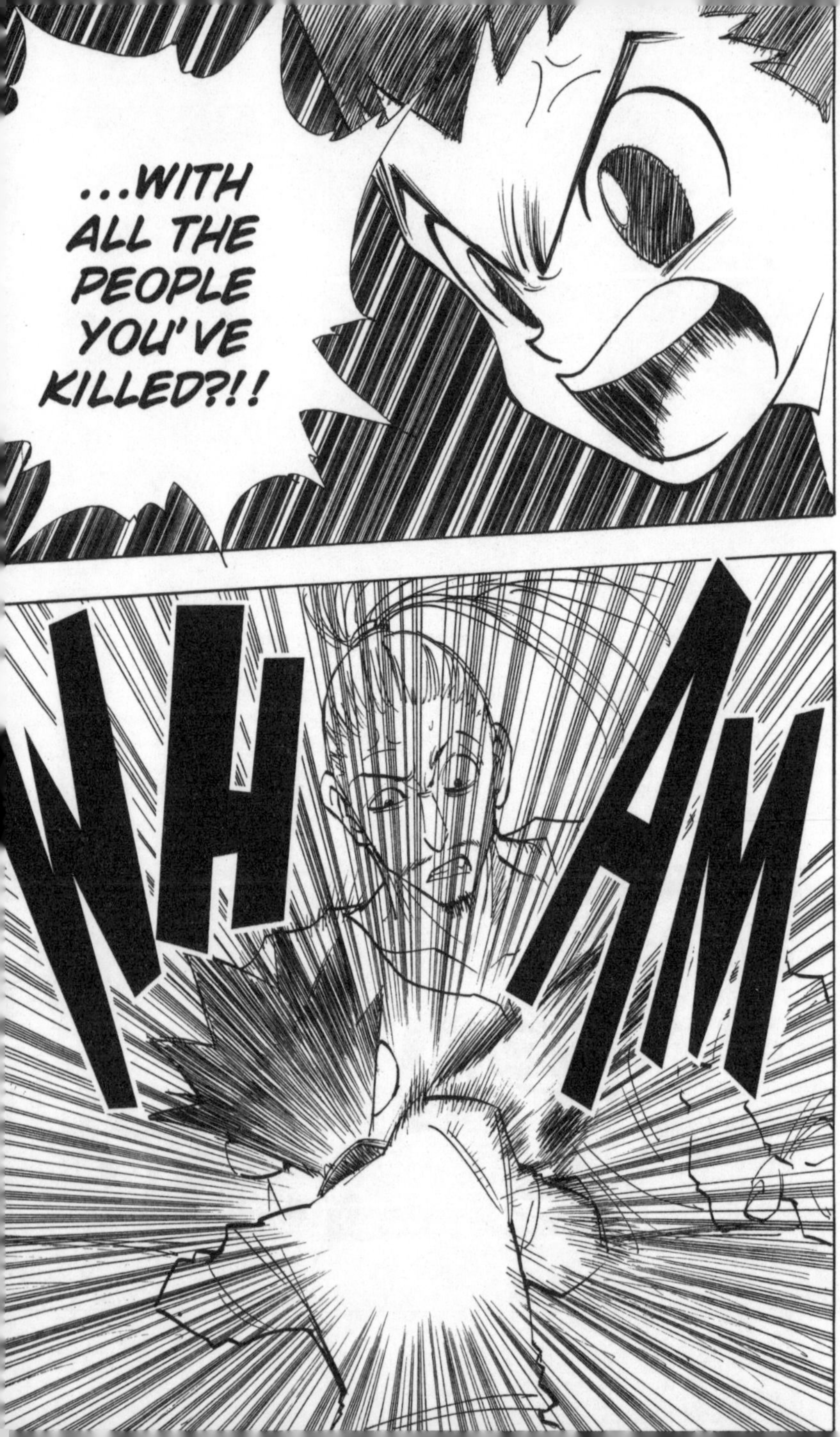
...WITH ALL THE PEOPLE YOU'VE KILLED?!!
WHAM

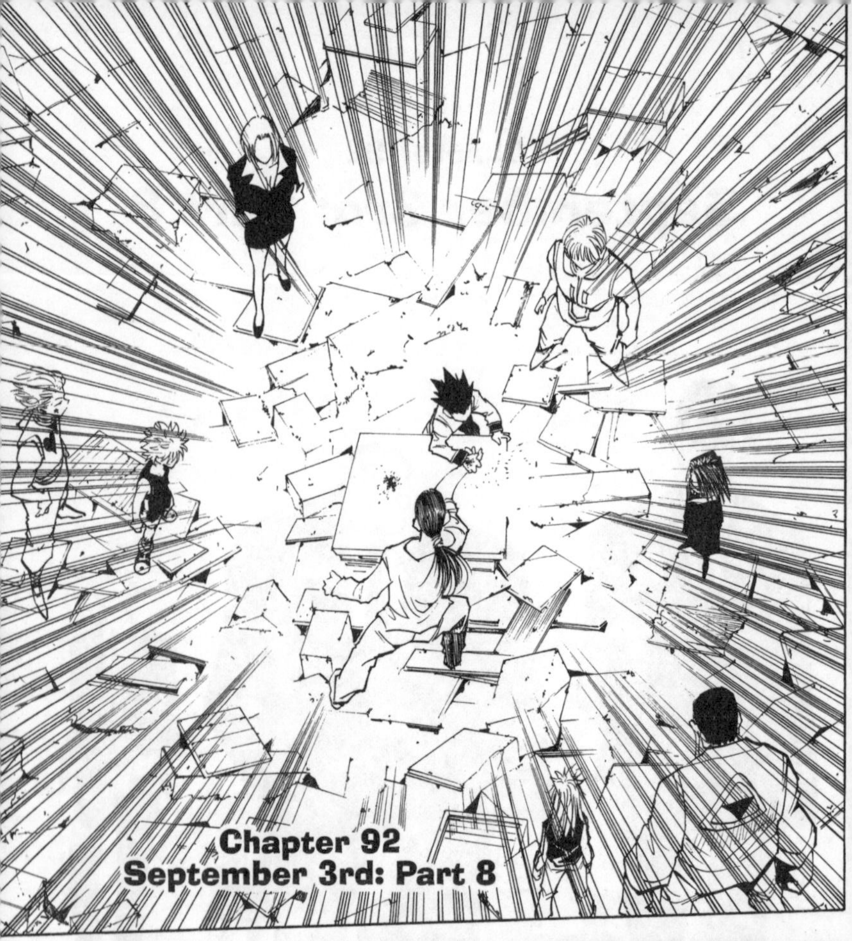
Chapter 92
September 3rd: Part 8
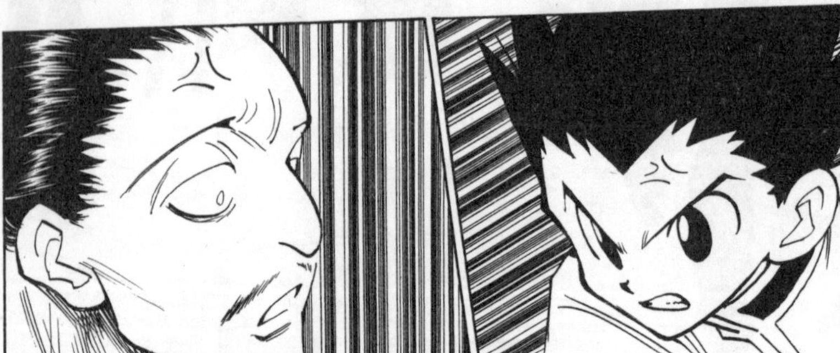

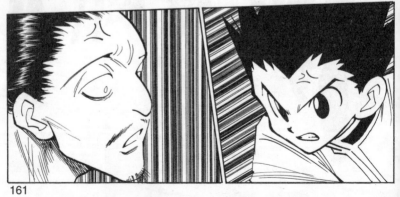

Chapter 92

September 3rd: Part 8

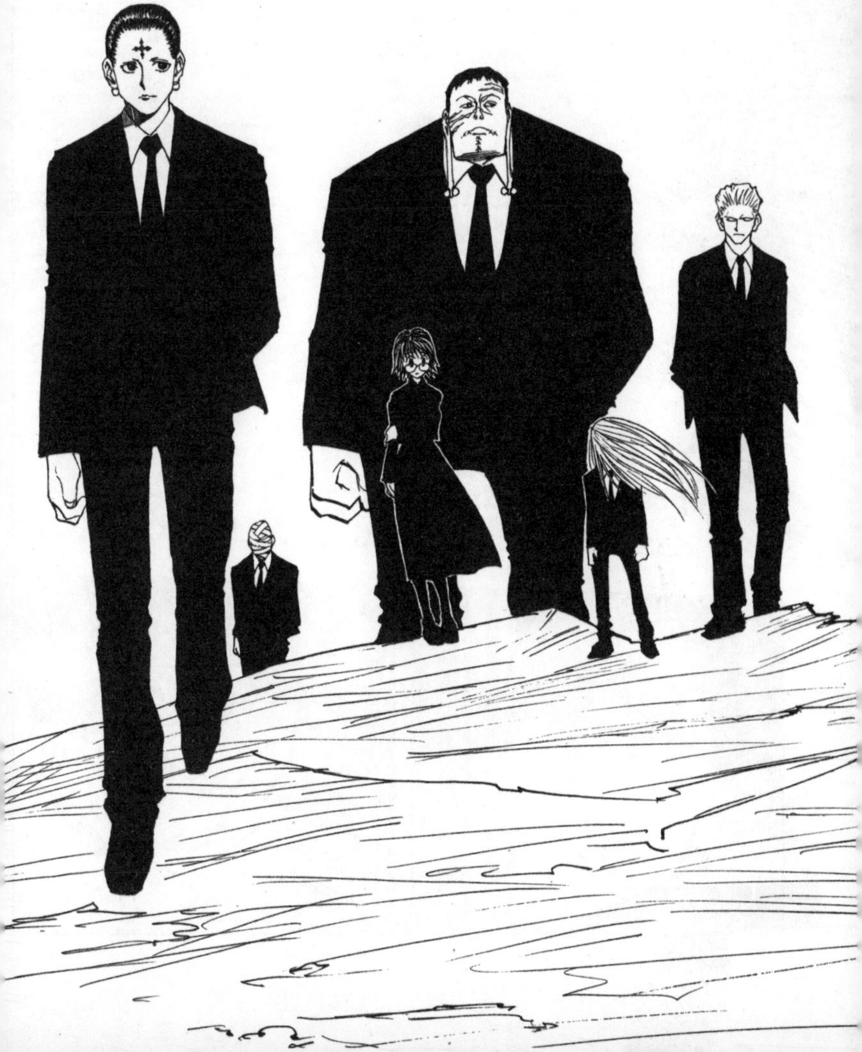

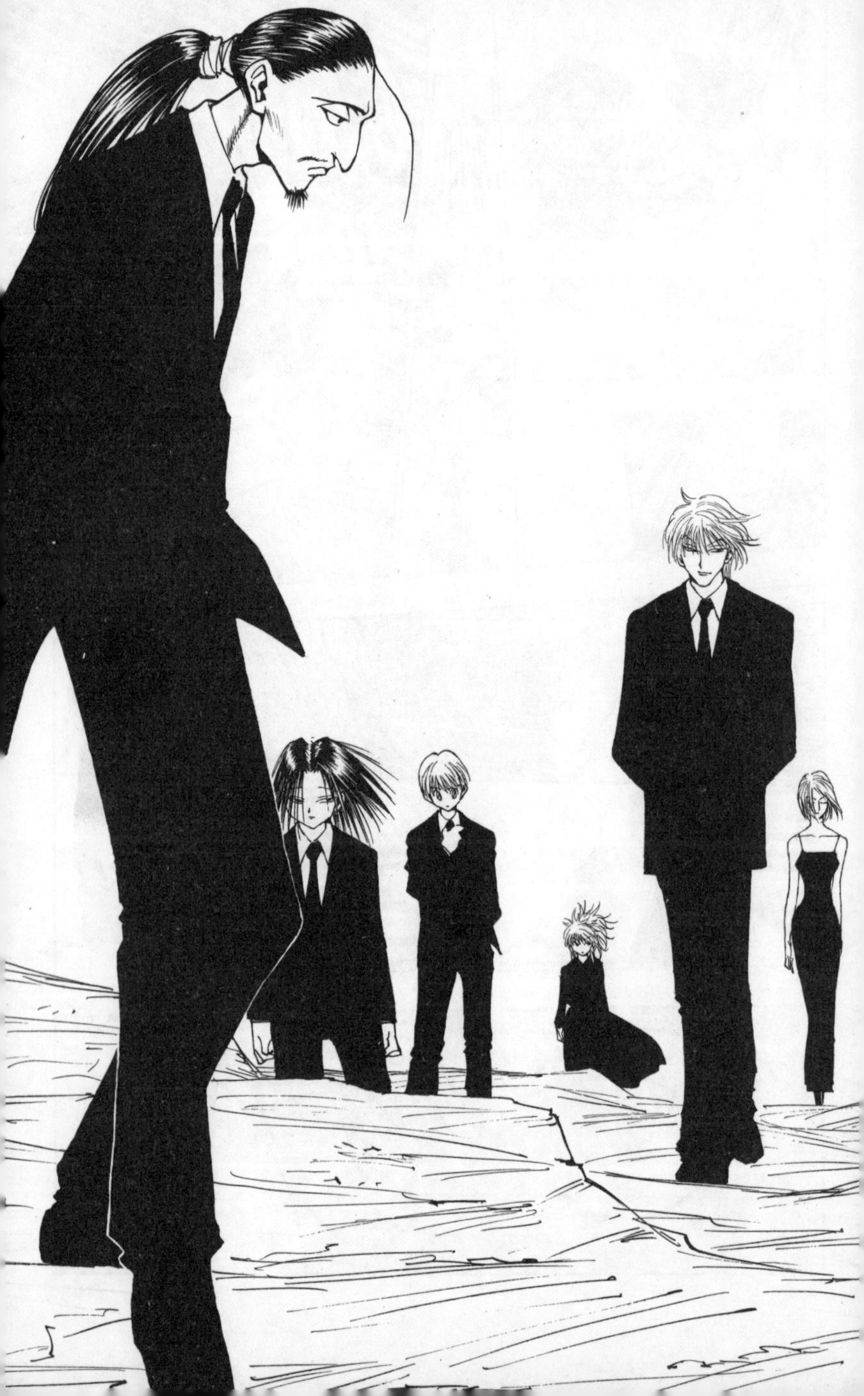

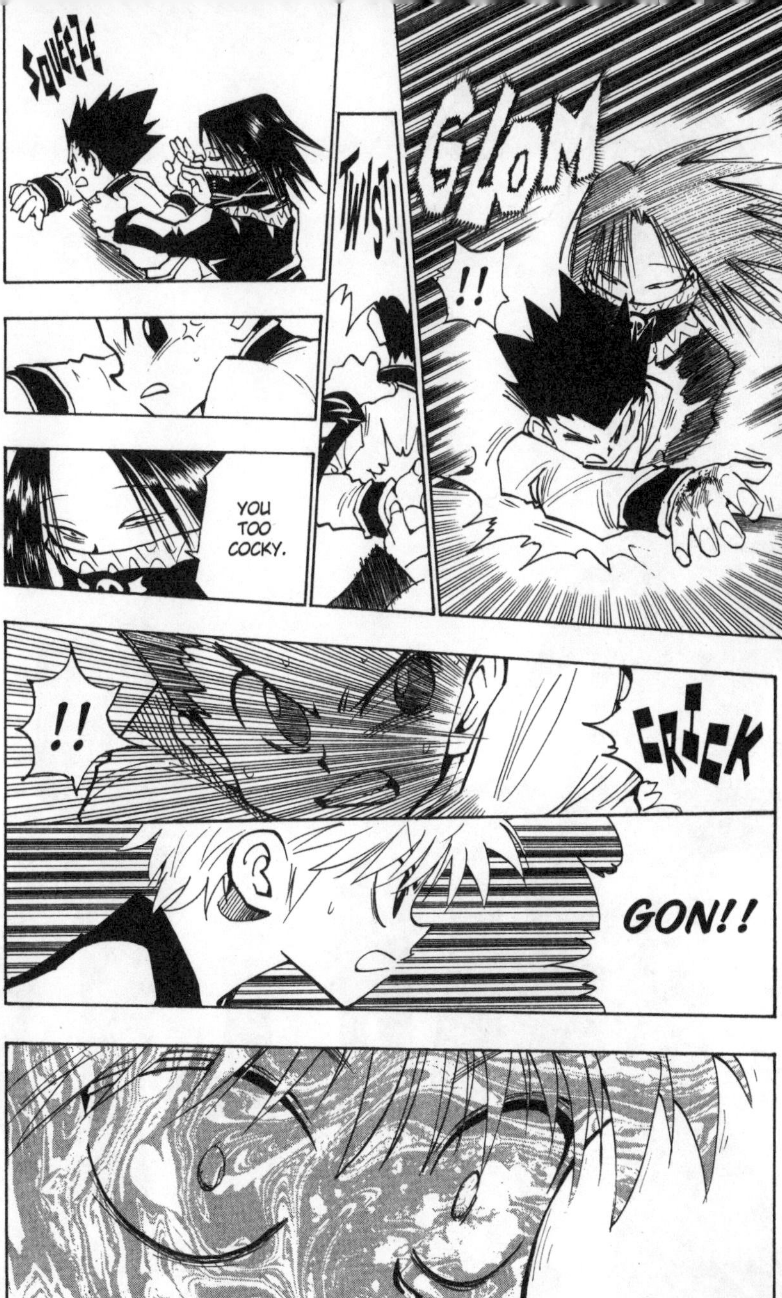
GLOM
!!
TWIST!!
SQUEEZE
YOU TOO COCKY.
CRACK
!!
GON!!

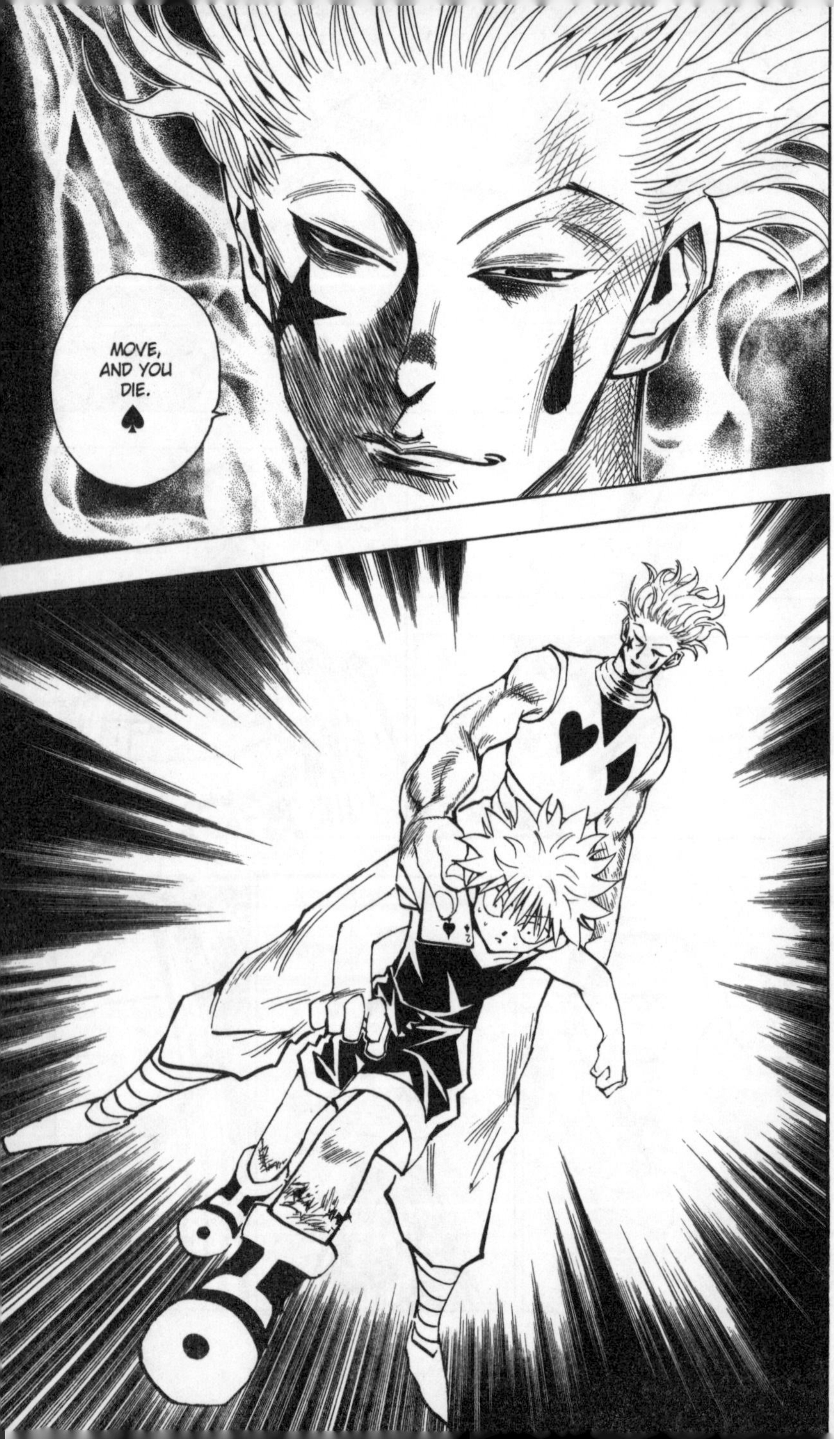
MOVE, AND YOU DIE. ♠

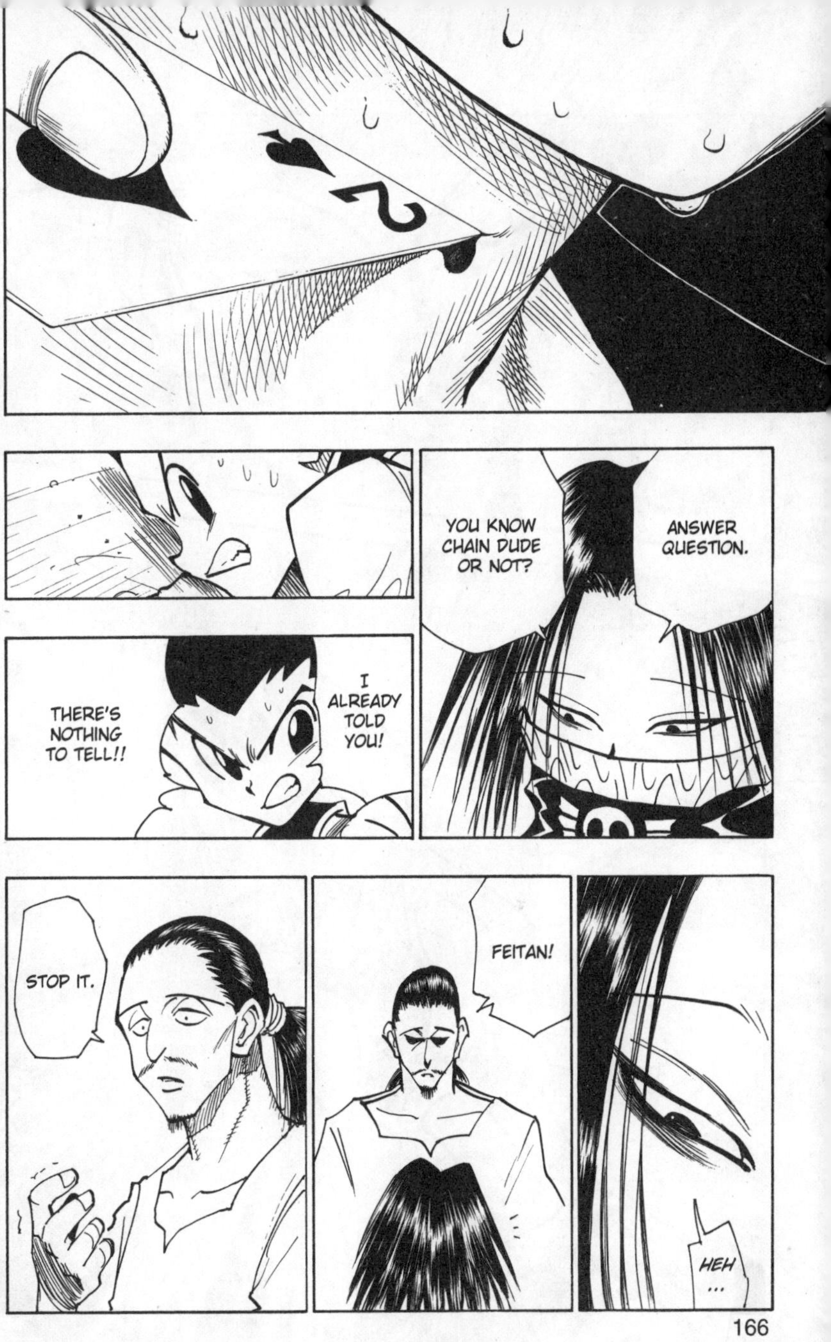
ANSWER QUESTION.
YOU KNOW CHAIN DUDE OR NOT?
I ALREADY TOLD YOU!
THERE'S NOTHING TO TELL!!
HEH ...
FEITAN!
STOP IT.

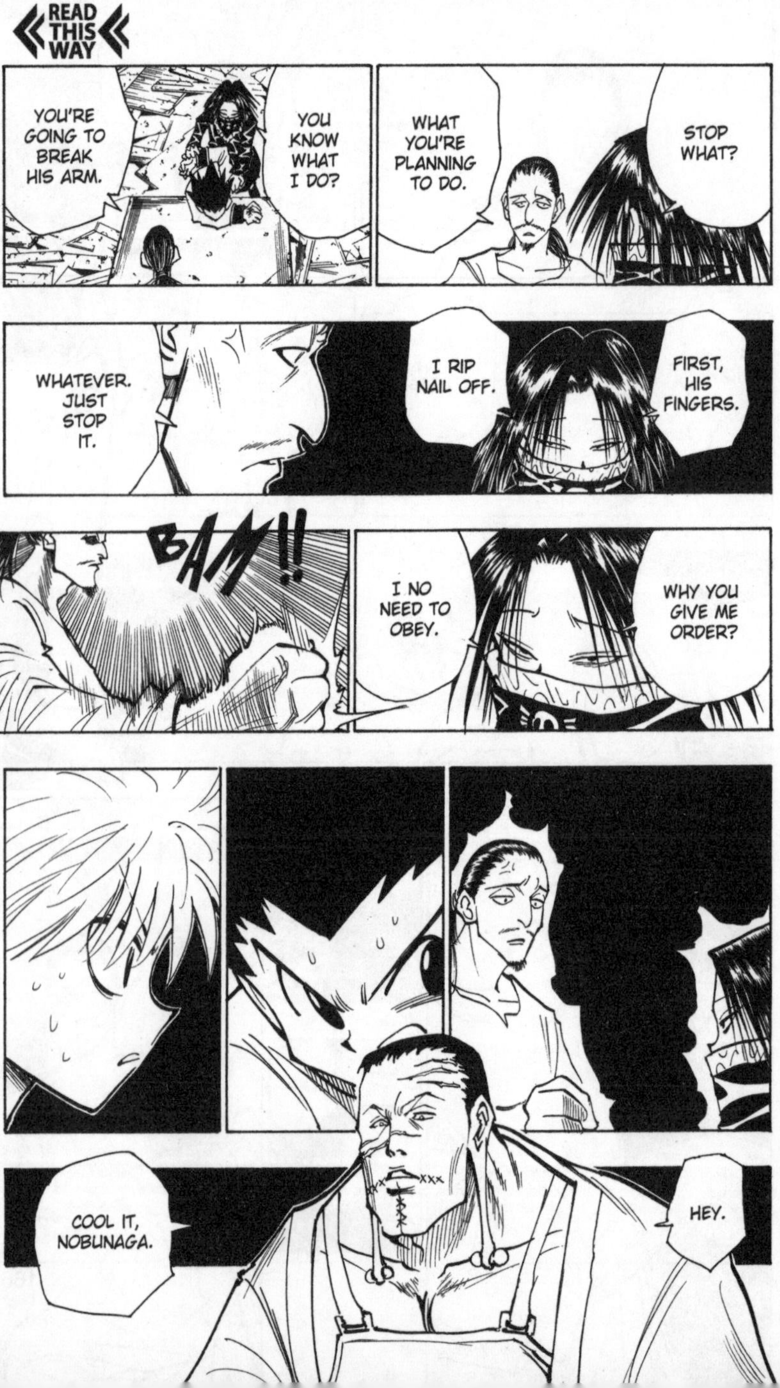
READ THIS WAY
STOP WHAT?
WHAT YOU'RE PLANNING TO DO.
YOU KNOW WHAT I DO?
YOU'RE GOING TO BREAK HIS ARM.
FIRST, HIS FINGERS.
I RIP NAIL OFF.
WHATEVER. JUST STOP IT.
WHY YOU GIVE ME ORDER?
I NO NEED TO OBEY.
BAM!!
HEY.
COOL IT, NOBUNAGA.

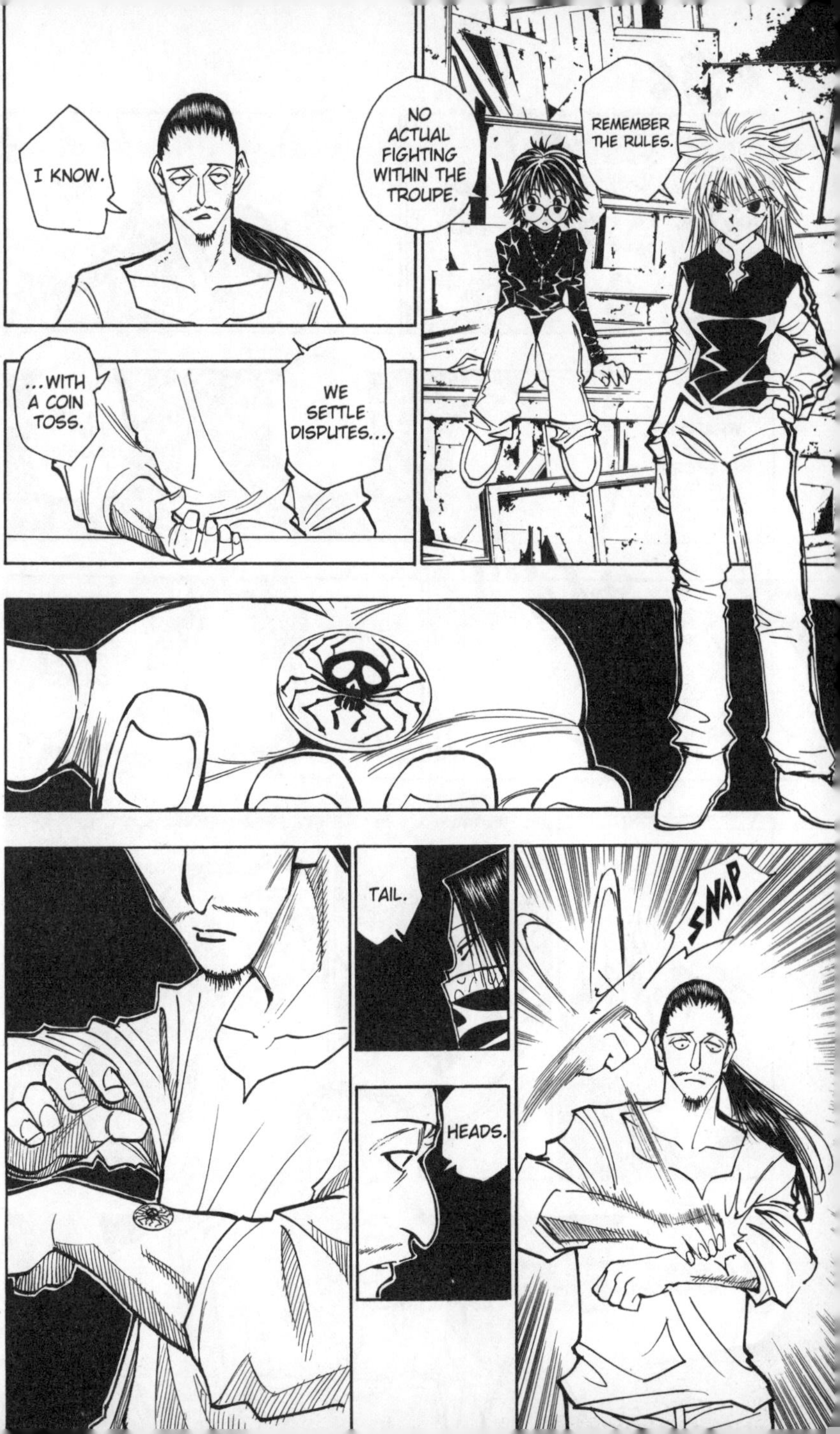
REMEMBER THE RULES.
NO ACTUAL FIGHTING WITHIN THE TROUPE.
I KNOW.
WE SETTLE DISPUTES...
...WITH A COIN TOSS.
SNAP
TAIL.
HEADS.

READ THIS WAY

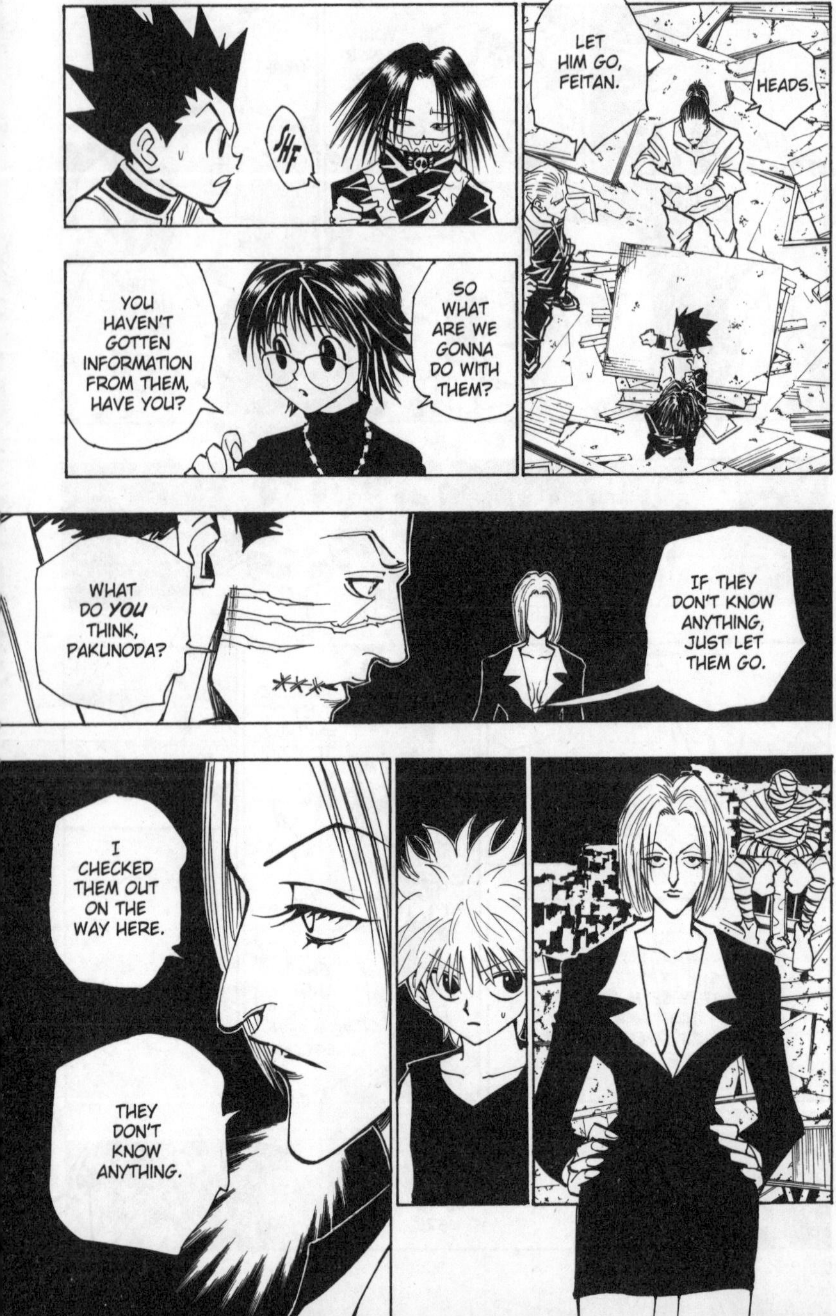
HEADS.
LET HIM GO, FEITAN.
SHF
SO WHAT ARE WE GONNA DO WITH THEM?
YOU HAVEN'T GOTTEN INFORMATION FROM THEM, HAVE YOU?
WHAT DO *YOU* THINK, PAKUNODA?
IF THEY DON'T KNOW ANYTHING, JUST LET THEM GO.
I CHECKED THEM OUT ON THE WAY HERE.
THEY DON'T KNOW ANYTHING.

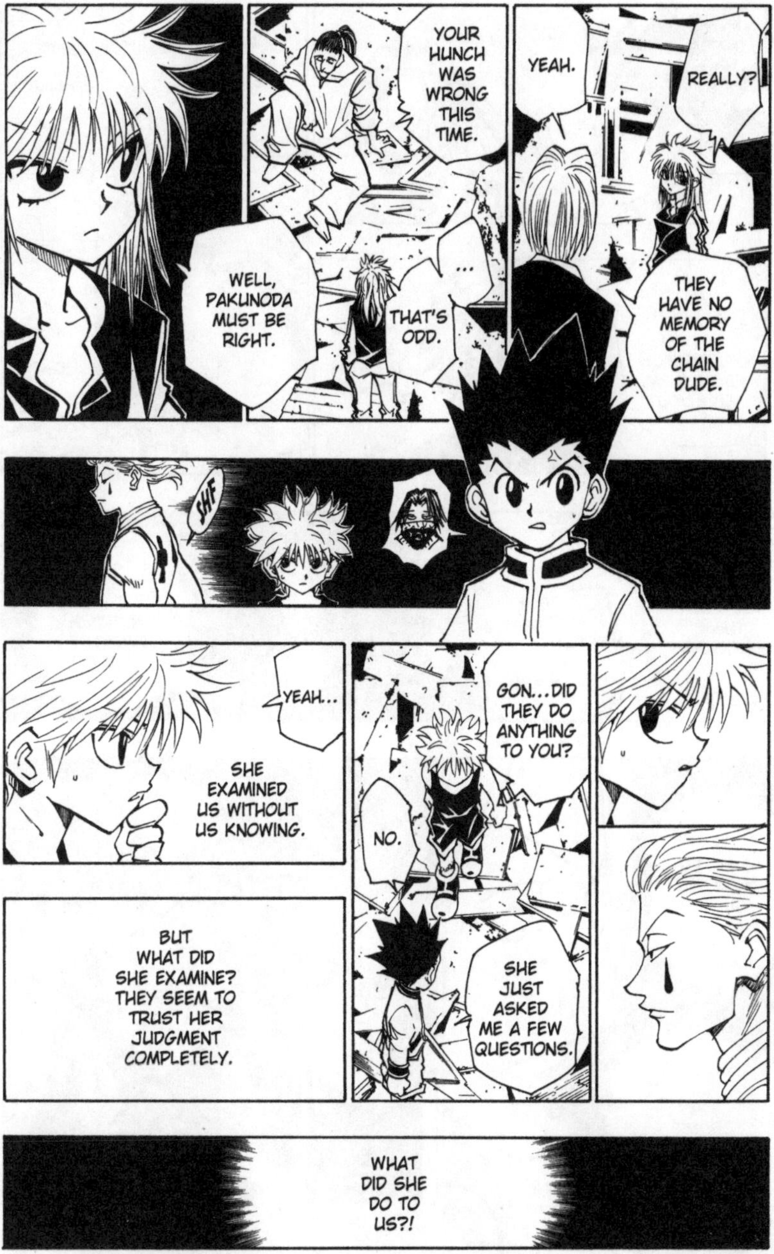
REALLY?
YEAH.
THEY HAVE NO MEMORY OF THE CHAIN DUDE.
YOUR HUNCH WAS WRONG THIS TIME.
...
THAT'S ODD.
WELL, PAKUNODA MUST BE RIGHT.
SHF
GON...DID THEY DO ANYTHING TO YOU?
NO.
SHE JUST ASKED ME A FEW QUESTIONS.
YEAH...
SHE EXAMINED US WITHOUT US KNOWING.
BUT WHAT DID SHE EXAMINE? THEY SEEM TO TRUST HER JUDGMENT COMPLETELY.
WHAT DID SHE DO TO US?!

READ THIS WAY

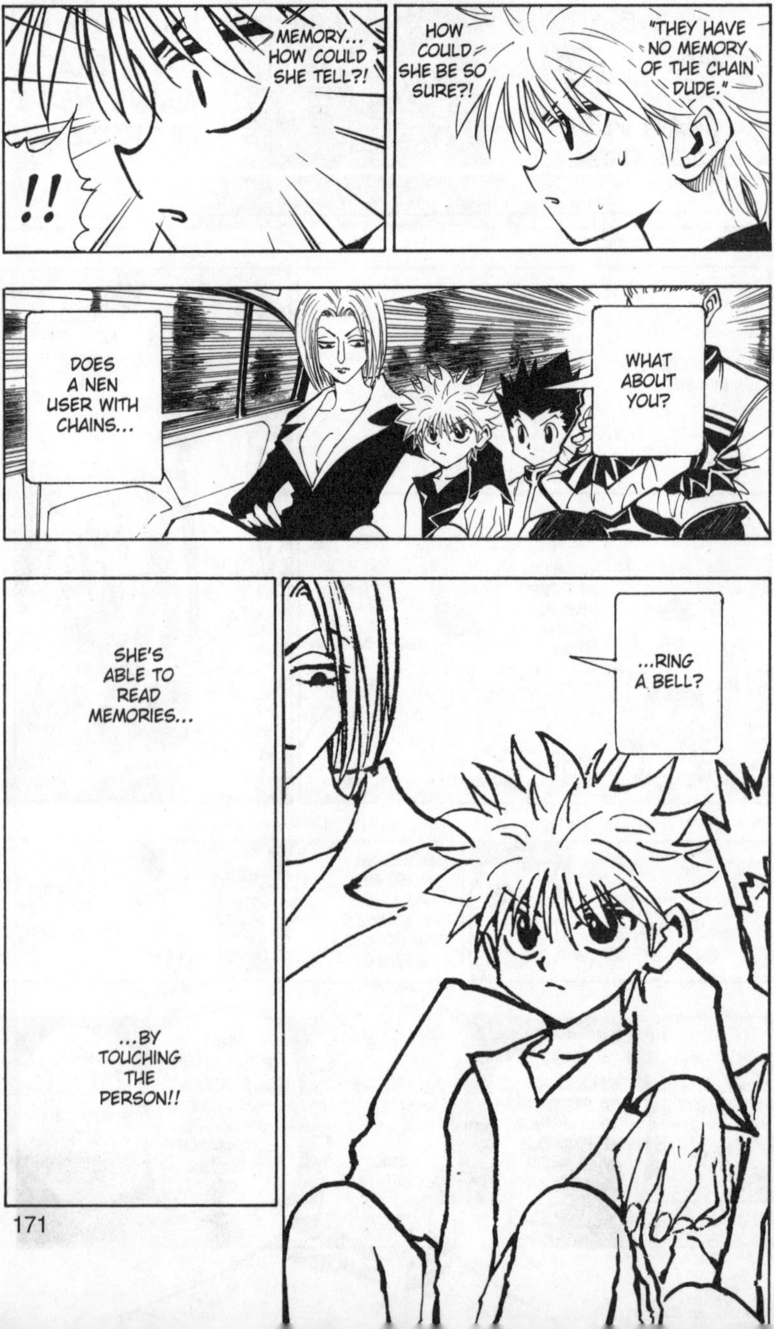

"THEY HAVE NO MEMORY OF THE CHAIN DUDE."
HOW COULD SHE BE SO SURE?!
MEMORY... HOW COULD SHE TELL?!
!!
WHAT ABOUT YOU?
DOES A NEN USER WITH CHAINS...
...RING A BELL?
SHE'S ABLE TO READ MEMORIES...
...BY TOUCHING THE PERSON!!

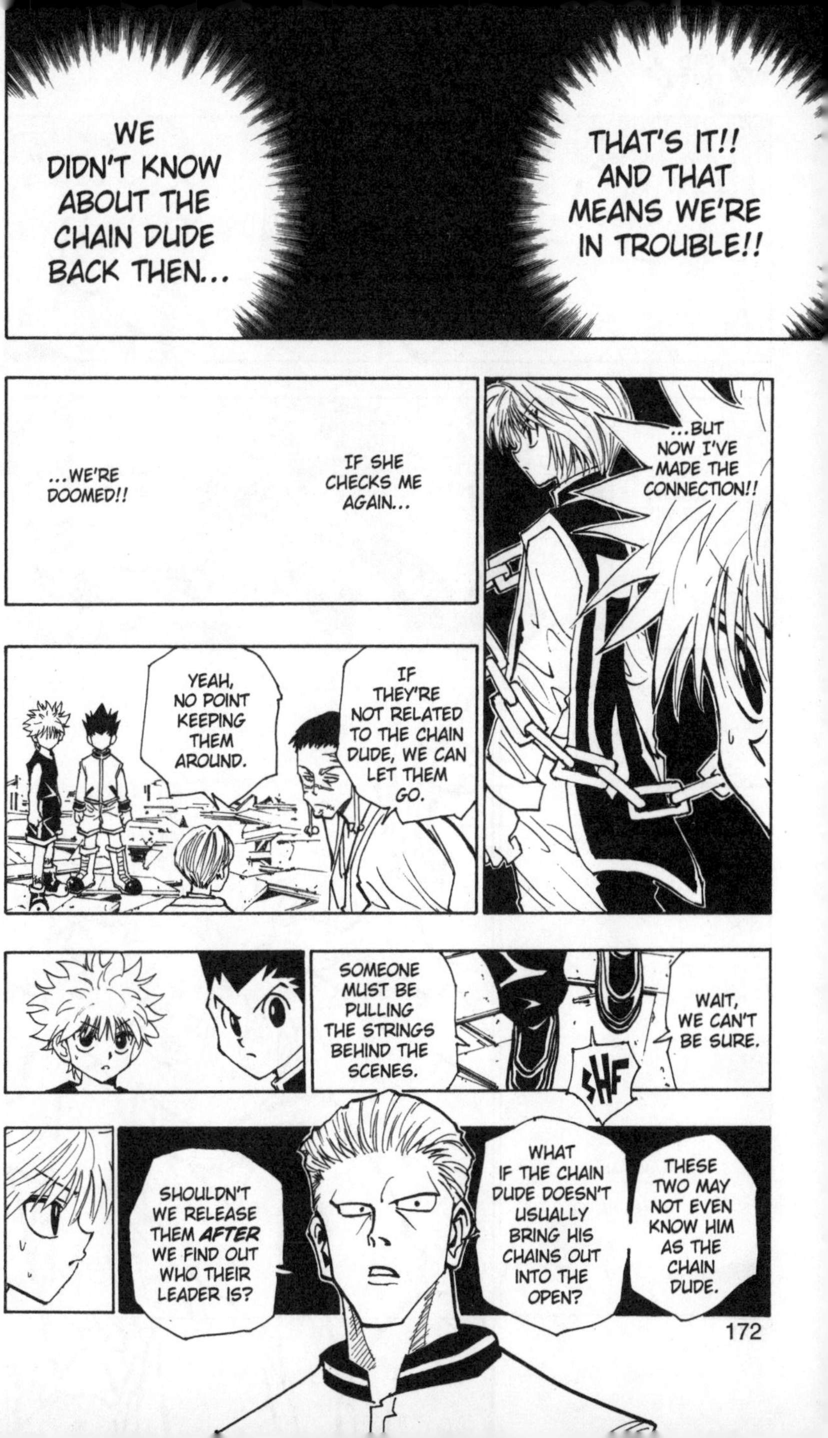
THAT'S IT!! AND THAT MEANS WE'RE IN TROUBLE!!
WE DIDN'T KNOW ABOUT THE CHAIN DUDE BACK THEN...
...BUT NOW I'VE MADE THE CONNECTION!!
IF SHE CHECKS ME AGAIN...
...WE'RE DOOMED!!
IF THEY'RE NOT RELATED TO THE CHAIN DUDE, WE CAN LET THEM GO.
YEAH, NO POINT KEEPING THEM AROUND.
WAIT, WE CAN'T BE SURE.
SHF
SOMEONE MUST BE PULLING THE STRINGS BEHIND THE SCENES.
THESE TWO MAY NOT EVEN KNOW HIM AS THE CHAIN DUDE.
WHAT IF THE CHAIN DUDE DOESN'T USUALLY BRING HIS CHAINS OUT INTO THE OPEN?
SHOULDN'T WE RELEASE THEM *AFTER* WE FIND OUT WHO THEIR LEADER IS?

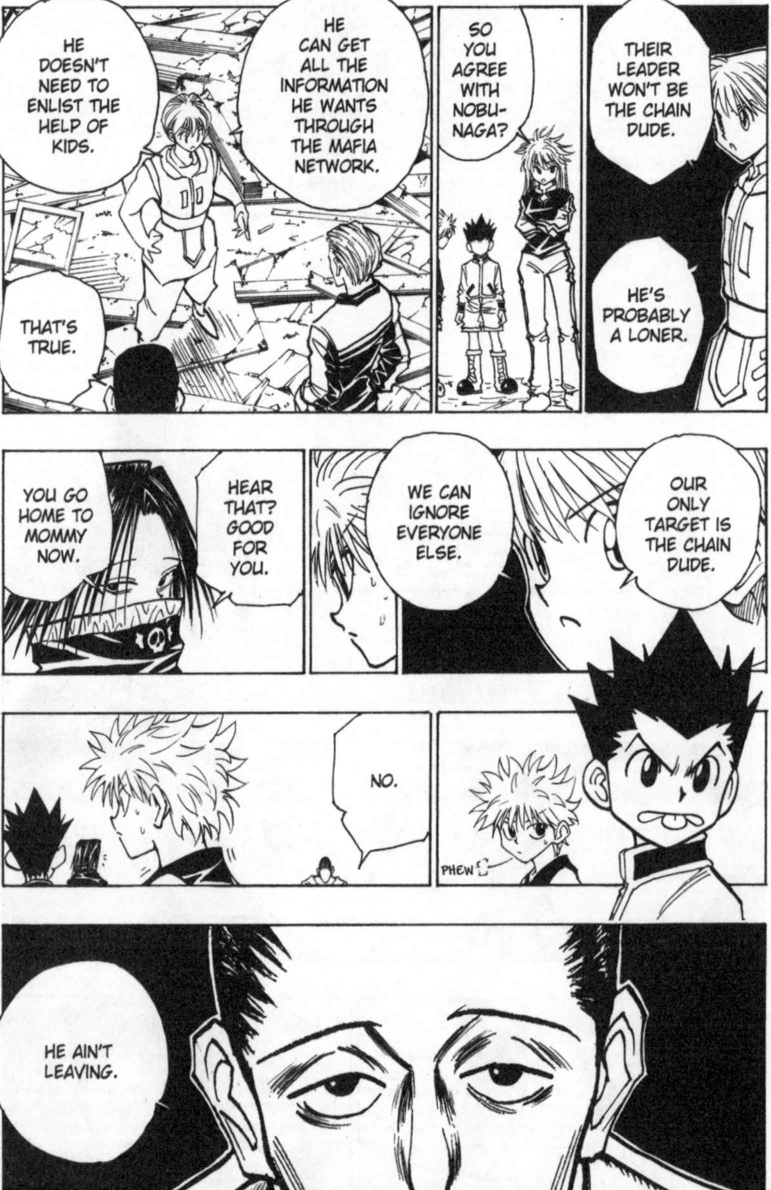
THEIR LEADER WON'T BE THE CHAIN DUDE.
HE'S PROBABLY A LONER.
SO YOU AGREE WITH NOBU-NAGA?
HE CAN GET ALL THE INFORMATION HE WANTS THROUGH THE MAFIA NETWORK.
HE DOESN'T NEED TO ENLIST THE HELP OF KIDS.
THAT'S TRUE.
OUR ONLY TARGET IS THE CHAIN DUDE.
WE CAN IGNORE EVERYONE ELSE.
HEAR THAT? GOOD FOR YOU.
YOU GO HOME TO MOMMY NOW.
PHEW
NO.
HE AIN'T LEAVING.

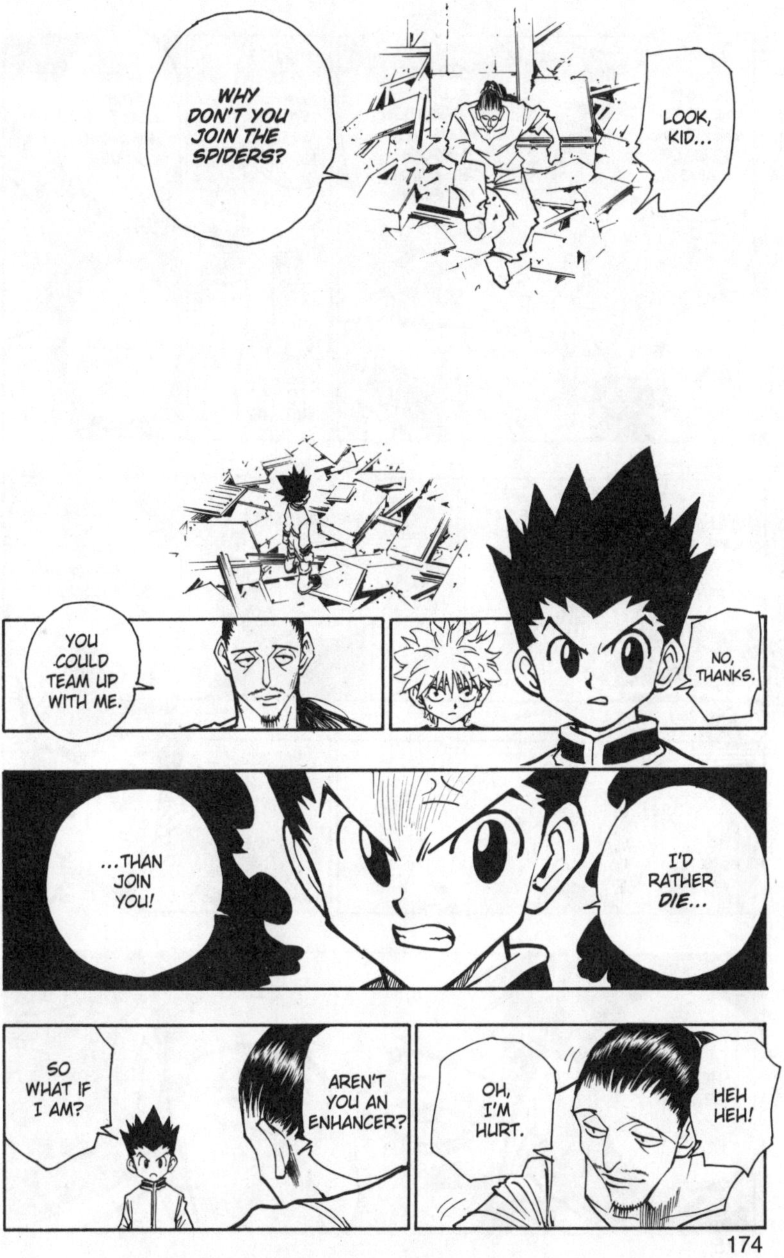
LOOK, KID...
WHY DON'T YOU JOIN THE SPIDERS?
YOU COULD TEAM UP WITH ME.
NO, THANKS.
I'D RATHER *DIE*...
...THAN JOIN YOU!
HEH HEH!
OH, I'M HURT.
AREN'T YOU AN ENHANCER?
SO WHAT IF I AM?

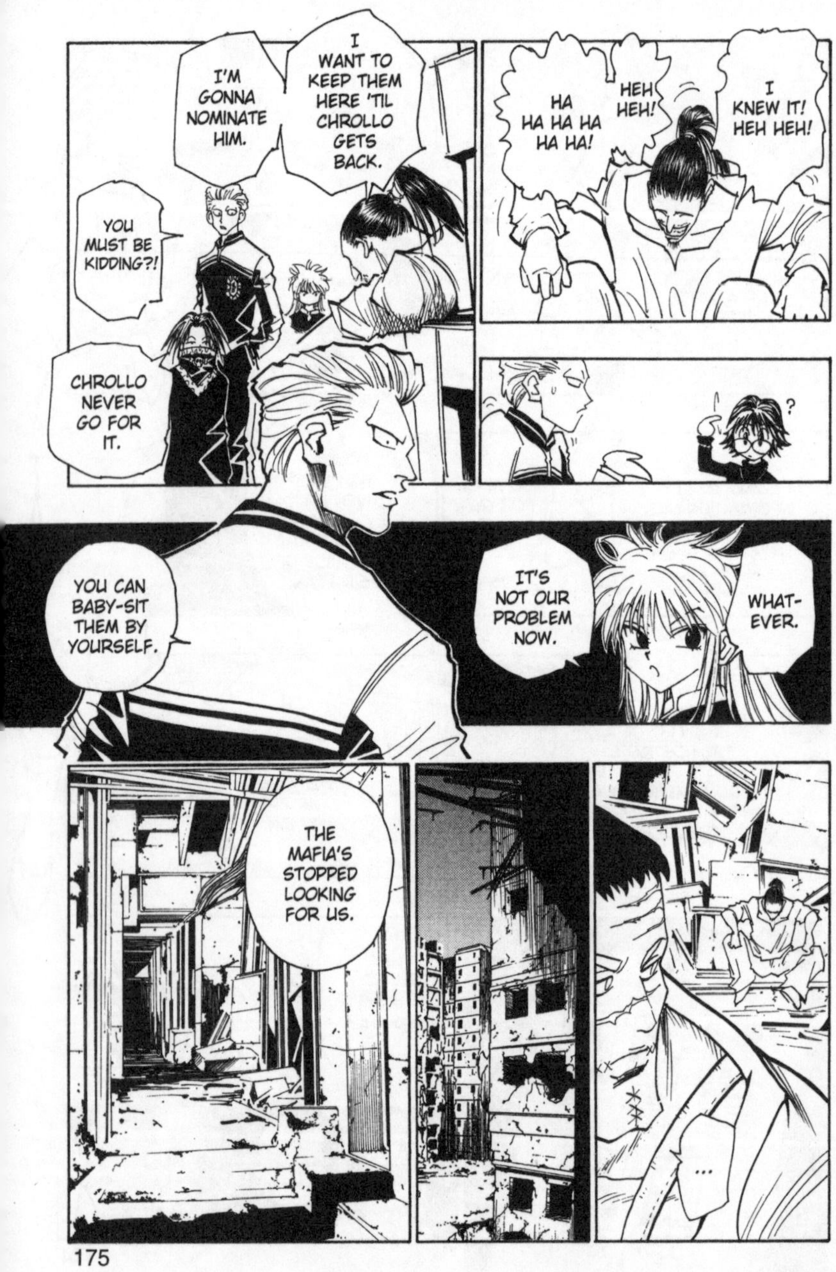
I KNEW IT! HEH HEH!
HEH HEH!
HA HA HA HA HA HA!
?
I WANT TO KEEP THEM HERE 'TIL CHROLLO GETS BACK.
I'M GONNA NOMINATE HIM.
YOU MUST BE KIDDING?!
CHROLLO NEVER GO FOR IT.
WHAT-EVER.
IT'S NOT OUR PROBLEM NOW.
YOU CAN BABY-SIT THEM BY YOURSELF.
...
THE MAFIA'S STOPPED LOOKING FOR US.

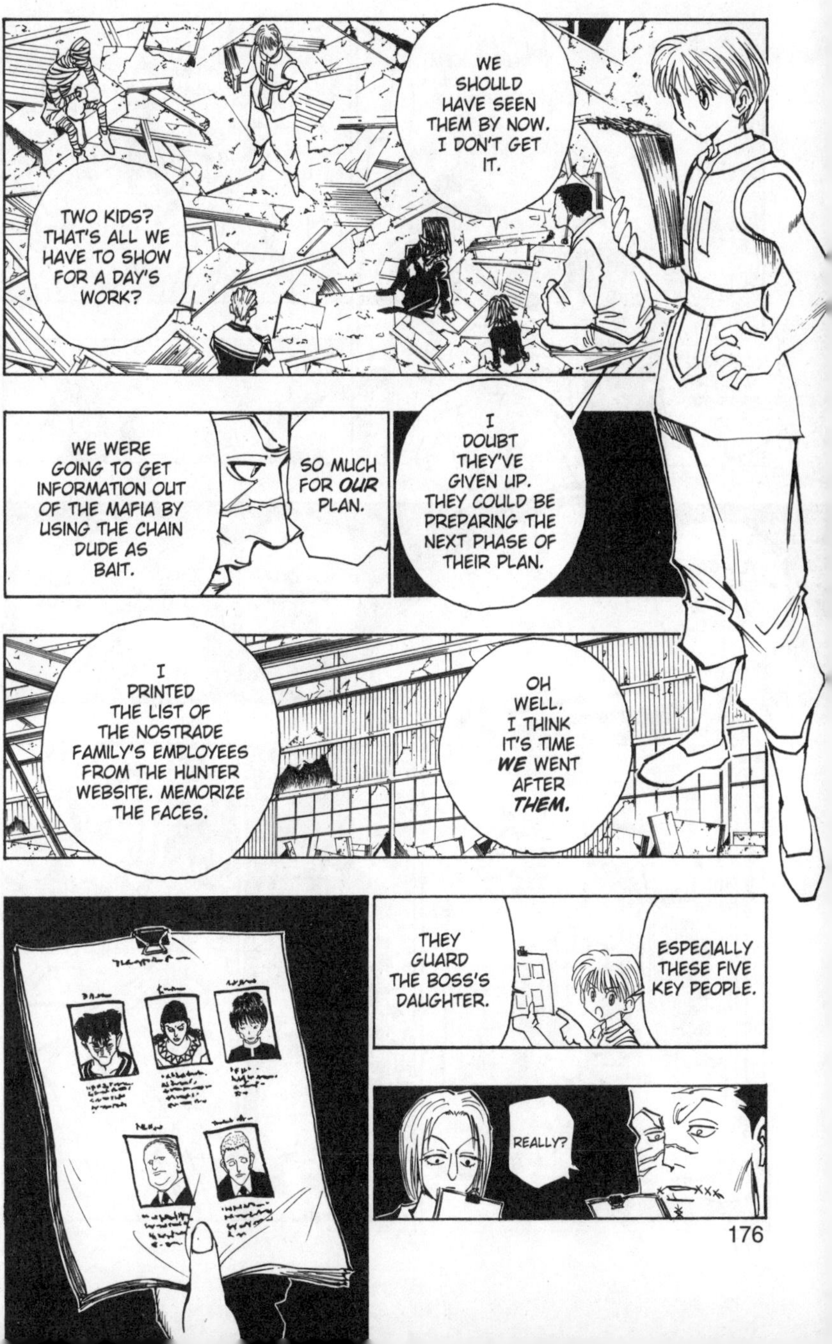
WE SHOULD HAVE SEEN THEM BY NOW. I DON'T GET IT.
TWO KIDS? THAT'S ALL WE HAVE TO SHOW FOR A DAY'S WORK?
I DOUBT THEY'VE GIVEN UP. THEY COULD BE PREPARING THE NEXT PHASE OF THEIR PLAN.
SO MUCH FOR *OUR* PLAN.
WE WERE GOING TO GET INFORMATION OUT OF THE MAFIA BY USING THE CHAIN DUDE AS BAIT.
OH WELL. I THINK IT'S TIME ***WE*** WENT AFTER ***THEM.***
I PRINTED THE LIST OF THE NOSTRADE FAMILY'S EMPLOYEES FROM THE HUNTER WEBSITE. MEMORIZE THE FACES.
ESPECIALLY THESE FIVE KEY PEOPLE.
THEY GUARD THE BOSS'S DAUGHTER.
REALLY?

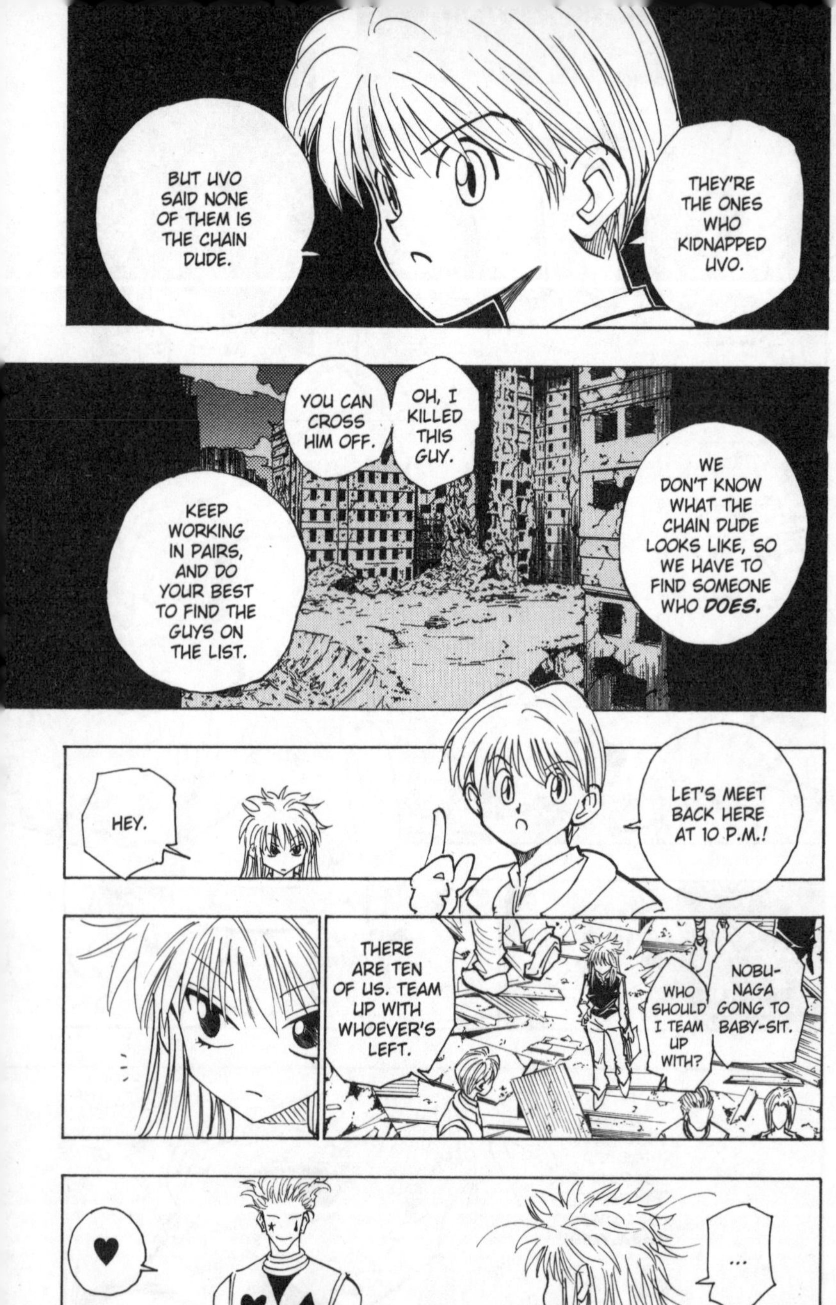
THEY'RE THE ONES WHO KIDNAPPED UVO.
BUT UVO SAID NONE OF THEM IS THE CHAIN DUDE.
WE DON'T KNOW WHAT THE CHAIN DUDE LOOKS LIKE, SO WE HAVE TO FIND SOMEONE WHO **DOES.**
OH, I KILLED THIS GUY.
YOU CAN CROSS HIM OFF.
KEEP WORKING IN PAIRS, AND DO YOUR BEST TO FIND THE GUYS ON THE LIST.
LET'S MEET BACK HERE AT 10 P.M.!
HEY.
NOBU-NAGA GOING TO BABY-SIT.
WHO SHOULD I TEAM UP WITH?
THERE ARE TEN OF US. TEAM UP WITH WHOEVER'S LEFT.
...
♥

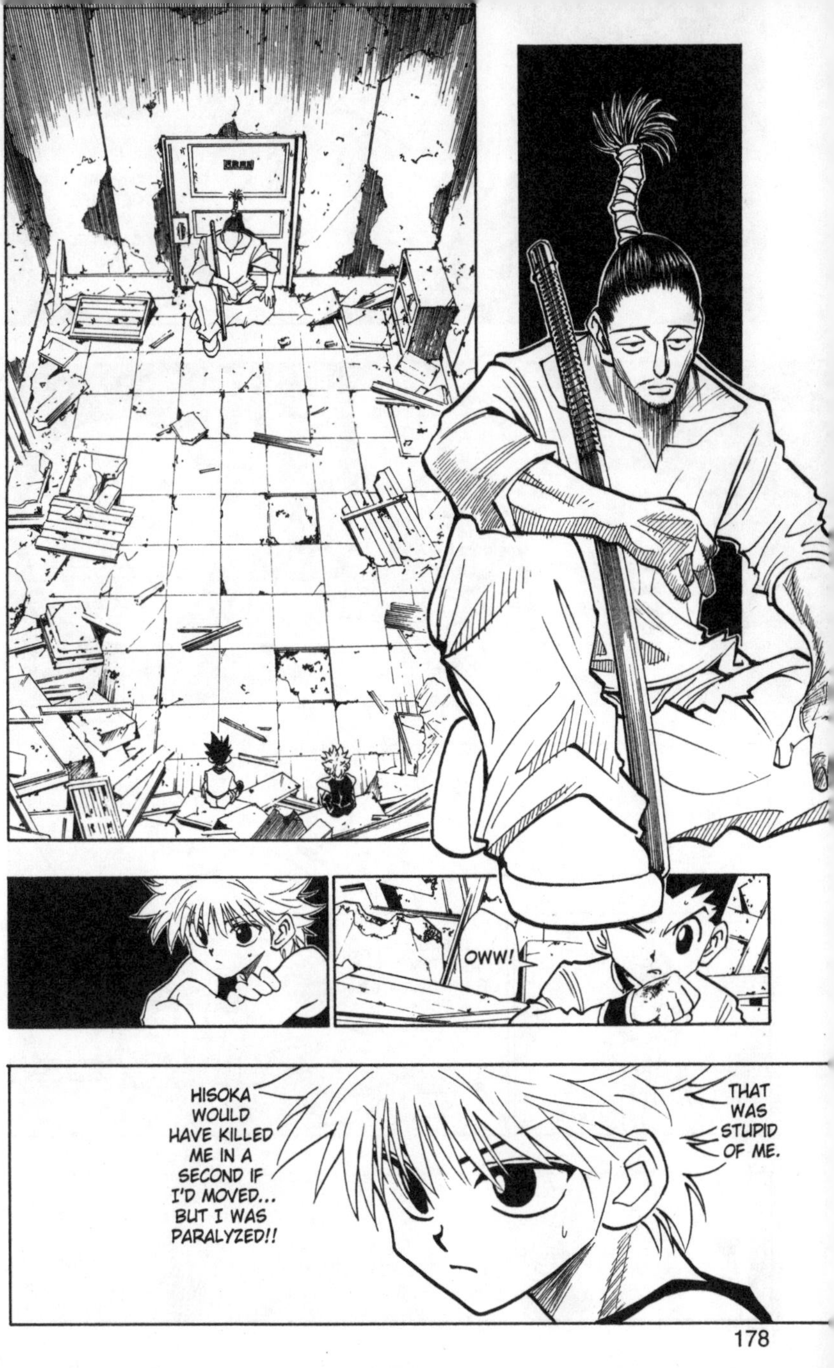
OWW!
THAT WAS STUPID OF ME.
HISOKA WOULD HAVE KILLED ME IN A SECOND IF I'D MOVED... BUT I WAS PARALYZED!!

READ THIS WAY

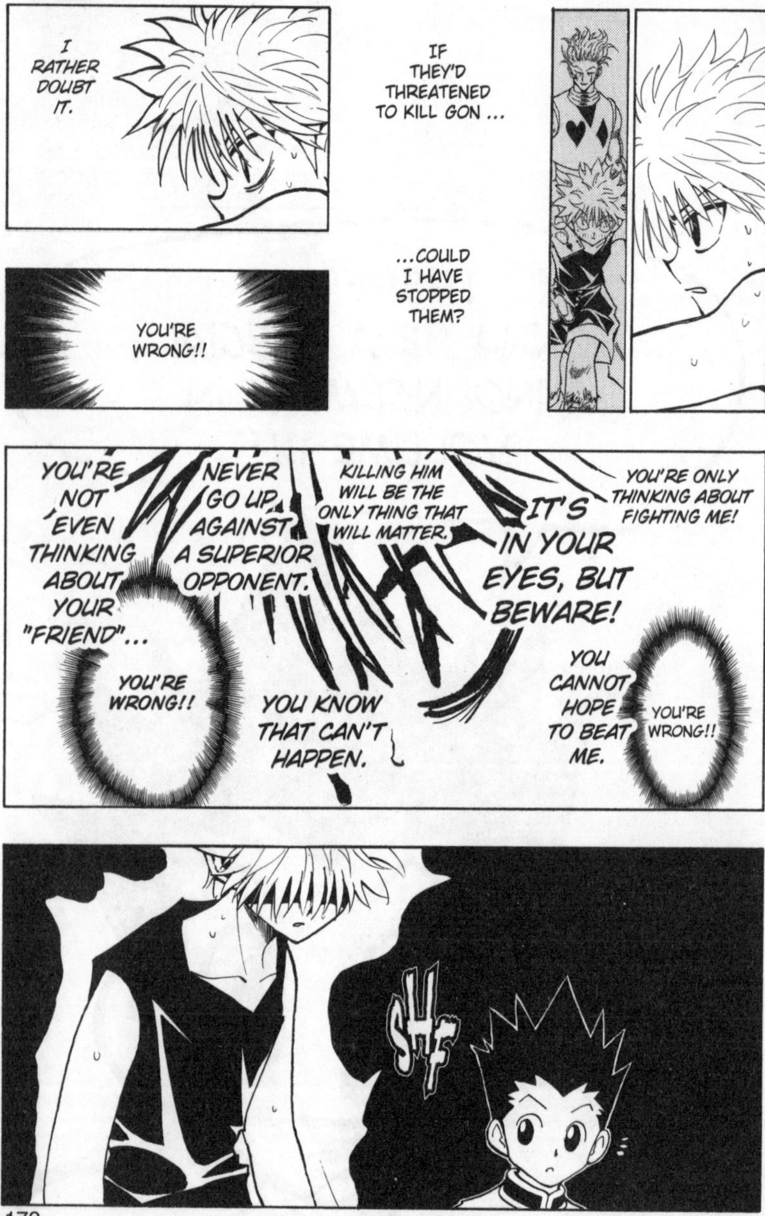

IF THEY'D THREATENED TO KILL GON ...
...COULD I HAVE STOPPED THEM?
I RATHER DOUBT IT.
YOU'RE WRONG!!
YOU'RE ONLY THINKING ABOUT FIGHTING ME!
IT'S IN YOUR EYES, BUT BEWARE!
YOU CANNOT HOPE TO BEAT ME.
YOU'RE WRONG!!
KILLING HIM WILL BE THE ONLY THING THAT WILL MATTER.
NEVER GO UP AGAINST A SUPERIOR OPPONENT.
YOU KNOW THAT CAN'T HAPPEN.
YOU'RE NOT EVEN THINKING ABOUT YOUR "FRIEND"...
YOU'RE WRONG!!
SHF

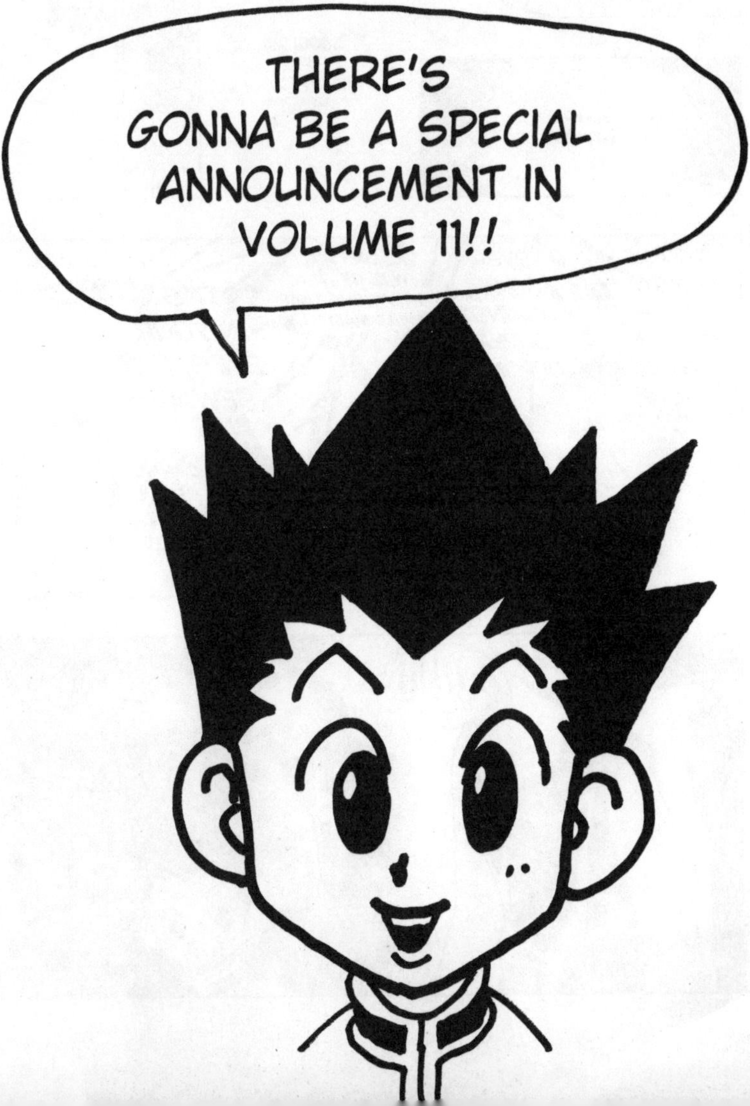
THERE'S GONNA BE A SPECIAL ANNOUNCEMENT IN VOLUME 11!!

Chapter 93
September 3rd: Part 9

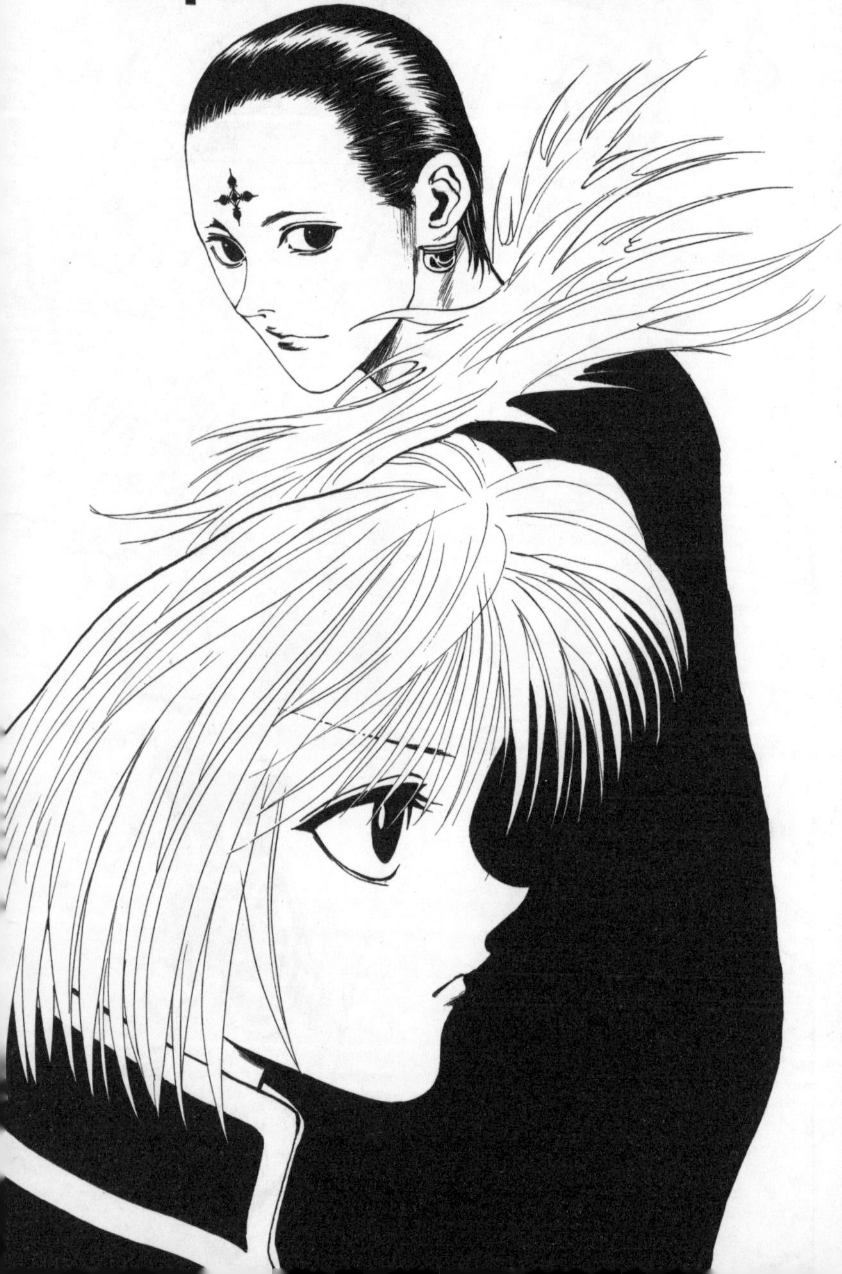

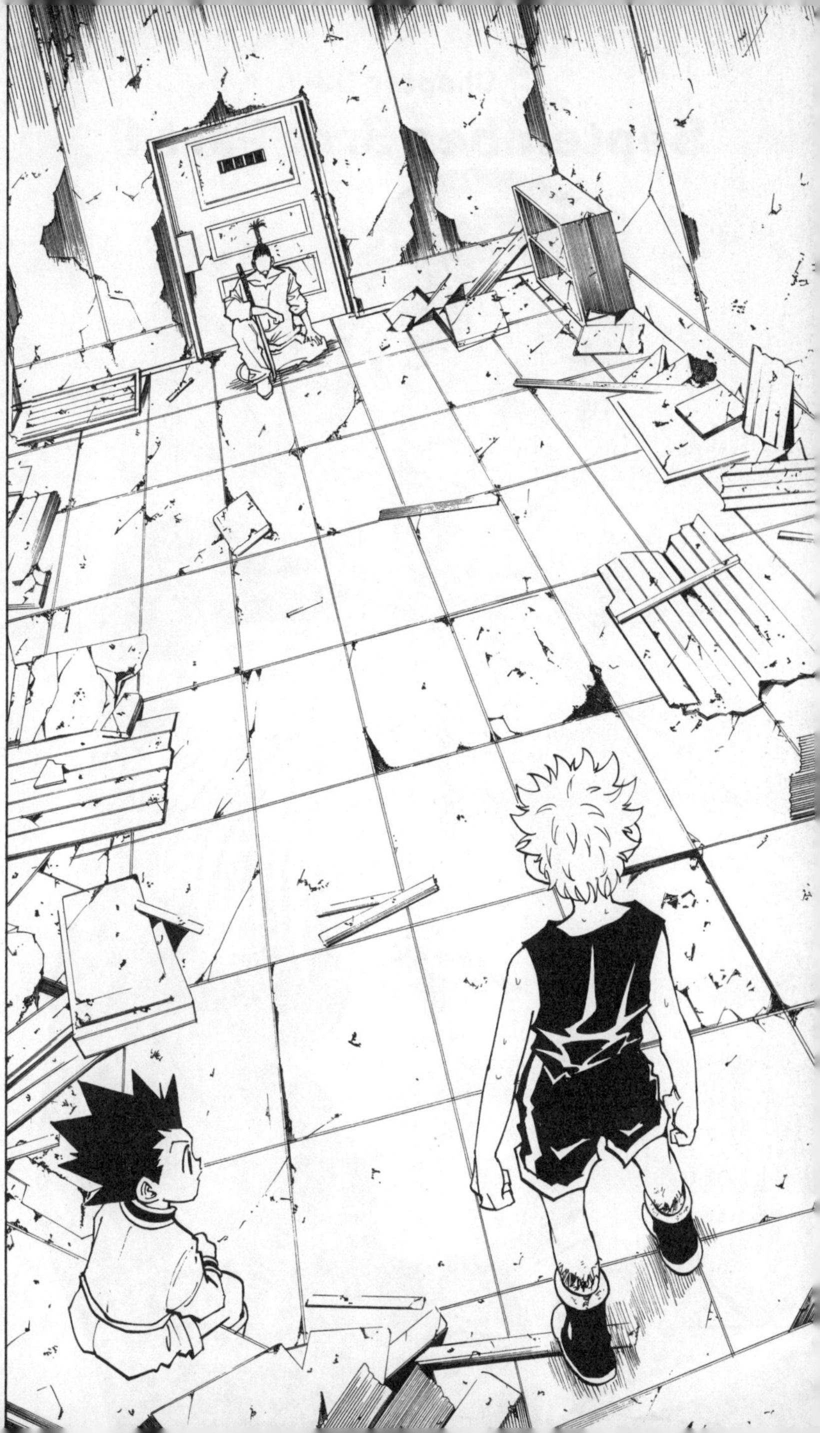

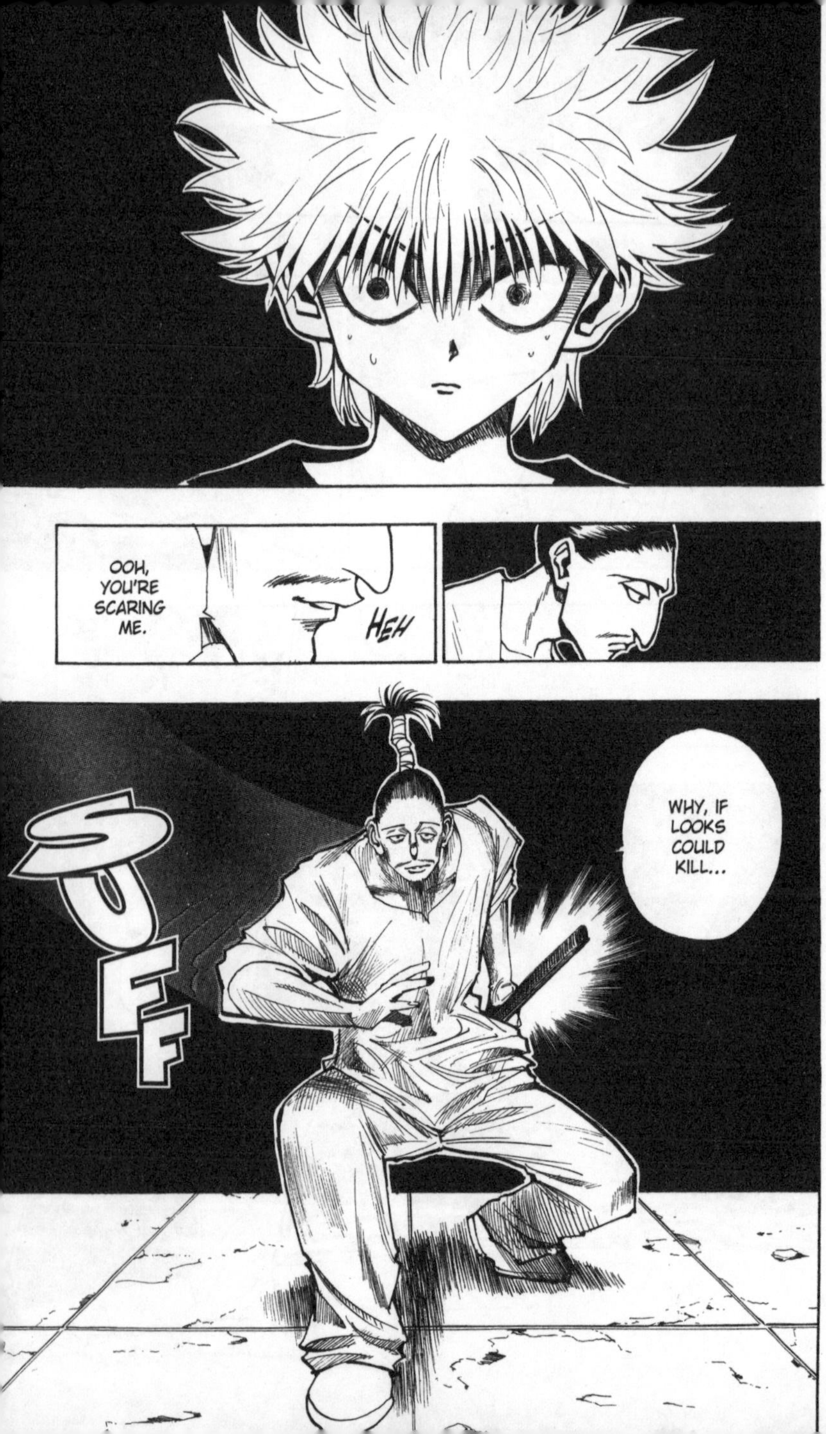
OOH, YOU'RE SCARING ME.
HEH
WHY, IF LOOKS COULD KILL...
SUFF

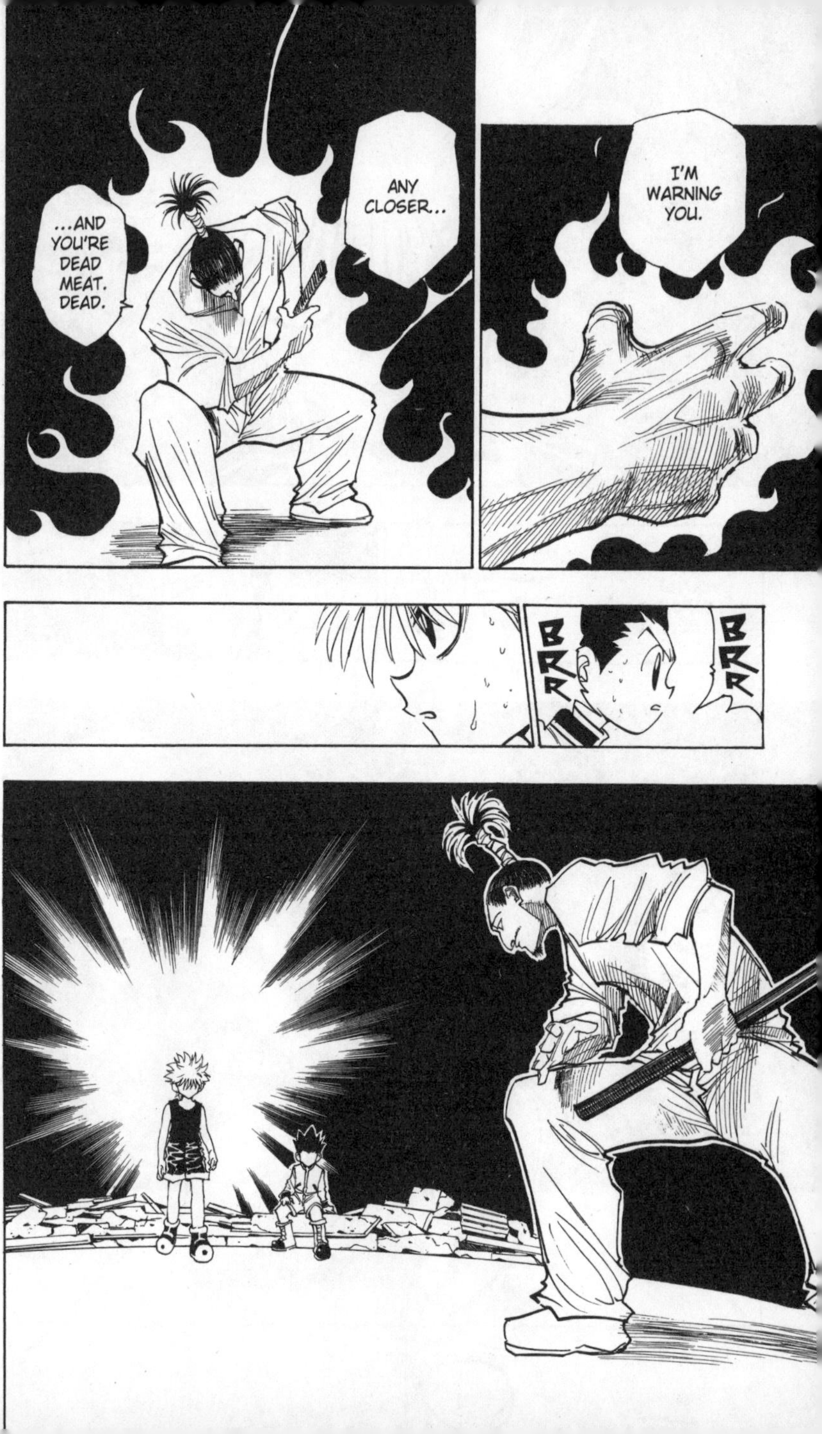
I'M WARNING YOU.
ANY CLOSER...
...AND YOU'RE DEAD MEAT. DEAD.
BRR
BRR

READ THIS WAY

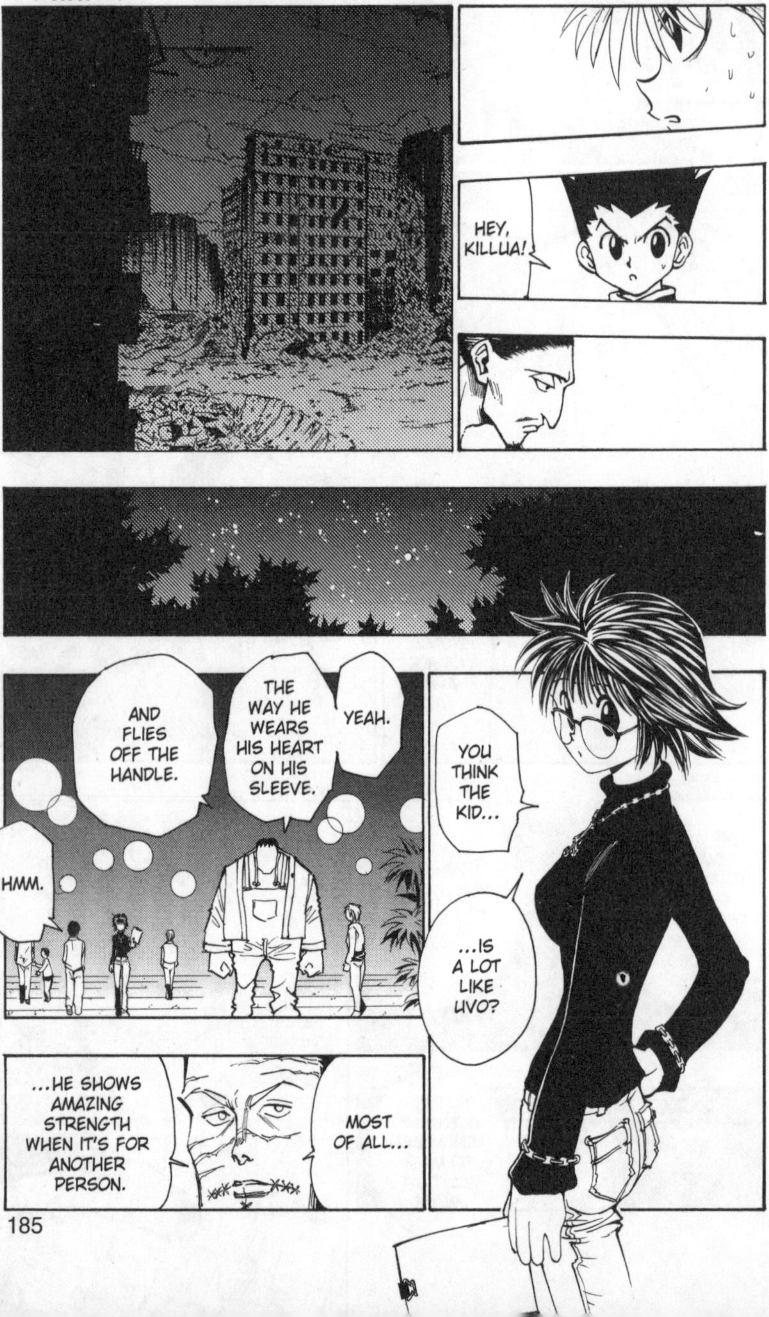
HEY, KILLUA!
YOU THINK THE KID...
...IS A LOT LIKE UVO?
YEAH.
THE WAY HE WEARS HIS HEART ON HIS SLEEVE.
AND FLIES OFF THE HANDLE.
HMM.
MOST OF ALL...
...HE SHOWS AMAZING STRENGTH WHEN IT'S FOR ANOTHER PERSON.

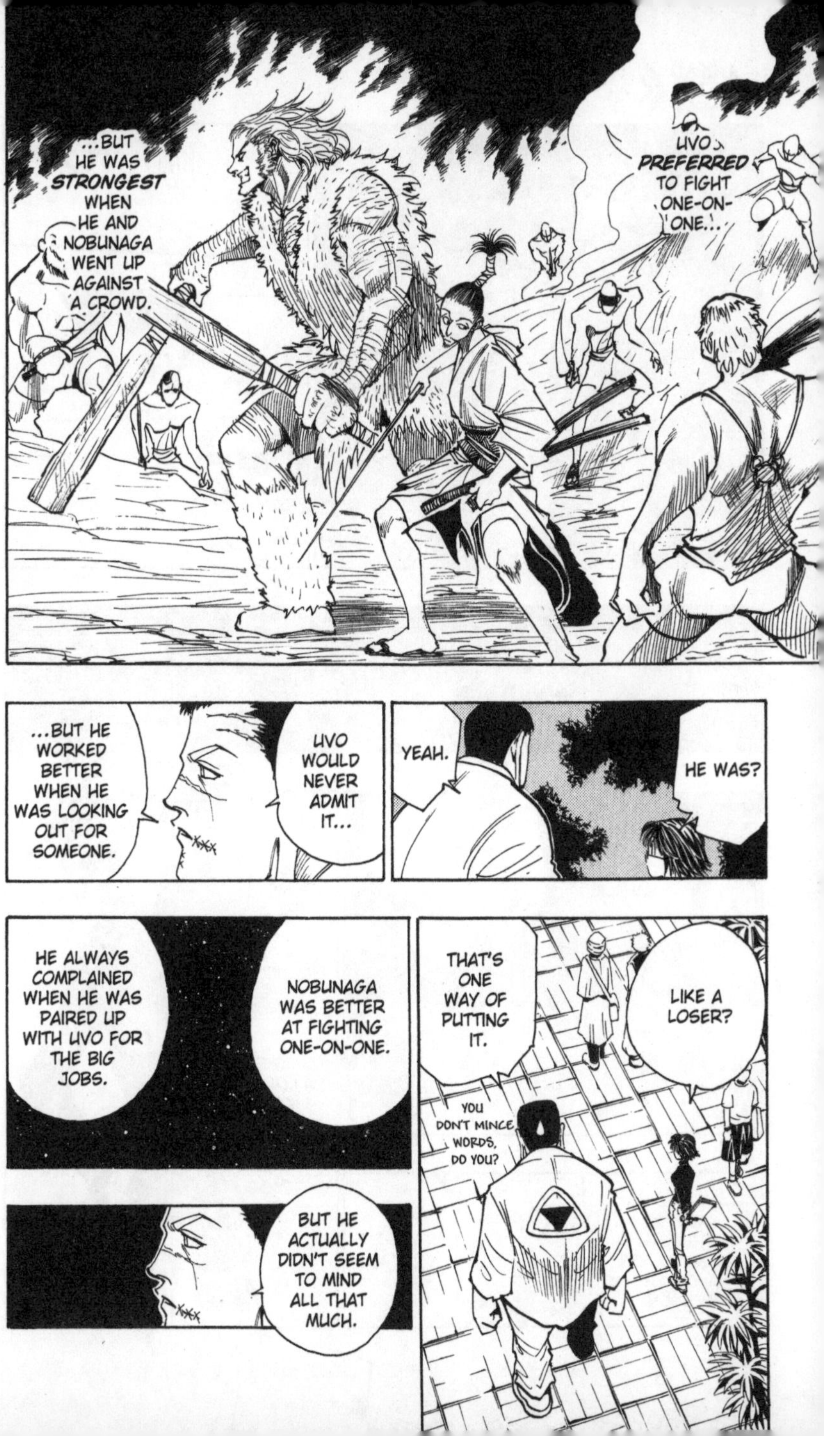
UVO PREFERRED TO FIGHT ONE-ON-ONE...
...BUT HE WAS STRONGEST WHEN HE AND NOBUNAGA WENT UP AGAINST A CROWD.
HE WAS?
YEAH.
UVO WOULD NEVER ADMIT IT...
...BUT HE WORKED BETTER WHEN HE WAS LOOKING OUT FOR SOMEONE.
LIKE A LOSER?
THAT'S ONE WAY OF PUTTING IT.
YOU DON'T MINCE WORDS, DO YOU?
NOBUNAGA WAS BETTER AT FIGHTING ONE-ON-ONE.
HE ALWAYS COMPLAINED WHEN HE WAS PAIRED UP WITH UVO FOR THE BIG JOBS.
BUT HE ACTUALLY DIDN'T SEEM TO MIND ALL THAT MUCH.

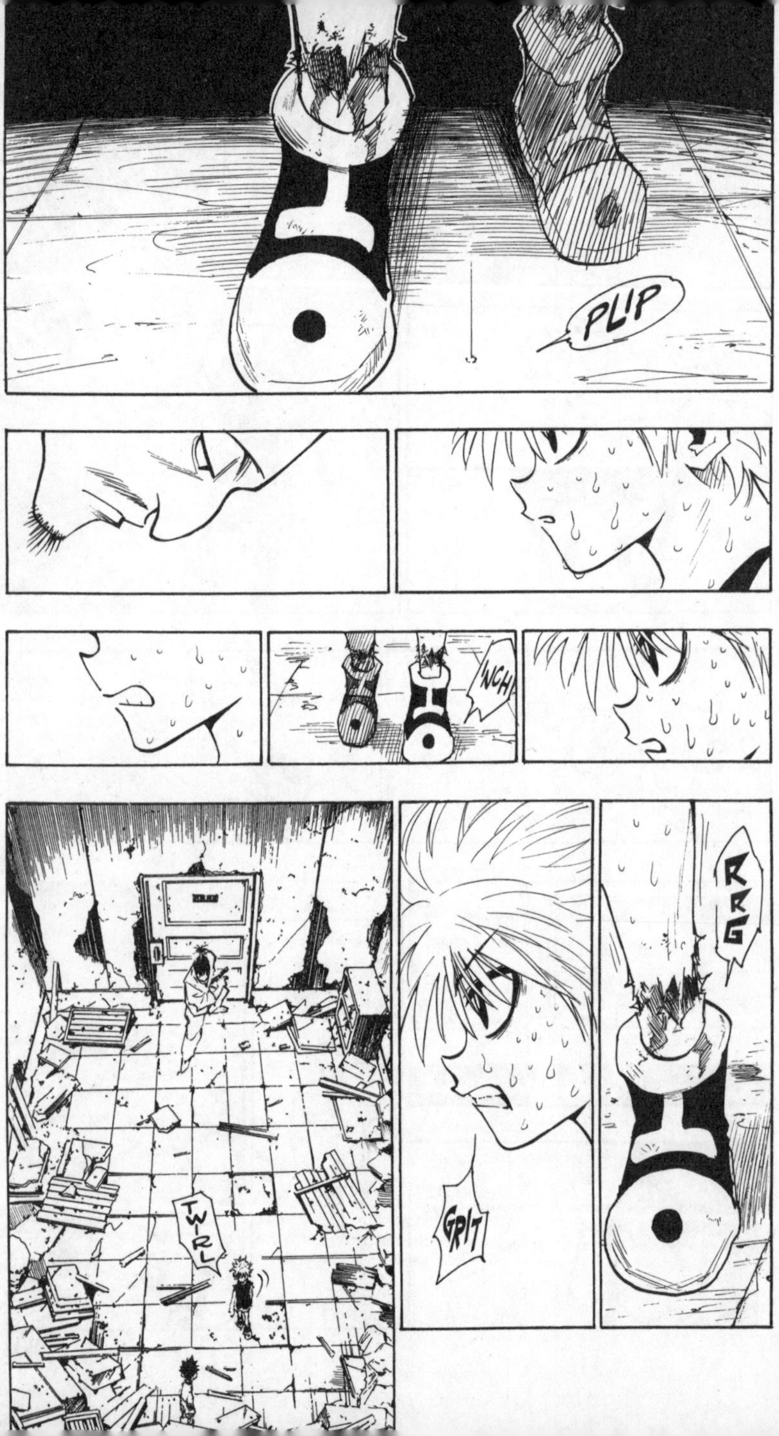
PLIP
'NCH
RRG
GRIT
TWIRL

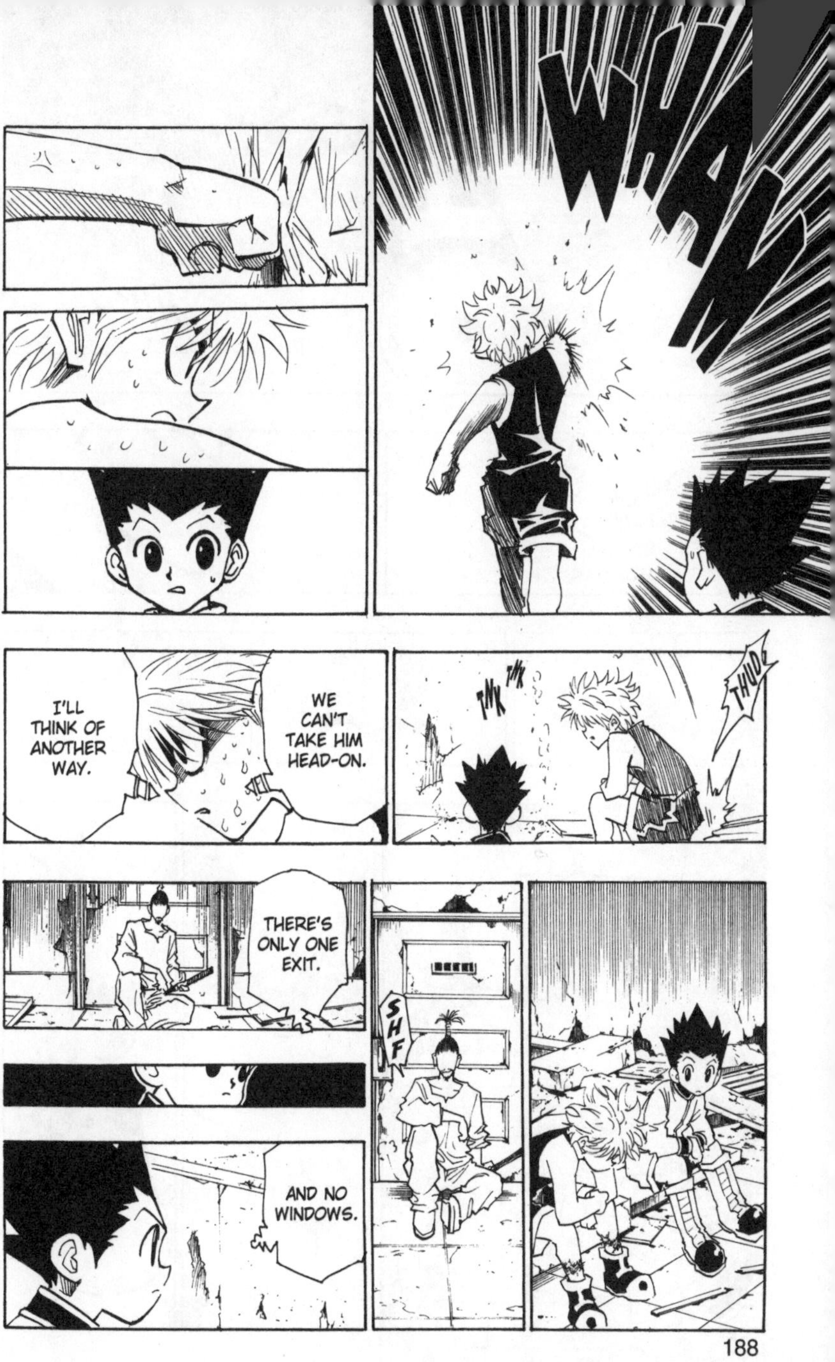
WHAM
TNK TNK
THUD
WE CAN'T TAKE HIM HEAD-ON.
I'LL THINK OF ANOTHER WAY.
SHF
THERE'S ONLY ONE EXIT.
AND NO WINDOWS.

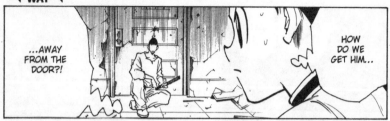

READ THIS WAY

HOW DO WE GET HIM...
...AWAY FROM THE DOOR?!
IT'S GETTING DARK.
PFF
I WONDER HOW LEORIO'S DOING?
I HOPE HE FOUND ZEPILE.

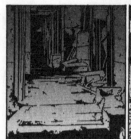

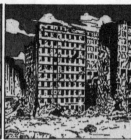

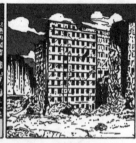

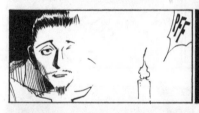

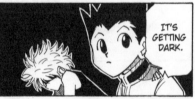

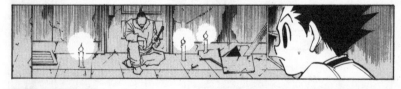

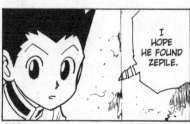

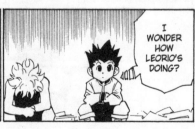

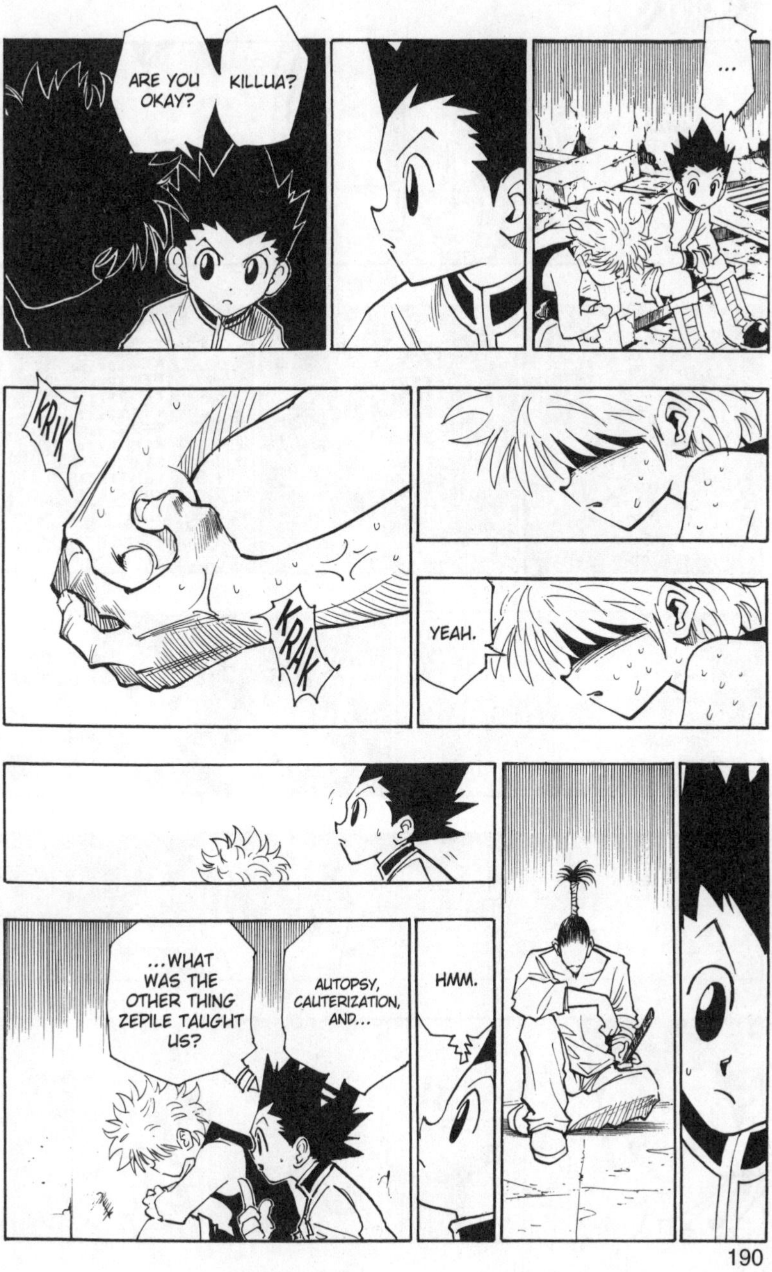
...
KILLUA?
ARE YOU OKAY?
YEAH.
KRIK
KRAK
HMM.
AUTOPSY, CAUTERIZATION, AND...
...WHAT WAS THE OTHER THING ZEPILE TAUGHT US?

READ THIS WAY

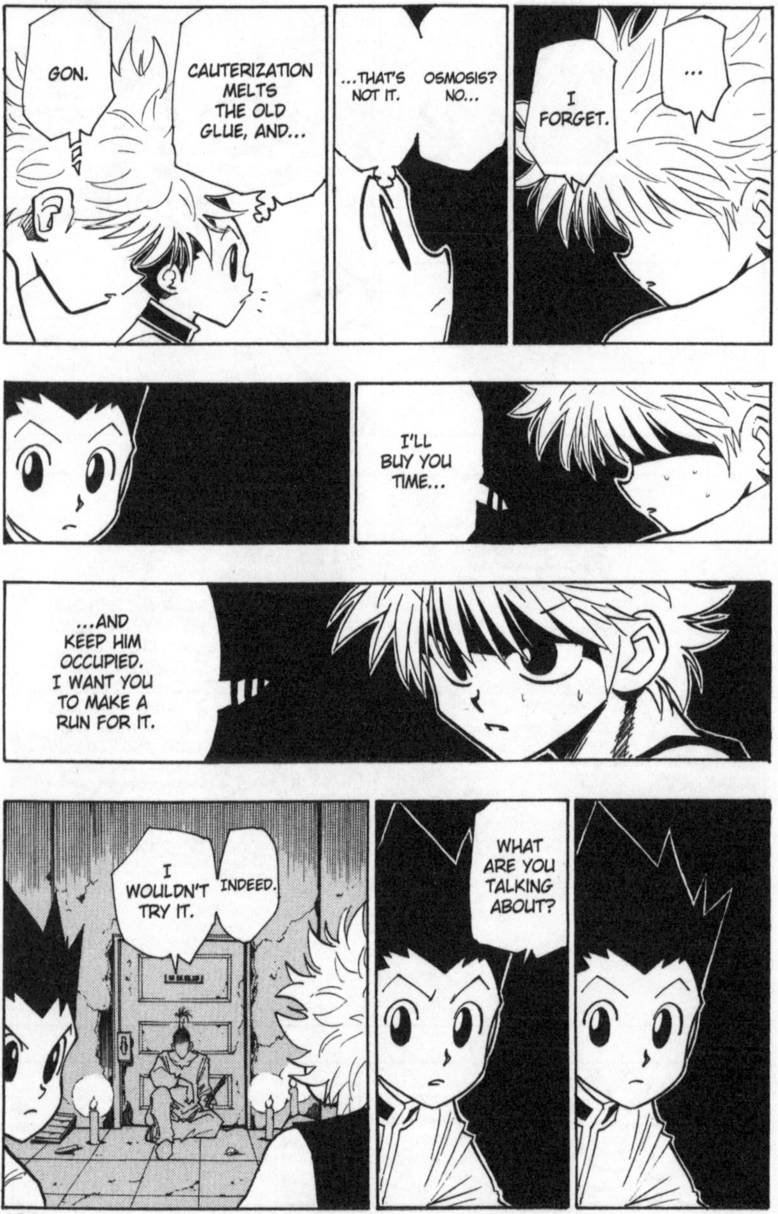
...
I FORGET.
OSMOSIS? NO...
...THAT'S NOT IT.
CAUTERIZATION MELTS THE OLD GLUE, AND...
GON.
I'LL BUY YOU TIME...
...AND KEEP HIM OCCUPIED. I WANT YOU TO MAKE A RUN FOR IT.
WHAT ARE YOU TALKING ABOUT?
INDEED.
I WOULDN'T TRY IT.

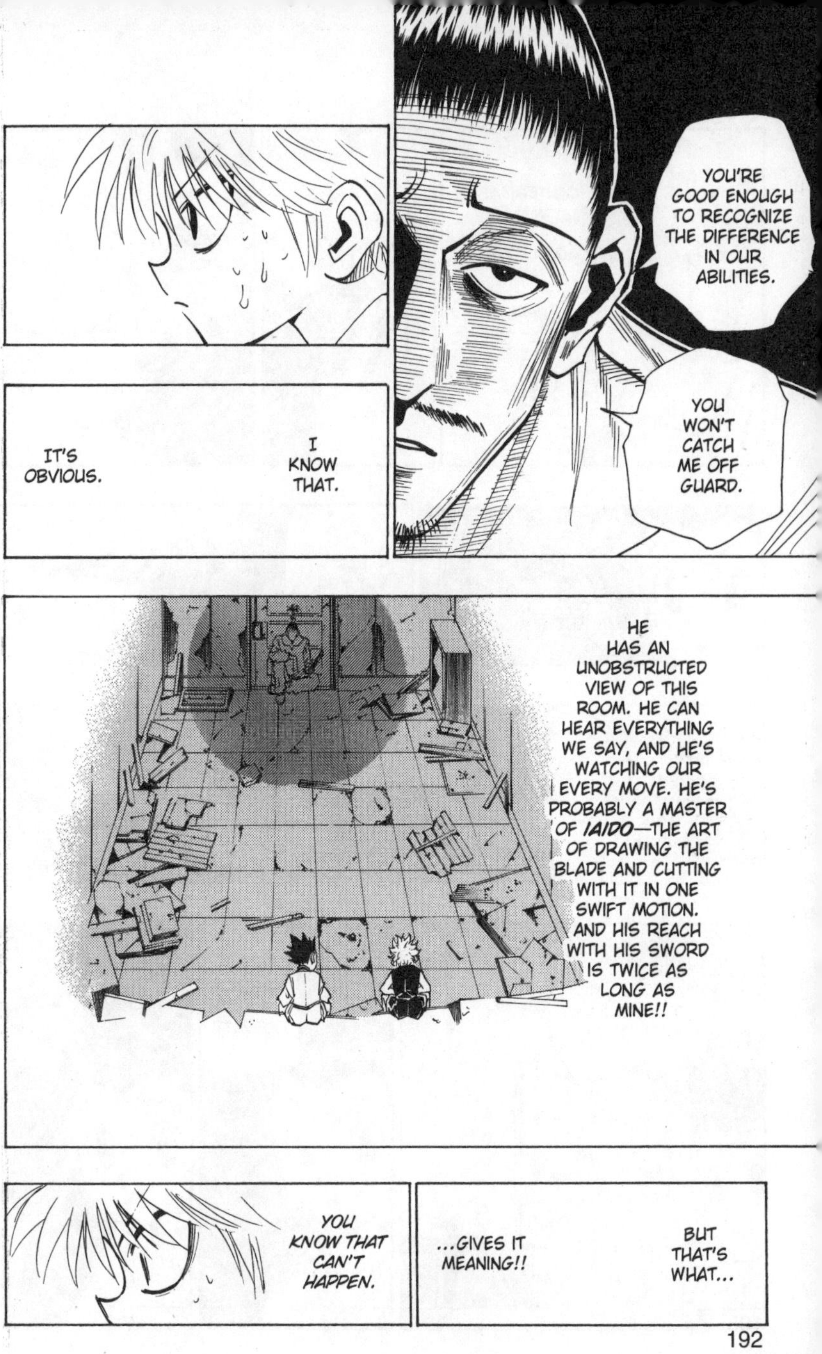
YOU'RE GOOD ENOUGH TO RECOGNIZE THE DIFFERENCE IN OUR ABILITIES.
YOU WON'T CATCH ME OFF GUARD.
I KNOW THAT.
IT'S OBVIOUS.
HE HAS AN UNOBSTRUCTED VIEW OF THIS ROOM. HE CAN HEAR EVERYTHING WE SAY, AND HE'S WATCHING OUR EVERY MOVE. HE'S PROBABLY A MASTER OF *IAIDO*—THE ART OF DRAWING THE BLADE AND CUTTING WITH IT IN ONE SWIFT MOTION. AND HIS REACH WITH HIS SWORD IS TWICE AS LONG AS MINE!!
BUT THAT'S WHAT...
...GIVES IT MEANING!!
YOU KNOW THAT CAN'T HAPPEN.

READ THIS WAY

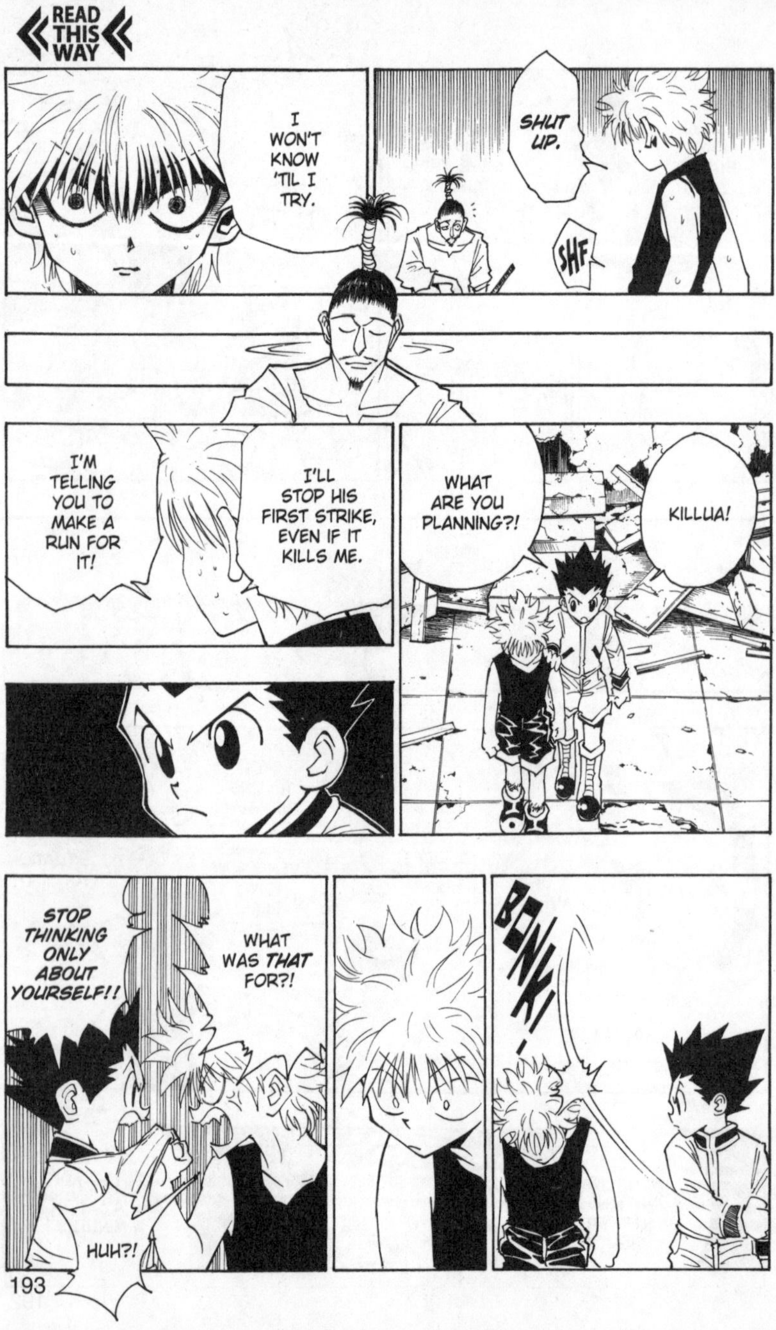
SHUT UP.
SHF
I WON'T KNOW 'TIL I TRY.
KILLUA!
WHAT ARE YOU PLANNING?!
I'LL STOP HIS FIRST STRIKE, EVEN IF IT KILLS ME.
I'M TELLING YOU TO MAKE A RUN FOR IT!
BONK!
WHAT WAS THAT FOR?!
STOP THINKING ONLY ABOUT YOURSELF!!
HUH?!

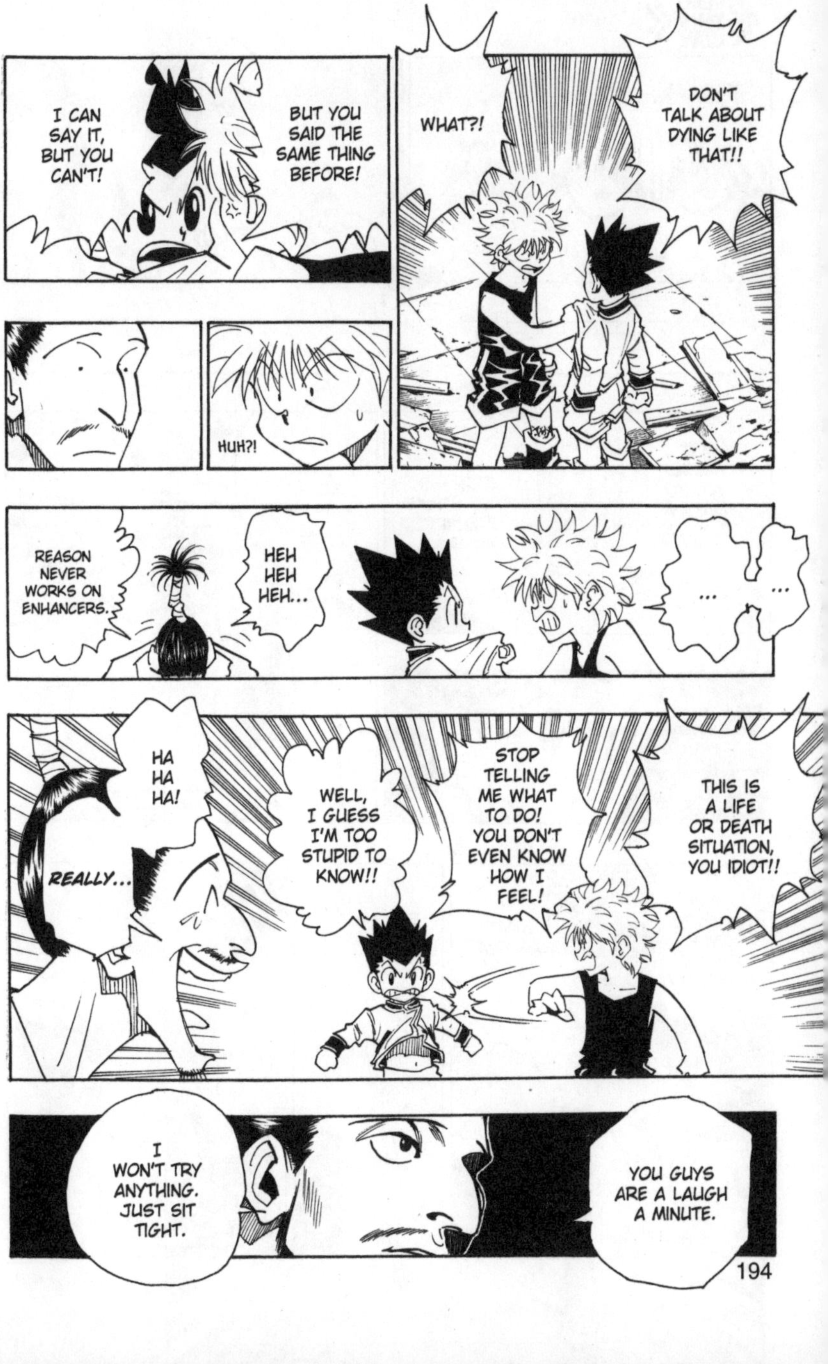
DON'T TALK ABOUT DYING LIKE THAT!!
WHAT?!
BUT YOU SAID THE SAME THING BEFORE!
I CAN SAY IT, BUT YOU CAN'T!
HUH?!
... ...
HEH HEH HEH...
REASON NEVER WORKS ON ENHANCERS.
THIS IS A LIFE OR DEATH SITUATION, YOU IDIOT!!
STOP TELLING ME WHAT TO DO! YOU DON'T EVEN KNOW HOW I FEEL!
WELL, I GUESS I'M TOO STUPID TO KNOW!!
HA HA HA!
REALLY...
YOU GUYS ARE A LAUGH A MINUTE.
I WON'T TRY ANYTHING. JUST SIT TIGHT.

READ THIS WAY

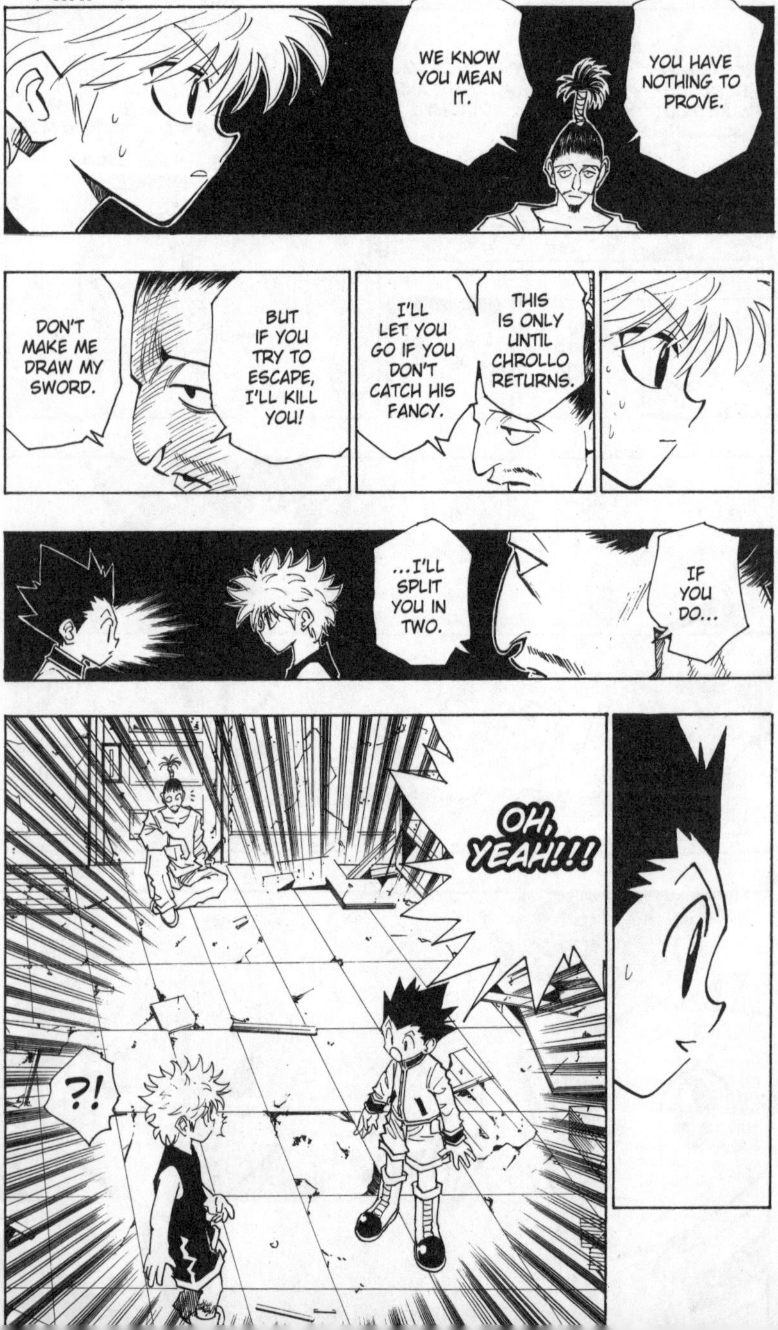

YOU HAVE NOTHING TO PROVE.
WE KNOW YOU MEAN IT.
THIS IS ONLY UNTIL CHROLLO RETURNS.
I'LL LET YOU GO IF YOU DON'T CATCH HIS FANCY.
BUT IF YOU TRY TO ESCAPE, I'LL KILL YOU!
DON'T MAKE ME DRAW MY SWORD.
IF YOU DO...
...I'LL SPLIT YOU IN TWO.
OH, YEAH!!!
?!

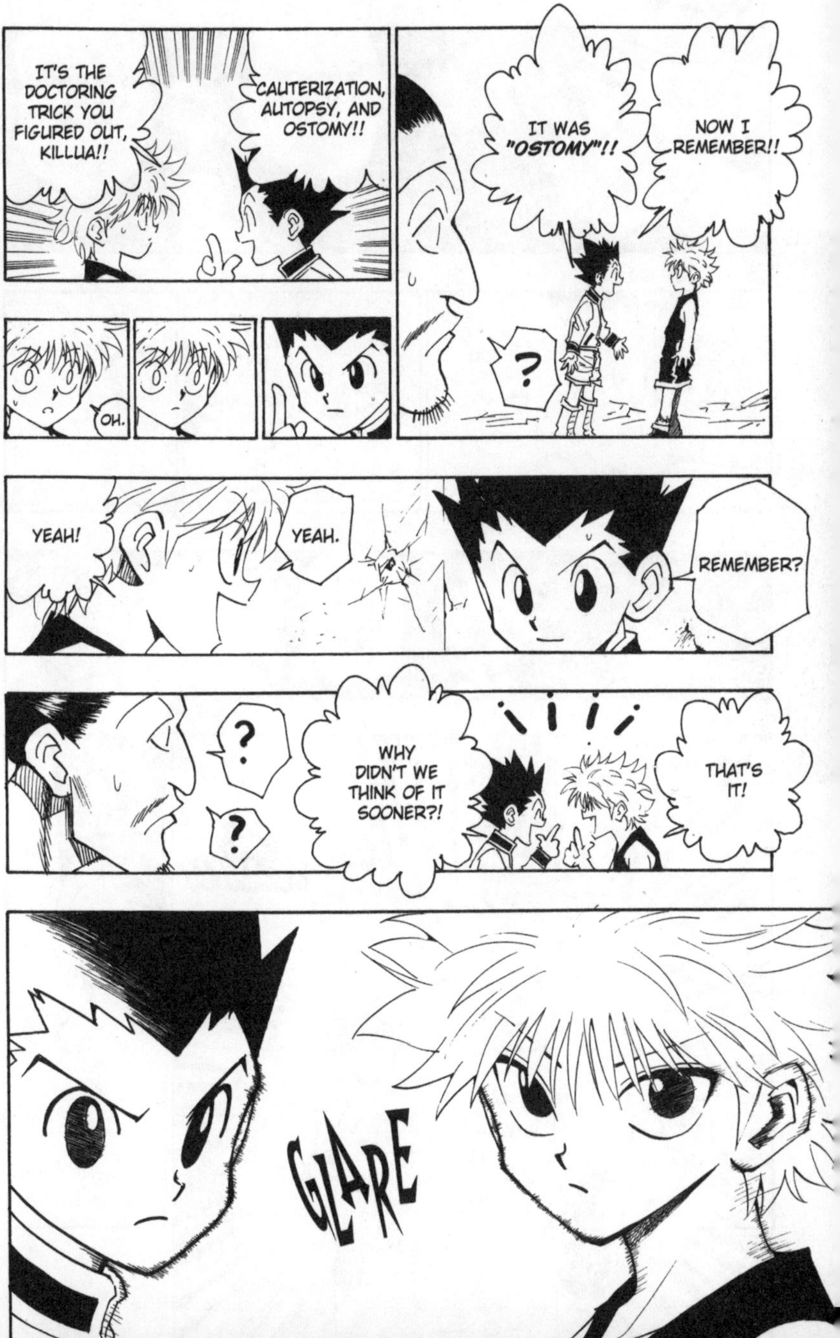
NOW I REMEMBER!!
IT WAS "OSTOMY"!!
?
CAUTERIZATION, AUTOPSY, AND OSTOMY!!
IT'S THE DOCTORING TRICK YOU FIGURED OUT, KILLUA!!
OH.
REMEMBER?
YEAH.
YEAH!
THAT'S IT!
WHY DIDN'T WE THINK OF IT SOONER?!
?
?
GLARE

READ THIS WAY

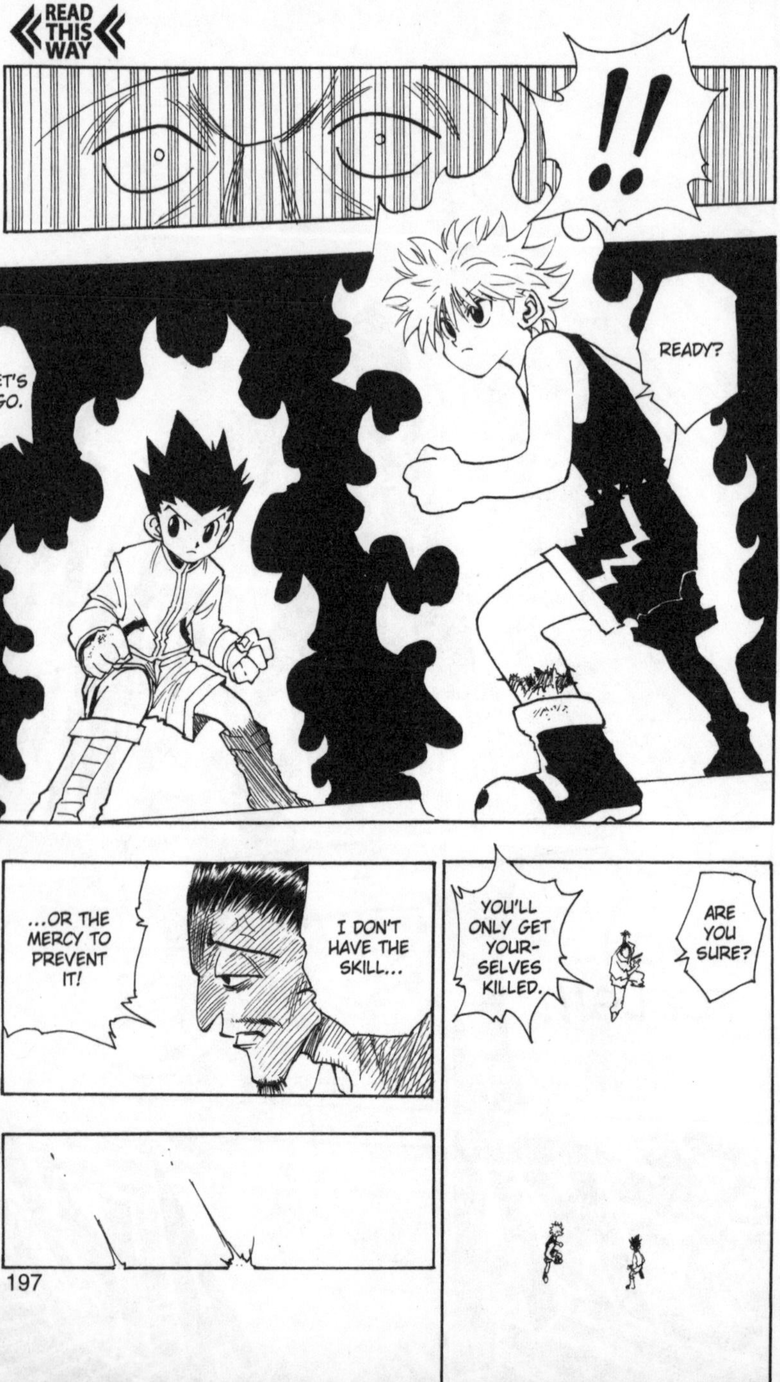
!!
READY?
LET'S GO.
ARE YOU SURE?
YOU'LL ONLY GET YOURSELVES KILLED.
I DON'T HAVE THE SKILL...
...OR THE MERCY TO PREVENT IT!

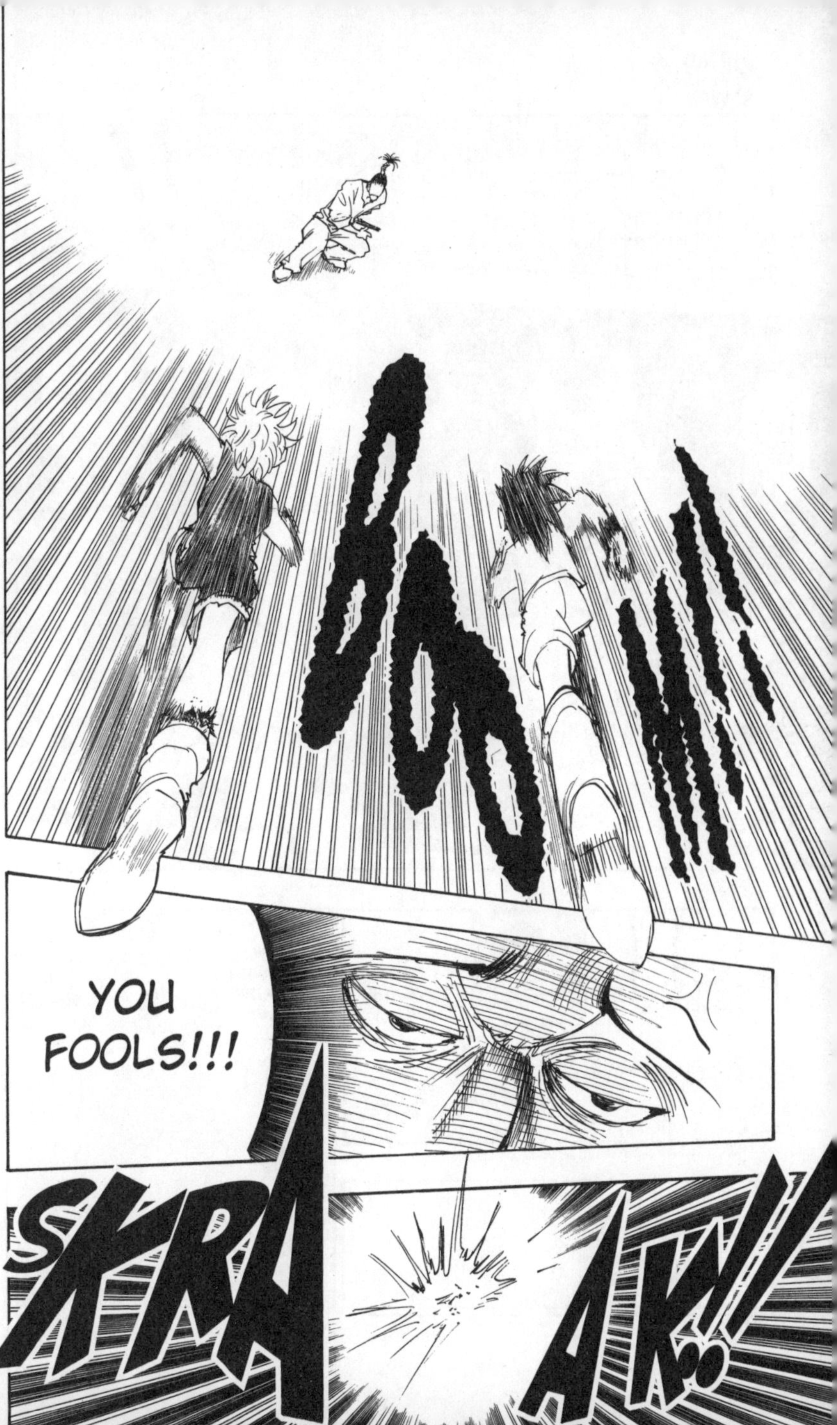
BOOM!!
YOU FOOLS!!!
SKRAAK!!

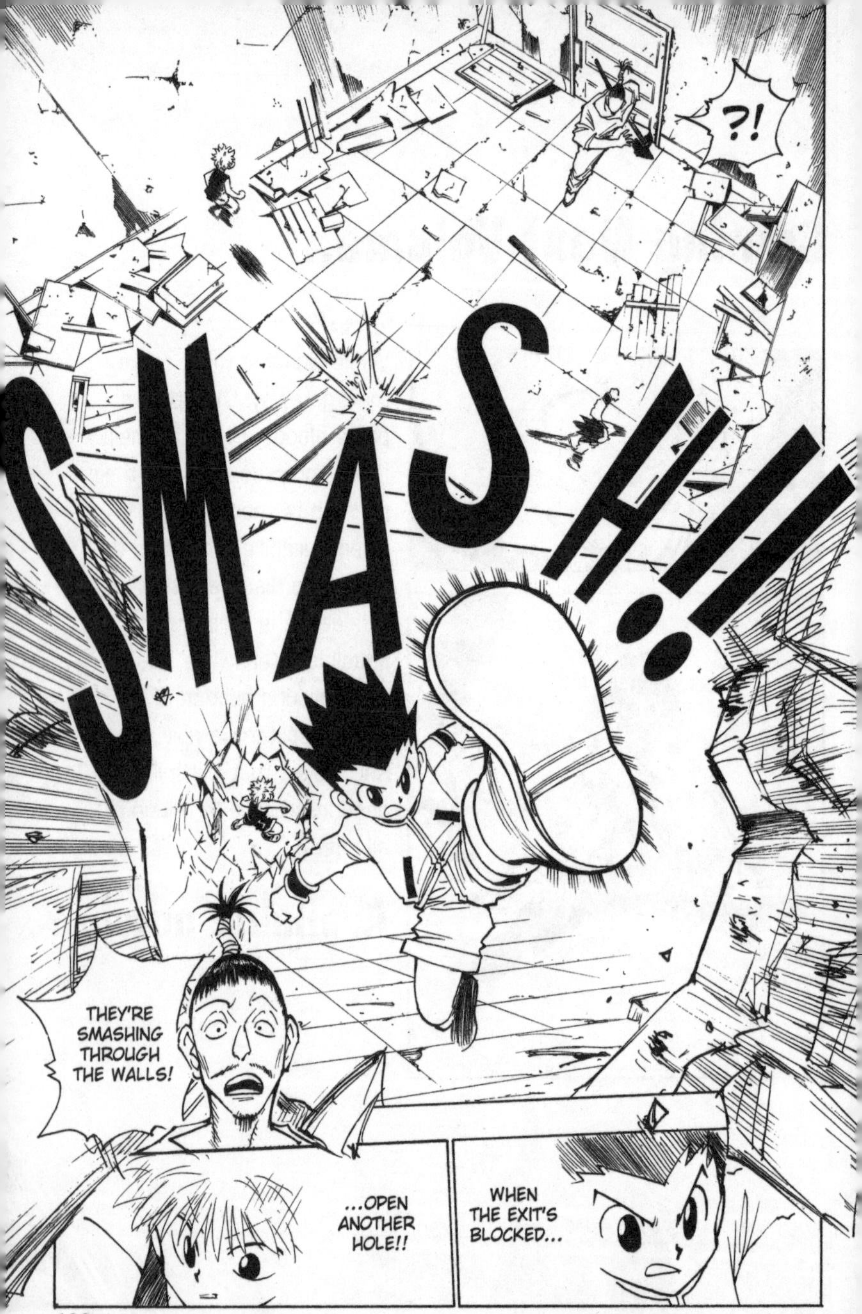
?!
SMASH!!
THEY'RE SMASHING THROUGH THE WALLS!
WHEN THE EXIT'S BLOCKED...
...OPEN ANOTHER HOLE!!

Coming Next Volume...

While Gon and Killua make their getaway, the Spiders pay a bloody tribute to their fallen comrade Uvo. But their triumph is short-lived, for when Kurapika arrives on the scene, he discovers that vengeance is no longer possible. Meanwhile, the underground auction is down to its last item: a pair of Kurta eyes that Kurapika has been instructed to obtain at all costs!

Available now!

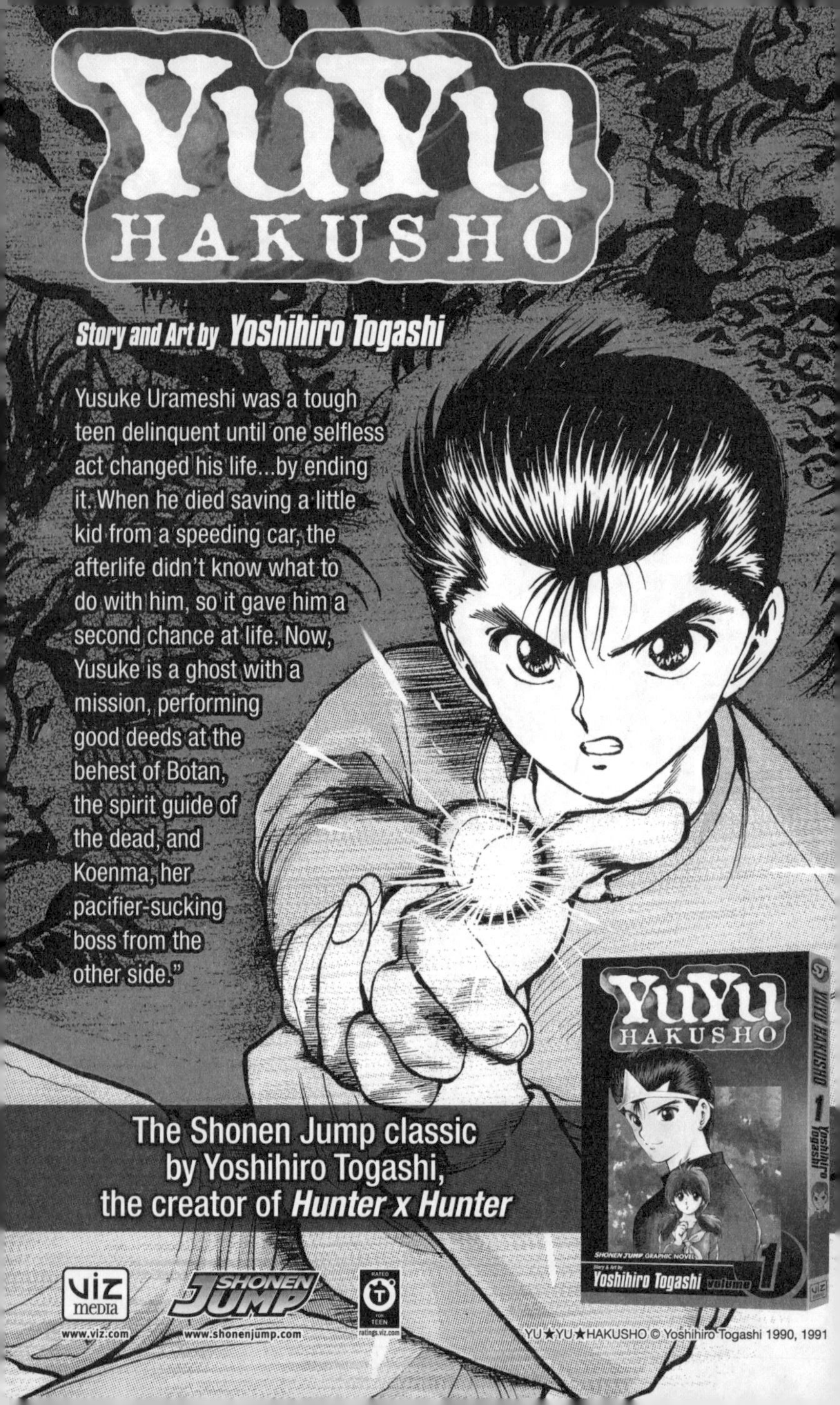
YuYu
HAKUSHO
Story and Art by Yoshihiro Togashi
Yusuke Urameshi was a tough teen delinquent until one selfless act changed his life...by ending it. When he died saving a little kid from a speeding car, the afterlife didn't know what to do with him, so it gave him a second chance at life. Now, Yusuke is a ghost with a mission, performing good deeds at the behest of Botan, the spirit guide of the dead, and Koenma, her pacifier-sucking boss from the other side."
The Shonen Jump classic by Yoshihiro Togashi, the creator of *Hunter x Hunter*
YuYu HAKUSHO
YUYU HAKUSHO
1
Yoshihiro Togashi
SHONEN JUMP GRAPHIC NOVEL
Story & Art by
Yoshihiro Togashi volume 1
viz media
www.viz.com
SHONEN JUMP
www.shonenjump.com
RATED T FOR TEEN
ratings.viz.com
YU★YU★HAKUSHO © Yoshihiro Togashi 1990, 1991

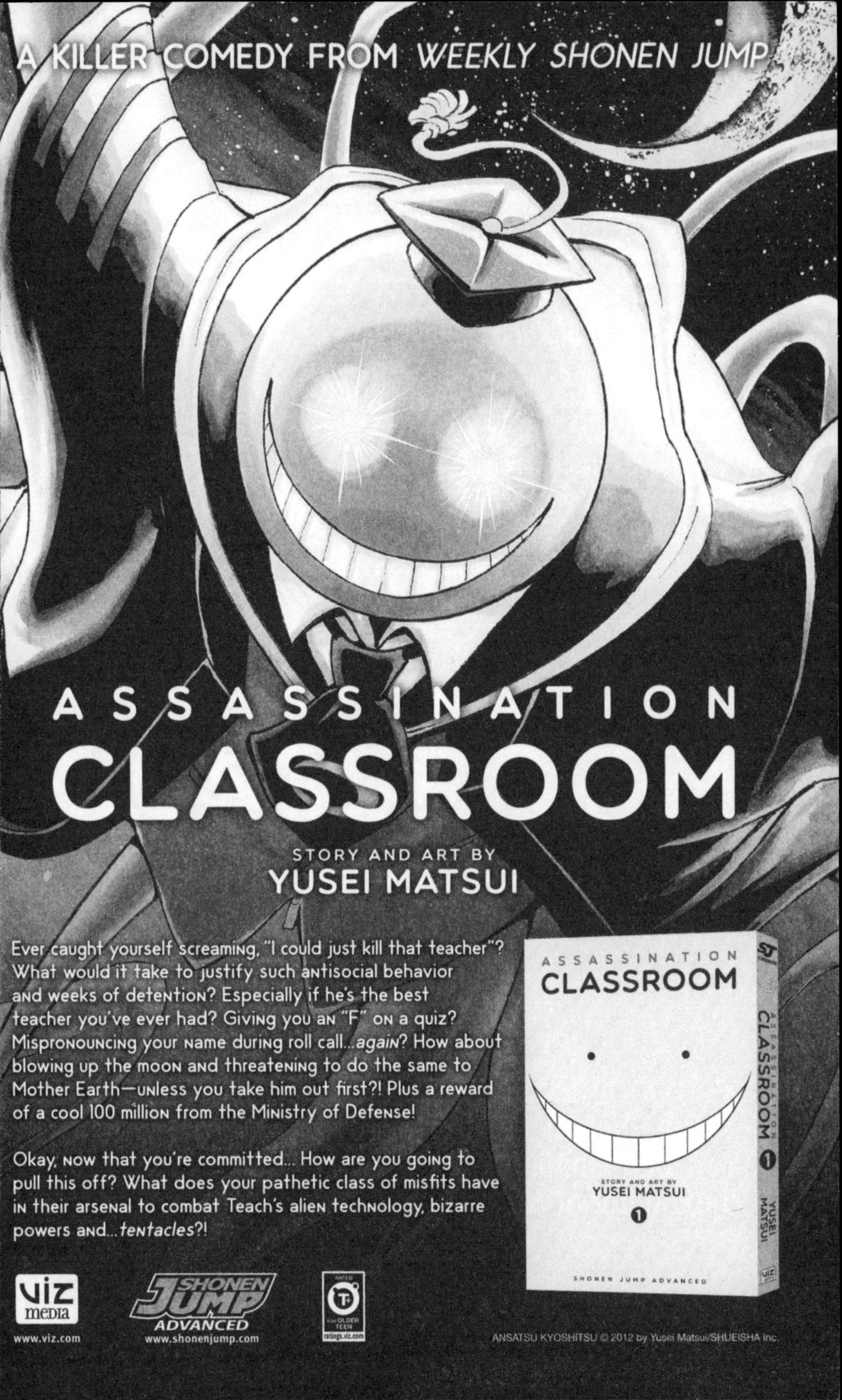
A KILLER COMEDY FROM WEEKLY SHONEN JUMP
ASSASSINATION
CLASSROOM
STORY AND ART BY
YUSEI MATSUI
Ever caught yourself screaming, "I could just kill that teacher"? What would it take to justify such antisocial behavior and weeks of detention? Especially if he's the best teacher you've ever had? Giving you an "F" on a quiz? Mispronouncing your name during roll call...again? How about blowing up the moon and threatening to do the same to Mother Earth—unless you take him out first?! Plus a reward of a cool 100 million from the Ministry of Defense!
Okay, now that you're committed... How are you going to pull this off? What does your pathetic class of misfits have in their arsenal to combat Teach's alien technology, bizarre powers and...tentacles?!
ASSASSINATION
CLASSROOM
STORY AND ART BY
YUSEI MATSUI
1
SHONEN JUMP ADVANCED
viz media
www.viz.com
SHONEN JUMP ADVANCED
www.shonenjump.com
RATED T+ FOR OLDER TEEN
ratings.viz.com
ANSATSU KYOSHITSU © 2012 by Yusei Matsui/SHUEISHA Inc.

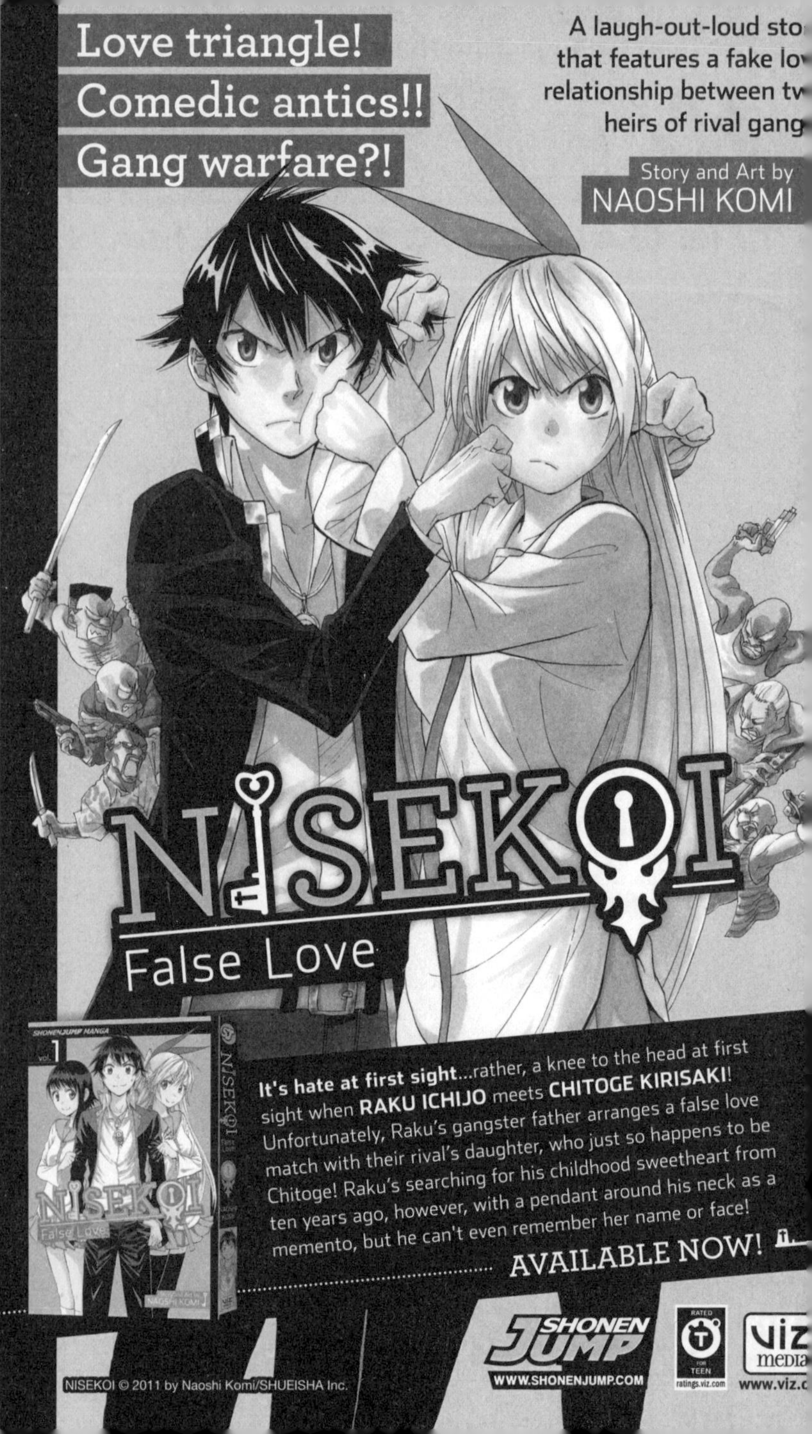
Love triangle!
Comedic antics!!
Gang warfare?!
A laugh-out-loud sto
that features a fake lo
relationship between tw
heirs of rival gang
Story and Art by
NAOSHI KOMI
NISEKOI
False Love
SHONENJUMP MANGA
It's hate at first sight...rather, a knee to the head at first sight when RAKU ICHIJO meets CHITOGE KIRISAKI! Unfortunately, Raku's gangster father arranges a false love match with their rival's daughter, who just so happens to be Chitoge! Raku's searching for his childhood sweetheart from ten years ago, however, with a pendant around his neck as a memento, but he can't even remember her name or face!
AVAILABLE NOW!
SHONEN JUMP
WWW.SHONENJUMP.COM
RATED T FOR TEEN
ratings.viz.com
viz media
www.viz.c
NISEKOI © 2011 by Naoshi Komi/SHUEISHA Inc.

Black Clover

STORY & ART BY YŪKI TABATA

Asta is a young boy who dreams of becoming the greatest mage in the kingdom. Only one problem—he can't use any magic! Luckily for Asta, he receives the incredibly rare five-leaf clover grimoire that gives him the power of anti-magic. Can someone who can't use magic really become the Wizard King? One thing's for sure—Asta will never give up!

THE PROMISED NEVERLAND

STORY BY **KAIU SHIRAI**

ART BY **POSUKA DEMIZU**

Emma, Norman and Ray are the brightest kids
at the Grace Field House orphanage. And under
the care of the woman they refer to as "Mom,"
all the kids have enjoyed a comfortable life.
Good food, clean clothes and the perfect envi-
ronment to learn—what more could an orphan
ask for? One day, though, Emma and Norman
uncover the dark truth of the outside world
they are forbidden from seeing.

You're Reading in the Wrong Direction!!

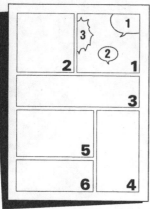

Whoops! Guess what? You're starting at the wrong end of the comic!

…It's true! In keeping with the original Japanese format, **Hunter x Hunter** is meant to be read from right to left, starting in the upper-right corner.

Unlike English, which is read from left to right, Japanese is read from right to left, meaning that action, sound effects and word-balloon order are completely reversed… something which can make readers unfamiliar with Japanese feel pretty backwards themselves. For this reason, manga or Japanese comics published in the U.S. in English have sometimes been published "flopped"–that is, printed in exact reverse order, as though seen from the other side of a mirror.

By flopping pages, U.S. publishers can avoid confusing readers, but the compromise is not without its downside. For one thing, a character in a flopped manga series who once wore in the original Japanese version a T-shirt emblazoned with "M A Y" (as in "the merry month of") now wears one which reads "Y A M"! Additionally, many manga creators in Japan are themselves unhappy with the process, as some feel the mirror-imaging of their art skews their original intentions.

We are proud to bring you Yoshihiro Togashi's **Hunter x Hunter** in the original unflopped format. For now, though, turn to the other side of the book and let the adventure begin…!

—Editor